# THE MAGIC HOUR

## FILM AT FIN DE SIÈCLE

## J. HOBERMAN

TEMPLE UNIVERSITY PRESS

Philadelphia

Temple University Press, Philadelphia 19122
Copyright © 2003 by J. Hoberman
All rights reserved
Published 2003
Printed in the United States of America

∞ The paper used in this publication meets the
requirements of the American National Standard
for Information Sciences—Permanence of Paper
for Printed Library Materials, ANSI Z39.48-1984

**Library of Congress Cataloging-in-
Publication Data**

Hoberman, J.
    The magic hour: film at fin de siècle / J.
Hoberman.
        p. cm. — (Culture and the moving image)
    Includes bibliographical references and index.
    ISBN 1-56639-995-5 (hard : alk. paper)—
ISBN 1-56639-996-3 (pbk. : alk. paper)
    1. Motion pictures.   2. Motion pictures—
Reviews.   I. Title.   II. Series.

PN1994 .H57 2003
791.43—dc21                    2002020423

# Contents

## III. ONCE AND FUTURE VANGUARDS

## IV. THE HISTORY OF FILM, THE FILM OF HISTORY

# V. OUR ROCK 'N' ROLL PRESIDENT

# THE FILM CRITIC OF TOMORROW, TODAY | 229

世界上最庞大的恐怖组织与世界上最强大的国家之间的抗衡！！

美国遭袭全记录

世界第一樓徹底坍塌
五角大樓面目全非
誰干的！？誰之過！？
布什會以牙還牙嗎？？？

世纪大灾难

美国遭袭与国际恐怖组织

一部詳盡記錄了世界貿易中心，

美國國防部五角大樓……

遭襲擊的詳細情況及

各國強烈的反應的紀錄片．

DVD
VIDEO

*The Century's Great Catastrophe* (Chinese DVD, 2001).

# INTRODUCTION

## ALL AS IT HAD BEEN

*Originally published in somewhat different form in
the* Village Voice *(September 25 and December 11, 2001).*

"He who imagines disasters in some ways desires them," Theodor Adorno noted a half century ago. Imagining this disaster is what the movies are all about. It was as though a message had bounced back from outer space. The giant dinosaurs, rogue meteors, and implacable insect-aliens who have destroyed movie-set Manhattans over the past few years were now revealed as occult attempts to represent the logic of inevitable catastrophe. The big-budget recreation of Pearl Harbor in particular seemed to have emerged from some parallel time-space continuum to provide an explanation for what was even now occurring.[1]

S O IT SEEMED TO THIS RESIDENT OF LOWER MANHATTAN, SEPTEMBER 12, 2001, the day after the volcano erupted, the asteroid crashed, the Martians landed, the Pacific fleet was destroyed, the big ship went down. Movies offered the only possible analogy for this "live" televised phantasmagoria of urban disaster, mind-boggling cartoon explosions, digicam special effects, and world-obliterating mayhem.

Blockbusters are what bring audiences together, all at once, around the world. Their lingua franca is violent action, and since the collapse of the Soviet empire, those sounds and images have belonged overwhelmingly to the American-run multinational force conveniently designated "Hollywood." Hence, the familiar sense of a scenario directed by Roland Emmerich for the benefit of Rupert Murdoch, the déjà vu of crowds fleeing Godzilla through Manhattan canyons, the bellicose rhetoric of *Independence Day*, the cosmic insanity of *Deep Impact*, the romantic pathos of *Titanic*, the national trauma of *Pearl Harbor*.

A psychotherapist I know told me of a patient who, since childhood, had the recurring nightmare of a low-flying airplane crashing into his apartment house. On September 11, he exited the subway at Chambers Street, saw a jet hit the World Trade Center, and assumed he had suffered a psychotic break. On September 11, then, the dream became reality—for the dreamer and for us. But what did that mean? As the German social critic Siegfried Kracauer was the first to argue, "The films of a nation reflect its mentality." Analyzing the popular movies of the Weimar Republic in the light of the Nazi rise to power, Kracauer wrote, "Germany carried out what had been anticipated by her cinema from its very beginning. It was all as it had been on the screen."

Do we live in a world of unmade film scripts that desire to go into production? Searching for an instant response to our leader's apparent confusion, the government incorporated elements of *Air Force One*, the 1997 hit in which blowback from a joint U.S.-Russian operation against neofascist, nuclear-armed Kazakhstan results in an attack on America—specifically the President's plane. (It was not the American people but their leader who was in danger.) Not only history but also film history changed. In retrospect, *Independence Day*, *Titanic*, et al. became the quintessential Hollywood movies of the fin de siècle.

*All as it had been on the screen.* The Events of September 11 were a 2001 scenario to rival that envisioned by Stanley Kubrick at the height of worldwide cinephilia back in the now-mythical year of 1968. Was the terror attack then a prophetic fantasy come true? A form of perverse wish fulfillment? For over half a century, the United States had bombed nations from Japan to Vietnam to Iraq to Serbia, without itself ever suffering a single bomb falling on its own cities. But even more—and for longer—we had bombarded the globe with our images. As *Variety* put it in one 1995 headline: "EARTH TO H'WOOD: YOU WIN."[2]

Some reverends and mullahs were quick to attribute September 11 to divine retribution. Other spectators understood the planet-transfixing Events as but one more spectacular world-dominating megabillion-dollar Hollywood science fiction extravaganza. (There were also those who imagined that, like the movie industry, this super production was organized by a conspiracy of Jews.) In his "Letter from China," published a month later in the *New Yorker*, Peter Hessler described the DVD quickies he found in Wenzhou video stores, displayed between the piles of *Jurassic Park* and *Planet of the Apes*: The cover of *The Century's Great Catastrophe* was appropriately garnished with a view of the twin towers aflame and portraits of the spectacle's rival stars, George W. Bush and the Dr. Mabuse–like mastermind Osama bin Laden—at that moment the biggest media personality since Adolf Hitler.[3]

Crediting *Armageddon*'s Jerry Bruckheimer as its producer, authors of *The Century's Great Catastrophe* combined American TV news footage with Chinese commentary, using the menacing shark theme from *Jaws* to underscore the north tower's slo-mo collapse and interpolating footage of Michael Douglas from *Wall Street* into a conclave of world leaders responding to the

Events. Other Chinese videos—*Surprise Attack on America* and *America's Disaster: The Pearl Harbor of the Twenty-first Century*—were more outrageous, sweetening the newsreel footage with (in)appropriate movie clips from *Godzilla* and *The Rock*. From the detached Wenzhou point of view, the Events were a study in dialectics: Jihad vs. McWorld. Suddenly, the Chinese were us—enjoying the spectacle of cataclysmic mass destruction from a safe vantage point.

André Bazin termed this particular cinematic pleasure the "Nero complex," referring to the decadent tyrant who supposedly supplied his own musical sound track as Rome burned. This rarefied aesthetic experience was democratized by motion pictures—which trafficked in disasters almost since the birth of the medium—and is even suggested by those televised movie critics who pass judgment on movies, thumbs up or down like parody Roman emperors.

▪▪▪▪▪▪▪▪▪▪

Fin de siècle cinema was nothing if not what the scholar of early movies Tom Gunning termed a "cinema of attractions," characterized by the production of F/X action blockbusters, grandiose disaster flicks, and other big loud movies, not the least of which was the first George Bush's Operation Desert Storm.

While *Titanic* (with its unprecedented, albeit digital, representation of mass death) displaced *Star Wars* as the top-grossing movie of all time, the Clinton impeachment and Y2K panic proved to be the much hyped doomsday thrillers that fizzled at the box office. In addition to the jihad terror of the first, 1993 WTC attack and the exploded federal building in Oklahoma City two years later, there was the "natural" terrorism of movies like *Twister*—not to mention "art" disaster films as varied as *Tribulation 99, The Rapture, Schindler's List, The Ice Storm, Crash, The Sweet Hereafter, Saving Private Ryan, Magnolia*, and *Thirteen Days*.

In the disaster cycle of the 1970s, calamity—like the loss of Vietnam, the Watergate scandal, and the Oil Shock recession—typically arrived as a punishment for some manifestation of the boom-boom sixties. Some disaster movies even blamed the catastrophe on rapacious, environment-raping corporations and craven, inadequate leaders. In the nineties, however, it was as though America was being punished just for being its own ever-loving, arms-dealing, channel-surfing, trash-talking, butt-kicking, world-historical Number One self.

Unchallenged hegemony created its own universal antithesis. In the absence of the Communist menace, the foe was everywhere. For Hollywood, this "unspecified enemy," in Gilles Deleuze and Felix Guattari's phrase, was variously visualized as Euroterrorists in *Die Hard* (1988), narco-terrorists in *Die Hard 2* (1990), neo-Nazi terrorists in *Die Hard with a Vengeance* (1995), homegrown terrorists in *Under Siege* (1992), "international" terrorists in *Under Siege 2*

(1995), extraterrestrial terrorists in *Independence Day* (1996), microorganic terrorists in *Outbreak* (1995), dino-terrorists in *The Lost World: Jurassic Park* (1997), Russian terrorists in *Air Force One* (1997), Bosnian terrorists in *The Peacemaker* (1997), and Islamic terrorists in *True Lies* (1994), *Executive Decision* (1996), and *The Siege* (1998), a movie that dramatized the wholesale roundup of Arab American suspects.

Meanwhile, Republican politicians and American jihadists argued that the real enemy was Hollywood itself—the movie industry had spent the past decade carrying out a form of soft terrorism. What force was more pervasive? Or persuasive? By positing several billion casualties, *Independence Day*—to name but one blockbuster, extremely popular in the Middle East as everywhere else on earth—pretended to massacre nearly as many people as paid to see it. Even at the time, audiences were observed to cheer the image of the vaporized White House. Who now will forget the stirring image of *Independence Day* good guy Will Smith fearlessly piloting his aircraft into the very citadel of alien power? And who cannot associate it with the fall of the Trades?

Hollywood's first response to September 11 was a fascinating exercise in magical thinking. Immediately after the Events, Warner Bros. postponed *Collateral Damage*, a movie in which Arnold Schwarzenegger plays a firefighter who wreaks cosmic vengeance when his wife and child die in a Los Angeles skyscraper blown up by narco-terrorists. Jerry Bruckheimer decided that the time might not be right for *World War III*, which simulated the nuking of Seattle and San Diego. MGM shelved *Nose Bleed*, with Jackie Chan starring as a window washer who foils a terrorist plot to blow up the WTC. ("It represents capitalism," one of the terrorists was to explain. "It represents freedom. It represents everything that America is about. And to bring those two buildings down would bring America to its knees.")

A new self-censorship was in place. The CBS show *The Agency* dropped a reference to Osama bin Laden. *Sex and the City* trimmed views of the Twin Towers; Paramount airbrushed them from the poster for *Sidewalks of New York*. Sony yanked their *Spider-Man* trailer so as to eliminate images of the WTC and similarly ordered retakes on *Men in Black 2* that would replace the Trades with the Chrysler Building. DreamWorks changed the end of *The Time Machine*, which rained moon fragments down on New York. It was as though the future might be made safe by rewriting the past.

Hollywood felt guilty. Only days after the towers fell, the studios eagerly reported that the FBI had informed them they could well be the terrorists' next target. On September 21, Los Angeles was swept with rumors of an impending attack. That great whirring sound wasn't the swallows returning to Capistrano but all those chickens coming home to roost. Not everyone was as blunt as director Robert Altman, who told the Associated Press, "The movies set the pattern, and these people have copied the movies. Nobody would have thought to commit an atrocity like that unless they'd seen it in a movie.... I just believe we created this atmosphere and taught them how to do it."

■■■■■■■■■■■■■

Such megalomania might seem unwarranted but, as the Chinese videos suggested, the Events of September 11 would be a hard act to top. It was the end of the End of History, the beginning of the Clash of Civilizations. In the days following the disaster, the *Los Angeles Times* reported entertainment industry concern that "the public appetite for plots involving disasters and terrorism has vanished."

What then would movies be about? A prominent TV executive hastily assured the *New York Times* that entertainment, post–September 11, would be "much more wholesome" and that "we are definitely moving into a kinder, gentler time" (presumably 1988). A DreamWorks producer explained that the present atmosphere precluded his studio from bankrolling any more movies like *The Peacemaker* and *Deep Impact*: "We make the movies that reflect, in one way or another, the experiences we all have. There are just some movies that you can't make from here on in."

Hollywood expected to be punished. Instead, it was drafted. Before long, the Pentagon-funded Institute for Creative Technologies at the University of Southern California convened several meetings with filmmakers to "brainstorm" possible terrorist scenarios and then offer solutions. For the first time since Ronald Reagan left office, it has become all but impossible to criticize the movie industry. After George W. Bush's late September suggestion that Americans fight terrorism by taking their families to Disney World, Disney chief Michael Eisner reportedly sent out an e-mail praising the president as "our newest cheerleader."

The reign of movie lover Bill Clinton was over. Yet, as the theater of battle moved from New York and Washington to Afghanistan, even Representative Henry Hyde—implacable scourge of Clinton's Hollywood amorality— requested motion picture industry input into a congressional hearing on how the United States might successfully win the "hearts and minds" of the Arab world. Unable to ignore the similarity between their religious fundamentalism and ours, the Bush administration now wanted to promote the traditional American values of "tolerance" and entertainment.

Among their other crimes, the iconoclastic Savonarolas of the Taliban had proscribed the sale of television sets and banned all movies—even subjecting them to public burning. Hence the phenomenal photograph printed

November 20, 2001, by the *New York Times*, page one above the fold, captioned "Kabul Cinema Opens to Joy and Chaos." In an image that would do the professional hysteria stokers of the Cannes Film Festival proud, a mob of smiling Afghan men were shown storming and even scaling the walls of the 600-seat Bakhtar Cinema to participate in Kabul's first public movie screening in five years. Not since *Independence Day* . . .

Never mind that women were banned and that the Afghans were fighting to see the 1995 *Uruj*—a movie celebrating those same mujahideen heroes whose war against the Communist infidels had brought bin Laden to Afghanistan in the first place. *Shrek* would surely follow—and maybe even *Pearl Harbor*. Kabul had rejoined our civilization.

## CODA

Will the dozen years between the fall of the Berlin Wall and the collapse of the World Trade Center ultimately be perceived as a golden age? American movies reigned supreme in the international marketplace; but, for no small number of cineastes, this happy period was understood not as the end of history so much as the end of movie culture.

Only a few months past the centennial anniversary of Auguste and Louis Jean Lumière's first public exhibition of their cinematograph, Susan Sontag wrote that "cinema's 100 years seem to have the shape of a life cycle: an inevitable birth, the steady accumulation of glories and the onset in the last decade of an ignominious, irreversible decline." (Yet, such directors of the fin de siècle as Hou Hsiao-hsien and Wong Kar-Wai, David Lynch and David Cronenberg, Chantal Akerman and Béla Tarr, can be legitimately counted among cinema's glories—and has there ever been an individual film artist more powerful than Steven Spielberg?)

Something else may be irreversible. Perhaps the projection of the disaster, years before it occurred, was a form of bravado: How could ordinary life, after all, possibly match the magical make-believe of virtual reality? Or possibly, by pretending to destroy the world, Hollywood's mindless demonstrations of cinematic might acknowledged the impending obsolescence of the motion picture apparatus that had so conveniently defined the twentieth century. It was as though the machine could sense the waiting junkyard. How striking that much current vanguard work—as well as academic film theory—should be focused on primitive cinema and the soon-to-be-anachronistic movie projector. Similarly, the quasi avant-garde Dogma movement—whether a quaint European reaction against Hollywood economic dominance or a cynical branding strategy—takes its stand on the endangered status of cinema's indexical relationship to that which has actually been.

Even as audiences continued to wander in dreamland, melancholy—if not sentimental—movie-movies from *Blade Runner* to *Memento* acknowledged their own mortality by insisting that memory, at least as we know it, is based on photography. A less humanist message from the future, George Lucas's long-awaited *Phantom Menace* turned out to be essentially an animated cartoon fashioned from photographic material—and thus a movie without external reference (unless it was the analogous form of the Japanese *anime*). The political possibilities of such digitally produced fantasies may be extrapolated from the melodramatic pageant *Forrest Gump* as well as the topical satire *Wag the Dog*. As the nature of the movie apparatus changes, so will our sense of the past— including the artifact that is the movie past.[4]

Cinematographers know that objects filmed in the "magic hour" before dusk are often suffused with an unpredictable golden glow. If the century's end cast a late-afternoon light on all films released during the 1990s, nostalgia for the photographic era—as well as that of serious moviegoing—can also be deduced from those adaptations of classic novels so characteristic of fin de siècle cinema. Just as the phrase "nineteenth-century novel" now conjures the richly populated, self-contained worlds of Dickens and Dostoyevsky, so the old-fashioned "twentieth-century movie" may come to represent a lost fusion of modernist aspiration and mass appeal—what the critic Raymond Durgnat meant by "the wedding of poetry and pulp" and neo new wave filmmaker Quentin Tarantino called "pulp fiction." The catastrophe then is to no longer remember what that fusion meant.

**NOTES**

1 J. Hoberman, "News of the World," *Village Voice*, September 25, 2001.

2 For most of the 1990s, the national film industries that inspired the greatest degree of cinephilic enthusiasm developed in countries outside the American cultural sphere: Iran and China (which itself had three centers). A measure of resistance was also provided by a few strong individuals who developed under the regime of the former Soviet empire—Krzysztof Kieślowski, Jan Svankmajer, Béla Tarr, Alexander Sokurov—as well as the cultural protectionism practiced by France.

3 Writing in the *Village Voice* (January 8, 2002), Mike Rubin speculated that the Osama bin Laden video-tape discovered in Kandahar and widely telecast in early December 2001 was "for most American viewers, probably their first experience watching something with subtitles."

4 In that spirit, the pieces that are here collected appear as originally published, save for the elimination of topical references and repetitions.

*Dr. Mabuse, the Gambler* (Fritz Lang, UFA, 1922).

# I

## PULP FICTIONS

### THE LANG TWENTIETH CENTURY

Originally published as "Old Lang Zeit," the *Village Voice*
(January 5, 1993).

THE NOTION OF HITLER AS MASTER CRIMINAL UNDERSCORES WORKS AS DISPARATE as Brecht's *Resistible Rise of Arturo Ui* and John Farrow's *The Hitler Gang*. It's another personality, however, who dominates the Goethe Society program "Out of the Dark: Crime, Mystery, and Suspense in the German Cinema." The central figure in this 16-film series is Hitler's fellow Austrian and near contemporary, the painter-turned-filmmaker Fritz Lang.

Lang, whose 1990 centennial passed virtually unnoticed (at least in New York), was a pulp fiction maestro—perhaps the greatest in movie history. His official masterpiece, *M*, is the original portrait of a serial killer, but there is scarcely a popular genre—sci-fi, sword and sorcery, espionage, gangster, horror—that did not pass through Lang's hands and does not bear his mark. (That was just in Germany. Once in America, Lang directed a proto–*Bonnie and Clyde* and helped invent film noir.)

Even more pop and less literary than his precursors D. W. Griffith and Louis Feuillade, Lang can scarcely be recuperated as anything other than the mad genius of juvenile trash. His worldview seems eternal. As Stan Brakhage put it, Lang sought to fashion a religion out of his adolescent daydreams, the "sexiest simplicities ... crudest power madness ... meanest worship—that which effects masturbation most easily." Lang's silent movies even have a built-in Oedipal kick; they were mainly written by his then-wife Thea von Harbou and often starred her ex-husband Rudolph Klein-Rogge in villainous roles.

*The Spiders* (1919), Lang's first success, concerned the megalomaniacal head of a clandestine organization. So, too, did the sumptuous and snappy *Spies* (1928). But the most celebrated of Lang's criminal geniuses—the one who, for him, personified the zeitgeist—was introduced in *Dr. Mabuse, the Gambler*, a two-part epic based on Norbert Jacques's self-consciously "modern" settings—

the art nouveau nightclubs and art deco gambling dens populated by cocaine-snorting aristos. Early audiences were more impressed by the car chases through the Berlin night: "Speed, horrifying speed characterizes the film," one reviewer wrote. But even then, Mabuse was employed to epitomize the postwar period of political instability, social turmoil, and crazed hyperinflation.

In the person of Mabuse, Lang gave Germany's breakdown a single cause. The gambler is a master of disguise and hypnotism, exerting his will over cabaret dancers and millionaires alike. Hidden yet ubiquitous, Mabuse is history's secret agent. It is he who masterminds the long-distance murder of a courier and panics the German commodity exchanges; he who wrecks the economy by flooding it with counterfeit dollars. According to Lang, the movie was originally introduced with a montage that skipped from the 1919 Spartacist uprising and 1920 Kapp Putsch through various disorders to the assassination of finance minister Walter Rathenau, to ask, "Who is behind this?" (Who, indeed? Rathenau was not assassinated until nearly two months after *Mabuse*'s release.)

The history of film or the film of history, as Jean-Luc Godard might ask: Mabuse was responsible for the lunacy of postwar Germany; the movie fittingly ends with his confinement to a madhouse. But Lang was persuaded to resurrect, if not precisely spring, Mabuse 10 years later—in the aftermath of *M* and on the eve of Hitler's election. In *The Testament of Dr. Mabuse*, the seemingly catatonic gambler takes control of the asylum doctor, who is soon ranting that Mabuse's *übermensch* brain will "smash our rotten world." Through mysterious recording devices and the pliant Dr. Baum (his study crammed with human skulls, primitive masks, and expressionist paintings), Mabuse plunges Germany into "an abyss of terror." His minions are everywhere; the normal world barely exists.

As *M* was predicated on an actual case, so *The Testament of Dr. Mabuse* was presented as the explanation for the crime wave Germany experienced during the early thirties, and the movies are further connected by presence of the earthy, cigar-smoking commissioner Lohman (a kind of Berlin Kojak). Although less methodical than *M*, *The Testament* is brisk and often brilliant filmmaking. As a master of suspense, Lang is the bridge between Griffith and Hitchcock. *The Testament* opens in the midst of an unexplained incident—a frantic man concealed in a print shop, playing cat and mouse with his armed pursuers to the overwhelming pounding of the unseen press. "Life under a terror regime could not be rendered more impressively," observed Siegfried Kracauer in hindsight.

Reveling in rhapsodic destruction and purveying a universal fear of authority, *The Testament of Dr. Mabuse* was scheduled to open on March 23, 1933—the same day, as it turns out, that the Reichstag voted Hitler dictatorial powers. But the movie was banned; its "presentation of certain criminal acts" was deemed "so detailed and fascinating" authorities feared it might inspire "similar" incidents of antistate terror. In an introduction written for the 1943 U.S. release (which was shown to coincide with Lang's anti-Nazi feature *Hangmen Also Die*), the director, now an American citizen, maintained that *The Testament* was made as an "allegory" of Hitler's terror. "Slogans and doctrines of the Third Reich [were] put in the mouths of criminals." But if *The Testament* attacked Hitler it may only be in retrospect. Mabuse represents disorder, not fascism—and von Harbou was a member of the Nazi party when she wrote the script.

Goebbels evidently banned *The Testament* sight unseen. After he saw it, he told Lang that the only thing wrong with the movie was the absence of a proper Führer to defeat Mabuse. It was at this meeting, by Lang's account, that Goebbels wondered if the director might like to head the German film industry. Lang would maintain that he closed out his bank account and left the Reich that evening.

In early 1958, an elderly Lang returned to Germany at the behest of producer Artur Brauner to make The *Tiger of Eschnapur* and *The Indian Tomb*; the success of this two-part feature, based on a script Lang wrote in 1920, prompted Brauner to suggest another *Mabuse*.

Lang decided to make a "brutal" film, evoking "the cold reality of today." That icy world was, of course, the Cold War and its epicenter, Berlin—a still undivided city where the hallucinatory prosperity of the rebuilt Western zone was surrounded by desolation and misted in intrigue, where Allied military sedans daily cruised one another's sectors, and no one was sure who was counter-spying for whom. As *The 1000 Eyes of Dr. Mabuse* went into production, the Soviets called for the withdrawal of all foreign troops: "Only madmen can go to the length of unleashing another world war over the preservation of occupation privileges in Berlin."

According to a reminiscence published by Volker Schlondorff, "Lang was past recognition. Since he couldn't go out without feeling like a stranger, he confined himself to the international anonymity of a hotel room. . . . His only thoughts were of Germany, of what it had been, of what it had done, of what it had become." Almost ridiculously straightforward, *The 1000 Eyes* is a work of studied geometry in which B-movie automatons glide through a constricted version of prewar Berlin, replaying incidents from the earlier *Mabuse* films (as well as *Spies*) in the zombie nightclubs and bunkerlike sets of the "Hotel Luxor."

Is it really the same map of the city splayed across the wall behind the jolly, *echt* Berlin police chief? (He's played by Gert Frobe, soon to embody the Langian figure of Goldfinger.) Mabuse is now pure *geist*. The megalomaniacal "genius of diabolism" who died in 1932 has been reincarnated as another hypnotist who plans to rule the world by gaining control of a millionaire American rocket scientist cum industrialist. Mobile spy units cruise the streets; the Hotel Luxor is not only a nexus of unsolved murders but also an unholy relic of the Nazi era, designed by the Gestapo to monitor, as well as house, foreign diplomats. Every room is under constant surveillance through a combination of hidden microphones, secret cameras, and one-way mirrors (which allow the innocent Ami to observe the German mystery woman in her underwear). But, if much of the action is framed by TV monitors, nothing is exactly what it seems.

No less than his pre-Nazi German films, Lang's swan song is a trove of prophetic paranoia. A séance arranged by a blind clairvoyant in a chamber where constellations are marked in phosphorescent stars offers a bizarre fore-taste of the Pentagon war room and title character from *Dr. Strangelove*. On May 1, 1960, an American U-2 spy plane was shot down over the Urals; on May 14, *The 1000 Eyes of Dr. Mabuse* opened in Stuttgart. The following summer, the Berlin Wall went up and an American defector named Lee Harvey Oswald applied to return home. . . . The Lang century continued.

## WHITE DOG

Originally published as "Howl," the *Village Voice*
(July 16, 1991).

THE MOST SOUGHT-AFTER AND ELUSIVE OF SHELVED STUDIO RELEASES, Samuel Fuller's *White Dog* has finally been unleashed. Inaugurating Film Forum's month-long Fuller retro, the movie gets its theatrical premiere nine years after Paramount decided it was too troublesome to open and sent it to the pound.

Adapted from Romain Gary's 1970 nonfiction novel, a section of which originally appeared in *Life* magazine, *White Dog* is an unusually blunt and sug-gestively metaphoric account of American racism. In the original story, Gary and his then-wife Jean Seberg find a stray German shepherd who, they soon discover, has been raised to attack blacks on sight. Although told that the dog is too old to be deconditioned, they ultimately turn him over to a black animal trainer who vengefully reprograms the creature to maul whites (including, at the book's climax, Gary himself). Paramount acquired the property in the mid-1970s; the project then went through seven scripts, with Roman Polanski, Arthur Penn, and Tony Scott variously named to direct, before it fell to Fuller, fresh from his comeback triumph, *The Big Red One* (1980).

In *Sam Fuller on the Set of White Dog*, the Christian Blackwood short that rounds out the Film Forum bill, producer Jon Davidson explains that he recruited Fuller because Fuller was the only man in Hollywood who could rewrite a script and be ready to start shooting in 10 days. It's also possible that Fuller was the only American filmmaker who could successfully short-circuit Gary's "civilized" irony and present *White Dog* head-on, treating the yarn with the sort of absurdist humor and unabashed didacticism the material warranted. Indeed, intuiting his potential audience, Fuller reconceptualized the movie to put the conflict inside the dog's brain: "You're going to see a dog slowly go insane and then come back to sanity in front of you," he promised *Variety*.

Fuller altered Gary's ending (making it more pessimistic and irrational), modified the character of the black trainer (Paul Winfield), and changed the protagonist from an activist movie star into an aspiring actress (childlike Kristy McNichol in her first "adult" role), whom the dog initially saves from a white rapist. In Fuller's world, unlike Gary's, racial paranoia doesn't drop from the sky but is associated from the onset with the paternal protection of the Law.

That, in homage to Seberg and Gary, Fuller maintains the initials J. S. for McNichol's character and R. G. for that of her writer-boyfriend, is suggestive of his film's boldly abstract tabloid stylistics. Filmed in headlines, framed as allegory, *White Dog* combines hard-boiled sentimentality and hysterical violence, sometimes in the same take—as a director, Fuller has lost very little since his masterpieces of the early sixties. (Fuller was exiled from Hollywood at the moment when American public reality was beginning to rival his *Shock Corridor*, and *White Dog* attests to the sad waste of his talent; had his career not fallen apart after *The Naked Kiss*, he might have been making two comparable films a year between 1965 and 1980.)

*White Dog*'s iconic visuals and cartoon dialogue ("Your dog is a four-legged time bomb!") are given unexpected dignity by the somber piano doodling and tense, moody strings of Ennio Morricone's brilliant score. Still, this is an animal film—replete with dog-level tracking shots and frequent close-ups of the dog's eyes. Given the surplus violence of the animal's savage, not always predictable, attacks—their locations ranging from McNichol's living room (TV blasting) to a movie set (a process shot of Venice flickering in the background) to a church (St. Francis of Assisi looking on)—and Fuller's regard for the dog as an alien intelligence, *White Dog* infuses a politically conscious variant of *Jaws* with intimations of Robert Bresson's sublime *Au hasard Balthazar*, not to mention the director's own unclassifiable nuttiness.

Where else but in a Fuller film would a purveyor of trained animals (Burl Ives) hurl darts at a poster of R2D2 ("that's the enemy!") or, having doubled for John Wayne in *True Grit* by reaching into a nest of rattlesnakes, proffer his paw with the invitation to shake "the hand that helped Duke win the Oscar!" Of course, the choice contradictions are reserved for Fuller's hero. "To me, this is a laboratory that Darwin himself would go ape over!" Winfield exclaims of the animal farm where he works; "How I wanted to kill that son of a bitch!" he describes his response on discovering the white dog trotting away from his latest victim, "But you can't experiment on a dead dog!" By the time Winfield swears that if he fails to cure this animal, he'll find another and another until he does, he has come to seem like a black Captain Ahab.

Fuller—who strongly criticized American racial attitudes in a number of his fifties action flicks (and made them the subject of *The Crimson Kimono*)—is responsible for some of the toughest social-problem films ever made in the USA. It's understandable that the NAACP would have taken an interest in *White Dog*'s production; it's unfortunate that, by warning Paramount that the film might give racists ideas and encourage the production of actual white dogs, the NAACP provided the studio—and later NBC—with an excuse to suppress what seems to me one of the most unflinching statements to ever come out of Hollywood, something like *Rin Tin Tin Joins the Ku Klux Klan*.

*White Dog* "naturalizes" racism in a strikingly unnatural way. While the movie's white characters are invariably amazed by the whole idea of the "white dog," most of the black characters treat his existence as a brute fact of life. Unlike in Gary's novel, the dog here doesn't seem to have a name—he's referred to once as "Mr. Hyde," leaving us to consider just who "Dr. Jekyll" might be. Late in the day, we discover his creator is a kindly old codger, with two little granddaughters and a box of candy for the lady who sheltered his pet.

What's stunning about *White Dog* is how it gives race hatred both a human *and* subhuman face. Which is the mask? Conditioned as it is to fear Willie Horton, white America might well ponder the bloody image of that snarling canine.

## BASIC INSTINCT

Originally published as "New York Letter: Fantastic Projections," *Sight and Sound* (June 1992).

THE MIRRORED CEILING IS STANDARD BOUDOIR ISSUE IN PAUL VERHOEVEN'S *Basic Instinct*—a movie that's been refracted through the American media for so long, it seems to get off on watching itself. The camera somersaults out of the looking glass in the very first shot to glom a naked couple grinding loins on silken sheets. She straddles him, ties his wrists to the bedpost, then arches her back to rebound with an ice pick. . . . Clearly, Verhoeven wants to give new meaning to the phrase over the top.

More inadvertently self-revealing than effectively malign in positing a sinister conspiracy of rich, beautiful, man-slashing crypto-lesbians, *Basic Instinct* is a film whose goofball preening is exceeded only by its ham-fisted dialogue. Offering his instant diagnosis of the ice-pick killer, a forensic psychologist tells the cops who found the grisly remains that they're "dealing with a devious, diabolical mind . . . a deep-seated obsessional hatred . . . someone very dangerous and very ill." Yeah, like the murderer and who else?

Reaping a whirlwind of publicity (and receiving violently mixed notices in the daily press), *Basic Instinct* grossed $15 million over its opening weekend to displace the teen comedy *Wayne's World* atop the national box office charts, before being succeeded by Ron Shelton's basketball buddy-drama *White Men Can't Jump*. In New York, where it was released the same day as a report detailing the rise in gay–bias victim attacks, *Basic Instinct* was protested by a coalition of gay and lesbian groups—as it had been while in production last spring. Still, the movie's basic instinct is not simply homophobia. As expulsive as the opening attraction proves to be, it's a veritable geyser of pathology.

*Basic Instinct* is nominally set in San Francisco (and thus an anthology of allusions to *Vertigo*, *Bullitt*, and *Dirty Harry*) but actually unfolds in the realm of unfettered desire. The atmosphere of superconsumption—the cops operate out of posh burnished-wood executive offices, interrogate suspects in a junior version of the Pentagon war room—is reinforced by the full panoply of ostentatious dolly and crane shots, the carefully dappled light that falls across the elevators, the casually superfluous helicopter overheads. (The film's budget has been put at $49 million.)

As with *Robocop* and *Total Recall*, Verhoeven places a Hollywood genre between quotation marks. It's as if he gave the routine *policier* the same madcap treatment he accorded middle-period Bergman in his last Dutch feature, *The Fourth Man*; as a thriller, *Basic Instinct* is more baroquely twisted than it is suspenseful, closer to De Palma than Hitchcock. The biggest tension builder is the shot-countershot montage that proceeds cop Michael Douglas's going down on suspect Sharon Stone in one of the film's hypertheatrical hot and slurpy sex scenes.

A hard-boiled wise guy who leads with his putz, Douglas here synthesizes all previous roles from *Fatal Attraction* and *The War of the Roses* to *Black Rain* and the long-running TV series *The Streets of San Francisco*. He's a superego tied into a pretzel, a cop with an addictive personality who con-sistently does the wrong thing—most spectacularly, we gather, when two tourists wandered into his line of fire. (It's also suggested that he drove his wife to suicide.) As a result, *Basic Instinct* opens with Douglas in a heightened state of deprivation, having temporarily given up cigarettes, sex, booze, and cocaine.

American movies, at least those directed by Howard Hawks, used to make a fetish of professionalism. *Basic Instinct* is almost delirious in celebrating the absence of ethics. Or maybe it's a form of social criticism. The movie is so opportunistic it could be taking place in the brain of Donald Trump—this fantasyland is sprinkled with sleaze instead of Disney dust. Sentenced to psychi-atric care after the tourist incident, Douglas sleeps with the police psychologist assigned to be his therapist (Jeanne Tripplehorn) while she, in turn, circulates his confidential file—ultimately sold off to Stone's mystery novelist cum murder suspect, who explains that writers are amoral by nature.

This blithe lack of scruples has been recapitulated after a fashion both by Verhoeven's bland assertion that the crypto-lesbians are the movie's most posi-tive characters and screenwriter Joe Eszterhas's campaign to distance himself from a script for which, despite its being a virtual retread of his *Jagged Edge*, he received $3 million. But the scenario also evokes the paranoid domestic mind-fuck of *Total Recall,* and chief among the movie's cartoonish pleasures is the spectacle of Stone playing Madonna to Douglas's Arnold.

Stone is the ultimate bad girl—it's interesting that, in general, men (straight and gay) have been far more disapproving of the film than have women. In every instance, the Stone character flaunts her trangressive power. Questioned by the police, she not only brazenly smokes in a no-smoking zone and con-founds six seasoned cops (their faces pouring sweat into the camera) with frank sex talk but reveals that she's donned her miniskirt *sans* knickers. Whether or not the scene sells the movie, it's enough to send Douglas pirouet-ting off the wagon into a rough sex *pas de deux*: "You've never been like that before," Tripplehorn observes after he brings her home, slams her against a wall, kisses her, rips apart her underwear, kisses her again, then pushes her face down onto a chair and takes her from behind.

From the Douglas perspective, *Basic Instinct* is one long confusing come-hither look. (To reinforce the point, Dorothy Malone periodically traipses out of the woodwork to reprise her fifties impersonation of nympho excitement—rubbing her back against the wall, sucking in her cheeks, batting her bedroom eyes.) Stone pals around with female multiple-murderers—as opposed to killers of multiple females—and, perhaps, lives out her bestsellers. She explains her relentless interest in Douglas in terms of a work in progress about a detective who "falls for the wrong woman" and gets himself killed. It's the boudoir-mirror principle, life imitating art imitating life . . . Ultimately, Douglas will propose an alternative ending to Stone's scenario: "How about we fuck like minks, raise rug rats, and live happily ever after." Too bad for him, the completed manuscript is already spewing out of her printer.

"My wife says it comes out of all my sexual fantasies," has been Eszterhas's convoluted explanation for *Basic Instinct.* Mrs. E. notwithstanding, the women here are all infinitely manipulative. Douglas is confused by two duplicitous shrinks—Stone's character having graduated from Berkeley with a double major in literature and psychology. Every female in the film is not only a possible or actual killer but also a potential lesbian. The running joke is that each, however, can be temporarily awed by the power of Douglas's wand. The most comic demonstration of this feat comes after the first Douglas-Stone tryst when, having spent the night watching the action, Stone's leather-clad consort (Leilani Sarelle) menacingly materializes in the bathroom and Douglas outmachos her, bare ass to the viewer.

As this coy camera placement suggests, it is Douglas who is the movie's real love object—his reported $14 million paycheck dwarfs Eszterhas's. (It is also Douglas who has been pressed into service to give *Basic Instinct* a "progressive"—or at least "libertarian"—reading.) So, is the movie being homophobic or naturalistic when it gives his lumberingly faithful partner (George Dzundza) an unrequited crush? Deducing that Douglas has been to bed with Stone, Dzundza is just as jealous as Sarelle: "Goddam sonafabitch, you fucked her. How could you fuck her!" That this public tantrum was evidently shot at a gay-and-lesbian country-western bar called Rawhide II suggests that Verhoeven, at least, understood the implications of this scene.

Less homophobic than misogynist, more ridiculous than not, *Basic Instinct* is full of fantastic projections—with all manner of doubling, evil twins and shadow selves. (There's even a character named "Hoberman," although I consider that less an acknowledgment of my panning Eszterhas's *Music Box* than a reference to the current Touchstone president.) If half the murders go absurdly unsolved—well, Freud would understand that too. Just what do these women want? The lesbian activity, such as it is, is a surplus of sexual heat, a factor of an overall female uncanniness, the manifestation of a male's fear that he might be expendable.

*Basic Instinct* is undoubtedly exploitative, but it's also unsettling—it's as if the female sex-toys in a garden-variety porn flick suddenly developed an unpredictable, shocking, vengeful autonomy. "Funny how the subconscious works," somebody muses late in the film. I dare say, it's a riot. One man's basic instinct is another's high anxiety.

## BLADE RUNNER

Originally published as "City of Dreadful Night,"
the *Village Voice* (September 15, 1992).

S OME MOVIES APPEAR IN TANDEM, SO PERFECTLY MISMATCHED THEY MIGHT HAVE been produced by the force that zapped the rocket fleeing Krypton and split Bizarro from Superbaby. First materializing in June 1982, two weekends into the *E.T.* era, Ridley Scott's *Blade Runner* is the Spielberg film's evil twin— a competing fantasy for the Age of Reagan.

Where *E.T.* was set in an idyllic whitebread suburb, *Blade Runner* invented a horrific multicultural inner city. Humanist to the max, *E.T.* resurrected J. C. in the form of a lovable alien; *Blade Runner* featured robot "replicants" more soulful than the *Homo sapiens* who hunted them. And, as *E.T.* proved the most universal movie ever made, Scott's $30 million bomb was relegated to the midnight circuit almost immediately. (Indeed, *E.T.* made Reese's Pieces while *Premiere* once humorously listed the corporations that vanished after being plugged in *Blade Runner*, Atari, Bell Telephone, Cuisinart . . .)

But if *E.T.* was the ultimate middlebrow cult film, *Blade Runner* outflanked it at both ends of the spectrum. At once a touchstone for MTV and an avatar of cyberpunk (predating the publication of *Neuromancer* by two years), an F/X head trip and an object of academic discourse, praised in *Starlog* and parsed in *October*, *Blade Runner* spent a decade proselytizing itself on home video and in classrooms—despite the inherent loss of visual grandeur.

Thus, the very month that trendmeister Peter Wollen informed a scholarly conclave that *Blade Runner* was the lone "canonical" movie of the eighties, its unheralded rerelease in the "director's version" broke house records at the Nuart in L.A. and the Castro in San Francisco. The subject of two imposingly theoretical essays in *Camera Obscura*, *Blade Runner* reopens here timidly relegated by Warners to the less-than-Ziegfeld screen of the Loews Village.

---

Given *Blade Runner*'s current reputation, it's instructive to review the tenor of its notices. "All visuals and no story," David Denby complained in *New York*, the summa of a "hundred naively bad experimental films." Denby's verdict ("terribly dull") was mild compared to his colleagues'. "*Blade Runner* has nothing to give the audience," declared Pauline Kael, while Michael Sragow concluded his *Rolling Stone* pan by declaring *Blade Runner* "best suited for zombies" and Stephen Schiff, who may be found frolicking about the still-living corpse of Leni Riefenstahl in this month's *Vanity Fair*, condemned *Blade Runner* to a moral gulag as "a film without sense . . . a film without soul, without conscience."

The reasons that *Blade Runner* was hated are the very things that give it grandeur. Visual rather than literary, blatantly post-authorial, the movie is a kind of natural effluvium, a ready-made metaphor, a treasure trove of vulgar postmodernist "jesgrew," that seems to have escaped human control.

Indeed, like Orson Welles's *Touch of Evil*, *Blade Runner* is a film without a fixed version. The current release is evidently the cut shown (with disastrous results) to the original preview audiences. Harrison Ford's much-maligned hard-boiled voice-over has been subtracted (save for the terse eulogy describing the suicide of the replicant *Übermensch* Rutger Hauer). The tacked-on "happy ending" (which supposedly recycled aerial outtakes from *The Shining*) has been junked—the movie now ends with the melancholy reminder that Ford's replicant love (Sean Young) is fast heading for a pre programmed obsolescence.

Is this an improvement? The old *Blade Runner* was a movie that thrived on disjuncture. In an essay on cult films that has also become canonical, Umberto Eco writes that *Casablanca* is not a movie but *the* movies—it transcends personal artistry or even human intent, the clichés themselves are "having a conversation." So, too, *Blade Runner*—a glittering mishmash of *Frankenstein* and *The Big Sleep*, *Metropolis* and *Love Story*, Josef von Sternberg and George Lucas. The old phony ending was hardly inappropriate. After all, it's a secondhand image used to construct a pseudo-escape—precisely the sort of simulation that *Blade Runner* is all about.

The Philip K. Dick novel from which *Blade Runner* was adapted is set in a radioactive world abandoned by humans for space colonies and concerns a bounty hunter who "retires" rogue androids and who himself becomes a kind of android. The movie retains a number of Dick's details—notably the "empathy test," which defines humanity—while simplifying the plot, introducing its own jargon, and transposing the action to Los Angeles 2019, where it could be thoroughly overwhelmed by the mise-en-scène.

As splendid an assemblage as *Blade Runner*'s sources is its look—a fantastic amalgam of locations, back lots (including Warners' old New York set), and miniatures. Although this futuristic vision of acid rain and eternal night, where advertising is the landscape, and Hovercrafts zip past the animated billboards as punks slurp ramen in the casbah below, owes little to Dick, it does anticipate William Gibson ("Night City was like a deranged experiment in social Darwinism, designed by a bored researcher who kept his thumb permanently on the fast-forward button"), not to mention the hallucinatory inner city of Fredric Jameson's "Hysterical Sublime," in which the decay of urban life produces its own heightened exhilaration.

The inspiration must be Hong Kong, although Scott told one visitor to his set that he was "constantly waving [a reproduction of Edward Hopper's *Nighthawks*] under the noses of the production team to illustrate the look and mood I was after." Nevertheless, now more than ever, *Blade Runner* has come to seem the quintessential Los Angeles film. Mike Davis's *City of Quartz* has a chapter pitting *Blade Runner* against Gramsci while the 1988 report *L.A. 2000: A City for the Future* specifically invokes the "*Blade Runner* scenario" as "the fusion of individual cultures into a demotic polyglotism ominous with unresolved hostilities."

The *Blade Runner* dystopia is hardly novel—an oligarchy in which a corporate state presides over a squalid ecological nightmare, the population drugged and pacified by image-induced dreams of consumption.

As in *Metropolis*, capital transforms labor into machines. But here, where every desire is reproduced and amplified in an endless chain of simulation, there's a continual dialogue between human and replicant, nature and culture. The human protagonists are all defined by their relation to the replicants. Are the replicants people who are treated as objects or are they objects who have somehow become human? (The snapshots they use to document their simulated memories suggest another Jameson trope—the postmodern sense of the past as a shoe box full of old photographs.)

As the lacquered replicant of a noir heroine, Young's Rachel is a multiple simulation. (She's the ultimate android in that she has no awareness of being anything other than human—her implanted memories are identical to actual experience.) In the movie's most discomforting scene, the Ford character—who knows what she is—compels her to love him, prompting her response step by step. Does he feel so free to dominate her because she's female or because she's a machine? Is teaching a machine to love you a form of masturbation?

The replicants are products of human vanity—but with a difference. They bear the burden of existential angst and romantic rebellion. Thus, the Hauer character wrests the movie away from its nominal hero and the slogan of the Tyrell corporation turns out to be true: The replicants are "more human than human."

Call it the death of the subject (as well as the author). Predicated on the pathos of machines who know they are programmed to shut down, *Blade Runner* suggests that, far from a state of grace, humanity is barely a state of mind.

## KISS ME DEADLY

Originally published as "The Great Whatzit,"
the *Village Voice* (March 15, 1994).

**G**ENRES COLLIDE IN THE GREAT HOLLYWOOD MOVIES OF THE MID-FIFTIES THAW. The western goes South with *The Searchers*; the cartoon merges with the musical in *The Girl Can't Help It*. Science fiction becomes pop sociology in

*Invasion of the Body Snatchers*; noir veers into apocalyptic sci-fi with Robert Aldrich's 1955 *Kiss Me Deadly*.

*Kiss Me Deadly*, which opens the Walter Reade's monthlong Aldrich retro, tracks the sleaziest private investigator in American movies through a nocturnal labyrinth to a white-hot vision of cosmic annihilation. From the perversely backward title crawl (outrageously accompanied by orgasmic heavy breathing) through the climactic explosion, the film is sensationally baroque—eschewing straight exposition for a jarring succession of bizarre images, bravura sound matching, and encoded riddles.

Mike Hammer plays with fire and (literally) gets burned. Jagged and aggressive, *Kiss Me Deadly* is an extremely paranoid movie—with all that implies. The mode is angst-ridden hypermasculinity. Fear of a nuclear holocaust fuses with fear of a femme fatale. Hammer pursues and is pursued by a shadowy cabal—a mysterious "They," as they're called in the film's key exchange, "the nameless ones who kill people for the Great Whatzit."

Hammer's quest is played out through a deranged Cubistic space amid the debris of Western civilization—shards of opera, deserted museums, molls who paraphrase Shakespeare, mad references to Greek mythology and the New Testament. A nineteenth-century poem furnishes the movie's major clue. The faux Calder mobile and checkerboard floor pattern of Hammer's overdecorated pad—a bag of golf clubs in the corner and Hollywood's first answering machine built into the wall—add to the crazy, clashing expressionism.

Among other things, *Kiss Me Deadly* served to kiss off Mickey Spillane, the most successful American novelist of the Cold War. Spillane's violent thrillers sold 24 million copies between 1947 and 1954; in 1956, seven of the 10 best-selling titles in the entire history of American fiction were by Spillane. Filling a function now satisfied by talk radio, Spillane created a character who was God's Angry Man. Mike Hammer was a self-righteous avenger—judge, prosecuting attorney, jury, and executioner in one. His antagonists were gangsters and Communists. At the end of *One Lonely Night*, he exults that he "killed more people tonight than I have fingers on my hands. I shot them in cold blood and enjoyed every minute of it.... They were Commies."

Hammer knows why his "rottenness was tolerated." His mission was "to kill the scum.... I was the evil that opposed other evil." This ends-justify-the-means brutality had its contemporary political manifestation in Senator Joseph McCarthy, described by one colleague in suitably Hammer-esque terms as a "fighting Irish Marine [who] would give the shirt off his back to anyone who needs it—except a dirty, lying, stinking Communist. That guy, he'd kill." In late 1954, after McCarthy was under Senate investigation, the *Saturday Review* published an essay bracketing Hammer and McCarthy. The same analogy occurred to Aldrich. In some interviews he called Hammer "a cynical fascist" and Spillane "an antidemocratic figure," arguing before the MPAA Code Administration that the film demonstrated that "justice is not to be found in a self-anointed, one-man vigilante."

"He can sniff out information like nobody I ever saw," one cop says of Hammer with admiring disdain. As played by Ralph Meeker, Hammer exhibits a surplus of macho individualism, aggravated by sexual repression and crass self-interest, that is so exaggerated it ultimately becomes a criticism of itself.

A director who has several times gone in and out of popular and critical fashion. Aldrich sprang from a prominent Rhode Island family. His grandfather was a U.S. Senator, his uncle served as Eisenhower's ambassador to Great Britain, his aunt married John D. Rockefeller Jr., his first cousin was Nelson Aldrich Rockefeller.

Aldrich's early Hollywood associations were even more distinguished. He served as an assistant director for Jean Renoir, Lewis Milestone, William Wellman, Joseph Losey, and Charles Chaplin; he worked closely with leftists Abraham Polonsky, Robert Rossen, and John Garfield. (Introducing Losey's 1951 *M* remake, a who's who of future blacklistees, last year at the Museum of Modern Art, French film authority Pierre Rissient proposed it as the major influence on *Kiss Me Deadly*.)

Given the company he kept, Aldrich expected to be named during the Hollywood witch-hunt but wasn't; perhaps he was too unimportant or too well connected. When he teamed with producer Victor Saville to make *Kiss Me Deadly*, Aldrich hired A. I. Bezzerides, another Hollywood fellow traveler, to adapt the novel. (Bezzerides, who wasn't blacklisted as is sometimes written, served penance by furnishing the script for the anti-Communist thriller *A Bullet for Joey* as a vehicle for another recovering liberal, Edward G. Robinson.) Bezzerides imbued *Kiss Me Deadly* with a surplus of cynicism and free association: "I wrote it fast, because I had contempt for it. It was automatic writing. Things were in the air at the time and I put them in."

Defending film violence in an article written for the *New York Herald Tribune*, Aldrich blandly asserted that "we kept faith with 60 million Mickey Spillane readers" in making "a movie of action, violence, and suspense in good taste." Nevertheless, Bezzerides changed the novel considerably—eliminating the first-person narrative, downgrading Hammer from private eye to divorce dick while raising his status as a consumer. The novel's souped-up heap became a Jaguar. Hammer's secretary, Velda, is transformed from a chaste and adoring fiancée to professional sex bait. The location shifts from New York to L.A. The villains mutate from gangsters to atom spies.

Shortly before its scheduled opening in May 1955, *Kiss Me Deadly* was condemned by the Legion of Decency. Although United Artists made a few minor cuts, some TV stations and newspapers refused to accept advertising for the movie, and later, when the Kefauver committee visited Hollywood to investigate the effects of movies on juvenile delinquency, *Kiss Me Deadly* was one of the exhibits.

Never reviewed in the *New York Times, Kiss Me Deadly* was banned in Britain; in France, however, the newly founded *Cahiers du Cinéma* made it a cause. Aldrich was hailed as "the first director of the atomic age." Young critics Truffaut and Godard repeatedly cited the movie, whose traces can be seen in *Shoot the Piano Player* and *Alphaville*. (*Kiss Me Deadly* was not just a cult film for the *nouvelle vague*—the hissing, corrosive finale was even transposed to *Raiders of the Lost Ark*, another pulp fiction version of the Manhattan Project.)

Claude Chabrol, who called *Kiss Me Deadly* "the thriller of tomorrow," wrote the quintessential celebration: "It has chosen to create itself out of the worst material to be found, the most deplorable, the most nauseous product of a genre in a state of putrefaction: a Mickey Spillane story. Robert Aldrich and A. I. Bezzerides have taken this threadbare and lacklustre fabric and splendidly rewoven it into rich patterns of the most enigmatic arabesques."

## NATURAL BORN KILLERS

Originally published as "True Romance," the
*Village Voice* (August 30, 1994).

**M**ORE BOMBAST THAN BOMBSHELL, *NATURAL BORN KILLERS* IS STILL SUFFICIENTLY schizoid to infect the viewer with a nasty case of ambivalence. Two hours of Oliver Stone shadowboxing here should leave you impressed but unconvinced, torn between admiration and disgust, a desire to praise audacious filmmaking and the urge to laugh at rampaging idiocy.

It's hard to fault Stone's timing. *Natural Born Killers* is both an aesthetic throwback and a new advance in meta exploitation. Cosmic bummer or current affair? On the one hand, this is the most blatantly avant-garde studio release since Dennis Hopper delivered *The Last Movie* (not to mention the most solemnly ludicrous vision of evil since Luchino Visconti applied black lipstick to National Socialism in *The Damned*). On the other, it surfs into theaters on a tsunami of ancillary hype.

In theory, the movie sounded like a belated postscript to the serial killer craze. In practice it's fresher than fresh. The premise, adapted from a story by red-hot Quentin Tarantino, could have been the centerpiece of *New York*'s recent "White Trash" cover story. The *New Yorker*, meanwhile, used its Stone profile as a pretext to emblazon their cover with the magic letters "O. J." for the third time since the Night of the White Bronco.

Basically, *Natural Born Killers* posits a nouveau Bonnie and Clyde—Mickey and Mallory Knox, played to the max by Woody Harrelson and Juliette Lewis—as a pair of dada punk cartoon cracker *l'amour fou*–struck thrill-killer Mansonettes, and presents the tale of their telecelebrity beatitude as an exercise in frenzied montage. The opening desert diner massacre—a bungled jumble of pulverized scorpions and shifting angles, the film stock oscillating like an old TV between livid color and black and white—buries all horror and foreboding in a welter of gimmicks, including one of Lewis's patented writhing cooch dances. The performances are beyond Kabuki. While big-jawed Harrelson seems lit from within like a jack-o'-lantern, Lewis, her bulging forehead concealed beneath a blond Brunhilde wig, is so rabid she must have been bitten by De Niro on the set of *Cape Fear*.

Clearly, *Natural Born Killers* is meant to be a comedy—although Stone never fences with a rapier when he can wrap his mitts around a Louisville Slugger, presenting, for example, Mallory's life as a sitcom complete with laugh track and Rodney Dangerfield as her abusive lech of a father. As in *Badlands*, Terrence Malick's more subdued treatment of similar material, the delinquent couple begin their spree by disposing of the girl's parents—here, however, they bludgeon Dad and drown him in a fish tank, then torch Mom in her sleep, telegraphing Stone's strategy to obliterate David Lynch and beat Tarantino's premise to a hallucinatory pulp.

Shifting film stocks and formats, throwing up rear-screen projections or subliminal images of bloody horror, interpolating all manner of animation, stock footage, and stroboscopic monkey screams, Stone has no shortage of visual ideas—and, as in *JFK*, he's found the film editors to cope with them. *Natural Born Killers* is full of hellfire and Japanese movie monsters. In its creepy-crawly nature inserts and computer-distorted close-ups, *Natural Born Killers* suggests a whole culture on bad acid. With Trent Reznor's symphonic sound mix underscoring the montage hysteria, the effect is pulverizing: Stan Brakhage meets Sam Fuller, with a soupçon of Dalí-Buñuel insect fear. When Mickey and Mallory take refuge in a motel room (a hostage cowering in the corner), the TV erupts with images of Hitler, Stalin, and a mountain of corpses, as well as clips from *The Wild Bunch* and *Midnight Express*. As in a Hans-Jürgen Syberberg film, the window functions as yet another TV.

Stone's anthology of celluloid atrocities resembles Wilhelm and Birgit Hein's underground assemblage *Kali-Filme*—except that the Heins' flick, a homemade contraption meant for study in the affectless, half-deserted aesthetic catacombs of New York and Berlin, exhibits a certain anthropological detachment while cinema devil worship à la Stone is an overweening megamillion-dollar attempt to huff and puff and blow your house down. Every fade is the equivalent of an atomic blast.

Unlike Tarantino, Stone is obsessed with generating significance. Mickey and Mallory alternately reflect their society, represent an endless cycle of abuse, and enact timeless Jungian archetypes. Hence, the self-canceling aspect to Stone's mania: The body count rises but nothing can quite project the couple's absolute evil. The scenes in which she murders the hapless gas jockey she's seduced into going down on her or he shoots a happy snake-handling Indian shaman (Russell Means) are meant to show Mickey and Mallory's worst, most secret transgressions. But, after killing 12 cops and an unspecified number of civilians, they only achieve notoriety as the subject of the tabloid TV news show *American Maniacs*, hosted by Wayne Gale (Robert Downey, Jr.), a gross, braying Australian modeled on Steve Dunleavy and Robin Leach.

Like Bonnie and Clyde in their 1967 incarnation, Mickey and Mallory are adored by kids all over the world; bad as the Knoxes may be, society is even worse. The outlaws are caught by a lunatic cop (introduced throttling a sweet-faced hooker in another image-ridden motel) and sent to a hellish prison administered by Tommy Lee Jones. Wildly camping as the pomaded warden, Jones manipulates himself like a marionette. He's a dervish of stooped positions, enlivening every scene with his slack-jawed, rubber-faced contortions, looking like Charles Burns's Dog Boy fronting for an entourage culled from the pages of *Mad* magazine. Meanwhile, Wayne Gale contrives to make television history, following the Super Bowl with an exclusive interview with the condemned Mickey.

There's nothing new, except maybe in degree, to such Hollywood finger-pointing at big, bad TV. Still, unexpectedly improving in its final reel, *Natural Born Killers* plays to its own medium's strength to end with a blast of pure anarchy and mad release—Stone even tossing "Night on Bald Mountain" into the charnel house mix.

---

Among other things, we've been replaying Summer of '69 for the past two months. The macho-patriotic *True Lies* is our debased, current equivalent of the Apollo Project's techno-extravagant moon landing, and if *Forrest Gump* represents the counterculture's Woodshtick yin, *Natural Born Killers* is a blatant expression of its contemporaneous Mansonesque yang. Mickey's explanation of murder as cosmic and natural is pure Charlie—as is his observation that "media's like the weather, only it's man-made."

But just as pundits will inevitably trap themselves flogging the tar baby of Stone's scenario, so Stone can't bear to separate himself from the spectacle at large—topical to the last, he winds up *Natural Born Killers* by flashing Eric and Lyle, Lorena, Tonya, Waco, and the whole sick crew (including a last-minute insert of O. J.) in our face. *Natural Born Killers* demonstrates that there isn't anything Stone won't try for an effect—including strip-mining the integrity of his own strenuously achieved paranoia. The movie doesn't achieve full amorality when Harrelson crowns Charles Manson "king," but when he trashes JFK with the observation that "Oswald might have been a pussy, but he was a great shot." (Even so, the joke is evil with a small *e*.)

Having produced, in *JFK*, the most baroque snuff film in American history (and the most blatant since Thomas Edison documented the electrocution of an elephant), Stone is scarcely detached from the celebrity-death religion he burlesques. Indeed, given the megalomaniacal occultism that underscores Stone's enterprise, I wonder why he isn't afraid that this frenzy of subliminal "evil" images won't light some lunatic's fire. Perhaps he wants a Hinckley-style assassin to call his own.

---

## PULP FICTION

Originally published as "Pulp and Glory," the *Village Voice*
(October 11, 1994).

**M**ORE THAN ANYTHING ELSE, QUENTIN TARANTINO IS A SPINNER OF TALL TALES— the superbly garrulous, living embodiment of the movie enthusiast's hey-wouldn't-it-be-great-if aesthetic. *Pulp Fiction* trumps *Reservoir Dogs* to confirm the 31-year-old writer-director as current King of the Wild Frontier, but nearly as remarkable as *Pulp Fiction*'s loop-the-loop digressions, shock violence, and outrageous plot twists has been its capacity to mobilize media attention. There's a sense in which Tarantino's now legendary ascension from video store geek to Palme d'Or chic is his own greatest whopper.

A blood-soaked exercise in nihilo-Neanderthal absurdism, Tarantino's debut moved simultaneously backward and forward in cinema history. "The first coffee-house action movie," per *Vanity Fair* (forgetting *Breathless* and *Shoot the Piano Player*), *Reservoir Dogs* "spoke to Kurt Cobain" and attracted "people who thought they were too cool for *Lethal Weapon*" with, among other things, the ear slice the *New York Times Magazine* leapfrogged past *Psycho's* shower sequence to term "the nastiest bit of screen violence" since Luis Buñuel and Salvador Dalí slashed an eyeball in *their* 1929 debut, *Un Chien Andalou*. The comparison is not entirely inapt. Just as *Un Chien Andalou* travestied the poetic avant-garde of the 1920s, so the independently produced *Reservoir Dogs* single-handedly shifted the Sundance Film Festival diet from granola and skim milk to french fries smothered in ketchup, after its 1992 world premiere there.

No less aggressive or stylized than its precursor, *Pulp Fiction* is a movie of interlocking stories set in an imaginary demimonde and held together by languorous fades, humorous ellipses, and nonstop conversation. The comic structure is largely based on a series of two-handers: Tim Roth playing verbal footsie with Amanda Plummer, a goofily stoned John Travolta escorting the haughty Uma Thurman, world-weary Bruce Willis coming home to kittenish (and ultimately tiresome) Maria de Madeiros, *Die Hard* Willis battling volcanic Ving Rhames, rattled Travolta debating the wired, superbad Samuel L. Jackson.

Tarantino has an unerring command of slang and, in lieu of visual ambience, invents an aural one. Every character has a rap or a riff, if not a full-fledged theory of life. (At times, *Pulp Fiction* suggests a two-fisted Jarmusch film.) No wonder actors love Tarantino. Not only does he write hilarious, convoluted dialogue but he permits them to posture through every scene as an extended one-on-one gabfest confrontation. Call the mode "Talk Talk Bang Bang." The language is as calculatedly brutal as the action—full of baroque racial, xenophobic invective as well as continual profanity.

Tarantino's America is a wondrously wild and crazy place. "They robbed a bank with a telephone," says one character in amazement—especially as he, and nearly everyone else in the cast, is packing heat. Violence erupts out of nowhere—or rather, it erupts out of some kind of "innocent" fun. A fetishistic close-up of fixing, shooting, and booting smack leads, by the by, to a bloody, drooling OD, hysterical panic, and finally, the most successfully horrific comedy sequence in the movie. Tarantino is too fascinated by the nuance of situation to be a master of suspense, but *Pulp Fiction* is predicated upon his gift for abruptly raising the stakes. A couple talk themselves into robbing the joint where they're having breakfast—chitchat giving way to lunatic frenzy. Two professional killers riff on European taste in American fast food en route to a wildly theatrical hit. Toying with one victim, the gunman offhandedly shoots a second, then apologizes to the survivor: "I'm sorry—did I break your concentration?"

Despite its title, *Pulp Fiction* has less to do with the hard-boiled detective stories published 60 years ago in *Black Mask* magazine than with the déclassé action movies of the early seventies. The movie resonates with echoes of biker and doper flicks, vigilante sagas like *Dirty Harry* and *Walking Tall*, the genres *Variety* dubbed spaghetti westerns, chopsocky, and, especially, blaxploitation, as well as the contemporary art-splatter of Hollywood auteurs Peckinpah, Scorsese, and De Palma—movies that were not only violent but steeped in moral confusion. More generally, the title suggests Tarantino's spongelike capacity to absorb whatever he sees. The seventies is always a touchstone, but *Pulp Fiction* lifts bits of business from *Kiss Me Deadly* and *Psycho* and Jean-Luc Godard, the inventor of movie postmodernism who has spawned yet another disciple.

In *Reservoir Dogs*, Tarantino's fanciful creatures asserted their reality by analyzing Madonna or musing upon the TV series *Get Christie Love. Pulp Fiction* is an even more naturalized hall of mirrors. Thurman wears Anna Karina's wig-hat; Willis does Ralph Meeker doing Brando. Jackson's Fu Manchu mustache, fierce mutton chops, and oiled 'fro make him pure essence of 1974. (All he lacks is the lime-green leisure suit.) Travolta's character is *Welcome Back, Kotter*'s Vinnie Barbarino grown up into a hit man called Vincent Vega—as in star. "We're gonna be like three little Fonzies here," Jackson soothes the participants of one Mexican standoff by way of saying Be Cool.

*Pulp Fiction*'s most elaborate set piece endearingly sends up Tarantino's own mind-set, inventing a made-for-57th-Street theme restaurant populated by fifties icons. "It's like a wax musem with a pulse," Travolta smirks—as if he weren't sitting in his own personal Hall of Fame, particularly once Thurman maneuvers him into a Twist contest that quickly turns *Bandstand* extravaganza of tiptoe swiveling, lasso moves, and synchronized shoulder strokes.

*Reservoir Dogs* was so totally an exercise in style and attitude that one could rightly wonder if it had anything more on its mind. In fact, although populated almost exclusively by presumably straight male Caucasians, the movie was obsessed, in its own flavorsome terms, with niggers, bitches, and fags. (Tarantino's favorite compliment was L. M. Kit Carson's admiring observation that he had produced a real "white guy movie.") *Pulp Fiction* brings more to the surface. While a second viewing eliminates Tarantino's mainly excellent narrative surprises, it also reveals how cleverly he sets up his punch lines—the early reference to the gangster played by Rhames getting "fucked like a bitch," the instant hostility between the Travolta and Willis characters, the degree to which the elements in the latter's dream are reconfigured in a far more nightmarish reality.

Indeed, spinning variations on what Tarantino himself calls "the oldest chestnuts in the world" (the guy who takes out the mob boss's wife, the boxer who is supposed to throw the fight, and "the opening five minutes of every other Joel Silver movie"), *Pulp Fiction* manages to get more pathological than one could believe possible—whether transforming cold-blooded killers into philosopher dorks or seducing the opening night crowd at the New York Film

Festival into laughing appreciatively when someone gets his head blown off and drenches a car's interior with blood. Tarantino, who associates a jocular attitude toward onscreen violence with the blaxploitation audience, demonstrates his own particular power by casting himself as the one character who can make the terrifying Jackson shuffle, even as he manages to enunciate the phrase "dead nigger" four times in as many minutes.

Whether or not *Pulp Fiction* is, as Janet Maslin enthused in the *Times*, "a stunning vision of destiny, choice and spiritual possibility," it amply demonstrates Tarantino's particular sense of movies as a medium that permits the quasi-divine manipulation of time and space, including the ability to resurrect the dead. *Pulp Fiction's* narrative loops back on itself as elegantly as that of *Reservoir Dogs* but to far more self-consciously playful purpose. Butch not only escapes on a chopper emblazoned with the cockamamie "Grace," but his getaway is accompanied by the theme from *The Twilight Zone*.

Never mind that Tarantino lifted *Pulp Fiction's* riff on Ezekiel 25:17 from an old kung fu movie or Jackson's redemption from *Kung Fu*, he is some kind of miracle worker. Reminiscing (with Dennis Hopper no less) in the current *Grand Street*, the filmmaker recalls, with some bemusement, the powers of persuasion he honed during his years behind a video store counter: "I remember—this is really weird—I created a following for Eric Rohmer in Manhattan Beach and the South Bay area." That was talk talk without the bang bang.

## MEET "BEAT" TAKESHI

Originally published as "Beatitudes," the *Village Voice* (November 14, 1995).

FORGET FLACCID STALLONE, DER KNUCKLEHEAD ARNOLD, GRANDDADDY CLINT. KEEP your Bruce and those petulantly pumped-up plastic men Van Damme and Seagal. Jackie Chan is slowing down, Chow Yun-Fat will never cross over, Ice-T needs a new agent. The international film circuit's current tough guy du jour is a 48-year-old former stand-up comic nicknamed "Beat" Takeshi—a block of rage so square he's cool.

Shambling into town for the crescendo of the Walter Reade's Japanese indie series, Takeshi Kitano is blue-collar everyman turned hard-boiled absurdist. A superstar actor, novelist, sports commentator, and all-around media personality in Japan, Kitano is known here mainly for his indelible performance as the affably brutal Sergeant Hara in Nagisa Oshima's 1983 *Merry Christmas, Mr.*

*Lawrence.* (He more recently appeared as the heavy in *Johnny Mnemonic*, a part greatly expanded in the movie's more commercially successful Japanese cut.)

Kitano has directed five movies since 1989; the first two are having their belated local premieres. *Violent Cop* (1989) stars the director as a deadpan Dirty Harry, beating drug-dealer butt and stepping on authority's toes to the accompaniment of an infectious theme that reconfigures a melancholy Erik Satie refrain into something more appropriate to a seventies disco. Impassive, slightly quizzical, smiling no more than once or twice a movie, Kitano is most expressive when he's socking someone. His cop never misses an opportunity to stomp a suspect—even kicking his own partner when he gets in the way. The movie's original title translates as "Warning: This Man Is Wild!"

In Japan, Jolt supercaffeinated soda chose Kitano as its corporate spokesman. No less than Toshiro Mifune (the last Japanese action star to intrude on American consciousness), Kitano relies on distinctive body language. But where the young Mifune was hyperkinetic, middle-aged Kitano is a stolid rock of concentration in a treacherous world. *Violent Cop*, which features no guns in its first half, is a film of constant pummeling physicality. It's been suggested that the movies he directs recreate the distinctive rhythm of his heavy, hunched-over, off-kilter stride.

*Boiling Point* (1990), which Kitano directed from his own script, is a far more eccentric mélange of jump cuts, mood shifts, and oblique exposition. Simply put, the movie pits the lackadaisical member of an amateur baseball team against some neighborhood yakuza. Be that as it may, Kitano appears midway through and takes over as the debt-ridden ex-yakuza owner of an Okinawa hostess bar. A monster of sullen aggression, even crazier than the hero of *Violent Cop*, he brutalizes all he encounters—at one point casually smashing whiskey bottles over his customers' befuddled heads. The Japanese title is an imaginary base-ball score suggesting that the visiting team has won the game in extra innings (baseball is a recurring Kitano motif, although he's also made a movie about a deaf-mute surfer); conventional wisdom has it that *Boiling Point* has something to do with the Japanese conflict between team spirit and individualism.

As an actor, Kitano defends his screen space against all comers. In Takeshi Ishii's *Gonin*, the flashy but empty caper flick rounding out the Kitano sidebar, Kitano materializes in the last half hour to decimate the cast as a hit man with a bandaged eye and a bad attitude. But given the havoc he wreaks in character, Kitano is a surprisingly classical filmmaker. He makes exceedingly precise use of post-dubbed sound. His camera angles tend toward the coolly functional; they're setups for occasional overheads or choreographed chase scenes. *Violent Cop*'s signature piece is a botched drug bust in which the suspect takes out three detectives, decks a fourth in a slo-mo punch-out, then (his mad dash underscored by some unlikely cocktail jazz) sprints through an unheeding workaday neighborhood, lethal baseball bat in hand. Although this prolonged, naturalistically grueling pursuit ends with Violent Cop ramming the suspect with his squad car, Kitano more typically uses long shots to muffle or defamiliarize violence.

Meanwhile, the unfathomable *Boiling Point* offers as much moment-to-moment amazement as any movie has all year. The bit of business in which a machine gun concealed in a floral bouquet goes off prematurely, and the sequence in which Kitano demands that his sidekick and girlfriend screw each other and then, increasingly excited by watching them, pushes the guy off the doll and begins buggering him, are pure *Pulp Fiction*. Indeed, Quentin Tarantino has evidently acquired Kitano's best to date, the 1993 *Sonatine*, for theatrical release. To know where that's coming from, catch *Boiling Point* first.

## ASHES OF TIME

Originally published as "Stormy Weather," the *Village Voice* (May 21, 1996).

**W**AFTING SLOWLY INTO THE RAREFIED ATMOSPHERE OF CINEASTE CONSCIOUSNESS, the films of Wong Kar-Wai are as convoluted and circuitous as their New York distribution patterns. Before Miramax released *Chungking Express*, Wong's movies were fabled objects—found on the fading Chinatown circuit, at one-night festival stands, or in occasional museum shows.

Wong, a cosmopolitan hipster and the only director to enjoy successive retrospectives at the Rosemary Theater on Canal Street and the American Museum of the Moving Image in Queens, may yet catch fire here before the sun sets on Hong Kong cinema—but don't count on it. *Chungking Express* is still hanging on as a midnight show, but I wouldn't wait to catch *Ashes of Time*, Wong's outrageously mannered new wave sword film.

In adapting *The Eagle-Shooting Hero*, an extremely popular four-volume martial arts novel by Jin Yong (HK's equivalent of Sir Walter Scott), Wong focused on two marginal characters—a pair of old sword fighters recalling their youth. Thus, *Ashes of Time* is set in a golden desert populated by a gang of angst-ridden, lovelorn mercenary killers. Just another fatalistic hitman, the memory-haunted Ouyang (Leslie Cheung) runs a wilderness pit stop and serves as an agent for the younger swordsmen drifting through. One (Tony "*City of Sadness*" Leung) is going blind, another (the *other* Tony Leung) is losing his short-term memory, a third (Brigitte Lin) has a full-fledged split personality—the male Yang and female Yin.

*Ashes of Time* opens with a bravura bit of leap-thrust-parry, rendered in Wong's patented slo-mo blur. But although the sword fights—each making use of some elemental motif (water, fire, sandstorms) or startling detail (a severed hand launched across the screen like a rocket)—grow more spectacular as the movie progresses, *Ashes of Time* is more extravagantly moody than it is violent. This is a movie of languorous melancholy and symphonic yearnings in which the director's blatant showmanship continually confounds genre expectations.

It's typical of the pretzel logic that Ouyang would first be hired by Yang's old friend Huang because Huang dumped Yang's "sister" Yin, and then be hired by Yin to kill her jealous "brother" Yang. Thus ping-pong'd between the sibs, Ouyang realizes that they are the same lovely schizo. The episode's emotional climax comes, however, when dreamy Yin mistakes Ouyang for Huang while, in a sultry montage of substitute memories, Ouyang pretends that Yin is his own long-lost love (Maggie Cheung). Thus, *Ashes of Time* is mostly anticipation, interrupted by sudden slurred zaps of inexplicable martial-arts tumult, as well as mystically congruent earthquakes and geysers.

Notorious among Hong Kong film buffs well before its premiere at the 1994 Venice Film Festival, *Ashes of Time* not only cost a massive (for HK) $5.5 million but managed to prevail over an extremely troubled production history. The movie, whose exteriors were filmed in mainland China, was begun in 1992, interrupted, and then—thanks to the complex schedules of the all-star cast—postponed until the summer of 1993. In the interim, a number of the performers appeared in a parody version of *The Eagle-Shooting Hero*, directed by Wong's sometime partner Jeff Lau, while Wong himself knocked off the insouciantly experimental *Chungking Express*.

*Ashes of Time* was shot, like almost all of Wong's movies, by Chris Doyle, and is no less stylized than *Chungking Express*. The frame permanently askew, the action accompanied by a score that privileges wailing flutes, solo electric guitar, bagpipes, and a droning male chorus, with bits of Buddhist wisdom interspersed, this sensuous reverie manages to come on as pure kinesis, even when nothing narrative is happening. The wind is moving in every close-up and so is the light. The wicker birdcage that dominates Ouyang's shack has the effect of a mirrored ball in a discotheque. Just as a network of flickering shadows all but efface the identities of Wong's melancholy protagonists, so the complicated narrative is nearly overpowered by the film's lengthy buildups, cathedral lighting, handheld camera stunts, complicated flashbacks, and prophetic flash-forwards.

Although the names Akira Kurosawa and Sergio Leone (especially *Once Upon a Time in America*), Sam Peckinpah (not *The Wild Bunch* so much as *Pat Garrett and Billy the Kid*), and even Josef von Sternberg come tripping to the tongue, Wong's voluptuously mournful ambience is of a piece with his previous films. For all the extreme tilts, outlandish angles, and pungent ultraviolence, there's nothing more characteristic of this brooding director than the rainy-day crash-pad ambience of jilted swordsmen sitting around and watching the storm clouds pass over the desert.

## MARS ATTACKS!

Originally published as "Creature Feature," the *Village Voice*
(December 17, 1996).

IF THE MISSION OF THE MOVIES IS TO RENDER EPHEMERA MONUMENTAL, THEN Tim Burton's *Mars Attacks!* is pure cinema. This may not be the first megamillion-dollar Hollywood blockbuster based on a bunch of 35-year-old bubblegum cards, but it's surely the standard against which all such subsequent efforts will be judged.

No one will ever accuse Burton of betraying his supremely cheesy source. *Mars Attacks!* is less camp than hyperreal in adapting the Topps series, deemed too lurid for kids back in 1962. The movie is a taxonomy of Cold War extraterrestrial invasion clichés. The theremins wail overtime as a flotilla of rotating saucers clutter up outer space like so many hubcaps on the cosmic junk heap.

Like Rupert Murdoch's lugubrious *Independence Day*, Time Warner's rival special-effects extravaganza, *Mars Attacks!* is a what-me-worry celebration of the new Pax Americana, spiced with a dash of premillennial jitters. (Although *Mars Attacks!* often seems to parody *Independence Day*, their similarities are likely a function of market testing—both use the crowd-pleasing convention of a righteous black man punching out an alien's lights.) Personal and anarchic where *ID4* was corporate and patriarchal, *Mars Attacks!* has an even purer hatred of politicians—and adult authority in general. "Extraterrestrial life— the people are going to love it," President Jack Nicholson smirks on seeing the first photos of the approaching armada. A pompously rancid blend of Reagan and Clinton, Nicholson is truly the leader we deserve. Playing the nation's senior star as the Hollywood king he actually is, Nicholson's performance is so layered with insincerity, he's all but lost beneath the waxy buildup.

Burton's fondness for strapping performers into bondage drag not withstanding, actors must enjoy working with him. Nicholson throws in a bonus stint as a leathery Las Vegas wheeler-dealer in a red-on-red cowboy suit and Stetson with attached orange wig. *Mars Attacks!* is overstuffed with cameos by other Burton alumni, including Sarah Jessica Parker as a Barbara Walters in go-go boots, Danny DeVito as a Vegas gambler, octogenarian Sylvia Sidney as a duplex planet diva, and, topping her Vampira turn in *Ed Wood*, Lisa Marie as a gum-chewing bubble-coiffed torpedo-breasted alien-designed sex doll.

The most sensitive director of live cartoons since Frank Tashlin put Jerry Lewis and Jayne Mansfield through their paces, Burton here achieves a near Preston Sturges–like density of character: He casts blaxploitation superstars Pam Grier and Jim Brown as an estranged couple; gets Annette Bening to play a New Age Spielbergette; recruits Glenn Close as the fatuous First Lady and Pierce Brosnan as a suavely inane scientist with a pipe attached to his jaw; rehabilitates Martin Short, bobbing and grinning as the president's mutant Stephanopoulos. (That some of Short's tawdry antics anticipate those of Dick Morris only demonstrates that politics and show biz are two hemispheres of the same galactic brain.)

All the more remarkable is that the human stars have to compete for attention with a screenful of computer-generated Martians. Their oversized iridescent heads half skull, half lushly exposed cerebrum, these quacking, eye-rolling diminutive cuties are as ferociously scene-stealing as they are lethal. Indeed, half the cast is wiped out in the first spectacular attack of these killer toys who—as gleeful in their destruction as Joe Dante's gremlins—pack heat-zapping ray guns that char their victims down to their orange-glowing skeletons.

The *Mars Attacks!* narrative is so inconsistent that screenwriter Jonathan Gems might have generated his script William Burroughs style by tossing the Topps cards in the air and tracking their random pattern. Who cares? No effect is too tacky—a herd of flaming cows, a couple of transposed heads, flying saucers over Vegas. Burton dresses a set with violently polka-dot spherical chairs, locates his trailer park in the shadow of a massive Donut World, sets an AA meeting in a Pepto Bismol–pink prefab church. (The movie's radioactive palette seems based on mood rings, lava lamps, and tropi-holic slurpies.)

Fittingly, the Martians are defeated not by Earth's indigenous microbes but America's native vulgarity. This is the sort of movie in which the resident nerd triumphant (Luke Haas) is serenaded by a mariachi band's "Star-Spangled Banner." God bless America. When the president takes to the tube to tell us that "a powerful memory is in the making. . . . This is the perfect summation to the twentieth century," he's providing *Mars Attacks!* with its perfect pull quote.

Originally published as "Among the Bugs," the *Village Voice*
(November 11, 1997).

**A**LL HAIL THE NEW SECULAR HUMANISM: INSTINCTUAL INSECT FEAR MIXES WITH goofy macho in *Starship Troopers*, Paul Verhoeven's long-awaited adaptation of Robert Heinlein's once controversial, sternly ideological ray-gun blaster.

Not for the arachnophobic, this intergalactic Raid campaign is surely on Verhoeven's wavelength. After *Robocop* and *Total Recall*, *Basic Instinct* and *Showgirls*, the transplanted Dutchman has become something like our Fritz Lang—Hollywood's comic-book artist deluxe, the suavely brutal purveyor of hardcore pulp. Verhoeven may lack Lang's visionary conviction and cultural pessimism, but he has a boldly cartoonish graphic sensibility and a corresponding gusto for caricatured postmodern shibboleths. Somewhere beyond irony, *Starship Trooper*'s clever opener dares the viewer to position the movie as kissing cousin to a Hitler Youth recruitment ad.

More than one observer has called Heinlein's novel borderline fascist. *Starship Troopers* was written during the period of Sputnik anxiety to protest a proposed suspension of nuclear testing and, rejected by Heinlein's longtime publisher as too militaristic for kids, was brought out in 1959 by another house as an adult novel. Baldly synopsized, it sounds like a straight-arrow precursor of William S. Burroughs' *Nova Express*. Heinlein's philosophical treatise transposes the World War II–platoon scenario to outer space, anticipating the New Frontier mystique of the Green Berets as rich kid Johnny Rico achieves his battle-field destiny amid the Terra Federation's struggle for control of the galaxy against the arachnoid collectivists known as the Bugs.

Verhoeven ups the Darwinian ante by casting his movie with (mainly unknown) prime young human specimens—the square-jawed Casper Van Dien and dishy Denise Richards are not only the most physically perfect but also the most enthusiastic of warriors, surviving a basic-training regimen that includes routine bone-breaking and public floggings. The movie has no difficulty conceptualizing the human race as fundamentally American. (Buenos Aires, where Van Dien and Richards are introduced graduating high school, is here less Latin than *Beverly Hills 90210*.)

Cynical enough to stage an attack with 10 million casualties, then riff on audience outrage at the death of a single dog, Verhoeven doesn't dwell unduly on the Heinlein worldview. A class on "the failure of democracy" briefly alludes to the process by which veterans took over and made citizenship contingent on military service. The atmosphere of steroid-pumped survivalism seems extrapolated from Desert Storm USA. In this postliterate world, personal letters can wind up publicly broadcast, the Internet advertises televised executions, and football has mutated into an even more violent indoor sport. Perhaps because the film was not bankrolled by Warner Bros., CNN is not on hand to cover the apocalypse—or is it that the script called for the battlefield reporter ("This is a bug planet, an ugly planet") to be dismembered midtelecast.

An altogether more stylish, sardonic, and efficient entertainment machine than *Independence Day*, *Starship Troopers* substitutes gender equality for ethnic balance. Showgirls go to war. The army is coed. Male and female soldiers get to shower and, on at least one occasion, bunk down together . . . in the name of species solidarity? The most intense sci-fi combat film since James Cameron's *Aliens*, *Starship Troopers* subsumes a plot-driven class struggle between infantry and air force in the visceral excitement of all-out, hand-to-tendril interspecies warfare—most spectacularly in the sensationally animated, artfully corpse-splattered, nerve-wracking attacks of the scuttling, screaming crustacean-spider hordes.

That the movie has no more depth than the early eighties video games that were based on Heinlein's novel is Verhoeven's ultimate joke. Every planet not only resembles the Dakota badlands but has an earthling-compatible atmosphere. Oxygen is everywhere. Considering that the spider-monsters are apparently capable of targeting earth cities with meteors launched from deep space, it takes the Terra Federation a remarkably long time to realize that the Bugs might actually be intelligent.

## SAN SERGIO LEONE

Originally published as "Finding Their Religion," the
*Village Voice* (August 24, 1999).

**I**N THE RELIGION OF THE MOVIES, SERGIO LEONE IS A PRIME CANDIDATE FOR BEATITUDE. Among his miracles, the Italian director—who is getting his first local retro at the American Museum of the Moving Image on the 10th anniversary of his death—reinvented a genre (the western) and created a star (Clint Eastwood). Leone made plenty of money spinning dross into gold but he endured martyrdom as well, struggling for 15 years to make a would-be masterpiece (*Once Upon a Time in America*), only to see it butchered by the studio.

Mainly, however, Leone created a totally distinctive place—voluptuous, even elegiac, in its rabble-rousing cynicism. ("To me, cinema is adventure, legend," was his suitably kitsch credo.) Frontier towns with the look of decaying movie sets nestle in landscapes of Martian desolation. Everyone needs a bath and drinks their whiskey from the bottle. Biblical plagues—dust, flies, thirst— underscore an ethos of universal sadism. You know you're in Leone country the moment a huge, unshaven face lolls across the wide, wide screen and one of Ennio Morricone's twanging, banshee-shriek themes rises on the sound track like a vamp for the Last Judgment.

These movies can never work on TV; their use of space is tonic. Epic vistas are joltingly juxtaposed with mega-close-ups. The three-way shoot-out that ends *The Good, the Bad, and the Ugly* (1967), amid *corrida* fanfares and tolling bells in a graveyard half the size of Texas, is one of the great set pieces in western history. The outrageously prolonged *Once Upon a Time in the West* credit sequence exemplifies the whole Leone aesthetic of exaggerated spectacle and revisionist grunge. Three gruesome plug-uglies wait in a dilapidated station for the train that will bring their intended victim. Framed so tightly that each drop of sweat becomes a visual event, the sequence is less a parody of *High Noon* than of Mount Rushmore.

The son of a director and an actress, Leone was born into the faith. He was a teenage extra in *The Bicycle Thief*, worked on half the Hollywood movies made at Cinecittà during the fifties, and broke into direction with the cheesy Supertotalscope sword-and-sandal muscle-man flicks the French call *peplums*—the 1959 remake of *The Last Days of Pompeii* and the surprisingly credible *Colossus of Rhodes* (1961). Perhaps something of a rogue—in 1961 Robert Aldrich fired him, for loafing, from the *Sodom and Gomorrah* second unit—Leone had an epiphany when he saw the 1962 Akira Kurosawa samurai flick *Yojimbo*, shamelessly plagiarizing it in his first, enormously successful low-budget western, *A Fistful of Dollars* (1964).

There had been 25 Italian oat operas made before Leone's, but he put the mode on the international map. *A Fistful of Dollars* and its follow-ups, *For a Few Dollars More* (1965) and *The Good, the Bad, and the Ugly* (1967), rehabilitated TV cowboy Clint Eastwood as the last western hero. Leone's sense of the quintessential American genre was at once more abstract and more violently naturalistic than Hollywood's. Bringing a taste for recurring flashbacks and a knack for *peplum* crowd shots, he raised the magnitude of the slaughter while eschewing the patriotic self-glorification that traditionally came with the territory.

Throughout the convoluted course of *The Good, the Bad, and the Ugly*, Eastwood's scuzzy bounty hunter, Lee Van Cleef's reptilian hired killer, and Eli Wallach's blasphemous bandit (an infinitely sly, violent, opportunistic Everyman) form and dissolve various alliances, littering the screen with corpses as they search for an elusive box of gold coins. The plot keeps intersecting the fringes of the Civil War, consistently presented as a far larger and more meaningless bloodbath than anything in which the principals get mixed up.

Flush with the success of the *Dollars* trilogy, Leone journeyed to Hollywood to find backing for a gangster epic. But *The Godfather* was still several years in the future and instead, Paramount made him an offer he couldn't refuse: carte blanche to do another western with Henry Fonda as star. Thus, even as Sam Peckinpah embarked on *The Wild Bunch*, Leone conceived of *Once Upon a Time in the West* (1969) as his western to end all westerns—"a ballet of the dead." There was nothing else quite like it. As coaxed and teased by Morricone's remark able score—a swelling, keening mélange of slowed-down Neapolitan street songs, yé-yé, choral requiems, and Ventures guitar licks—the film is constantly reading and readjusting its thermostat, from self-parody to nostalgia, from myth mongering to spectacle.

But this exercise in glacial pacing and rampant grandiloquence proved as dormant at the box office as its predecessors were successful. Leone was cast into darkness. He directed only two more movies—both male love stories in the form of flawed, violent epics. Revisiting the lumpen leftism of the *Dollars* trilogy—although the introductory quote from Chairman Mao is missing from the studio print AMMI is screening—*A Fistful of Dynamite* (a/k/a *Duck, You Sucker*, 1972) has an exiled Irish terrorist (James Coburn) and a Mexican bandit (Rod Steiger in the Eli Wallach part) inadvertently swept into the revolutionary maelstrom of 1913 Mexico. Overtly Third Worldist (and at times almost Eisensteinian in its class-conscious agitprop), the movie dwells on the wreck of revolutionary dreams, Leone's not the least.

Then, after years in the wilderness, Leone got to make his gangster film. The story of two star-crossed *shtarkes* (Robert De Niro and James Woods) rising from the gutters of Jewish Williamsburg to rag-trade racketeering and the lavish splendor of a palatial speakeasy above Fat Moe's Deli, *Once Upon a Time in America* (1984) is brutal, inventive, and daringly cerebral. Closer in mood to Coleridge's "Kubla Khan" than to Coppola's *Godfather*, it made for a stunning swan song. Beginning with a mystery and ending in an opium den, *Once Upon a Time in America* hopscotches from 1933 to 1968 to 1921 back to 1968.

All is vanity—*peplum* grandiosity, spaghetti western savagery, the so-called American dream. It's not Leone's greatest pulp fiction, but who else could have conceived an action flick in the form of a reverie? The brute delicacy with which the resurrected artist took leave of his medium was the greatest miracle of all.

*In the Mood for Love* (Wong Kar-Wai, Block 2 Pictures, 2000).

# 11

## ADVENTURES IN DREAMLAND

### THE LONG DAY CLOSES

Originally published as "The Rapture," the *Village Voice*
(June 1, 1993).

THE CREDITS TO *THE LONG DAY CLOSES*, TERENCE DAVIES' MESMERIZING FOLLOW-UP
to his 1988 *Distant Voices, Still Lives*, have the ceremonial look of an
engraved wedding invitation—yet the film itself is profoundly solitary. It's as
though the union Davies has in mind is a marriage of individual and collective
memory consecrated by the movies.

The Long Day Closes is the bridge between the prenatal memories of
Davies' two-part *Distant Voices, Still Lives* and the anguished homosexuality of
his earlier *Trilogy*. Set during World War II, *Distant Voices* revolved around
family memories of a stubborn, furious father as framed by the marriage of his
oldest daughter; *Still Lives* picked up the thread of the daughter's unhappy
married life, refracted through a succession of celebrations in which the entire
family comes together in the local pub to quarrel with their spouses and sing
popular songs. *The Long Day Closes*, which Davies says will be his last autobiographical film, takes place a few years later, in 1955–56, with the hero, Bud, a
severe-looking, friendless child of 11.

No less than Davies' previous movies, *The Long Day Closes* is charged by a
love for the ineffable—in this case, Bud's fascination with that world on the screen
we never see. The play of light on transfixed faces, the austere illumination of
the projection beam, are counterpointed by something blatantly material—the
hurdy-gurdy waltz from *Carousel* or a sound clip from *Kind Hearts and
Coronets*. Representing daily life as the series of heroic friezes that link one
bijou epiphany to the next, Davies' mise-en-scène combines hyperrealist clarity
with stylized theatrical lighting—much of the action staged from the head-on
perspective of a viewer in the sixth row.

For those who have seen *Distant Voices, Still Lives, The Long Day Closes* will
scarcely seem exotic. Davies repeats many of the lessons of the earlier film.
Here again are the etched period details and intensely subdued colors, the a

cappella group sings and voluptuous gestures: The first scene uses the 20th Century Fox fanfare to underscore a close-up of a soggy, disintegrating movie poster in a rain-drenched back alley, Nat King Cole crooning "Stardust" as the camera dollies forward, around the corner, and up some stairs to light upon Bud plaintively asking his mother for money to go the pictures. But *The Long Day Closes* is less bound by narrative than Davies' earlier films—the disappearance of the oppressive father has freed the movie to become a chain of associations.

The youngest of 10 children, born in working-class Liverpool in 1945, and thus a younger contemporary of the Beatles, Davies deals in re-creation, constructing his films out of the sharp shards of childhood memories, assembling his own rarefied world of precious objects and sacred presences. His studio Liverpool is usually cold and dark and as hermetic as a bell jar. (In one evocative bit of business, the family is frightened by the appearance of a black West Indian at their front door.) There are no street noises. The weather is a near perpetual monsoon—the set more drenched with precipitation than the MGM back lot where they shot *Singin' in the Rain*, the film Davies remembers as the first he saw.

Introverted and uncompromising, Davies treats each remarkably studied image as though exhuming some sepia-tinted relic from the archeological site of Catholic, working-class Liverpool. "I try to celebrate Englishness with the panache of the Americans," Davies told *Sight and Sound*. *The Long Day Closes* occasionally mutates into a fairy-tale England—the fantasy of snow for Christmas, a candlelight vigil, and the mass singing of "Auld Lang Syne" on New Year's Eve 1956—but there's a stillness here that distinguishes Davies' reconstructions from those of Hollywood nostalgists like Steven Spielberg or Joe Dante.

Davies may aspire to a collective dreamland, but as a director, he exhibits a startling absence of hubris. (His excavation of childhood wonder suggests the Fellini-esque without the overbearingly expansive Fellini personality.) The Davies mode is a controlled, perhaps depressed, ecstasy. It's a fundamentally religious worldview whose characteristic camera maneuver is a slow lateral pan that gazes down on the action like a low-flying angel. He's a humble devotee with a sense of the audience as the conglomerate of intensely focused solitudes. When Bud's mother sings "Me and My Shadow," she's providing the anthem for the entire movie.

*The Long Day Closes* is not only haunted by the sound track from *The Magnificent Ambersons* but the way in which movies get mixed up with life—the lumpy neighbor who embarrasses his acid-tongued wife with imitations of Edward G. Robinson and James Cagney. As Bud is a permanent observer, Davies keeps finding ways to create visual metaphors for the movie screen (sometimes even in CinemasScope) within the family's drab row house. Indeed, Davies' most remarkable visual epiphany redeems what would seem to be the most hopeless material. An overhead shot of an uncharacteristically playful Bud swinging

Tarzan style on a rusty piece of scaffolding somewhere outside the movie theater cues Debbie Reynolds' tremulously saccharine rendition of the title song from *Tammy*. The stately camera continues to track over the head of a rapt movie audience match-dissolved into first a church congregation, then children in a schoolroom, and finally a landscape of corroded metal and worn stone.

Although *The Long Day Closes* is undeniably beautiful, it's the purity of Davies' concentration that's ultimately most heartbreaking—the distillation of events, the sense of mental performance. For Davies, the projected shaft of light is a form of divine radiance. But *The Long Day Closes* is as tactile as it is ethereal. More redemptive than nostalgic, the movie is a celestial vaudeville in a fastidiously grubby heaven.

## EXOTICA

Originally published as "Ghost Story," the *Village Voice*
(March 7, 1995).

A DISTURBING AND ULTIMATELY HEARTBREAKING EROTIC REVERIE, ATOM EGOYAN'S *Exotica* lifts this gifted young Canadian filmmaker to a new level of achievement. Egoyan's previous movies were suffused with a powerful sense of his own voyeurism, but there's a vivid immediacy to this haunting, sensuous film that pushes it past self-consciousness—it has the quality of spooky, tragic porn.

Steeped in shame and limned with foreboding, *Exotica* is a movie made under the sign of the superego. The opening scene has a pair of airport cops spying through a two-way mirror on the customs procedure at the Toronto airport. The subject of their interest, a painfully meek pet shop owner named Thomas (Don McKellar), isn't busted until later in the movie, but in *Exotica*, the search for secrets is universal. Everyone has something concealed in their psychological baggage; no one is precisely who they seem to be. ("You're invited to misperceive as well," the filmmaker enthusiastically confided in *Interview*.)

*Exotica* is more supple and accomplished than its predecessors but is still the characteristic Egoyan nexus of tangled relationships and crisscrossing narratives. The story unfolds at several sites at once, each with its own distinctive ambient music. The most spectacular location is the nightclub Exotica. Almost a parody of Egoyan's previous sinister, sexually charged films, it's a mock jungle harem of Roman pillars and potted palms, wailing Asian music, and lushly naked women voguing under the blue lights. Humid as the environment seems, the patrons are impassive business types, cool to the point of frozen solid. The gaze rules. The iron law here (as in the movies) is look but don't touch.

Given his long-standing fascination with surveillance and guilty pleasures, technologically enhanced sexual relations and video simulation, dysfunctional patriarchy and incestuous families, Egoyan has always balanced on the knife-edge of exploitation. In *Exotica* that aspect of his project is articulated by the club's smarmily insinuating master of ceremonies, Eric (Elias Koteas, the manipulative insurance man in *The Adjuster*). From his aerie above the dance floor, Eric watches and narrates over the revels. "What is it that gives a school-girl her special innocence?" the tormented MC asks his listeners as a lithe, solemn dancer, dressed in a schoolgirl's uniform to look even younger than she is, wanders out under the lights and breaks into a slow-motion, spastic per-formance, raising her tartan skirt and gyrating her hips to the unlikely accom-paniment of Leonard Cohen's sepulchral drone.

Thus presented, the enigmatic Christina (Mia Kirshner) is *Exotica*'s focal point. She obsesses Eric, her former lover (who claims that it is "therapeutic" for him to offer long and personal introductions to her act). She has some sort of liaison with Zoë (Arsinée Khanjian), the woman who owns the club. And, night after night, she is hired to dance at the table of the markedly melancholy customer, Francis (Bruce Greenwood). As spied upon by jealous Eric, Christina exhibits herself for Francis with an angel's tender solicitude. They even have their rehearsed dialogue. "How could anyone want to hurt you?" he asks while she solicitously reassures him that "You'll always be there to protect me."

While the nature of Francis's desire remains, for much of the movie, some-thing of an unknown, it develops that, in the daytime world, he himself is an investigator—arriving at Thomas's pet store to audit the company books. The pet store provides a dusty, comic analogue to the Club Exotica. It, too, is a family business, as well as both a repository of unusual fetishes and a kindred terrarium in the orderly if anxiety-charged night town Egoyan has made of bland Toronto. Like the nightclub, the store is eerily entropic—a greenish light emanating from the rows of fish tanks waiting to encompass who knows what fantasy.

Employing a typically prismatic Egoyan structure, *Exotica* is a series of repeated set pieces, connected by dreamy sound bridges and interspersed with flashbacks in which more youthfully innocent versions of Eric and Christina meet while combing a rural field for a missing child. The narrative inches simultaneously forward and backward as Francis engages in his nightly ritual at Exotica. Thomas, meanwhile, has developed his own primal scene, using an extra ballet ticket to pick up a succession of racially "exotic" one-night stands.

Such role-playing and compulsive behavior are scarcely unusual in the Egoyan cosmos. The hero of his first feature, *Next of Kin*, presented himself to a bereaved family as their long-lost son; the heroine of *Speaking Parts* obses-sively rented movies on videotape in order to track the career of a particular film extra. In last year's *Calendar*, Egoyan himself played a photographer who, having separated from his wife, invites a different woman home for dinner each month, then eavesdrops as she makes an impassioned phone call to her lover in a foreign language. But no previous Egoyan film has been as founded as *Exotica* on the use of repetition to assuage trauma and conjure absence—raising the compulsion to repeat to the level of ceremonial performance.

*Exotica* is also a movie about parents and children—something clearly on the filmmaker's mind. (Exotica's heavily pregnant proprietress is played by his wife and frequent star.) Every house has its ghosts; each love is founded upon some sort of spiritual possession. As Francis has constructed a complicated neurotic scenario around his own lost family, so Zoë has inherited the club from her late mother, whose clothes and wig she habitually wears. Eric was contracted to father Zoë's child; even Thomas, left his shop by his father, has smuggled in a rare egg. Christina is the only central character without evident family relations, although that which Eric advertises as "the mystery of her world" is finally revealed as well.

Egoyan has always shown a greater interest in structure than narrative, but *Exotica* is less stilted and more emotional in its development than his earlier features. A hissing snake, Eric sets up unhappy Francis for the further shock of expulsion from Exotica's ersatz Eden. The narrative tension builds through the gradual elucidation of the various characters' connections—including past and present blackmail, murder, and adultery—to a climactic flashback offering a revelation at once powerfully ordinary and extraordinarily sad.

While earlier Egoyan films were set in a video phantom zone, *Exotica* takes as its subject the loneliness of life amid a paradise of paid surrogates. As Zoë tells Christina, "We're here to entertain, not to heal." The taboos are never broken on screen; the film's argument is only played out in images or the imagination. For the audience as much as for the characters, *Exotica* expresses a longing beyond its frame, beyond words.

## DIE HARD WITH A VENGEANCE

Originally published as "Bomb, Baby, Bomb," the
*Village Voice* (May 30, 1995).

**A**NNOUNCING ITSELF AS THE ULTIMATE NEW YORK CITY SLAM DANCE, *Die Hard with a Vengeance* opens with a blast of "Summer in the City," a mosh-pit montage of sweaty Midtown, and then, in panoramic long shot ... a department store casually exploding in your face.

That opening salvo should, by now, have gotten the movie some negative attention. (Well before the premiere, 20th Century Fox had the stars on TV doing damage control.) But the barn door has long since been blown away. If this latest installment of the *Die Hard* saga was inspired by the 1993 World Trade Center bombing, it's also possible that the original *Die Hard*—in which Bruce Willis's NYPD street cop McClane battled international terrorists in an L.A. skyscraper—may have contributed to the WTC scenario. Like the Oklahoma City explosion of April 1995 and subsequent terror attacks in the New York and Tokyo subways, *Die Hard with a Vengeance* is a post-WTC production—which is why it's hard to laugh (even with a vengeance) at the bomb jokes, especially when the resident (or rather, resident alien) terrorist, Simon (Jeremy Irons), threatens to blow up a public school full of kids. Oklahoma City has definitely taken some of the fun out of the situation.

*Die Hard with a Vengeance* has its share of free-floating social metaphors. The bad guys are a paramilitary bunch of crypto-Nazi German skinhead thugs, and Simon uses talk radio to panic the population. Despite the requisite anti-FBI scene, *Vengeance* lacks the antibureaucratic edge of *Die Hard* and *Die Hard 2*—although the Rambotic premise remains that one man can do it, almost alone, even with a monstrous hangover. For the most part, the movie is played as a total grudge match in which Simon spends the first and best 45 minutes running McClane all over our hostagized city in much the way that, two dozen years ago, Zodiac tortured Dirty Harry. The mood is a bit more jocular. Clint never had to position himself on West 138th Street in boxer shorts and a sandwich sign reading "I Hate Niggers." The setup enables Willis to be rescued by (and eventually bond with) Samuel L. Jackson, playing a testy black nationalist with even more attitude than McClane.

The buddies absorb much punishment—by the end of the movie they're slimy with blood—but the money scenes are mainly vehicular. In the most impressive, McClane requisitions a cab, then runs a light and makes like the taxi has four-wheel drive by plowing off the road in Central Park (positioned in the movie as a shortcut to Wall Street), barreling through Columbus Circle behind the ambulance he's conned into running interference in order to catch up with, and jump atop, the moving subway on which Simon has planted yet another bomb. When the station does explode, you get a sense of how the movie views us. A vapid bunch of popcorn-chomping spectators are shown watching from their office towers: Cool.

New Yorkers may remember that *Die Hard with a Vengeance* tied up a considerable portion of Manhattan real estate during the summer of 1994—which is perhaps why the city appears here as an unfathomable terrain of crazed natives and hassled unflappable cops. Strictly as a local, I appreciated the scene where McClane drives through Water Tunnel 3 as well as the shoot-out and bumper-car crash on the Saw Mill River Parkway. (But why is it raining in

Westchester and sunny in the Bronx?) Unfortunately, the movie lacks consistent velocity. The Steadicam immediacy of director John McTiernan's hectic, bruising style gives the sensation of being trapped in a speeding taxi that repeatedly stops short. McClane's recurring complaint—"I've had a bad fucking headache all day"—is contagious.

The movie's lumpen James Bond always shoots first and never loses his bad attitude, but his bon mots aren't even wisecracks, just bellicose insults. Although the movie's most emotionally satisfying moments are those in which McClane liberates a car phone from a Wall Street yuppie or blows away six neo-Nazis at outrageously close quarters, *Die Hard* is basically a fantasy of oral aggression where the bloody, unbowed hero can stop the villain in his tracks with a brusque "Hey dickhead."

## I SHOT ANDY WARHOL

Originally published as "SCUM Like It Hot," the
*Village Voice* (May 7, 1996).

FROM *THE PHILOSOPHY OF ANDY WARHOL*: "I ALWAYS WORRY THAT WHEN NUTTY people do something, they'll do the same thing again a few years later without ever remembering that they've done it before—and they'll think it's a whole new thing they're doing. I was shot in 1968, so that was the 1968 version. But then I have to think, 'Will someone want to do a 1970s remake of shooting me?'" Or, as Karl Marx (a sort of nineteenth-century Warhol) once almost said: The first time as tragedy, the second as a made-for-TV movie.

*I Shot Andy Warhol*, Mary Harron's entertainingly kicky, unexpectedly sharp and thoughtful docudramatized saga of Warhol's assassin Valerie Solanas, is itself a triumph of Warholism—illuminated by Lili Taylor's performance as the founder, chief theorist, and sole member of the Society for Cutting Up Men (SCUM). "If anyone can make you a star, Andy can," butch lesbian Solanas is at one point advised by drag queen Candy Darling (Stephen Dorff). It's the aspiring superstar giving career guidance to the would-be exterminating angel—a prophetic aside that turns out to be doubly true.

As pithy as its tabloid title (the words with which Solanas gave herself up to a rookie cop in Times Square), *I Shot Andy Warhol* is a modest recreation of the high sixties—the antithesis of Oliver Stone bombast. Harron, a former journalist, stages the title crime beneath the credits, then plunges into its aftermath—the Warhol Factory in hysterical mourning. Picking up the Solanas story during her college years, *I Shot Andy Warhol* establishes its protagonist as a saucy borderline case and panhandling sexual bohemian adrift on a social undercurrent that, by the mid-sixties, would seep through the floorboards and flood the Factory.

In this milieu, Solanas is one more self-invented, hyperarticulate philosopher of the bedroom. The economical script, written by Harron and Daniel Minahan, is a scrupulous work of pop scholarship (anyone familiar with the literature can spot the footnotes) that contrives, as often as possible, to work in passages from Solanas's outrageous *SCUM Manifesto*—pegged by its first publisher Maurice Girodias as a Swiftian satire on the depraved behavior, genetic inferiority, and ultimate disposability of the male gender. Occasionally the material is delivered stand-up style—a more glamorous Solanas imagined as the radical feminist Lenny Bruce—but no frills are needed to put across a line like the male will "swim a river of snot, wade nostril-deep through a mile of vomit, if he thinks there'll be a friendly pussy awaiting him."

In the first of several polemical fictionalizations, Harron and Minahan bracket Solanas with the most convincingly femme of Factory drag queens, Candy Darling. ("You're a guy? My God, I thought you were a lesbian," Solanas exclaims in a typically hall-of-mirrors gag when first they meet in Washington Square Park.) It's Candy who, against her will, introduces Solanas to the silver-painted wonderland, first glimpsed with an aria from *Rigoletto* echoing through its vast, enchanted expanse. Venting her urge to desecrate, Solanas decides that Warhol will produce her wildly scatological play *Up Your Ass*. "I dedicate this play to me!" she exults, and she is, it would seem, the only true spectator. An abortive reading in the old 8th Street Nedick's is crosscut with a gaggle of female Factory hands leafing gingerly through the manuscript: "It's way too disgusting even for us."

Harron suggests that Solanas, in her bop cap and ratty pea coat, was too real (and in a perverse sense too female) for the Factory. "What is that horrendous monstrosity?" someone trills when Solanas's Factory screen test flashes on the screen. Solanas herself did make a brief, fabulously hostile appearance in *I, A Man*—cornering the star Tom Baker in a tenement hallway, grabbing his ass and demanding he tell her how he keeps it so "squishy." This movie, one of the worst the Factory ever released, is notable mainly in that everybody in it save Solanas keeps acting like they're acting in an Andy Warhol movie.

More connected with the audience, Taylor plays Solanas as Dead End Kid, at once street smart and clueless, weirdly cuddly and imbued with antiglamour—there's nothing funnier than her incredulous glare when, during her perp walk, one newshound yells, "Hey Valerie, you got a boyfriend?" or her drunken dinner with the suave and sleazy Girodias (a wittily concocted performance by

Canadian actor Lothaire Bluteau). What's most authentic is her yearning for a "magic world," and her visceral experience of sexual oppression.

As Tim Burton's *Ed Wood* offered a hyperreal remake of *Bride of the Monster*, so *I Shot Andy Warhol* reproduces Solanas's scene from *I, A Man*. Hyperreal too is the dead sun around which Solanas orbits. Played by Jared Harris with bad skin and a perpetual sneer, the movie's Warhol is a kind of self-conscious waxwork. What goes around comes around: Harris seriously projects a copy of the affectless, mumbling public persona that Warhol himself projected as a joke. He's surrounded by a variety of Factory superstars—the most vivid, by far, being Michael Imperioli's snarling speed freak Ondine.

What the movie cannot recreate, however, is the Factory ambience. An ambitious party scene, complete with light show and ersatz Velvet Underground, plays like dinner theater at the mall. (Each superstar is encased in his or her own vitrine.) Unfortunately, this monumental fizzle has been designed to frame the movie's key thesis. Trapped in the ultimate high school party, as well as their respective sexual purgatories, deadpan Andy and feral Valerie watch the cool kids dance—clinching their kinship as they wind up together on the infamous Factory couch. Thus encouraged, Solanas spends the rest of the movie skulking through the back room at Max's, hassling Andy to produce her play or at least return the manuscript.

Unlike the other Factory regulars, Solanas didn't need drugs to go paranoid or delusional. Harron nevertheless makes a causal link between Solanas's violence and the revolutionary rhetoric of the day: Solanas picks up a member of the anarchic SDS offshoot that called itself Up Against the Wall Motherfuckers at an East Village copy shop and rolls him for the gun he keeps in his extravagantly sordid pad. Similarly, the script takes advantage of Solanas's abortive TV appearance as a guest of the ultraconfrontational Alan Burke to suggest a freak show far more vulgar than Warhol's.

Valerie Solanas really was a nobody until she shot Andy Warhol. But once *The SCUM Manifesto* was underlined in blood, Solanas hardly had to wait for admirers. Just as the Weathermen would champion Charles Manson some 18 months later, so Solanas was claimed as an "important spokeswoman" by the radical wing of NOW, written up at regular intervals in the *Voice,* and celebrated by the Motherfuckers ("Plastic Man vs. the Sweet Assassin ... The Camp Master slain by the Slave—and America's white plastic cathedral is ready to burn"). Yippie provocateur Paul Krassner provided the postscript for the first edition of *The SCUM Manifesto* (which was itself excerpted in *Sisterhood Is Powerful* and included in *The Sixties Papers*).

Having died in 1988, Valerie is pure celebrity. Lou Reed may have kept his distance from this project, but the movie has been avidly embraced by numerous

Factory hands, as well as Warhol's erstwhile journal, *Interview* (which used it as a hook for last month's cover and is cosponsoring the New York premiere), not to mention the Andy Warhol Museum (hosting the Pittsburgh premiere). In his *Philosophy*, Warhol casts Solanas, at least by implication, as an aggrieved fan. Had he ever a more devoted one? If the artist had actually died in 1968, his place in the pantheon would be impregnable—particularly as the strongest 95 percent of his work was produced before the shooting.

Thanks to Harron, Warhol and Solanas have merged in death. The *I Shot Andy Warhol* poster is a pastiche of Warhol's "Triple Elvis"—a true simulacrum collectible, with Taylor-as-Solanas striking the gun-wielding Presley pose Warhol cribbed from a 1960 Don Siegel western. The name of that movie? *Flaming Star*.

## AVENTURERA

Originally published as "Border Lines," the *Village Voice*
(August 27, 1996).

**N**OW THAT WE'VE ALL LEARNED TO LOVE HONG KONG ACTION FLIX, IS IT TIME TO rediscover Mexican *cabaretera*? Starting near the top, Alberto Gout's 1950 *Aventurera* (The Adventuress), never to be confused with *L'Avventura*, may be the genre's supreme example—or at the very least its most daringly ridiculous.

Opening at Film Forum, having dazzled audiences at the Telluride Film Festival, *Aventurera* is one of a trilogy of musical melodrama noirs that were made back-to-back featuring the sensationally uninhibited Cuban *rumbera*, Ninón Sevilla. The British Film Institute's newly published anthology *Mexican Cinema* calls these films profoundly subversive works that even garnered the attention of the French press—yessiree and, according to Jack Smith's syllabus for a never-taught course in movie history, impressed Smith as well.

Truly, the tawdry lighting, bravura theatrics, shameless posturing, pulsating rhythms, and fantastic emotional intensity of something like *Aventurera*, or Emilio Fernández's nearly-as-sensational *Salón México*, provide an entirely new context in which to appreciate the camp excesses of current Latin melo-maestros Pedro Almodóvar and Arturo Ripstein, not to mention Luis Buñuel (who broke into the Mexican movie industry in the late 1940s with a pair of *cabareteras*) or the whole Telemundo roster of *telenovelas*.

A movie that could never have been produced in 1950s Hollywood, *Aventurera* establishes an immediate surplus of emotion when the proper bourgeois maiden, Elena (Sevilla), skips upstairs to discover her mother *en flagrante* with her father's business partner. Mother runs off, father blows out his brains, and dazed Elena leaves staid Chihuahua for the border-town sleaze of Ciudad Juárez, where she's betrayed by a suave gangster and drugged/raped into prostitution. The dance hall–bordello is administered by a madam tough and stately enough to give Joan Crawford pause; her enforcer is the tuxedoed, razor-wielding mute El Rengo (Miguel Inclán, a specialist in sinister disability, who played the blind musician in Buñuel's *Los Olvidados* the same year).

The transformation of the innocent Elena into the impulsive dance-hall dynamo celebrated in the movie's superbly overripe title song ("And he who awaits the sweet honey of your kiss/Must pay the price in diamonds for your sin") is only the beginning. *Aventurera*'s outrageous plot twist manages to implicate the Mexican upper classes in the sleaziest of exploitation gigs. Bound to expose their hypocrisy, Sevilla embarks on a marriage of vengeance—and this amid all manner of flaming rumbas, seductions, attempted murders, blackmail schemes, catfights, and deathbed conversions.

The rangy, long-stemmed Ninón Sevilla leads with her upthrust chin and plays directly to the camera. She's a confidently terrible actress, but why limit her performance to mere acting? With her determined flounce and volcanic rage, Sevilla is a force of nature worthy to be bracketed with Maria Montez and Carmen Miranda. You can watch her calculate every emotion that flickers across her determined face. She's pure kinesis—and we're not even talking about the hand-fluttering, eye-rolling, self-caressing, back-bending baroque that is Ninón dancing.

Sevilla's performances are typically set on impossibly large stages, cluttered with all manner of Arabian Nights exotica. At once stuck-up and trashy, she twirls and shakes, prancing around the set with her palms up, her nose in the air, her backfield in motion, her face frozen in a parody of haughtiness. Sevilla bases an entire number around a supplicating tambourine and pushes something sounding suspiciously like the old Chiquita banana commercial into a world beyond suggestive. If I know the Film Forum audience, they'll be screaming in the aisles long before the *rumbera*'s ringing declaration "My life has only been the road to perversion!"

## VERTIGO

Originally published as "Lost in Space," the *Village Voice* (October 15, 1996).

**A** MYSTERY THAT ONLY IMPROVES WITH KNOWLEDGE OF ITS "SOLUTION," *VERTIGO* is the ultimate movie—a movie that is, after all, concerned with being hopelessly, obsessively, fetishistically in love with an image. Or, as the *New York*

*Times* reported in June 1958, it is "all about how a dizzy fellow chases after a dizzy dame."

Back in the day, *Vertigo* was received with genial condescension. *Time* called it a typical "Hitchcock-and-bull story." Hitchcock was then heavily involved in television, and although "Hollywood's best-known butterball" (*Time*), he was perceived to be stretched a mite thin. Knowledgeable reviewers noted that, adapted from a novel by the same French authorial team that provided rival director H. G. Clouzot with his hit thriller *Diabolique*, *Vertigo* was a form of catch-up. Since it was less successful with audiences than *Rear Window, To Catch a Thief,* and *The Man Who Knew Too Much*, only *Cahiers du Cinéma* and the mavens who wrote for the Hollywood trade papers took the movie seriously.

A three-year, frame-by-frame restoration by James C. Katz and Robert A. Harris, the 1996 re-release uses 70-mm wide-screen to re-create the VistaVision version seen by *Vertigo*'s first-run audiences. (A clever wide-screen process, VistaVision was produced by positioning the movie camera horizontally to expose the equivalent of two 35-mm frames. Few theaters were equipped to project the larger image, however, and *Vertigo* was soon reduced to regular 35-mm.) While the original TechniColor is no longer available, Katz and Harris have remixed the sound track—thus burnishing Bernard Herrmann's hyper-moody score to an almost disconcerting brightness.

Quintessential film modernist though Hitchcock may have been, he was also a dedicated Pop Artist—the master not only of suspense but also self-promotion and gimmickry. (*Vertigo* was promoted with a party on the 29th floor of an unfinished East 42nd Street skyscraper.) Stars Jimmy Stewart and Kim Novak aside, the movie's main attraction was understood to be its wide-screen "travelogue" treatment of San Francisco. Thus, the restoration's major visual revelation is the additional weight given the prolonged, gliding, all but wordless automotive chase that made the *New Yorker*'s critic complain he was carsick: Stewart's Scottie pursuing the ghostly jade green Jaguar driven by Novak's Madeleine through S.F.'s hilly streets.

*Vertigo* bogs down more than once in tedious exposition. But, although literal-minded critics continue to knock Hitchcock's implausible narrative, this seems a bit like complaining that *Un Chien Andalou* is too discontinuous or the myth of Orpheus and Eurydice lacks the necessary verisimilitude. It would be tempting to call *Vertigo* the last masterpiece of movie surrealism were it not that Buñuel ended his career by making a comic analogue with *That Obscure Object of Desire*—another movie about a man obsessed with a woman who does not exist. *Vertigo*'s evocatively imminent, emptied-out world has the melancholy solitude of the de Chirico city just as Madeleine's uncanny movements in and out of frame suggest Maya Deren's montage.

There is a sense in which *Vertigo* sums up 30 years of Surrealist (and Surrealist-into-advertising) imagery. With its long late-afternoon shadows, pervasive anxiety, terrifying intimations of the void, frozen immobility, feeling of elastic time, charged symbols, uncanny portraits, and general sense of weirdness in broad daylight, *Vertigo* could have been subtitled after de Chirico (*Nostalgia of the Infinite*) or Deren (*Meshes of the Afternoon*). Taking the term that Joseph Cornell applied to the somnambulant star Hedy Lamarr, Madeleine describes herself as a "wanderer." Like the Surrealist heroine Nadja, Madeleine lives out her dreams—or are they Scottie's?

*Vertigo* is not without its dark humor, but it is an intensely, almost shockingly, romantic movie: like bereft Heathcliff in the second half of *Wuthering Heights*, shell-shocked Scottie pleads with his lost love to haunt him. And once she does return from the dead—her kiss obliterating time and space as Herrmann works variations on Wagner's *Tristan und Isolde*—the movie's own current resurrection becomes secondary. When its drama is distilled to overwhelming desire (and the desire to be desired), when its narrative is vaporized by the force of mutual (and mutually exclusive) longings, *Vertigo* could cast its spell from a nine-inch black-and-white TV set.

## THE TRUMAN SHOW

Originally published as "Thru a Lens Darkly,"
the *Village Voice* (June 9, 1998).

CELEBRITY IS THE COIN OF THE AMERICAN REALM, AND PETER WEIR'S *The Truman Show*, which opened on a crescendo of buzz, is a movie about celebritude that pushes the conventional wisdom on the subject to its logical extreme.

The movie's protagonist, Truman Burbank (Jim Carrey), is not just well-known for being well-known; he's well-known precisely because he's the most well-known person who ever lived. This star was born . . . at birth. His 15 minutes of fame have been extended into an entire lifetime; his daily existence is broadcast to millions of faithful viewers as the subject of a live, 24-hour-a-day television show. For 30 years, Truman has played a normal person on TV—but, of course, he's not really a normal person because he's the only one in the world unaware of his celebrity.

A similar premise served as the basis for an early episode of *The Twilight Zone*, in which a businessman suddenly found his office transformed into a movie set. It's also an elaboration on Chuck Jones's classic *Duck Amuck*, in which a capricious, unseen animator treats Daffy Duck as the Looney Tunes equivalent of Job. But *The Truman Show*, which was written by Andrew Niccol—the young author-director of last year's *Gattaca*—is an attempt to represent a total system. Just as the ambitious, if stultifying, *Gattaca* offered a sci-fi critique of genetic programming, so *The Truman Show* suggests that stardom too can be rationally produced. This spoof of what Mark Crispin Miller dubbed our National Entertainment State is a scenario that mixes the *1984* nightmare of absolute surveillance with the notion of an idiot-audience hooked on the vicarious thrills of virtual reality (or what André Bazin called the Myth of Total Cinema).

Truman's antiseptic hometown—seemingly modeled on the Disney planned community, Celebration—is a vast, domed movie studio. The show's somber, self-important creator, Christof (Ed Harris), broods in the fake sky overhead while the outside world is represented by occasional cutaways to Truman's cretinous devotees watching their idol on TV. Without doubt, *The Truman Show* has the most intriguing metaphysical premise of any Hollywood comedy since *Groundhog Day*, offers the most resonant showbiz metaphor since *The King of Comedy*, and executes the most ingenious mise-en-scène since *Defending Your Life*. But what's it up to?

Surrounded as he is by actors, including his wife (Laura Linney), and eternally observed by an unseen audience (not to mention his producer), there would seem to be two ways to allegorize Truman's condition. Either he's delusional, a paranoid schizophrenic, or else an existential victim, the subject of a brainwashed quasi-religious cult. Is it the movie or the town which is constantly awash in reverential theme music? Or has the sound track been implanted in our hero's brain? Truman's TV is only the most obvious part of his environment that is custom-programmed to control him. In the movie's grisliest joke, actors playing doctors have to stage an amputation for his benefit. Truman's wife is at once shrill and soothing, proudly announcing her latest brand-name purchase to the hidden camera. (Product placement substitutes for commercial breaks.)

Jim Carrey's Truman is even more insanely cheerful. Like Steve Martin and Bill Murray before him, Carrey is the master of "sincerity"—so much so that he often seems like a simulation himself. Initially oblivious to the production's various mishaps and miscues (a klieg light crashes down onto his street, a rainstorm follows him around), his Truman is just beginning to suspect something peculiar. As he explains to the actor who is cast as his best friend, he's wondering if, somehow, the whole world revolves around him. *The Truman Show* is less funny than clinically hysterical and, although the pathology isn't meant to be individual so much as social, what the movie suggests is the celebrity's view of celebrity.

The filmmakers might have done more with the backstage technology that makes the spectacle work, but then *The Truman Show*—like its TV counterpart—is a star vehicle. Crucial to the premise is the idea of high-paid, lowbrow maniac Jim Carrey taking his first "serious" role. Never mind that Carrey basically plays Truman as an overgrown kid, that *The Cable Guy*'s karaoke scene alone was more horrific than the entire *Truman Show*—or that, despite its flaws and lapses, *The Cable Guy* itself remains a far more serious and provocative social critique. There, truly working without a net, Carrey played a terrifyingly obnoxious personification of mass culture—not exactly a cover- friendly icon for *Time* magazine. (Good ol' boy Andy Griffith never revisited the demonic persona he exhibited in *A Face in the Crowd*; the same may be true for Carrey.)

The show within *The Truman Show* is good viewing. As Truman struggles against his fate, Christof resurrects the dead, adds a love interest, conjures up natural disasters to keep him in line. Like *Duck Amuck*, the movie builds to a confrontation between the star and his creator—except that this time, the whole world is watching. The filmmakers have succeeded in marshaling our attention, but neither their protagonist nor his interpreter has the depth or range to play the Jesus Christ Prometheus Joseph K. Frankenstein monster that the situation warrants. *The Truman Show* winds up by suggesting that this is just entertainment after all—poor dramaturgy, but the acme of social realism.

## THERE'S SOMETHING ABOUT MARY (AND MARY)

Originally published as "Boys to Men," the *Village Voice*
(July 21, 1998).

**T**HERE'S SOMETHING ABOUT MARY IS LESS AN ASTEROID SENT HURTLING TOWARD the audience than a great gobby spitball. Duck if you're squeamish. Proudly lowbrow, hopelessly incorrect, visually strident, and awash in bodily fluids, this third and funniest gross-out yuckfest by Peter and Bobby Farrelly goes a long way in establishing the auteurs of *Dumb and Dumber* and *Kingpin* as the cone-head's Coen Brothers.

A romantic comedy, if not exactly the sort that Nora Ephron would concoct, *There's Something About Mary* opens in the filmmakers' native Rhode Island and immediately establishes a typically Farrellian state of mind—Ben Stiller playing a high school senior afflicted with double braces and tormented by an advanced case of the nerds. Although the Farrellys derive considerable amusement from this prologue—which features the spectacle of thirtysomething actors in outlandish fright wigs reenacting their inarticulate, high school geekiness—the movie's level of humor is even more regressive, closer to that of a vicious 12-year-old.

Invited to the prom by the senior-class goddess and eponymous object of desire (Cameron Diaz), Stiller proves completely hapless—unwittingly alienating her excitable stepfather, innocently sending her mentally retarded brother into a frenzy, inadvertently peeping on her toilette, and then, in a paroxysm of embarrassment and the first of the movie's two never-to-be-forgotten bits of business, catching a bit of scrotum in his zipper. Can any amount of Cameron Diaz cheesecake compensate for what is arguably the most excruciatingly visceral castration metaphor in any Hollywood movie since Ronald Reagan had his legs lopped in *King's Row*? Even a cop shows up to gawk.

Thus arrested in his development, Stiller remains fixated on the lissome, unattainable Diaz for the next 15 years. His simian character is so dorky that even Tostitos corn-chip star Chris Elliot feels entitled to give him coolness tips—and so boring in his romantic obsession that his analyst sneaks out to have lunch as Stiller drones on about the trauma that ruined his date. (Is it a mercy or just another sadistic joke that America's shrinks will be on vacation as *Mary* plays the 'plexes?)

To further explicate Stiller's adolescent angst, Jonathan Richman—the king of greasy kid stuff—is on hand as a troubadour, serenading the principals as he periodically strolls on-camera to articulate his own peculiar brand of deadpan, earnestly dopey romanticism: "True love is not nice and it brings up hurt from when you were five years old/Oh pain, pain, pain is true love's name." Indeed. Although worthy of John Waters' *Pink Flamingos* (or even his gruesome *Desperate Living*), *Mary*'s fly-trap scene is scarcely the film's only venture into theater of cruelty.

*Mary*'s rude assortment of muscular dystrophy, psoriasis, and homophobic jokes might have been scripted by the Garbage Pail Kids for the cast of *South Park*. The material written for Farrelly axiom Lin Shaye—here elaborating her sexualized-hag cameos in their previous films—is approached only by the scene in which Stiller's sleazy rival Matt Dillon is compelled to perform CPR on the Shaye character's terrier. (The gag reflex is a double-edged sword in Farrellyworld.) A satire of inept male behavior predicated on the fear of sexual rejection, *There's Something About Mary* expresses an anxiety so funky that you can practically smell it. The jovially disgusting ribaldry suggests a hetero equivalent to the old Playhouse of the Ridiculous.

Could this be the Farrellys' moment? Their man Jim Carrey is being touted for an Oscar, *Kingpin*'s bowling set up *The Big Lebowski*'s, and the most notorious scene in *Dumb and Dumber* was ripped off by the ecstatically overpraised

*Henry Fool. There's Something About Mary* towers above the usual summer idiocy on its formal qualities alone—the slapstick timing, adroit sight-gag placement, choreographed Abbott-and-Costello misunderstandings. Dillon's stupid huckster not only sports a set of oversized choppers but surprising echoes of Groucho Marx. Not the least of the movie's triumphs is Cameron Diaz. At once eternal foil and holy grail, perfectly oblivious, always credulous, generous in her affection, she's a woman so perfect she even likes to talk football.

Good sport or plastic mannequin, Diaz's Mary is untouched by the stalking, stinking, all-round vulgarity that surrounds her even when it smears . . . never mind. As you are sure to hear around the schoolyard, *There's Something About Mary* has the most startling parody of a money shot—ever. Here, too, the unfailing Diaz radiance brings to mind novelist Fred Chappell's observation in his "Twenty-Six Propositions About Skin Flicks" that "If the whole of history, with its prostitution and unrelenting degradation, has not violated women in their essence, how shall the camera accomplish it?"

There's pathos in the pathology here—but, of course, only if you think about it. The worst thing about *There's Something About Mary* is the license it will extend to the next 50 gross-out comedies.

------

Even if homosexual panic were not an essential ingredient in the goulash of Farrelly humor, *There's Something About Mary* would merit a footnote in Mark Rappaport's new movie for its title alone.

More playfully subversive and less conventionally hand-wringing than Robert Epstein and Jeffrey Friedman's 1995 clip anthology *The Celluloid Closet*, Rappaport's *The Silver Screen—Color Me Lavender* takes the position that Hollywood is naturally gay or barely repressed. Rappaport, who first staked a claim to the territory of VCR-cheology with *Rock Hudson's Home Movies*, concentrates mainly on studio comedies from the mid-thirties through the mid-fifties, subjecting footage to extensive microanalysis or bringing out latent meanings by fooling with the sound track.

*The Silver Screen* begins by surveying the "unproclaimed homosexuals" who populate the world of Fred Astaire–Ginger Rogers musicals. Although Rappaport doesn't make the point that obvious sissies like Eric Blore or Franklin Pangborne were there to inoculate the less-than-macho Astaire against charges of effeminacy, he argues that these pansies disappeared after 1941 because effete behavior was no laughing matter during wartime (don't ask, don't tell)—especially when women were usurping male prerogatives on the home front.

Providing a taxonomy of Carmen Miranda impersonations (not forgetting Daffy Duck's), *The Silver Screen* goes on to celebrate the queeny aesthete played by Clifton Webb in *Laura* (and done "straight" by George Sanders in *All About Eve*) while touching briefly on the open homoeroticism of European sophisticates like Jean Cocteau and Luchino Visconti. But Rappaport is clearly most amused by parsing the Hollywood dance of insinuation and denial. "Defining and redefining masculinity is a particularly American trait," he asserts, piling on evidence of queer behavior by Jerry Lewis, Red Skelton, and, most hauntingly, Danny Kaye.

Having foisted Lin Shaye on the American public, the Farrelly brothers would no doubt appreciate Rappaport's explication of the "grizzled old prospector," namely Walter Brennan, in the many movies where he plays "boyfriend sidekick" to the Humphrey Bogart or John Wayne action hero. Rappaport's most apt contribution may be his deconstruction of Bob Hope's compulsive camping and impugning of Bing Crosby's masculinity: "What could be funnier than a straight guy pretending he's not as straight as he pretends?"

## HOW *STAR WARS* SUPPLANTED RELIGION, MUTATED THE SPECIES, AND CHANGED THE MOVIES

Originally published as "The Force Will Always Be
with Us," the *Village Voice* (May 18, 1999).
Postscript originally published as "All Droid Up," the
*Village Voice* (May 25, 1999).

LEAVE IT TO GEORGE LUCAS TO SCHEDULE THE MILLENNIUM TO PROMOTE HIS NEW movie. For millions, the second coming of *Star Wars* is a cosmic event of equal historical significance.

Opening (as if you didn't know) next Wednesday at 2,500-plus North American theaters, *Star Wars: Episode I—The Phantom Menace* is an event that brings together religion, entertainment, business, technology, weaponry, and publicity—the most powerful aspects of American culture—in one brain-dissolving package. The true believers—the children of *Star Wars*—have been awaiting this moment for nearly two decades.

The hype, which took off last fall when fans began paying full admission to witness the two-minute *Phantom Menace* trailer, has long since reached warp speed; the rapture has nothing on this baby. The costumed ticket lines are almost two weeks old. The *New York Post*, owned (like distributor 20th Century Fox) by Rupert Murdoch, has been running a daily *Phantom Menace* countdown for a month. If anything in showbiz was ever a sure thing, this is it. Even so, the notoriously reclusive Lucas has been a publicist's dream, flacking *The Phantom Menace* on TV, granting interviews, and furnishing "exclusive" pictures of Planet Naboo and the lovable Gungan called Jar Jar Binks to half the glossies on the newsstand.

Some believe that Lucas's self-financed $120 million production will make back its budget during its first week, en route to an eventual billion—and that's just box office. Merchandisers predict *The Phantom Menace* will sell a billion dollars' worth of licensed toys. Pepsi has already paid Lucas twice as much for a sponsorship deal that includes a custom-made, four-armed digital huckster hobbit called Marfalump and 24 collectible soda cans.

No one doubts that this still-unseen attraction is destined to sink *Titanic*, just as *Star Wars* swamped *Jaws* 22 years ago. Even the old "Star Wars" missile-defense scheme has been revived in scaled-down fashion to be operational by 2005—to coincide with the culmination of Lucas's second trilogy. (It is only a matter of moments before politicians begin to refer to Russia, China, or Slobodan Milosevic as the Phantom Menace.) Why is this blockbuster different from all other blockbusters? *The Godfather*, *The Exorcist*, and *Jaws* inspired repeat viewings, spawned sequels, and revitalized genres. *Star Wars*, however, was always something more.

*Star Wars* would establish a franchise, but back in May 1977, *Variety* was too awestruck to consider the bottom line: "Like a breath of fresh air, *Star Wars* sweeps away the cynicism that has in recent years obscured the concepts of valor, dedication and honor. Make no mistake—this is by no means a 'children's film' … This is the kind of film in which an audience, first entertained, can later walk out feeling good all over."

What is overdetermined now was spontaneous then. Lucas's geeky pulpfest caught the movie studios, the toy stores, and the media by surprise. As late as Christmas 1977, a month after *Star Wars* topped *Jaws*, theater owners were still fighting to keep it on their screens. Not since Chaplinitis swept America in 1915 had cinema inspired so heady a craze. Perhaps we can date the decline of mere movies to that moment. A year after *The Rocky Horror Picture Show* began building its fanatical midnight following, *Star Wars* established a cult on an unprecedented scale. Francis Ford Coppola wasn't entirely kidding when, according to Lucas, he suggested his onetime protégé turn *Star Wars* into a religion: "With religion, you *really* have power."

Coppola needn't have worried. Established faiths were already on the case. Lucas's creation was celebrated by *Christian Century* and *The Lutheran*. In *The Force of Star Wars*, an original Bible Voice paperback published while the movie was still in first release, a born-again former Disney publicist with the

Dickensian name Frank Allnutt compared the plucky crew of the Millennium Falcon to the early Christian true believers. Allnutt expressed his belief that *Star Wars* presaged another imminent "invasion from outer space"—namely, the triumphant return of Jesus Christ to Earth.

The *Star Wars* resurrection has been heralded by hundreds of Web sites, some submitting the Lucas text to scriptural exegesis and Talmudic interpretation. Lucas recently described *Star Wars* as a sort of drive-in McChristianity, "taking all [*sic*] the issues that religion represents and trying to distill them down into a more modern and easily accessible construct." Obi-Wan Kenobi may not yet be recognized as Lord Krishna's avatar, but I have seen a Darth Vader action figure incorporated into a voodoo altar—just as it was fetishized in the bedrooms of 10 million American kids.

*Star Wars* may not have inspired the first sci-fi church (L. Ron Hubbard was already in business). Nor was it the first movie to bring divine revelation to the screen (although it did render DeMille's *Ten Commandments* obsolete). But, unlike any previous religion, *Star Wars* used late-twentieth-century technology to bypass church, state, and parental authority in mass-marketing its vision. What then was George Lucas's burning bush?

A long time ago in a galaxy far, far away, lived a little boy without TV: me. I remember the day that, after much lobbying, my dad brought home a boxy Emerson and installed it in a living-room bookcase. I even more vividly recall my pleasure as a five-year-old in the Wednesday night telecast of *Disneyland* and enormous satisfaction in the innocent belief that right then sets were blasting on all over America. Every kid in the country was watching Tinkerbell shake her booty around Cinderella's castle and, what was more, *we were all watching it at the exact same instant*—experiencing the feeling that Benedict Anderson would eventually characterize as the "deep horizontal comradeship" of an "imagined community."

When *Disneyland* began to televise the adventures of Davy Crockett, every kid on my block had a coonskin cap and could chant "The Ballad of Davy Crockett"—and not just on my block. The boomers entered the marketplace. A generation recognized itself in the greatest merchandising bonanza of the age. The child George Lucas was watching TV then too. Thus, as prophesied by Uncle Walt, *Star Wars* was a religion founded on the imagined community of Disneyland and the cash-cow collectibility of Davy Crockett.

A man with a mission, Lucas would explain that whereas he made *American Graffiti* (the movie that effectively ended the sixties when it was released during the summer of 1973) for 16-year-olds, *Star Wars* was created for a younger audience. The filmmaker was addressing those 10-year-olds who—in his opinion—had been deprived of their mass cultural birthright. As

Lucas remembered, western movies had been the great repository of mythic narrative and moral value when he and we were growing up post–World War II. Cowboys and Indians, every night on TV and every week at the movies, taught us right from wrong, good guys from bad. But somehow the genre failed to survive the tumult of the Vietnam era—as did many thousands of little western devotees. Lucas took it upon himself "to make a film for young people that would move forward the values and the logical thinking that our society has passed down for generations."

*Star Wars* was not just a seamless blend of Walt Disney and Leni Riefenstahl, *The Searchers* and *2001*, *The Wizard of Oz* and World War II. Lucas had not only studied Akira Kurosawa but also Carlos Castaneda and even Joseph Campbell's 1949 pop Jungian treatise on the monomyth, *The Hero with a Thousand Faces*. Moreover *Star Wars* had politics. Clancy Sigal soon noted in *The Spectator* that Lucas had synthesized "the most imaginatively compelling aspects of the Vietnam-era culture: the technical achievements of scientific hardware (from NASA space probes to helicopter gun ships used in search-and-destroy operations) and the ascendancy of mushy mysticism." *Star Wars* was an antitechnological technological wonder—an ultra-authoritarian presentation with an antiauthoritarian message.

Sigal cited *Star Trek* as *Star Wars*' precursor: "a substitute classroom-church for millions of American kids." But I was in grad school when *Star Wars* opened and, as Fox dumped a bunch of invites at Columbia, managed to be present when the sacred text first scrolled upon the screen. For me, *Star Wars* was a new wave nightmare—sanctimonious and soulless, a jet-propelled smile button with a raucous blitzkrieg ending. But what did I know? As the lights rose I was amazed to see the middle-aged face of my department chairman redder than usual and creased with childlike delight. (I'd be less surprised six years later when President Ronald Reagan appropriated the movie for his own political agenda.)

So I thought *Star Wars* was a bore—but so what? I was hardly the target. A movie about teenage heroism in an adult universe, *Star Wars* created a pop-cultural generational divide comparable to the chasm that had split the nation with the arrival of Elvis Presley 21 years before. (In a convenient bit of Jungian synchronicity, the King OD'd the summer of *Star Wars*' release—never to be introduced on planet Vegas by a blast from the cornball migraine-maker that was John Williams' instantly disco-ized theme.) Just as few born before 1938 would ever truly believe in the "magic" of rock 'n' roll, those born after 1968 experienced a force that their elders could barely imagine. Call these mutants the Star Woids. There is not one person that I've asked between the ages of 25 and 30 who doesn't have some powerful *Star Wars* association. An artist remembers leaving the movie house and hallucinating Darth Vader in the streets.

A writer who has no memory of the movie recalls organizing the neighborhood kids in a *Star Wars* pageant.

When I surveyed my college students on the occasion of the twentieth-anniversary re-release, their responses were scarcely less cosmic. "*The Empire Strikes Back* was the first event in my life," one wrote. "My brother remembers the exact time and the position of the sun when he first saw *Star Wars*," another maintained. If some couldn't bring to mind the first time they saw the movie, it was because they felt they'd always known it. One found it more powerful than Catholic school. Another described his grade-school trauma—being asked the "horrifying question: 'You really haven't seen any *Star Wars* movies?'" A boy from South America recounted a similar moment of truth. "When I raised my hand telling I had not yet seen *Star Wars*, my friend looked at me sideways and whispered, 'Freak.'" As one Russian student described the heroic risks that his family took to see *Star Wars* in Odessa, a Caribbean girl remembered recognizing that this movie was the "symbol of America," and a Pakistani boy, brought to the U.S. at eight, knew then that knowledge of *Star Wars* was "required if I was to be Americanized."

Was there a choice? In the half dozen years between the opening of *Star Wars* and Reagan's "Evil Empire" speech, kids wore *Star Wars* sweatshirts, carried *Star Wars* lunchboxes to schools where they wrote with *Star Wars* pencils in *Star Wars* notebooks, lobbied for *Star Wars* light sabers, role-played *Star Wars* and played *Star Wars* videos, read *Star Wars* books, listened to *Star Wars* records, attended *Star Wars* birthday parties, donned *Star Wars* Halloween costumes, and, each night, brushed with *Star Wars* toothbrushes and slept in *Star Wars* pajamas, between *Star Wars* sheets, to dream *Star Wars* dreams.

Endless regression: By the time of *Star Wars*' 1987 and 1997 anniversary reissues, the horizontal comradeship of the initial craze had been transmuted into the premature nostalgia that is fueling the current hysteria. The audience for *The Phantom Menace* is not 10 but 30. For *Star Wars* not only resurrected the entire sci-fi fantasy genre and reconfigured modern warfare; it created a new cinematic paradigm. For studios, *Star Wars* seemed the ultimate moneymaking machine, one to be emulated into eternity. For impressionable viewers, Lucas produced an experience so intense, provided a worldview so participatory, and created a narrative so totally awesome that, however craved, the effect can never be equaled.

The sense of a spurious reality is the theme of the season's sci-fi sleeper. Indeed, back in 1977, Frank Allnutt praised *Star Wars* in terms suggestive of *The Matrix*. Rather than believing that the movie allowed audiences to relive childhood fantasies (per Lucas), Allnutt thought *Star Wars* did the opposite. "Perhaps the youth of today, especially, see the world they are living in as artificial, a fantasy, if you will, and really want to find reality. *Star Wars* gives them a glimpse of reality—a hope for something more meaningful than the fantasy of everyday life so many people are living."

On the other hand, *The Matrix* might be an allegory for the *Star Wars* world. *The Phantom Menace* is 95 percent digitally realized. Lucas has compared this technology, pioneered by his Industrial Light and Magic, to the invention of sound or color. His new movie is essentially an animated cartoon fashioned from photographic material—not just backdrops and stunt-doubles, but entire worlds and characters are computer-generated.

As the spectacularly alienated aerial battle that ended *Star Wars* predicted video and computer games to come (not to mention the sanitized air war of Desert Storm), so *The Phantom Menace* demonstrates the history of the future—literally. Years ago, Siegfried Kracauer linked the development of historicist thinking to the mid-nineteenth-century rise of photography: "The world has become a photographable present and the photographed present has been entirely eternalized." History was the attempt to "photograph time" and photography was memory made material.

But, infinitely malleable, digital imaging does not share photography's indexical relationship to the real—it doesn't produce a document (admissible as evidence) but rather a fiction. Will this mastery over the photographic record inspire a new historicism or inspire a continually "improved" past? It is telling that where politics made it impossible for the National Air and Space Museum to present a factual show marking the 50th anniversary of the Bomb dropped on Hiroshima, the same museum subsequently mounted a wildly successful, wholly fictional exhibit called "Star Wars: The Magic of Myth."

Purists screamed when *Casablanca* was colorized, but Star Woids were thrilled when Lucas digitally added Jabba the Hutt to the *Star Wars* reissue. Few were disturbed when he improved Han Solo's character by changing a scene so that villainous Greedo fired on the good guy first, rather than vice versa. Rewritten history or only a movie? For some, the *Star Wars* saga is already the essential past. Where *Time* hailed *Star Wars* as a "subliminal history of movies," filmmaker (and Star Woid) Kevin Smith remembers encountering classical mythology in school and assuming that the Greeks had ripped off Lucas. And recently, *Newsweek* reversed another chronology. No longer did Lucas illustrate the ideas of Joseph Campbell: "In *The Hero with a Thousand Faces* and *The Power of Myth*," according to one commentator, "Campbell interprets the universal appeal of *Star Wars*."

The future revises the past. George Lucas owns the monomyth. Were Campbell still alive he might find himself sued for copyright infringement. As *Star Wars* ended with a scene cribbed from *Triumph of the Will*, so the tumult around *The Phantom Menace* suggests a slogan associated with that vision of totality. One people, one entertainment regime, one movie.

## POSTSCRIPT: THE PHANTOM MOVIE

There's a rough justice in the way the 24-hour news cycle devours its own. Bill Clinton was the first American president to enjoy a preinaugural "honeymoon"—the day he took office his poll numbers were already falling. If spouse Hillary's Senate campaign has faded from overexposure even before it could be declared, the same is true for George Lucas's *Star Wars* prequel.

*Star Wars: Episode I—The Phantom Menace* may be the first movie to peak before its opening. Last year's *Godzilla* was dead on arrival, but *The Phantom Menace*—which (finally!) has its premiere today—has enjoyed a six-month run in the media. Hence, the movie required scarcely more than six minutes to wear thin. There is nothing in this noisy, overdesigned bore to equal the excitement generated by the mere idea of the trailer. Indeed, days before *The Phantom Menace*'s high-security press junket, fans who penetrated a top-secret distributor's screening were venting their disappointment over the Net. By junket time, the backlash was evident. Several local and national periodicals broke the cardinal rule of studio PR and jumped the opening by 10 days to pan the most anticipated movie in living memory.

This, of course, scarcely matters. However anticlimactic, *The Phantom Menace* is not only critic-proof but audience-resistant as well. The movie has already made its money back 10 times over through Pepsi's merchandising blitz alone, and thanks to Lucas's pressure on theatrical exhibitors to guarantee lengthy exclusive runs (and the decision by rival distributors to cede him the rest of the spring), it would take the consumer equivalent of the Russian Revolution to keep *The Phantom Menace* from ruling the box office for weeks.

What else is new? In essence, *The Phantom Menace* remakes *Star Wars* with more elaborate effects, greater childishness, and weaker characters. The evil Darth Vader is here an innocent nine-year-old towhead named Anakin Skywalker (Jake Lloyd), while the absence of a Han Solo antihero further diminishes the humanity quotient. From the moment a pair of Jedi knights (Liam Neeson and Ewan McGregor) do battle with a treacherous gaggle of Trade Federation fish faces, the movie is steeped in déjà vu. If *Star Wars* was, as *Time* magazine once raved, a "subliminal history of movies," *The Phantom Menace* is a dreary recap of that synopsis. Thus cute li'l R2D2 saves another spaceship, Jabba the Hutt presides over a drag race through a digital Monument Valley, and Lucas rewards the faithful with the revelation that the future Darth Vader, who we already know fathered Luke Skywalker, was also a precocious mechanical genius who invented the dithering C3PO.

Yoda puts in a cameo, but the film's designated alien is Jar Jar Binks, a rabbit-eared ambulatory lizard whose pidgin English degenerates from pseudo-Caribbean patois to Teletubby gurgle. (Although Jar Jar can be construed as grotesquely Third World and the fish faces talk like Fu Manchu, the most blatant ethnic stereotype is the hook-nosed merchant insect who owns young Anakin.) Jar Jar and his fellow Gungans suck the oxygen out of every scene; their human costars seem understandably asphyxiated. In addition to dogged Neeson (whose presence gives Oskar Schindler a retroactive Jedi glow) and the embarrassed, smirky McGregor, the unhappy-looking cast includes the seemingly dubbed Natalie Portman as the elected queen of Naboo, a walking piece of japonaiserie; a ridiculously earnest Samuel L. Jackson as an über-Jedi; and Terence Stamp as the galactic pol Lucas has designated the Clinton character. The big tease is the close-up of Portman gazing fondly down at Jake Lloyd. All true Star Woids know that this little kid will father her children, doubtless offscreen—if not between episodes.

Climaxing instead with four simultaneous battles, *The Phantom Menace* is a war movie that's all the creepier for making the combat virtually cost-free. The two human Jedis decimate, dismember, and destroy several dozen digital droid armies—but these pesky critters feel no pain. Similarly, little Ani learns the magic of strategic bombing (or is it a video game?), blasting away at largely unseen as well as nonhuman targets. The extended carnage has none of the horror that characterized the digitally produced human-insect struggle of *Starship Troopers*. The most exciting action is also the most conventional—the Jedis' leaping light-saber fight with a horned, orange-eyed, camouflage-faced bogeyman could have been choreographed for Errol Flynn.

*The Phantom Menace* may strike even some kids as excessively cartoonlike, but then, as a director, Lucas remains the greatest exponent of the theme park aesthetic. As each character in *The Phantom Menace* has been designed with a molded plastic collectible in mind, almost every sequence suggests either Mr. Toad's Wild Ride or a Fantasyland it would be a pleasure not to visit. The production design is astonishingly crass. If Naboo City is a gussied-up Victorian vision of ancient Rome, the Gungan underwater civilization seems modeled on a Bowery lighting-fixture emporium. Most hideous is the galactic capital—a nauseatingly dense combination of Manhattan and L.A. in which every interior is furnished like a Reno carpet joint and every window reveals a sky in whirlybird gridlock.

Nor is the script much better. Most of the dialogue sounds like silent movie intertitles ("The death toll is catastrophic—we must bow to their wishes"). The rest, mainly intoned by Neeson, seems to have been found in a fortune cookie. "Our meeting was not a coincidence—nothing happens by accident," he explains to his little protégé. Representative of the Force, Neeson is the resident sage: "Fear leads to anger, anger leads to hate, hate leads to suffering"—which presumably promotes fear.

Religion may be a presence, but Lucas's magic kingdom is strikingly sterile. His creatures dwell in a perpetual present, devoid of sexual activity (Anakin, it is strongly hinted, was the product of an immaculate conception), historical con-sciousness, or even the most debased form of cultural expression (like advertising). Any of these would constitute a dangerous distraction. *The Phantom Menace* is simply a billboard for itself. Anyone who sees it will be experiencing it for the second time. The hype was not about the movie; the hype *was* the movie.

## RUN SHAG RUN

Originally published as "So Long a Go-Go,"
the *Village Voice* (June 22, 1999).

**J**EAN-LUC GODARD HAS LONG BEEN CONSIGNED TO THE MARGINS OF COMMERCIAL cinema, but the "new wave" cinema epitomized by his 1959 *Breathless* lives on and on, sometimes in forms that are barely recognizable. Based as much on attitude as methodology, new wave movies were blatantly cinephilic and radi-cally self-conscious—drawing attention to themselves as films not only through historicizing allusions to other movies, but through disjointed narratives, deconstructed genre references, sudden mood shifts, bizarre sight gags, and performances based on "movie acting."

Almost every film-producing nation had its sixties or seventies new wave equivalent; the Hollywood version stood Godard on his head with the seamless, reconstructed package that was *Star Wars*. Current neo–new wave filmmakers would include Wong Kar-Wai, the Olivier Assayas of *Irma Vep*, and, of course, the still-burgeoning Anglo-American tribe of Tarantinians. This week brings another variation on the formula in German filmmaker Tom Tykwer's bid for name-brand status, *Run Lola Run*.

An enjoyably glib and refreshingly terse exercise in big beat and constant motion, *Run Lola Run* hit the ground sprinting at the last Venice Film Festival. (Such was the reception that the movie's first North American showing—days later, in Toronto—occurred amid a buzzy crescendo of cell-phone static and ended with word that Sony Classics had clinched the U.S. distribution deal mid-screening.) Unfolding in near real time, this third feature by the 33-year-old writer-director hotshot is a sort of power-pop variation on the mystical time-bending Euro-art movies made by the late Krzysztof Kieślowski. In this tale of three alternate futures, the eponymous Berlin punk goddess (Franka Potente) has a mere 20 minutes to raise 100,000 deutsche marks (approxi-mately $60,000) and save the life of her gangster-wannabe boyfriend—a cute *dummkopf* named Manni (Moritz Bleibtreu) who, gofer in some sort of dope deal, managed to leave a bag full of banknotes behind him on the U-Bahn.

The doomed outlaw couple is a new wave standby, but *Run Lola Run* is far too businesslike to indulge anyone's romantic fantasy. (There is not a single musical interlude to tweak the viewer's nostalgia.) Nor is there the least hint of a class angle. That the film's heroine is a banker's daughter turns out to be mere plot contrivance. Ultimately less useful than the gift of her petulant supersonic, glass-shattering scream, Lola's provenance has scarcely more weight than the various robberies, shootings, and fatal accidents that occur in the several parallel universes.

*Run Lola Run* aspires to pure sensation. Whether the denouement of Tykwer's mock interactive, beat-the-clock chase is predicated on chaos theory or blind chance, Franka Potente personifies the movie's compact running time. Indeed, with her eye-catching vermilion hair, blue tank top, sherbet green dungarees, and expression of grim determination, she is a sort of all-purpose cinematic muse. Watching this virtual cartoon character dash through a nondescript residential district in summery Berlin, you can imagine her form enlivening anything from Eadweard Muybridge's precinematic locomotion studies to *Mad Max* to Metal Gear Solid.

Switching back and forth between 35-mm and video, color and black and white, live action and animation, *Run Lola Run* suggests an 80-minute chunk of MTV. Still, unencumbered by the narrative weight of kindred neo–new wave style parades like *Trainspotting*, *Lock, Stock and Two Smoking Barrels*, and *Go*, *Run Lola Run* maintains its forward momentum through all manner of split screens, replays, and rapid-fire digressions.

*Run Lola Run* manages to be both philosophical and brainless. As its title suggests the name of the original new wave film, so this go-go abstraction feels as inexorable as the millennium. Subtitles may keep the movie from being a hit, but given its punchy editing, pulse-pounding score, and calisthenically enriched protagonist, *Lola* could have a long nontheatrical afterlife in health clubs across the world as a hipster exercise video.

*Austin Powers: The Spy Who Shagged Me* would be a neo–new wave movie if only for existing largely in a realm of movie references—mostly taken from *Austin Powers: International Man of Mystery*, the 1997 movie which first defrosted Mike Myers' Carnaby Street relic. But it has additional relevance for its burlesque of Richard Lester's Swinging London commercialization of Godardian cinema.

Essentially the same sixties/nineties joke as the original *Austin Powers*, *The Spy Who Shagged Me*—also directed by Jay Roach from Myers' script—is no less funny, being similarly founded on groovy, pop-op set design and James Bond–parody parody, and enlivened by a now familiar mix of lewd anatomy jokes, bad puns, Mel Brooks character names (Ivana Humpalot) and Yiddishisms

(Kreplachistan, Frau Farbissina), free-floating scatology, prancing go-go girls, and tacky psychedelic effects. (Myers' other persona Dr. Evil isn't kidding when he cries, "Send in the clones!") Certain bits of business are simply repeated, with Burt Bacharach grinning zombielike through his requisite cameo as though being rediscovered for the first time.

In short, the sequel attempts to place the original within quotation marks—embellishing, rather than extending, the original premise. Well before the opening credits end, *The Spy Who Shagged Me* has demolished its predecessor's happy ending while reestablishing Myers' exhibitionist credentials. Austin's new bride turns out to be a fembot with machine-gun jumblies—giving him license to prance naked through the hotel lobby looking for birds. His replacement love interest (Heather Graham) is a luscious CIA operative who aspires to be the female Austin Powers.

Austin's shag-pad includes his own pseudo-Warhol portrait, and the plot contrives for him to be joined by his 10-minutes-future self, but the nominal hero is overshadowed by his various alter egos. The epicene Dr. Evil gets at least as much screen time as Austin, plus the theme song ("Evil is his one and only name"). There's also a scaled-down Dr. Evil replica (32-inch Verne Troyer), complete with a bald kitten to cuddle, whom the original dubs "Mini-Me." Myers further enhances the Peter Sellers effect and ups the gross-out quotient by appearing as Dr. Evil's most disgusting henchman, the F/X-padded, kilt-wearing, slobbering Scotsman accurately known as Fat Bastard.

Although not as brilliantly scored as the original, *Austin* redux is even more a musical. While the obligatory polka-dot swirl disco scene, in which Graham dances down from the balcony to "American Woman," prompts the unhappy—and accurate—suspicion that we'll never again get to watch her frug, Dr. Evil has a memorable Marvin Gaye pas de deux with Frau Farbissina. Even better, when he sings "Just the Two of Us" to Mini-Me, he turns Will Smith's rap ballad into the perfect anthem for a movie narcissistically encrusted with its own mythology.

## *EYES WIDE SHUT*

Originally published as "I Wake Up Dreaming,"
the *Village Voice* (July 27, 1999).

**T**HE BEST THING ABOUT *EYES WIDE SHUT* MAY BE ITS TITLE, BUT ANYONE PLANNING to see Stanley Kubrick's long-awaited, posthumously released swan song is advised to go with eyes open. Completed by Warner Bros. after the director's death last March (and shamelessly proclaimed a "brilliant," "haunting" "masterpiece" in the advance cover story provided by the studio's corporate sibling, *Time*), this two-hour-and-39-minute gloss on Arthur Schnitzler's fantasmagoric novella feels like a rough draft at best.

At worst, *Eyes Wide Shut* is ponderously updated—as though Kubrick had finally gotten around to responding to Michelangelo Antonioni's druggy *Blow-Up*—if not weirdly anachronistic. (It's difficult to make a movie about a city you last set foot in 35 years ago.) Shot in London, *Eyes Wide Shut* opens in a fabulous Upper West Side apartment filled with florid paintings, Alice (Nicole Kidman) stripping down to dress up—and not for the last time. She and her doctor husband Bill (Tom Cruise) have been invited to the splendiferous Christmas bash hosted by a wealthy sleazebag of mystery (Sydney Pollack).

Lit like Bloomingdales' window and shot as though for *The Shining*, the party is charged with telegraphed sophistication and rich with significant meetings. Bill encounters an old med-school buddy playing piano; Alice is swept away by a predatory Hungarian for a foxtrot so torrid they're practically horizontal. Just as Bill is being waltzed off to pleasures unknown by a pair of flirtatious models, he is summoned, at the host's behest, to revive a very naked lovely who has inconveniently OD'd in the master bathroom. *Eyes Wide Shut*, as you may know, is about sex—albeit mainly in the head.

In one of the movie's two bravura scenes, Bill and Alice smoke weed and rehash their confusing Christmas party encounters. Irritated (or is it stimulated?) by Bill's smug denials, Alice launches into an impassioned riff on marriage, jealousy, and the alleged difference between the genders. Bill remains clueless: "Relax, Alice, this pot is making you aggressive." The scene demonstrates why Kubrick wanted a real-life couple—Cruise's evident discomfort is no less crucial than Kidman's ecstatic exhibitionism. The actress is not only a more assured performer than her husband but an incomparably greater showboat, almost absurdly comfortable acting without clothes. (A year spent shooting and reshooting this material must have propelled her into *The Blue Room*.)

The all-purpose conjugal argument, somewhat skewed by Kidman's stoned rantings and distracting dishabille, segues into a confession that she has only just finished making when the telephone rings. Summoned to his professional duties, the most boyish, least likely, doctor in New York City embarks on a stumbling sexual Cook's tour. Imagining his wife's imagined infidelity all the while, he is successively propositioned by a dead patient's neurotic daughter, gay-baited by six drunken teenagers, picked up by an exceedingly pretty hooker, made privy to a sordid instance of pedophilia, and ultimately transported to a masquerade orgy at a baronial estate somewhere in the richest, most Republican districts of Long Island.

The latter is the movie's set piece but, for all the bare breasts and velvet capes, black mass paraphernalia and strenuously implied in-and-out, it's less carnal cornucopia than a triumph of theatrical fustiness that effectively liquidates whatever mad oneiric momentum the movie has built up over the past hour. Hardly the sexual heart of darkness, this decorous gavotte is more studied than a fashion shoot and rather less explicit. The final shock: Two men dancing . . . together!

The story of a guy who crashes out of his bourgeois existence into a nocturnal world of sexual gangsters and femmes fatales, *Eyes Wide Shut* is a kind of primal noir. The script, which Kubrick wrote with novelist Frederic Rafael, is, for much of its length, surprisingly faithful to the 1926 Schnitzler original— a fluid exploration of the marital magnetic field that, successfully blurring the boundaries of the real, keeps telling the same story again and again, charging it each time with additional psychosexual material. (Physician, heal thyself: Schnitzler himself was a medical doctor and, like Kubrick, a doctor's son.)

While Bill's out exploring, Alice has been home in bed, dreaming. Far more cogent (and disturbingly erotic) than the vaunted orgy, Kidman's agonized recounting of her nocturnal adventure makes the movie's most compelling scene. Events staged are trumped by those imagined. *Eyes Wide Shut* is its own critique—no wonder Kubrick spent so many years pondering this project and so much time in production.

———

No small attention has been given to the digital figures that Warner Bros. introduced into Kubrick's footage, strategically positioned to block the action during the orgy scene. (The effect is not unlike the inscribed audience in *Mystery Science Theater 3000*.) Supposedly added to secure the movie's R rating, these computer-generated fig leaves may conceal something else.

Days after Kubrick's death, Warners' then co-chairman Terry Semel told the *New York Times* that *Eyes Wide Shut* was "totally finished." Save for "a couple of color corrections" and some unspecified "technical things," Kubrick had made "his final cut." From a semantic point of view, this last statement is undeniable— the director had made his last cut, at least on this earth. But *Eyes Wide Shut* may be scarcely more Kubrick's film than *Juneteenth* is Ralph Ellison's novel. Whether or not one believes the rumors that the *Eyes Wide Shut* release version was supervised by Steven Spielberg or Sydney Pollack or even Tom Cruise, the ponderous *Temple of Doom* orgy, crassly matched location inserts, overreliance on cross-cutting, and atrocious mixing (most obvious in the orgy's dreadful dubbing and oscillating hubbub level) all suggest the movie was quite far from completion when its notoriously perfectionist author passed away.

*Eyes Wide Shut* had more than a few problems for Kubrick to solve. Out of his depth playing out of his depth, Cruise is as blatantly miscast as his character is incoherent. (The role of this self-deluded society doc might have made more sense if Bill were unhappily Jewish, as Rafael wanted, or a closeted gay, as Kubrick sometimes hints.) The ridiculous orgy and the botched sense of place would have been difficult to repair, and I don't think there was any way to reconcile the cinematography's would-be grainy immediacy with the fastidious studio lighting and lavish New York street set. But although the sarcastic use of pop chestnuts like "Strangers in the Night" and "When I Fall in Love" sounds like Kubrick, it's difficult to find a precedent in his oeuvre for the embarrassingly insipid score.

Notwithstanding the misguided attempt in the movie's final half hour to rationalize Schnitzler's evocative material with a heavy-handed and ultimately nonsensical plot device, I'm not even convinced that this "haunting final masterpiece" has the tone that Kubrick intended. It requires but the barest familiarity with *Lolita* or *Dr.Strangelove* to see how *Eyes Wide Shut* might have been cut by 45 minutes and played for East European black comedy. (The movie is rife enough with broad performances—ranging from Sky Dumont's hokey Hungarian to the fey camping of Alan Cumming's desk clerk.) There may be a scandal behind *Eyes Wide Shut*—which, even in this forlorn state, has enough stuff to suggest a Kubrick film— but it has nothing to do with explicit sex. Someday some dogged cine-archaeologist will get to the bottom of this corporate restoration and, figuring out just who did what to whom, sort the potential film from the apparent one. For most people, though, a single viewing will be more than enough.

## IN THE MOOD FOR LOVE

Originally published as "High Lonesome," the *Village Voice* (February 6, 2001).

**W**ONG KAR-WAI MAY BE THE MOST FETISHIZED—AS WELL AS THE MOST FETISHIZING— of contemporary filmmakers, and with *In the Mood for Love* he takes this form of worship as his subject. Boldly mannered yet surprisingly delicate, *In the Mood for Love* is a wondrously perverse movie that not only evokes a lost moment in time but circles around an unrepresentable subject.

Mood is the operative word. A love story far more cerebral than it is emotional, *In the Mood for Love* invests most of its passion in the act of filmmaking . . . mainly by subtraction. Oblique events unfold in a sort of staid delirium. There may be no distinction between creating the memory and making the movie—"the past was something he could see but not touch," it is explained of the lead character—

except that *In the Mood for Love* is structured on a principle of selective amnesia. The movie's presumptive title song is scarcely the only absent element.

Wong's story is set, mainly among displaced Shanghainese, in the Hong Kong of the early 1960s—which is to say the period and milieu of the filmmaker's own childhood. Mrs. Chan (Maggie Cheung) and Mr. Chow (Tony Leung) simultaneously rent rooms in adjacent apartments in the same crowded building and are forever bumping into each other in the narrow corridor. Through a series of parallel conversations, they deduce that his wife and her husband— who are several times heard, but whose faces are never shown—are having an affair, seemingly on their frequent business trips abroad. As a result of this, Mrs. Chan and Mr. Chow are often alone and consequently drawn together.

This overdetermined symmetry is Wong's version of the urban romance epitomized by the 1928 silent picture *Lonesome,* in which a young couple meet, fall in love, and then lose each other in the mass-society frenzy of a Coney Island Saturday night only to discover that they actually live in adjoining rooms in the same anonymous boarding house. Wong begins where *Lonesome* ends and, in a sense, works the story backward as well as forward. (At times, Mrs. Chan and Mr. Chow pretend that they are their own adulterous spouses, rehearsing confrontations that may never take place.) With its blatantly manu- factured coincidences, *In the Mood for Love* works both as experimental character drama and ritual in transfigured time. (That Mrs. Chan is employed as the personal secretary for a boss who is juggling a wife and mistress adds another invisible character to the movie.)

A largely fluid succession of short, often shot-length scenes interspersed with tantalizingly incomplete interactions between its two stars, *In the Mood for Love* is rhythmically a matter of dramatic elision and elongated privileged moments. Wong is never more modernist than in his willingness to create a narrative out of trivial dailiness, the storyteller's equivalent of the painter's negative space. If the relationship between his two elegantly unhappy and impossibly beautiful losers is sexually consummated, the audience will never know it: *In the Mood for Love* is a family romance without a primal scene.

Because the stars almost never touch, the air between them accrues an electric charge. The slightly slow-motion interludes, accompanied by Michael Galasso's stringent, wistful score, allow for the enraptured contemplation of Cheung's moving form—seen from the perspective of her affably depressed admirer—as she recedes slowly into the past. There is a sense in which the movie is all about the pensive languor with which the actress models her *qipao*. *In the Mood for Love* has many clocks but no temporal signifiers. The viewer learns to tell time by the leading lady's dresses—she wears a new one in every scene. (The size of her closet is another off-screen mystery.)

Although *In the Mood for Love* is less frenetically new wave and more lacquered than previous Wong, its period stylizations hark back to his first hit, *Days of Being Wild*. Unlike the earlier Chris Doyle–shot films, the camera is relatively sedated. The movie feels as much designed as directed—it's a loving reconstruction in which fake rain gently erodes the doctored exterior of worn apartment buildings. (Wong's longtime art director and costume designer, William Chang, also edited the film.) Scenes are typically set in cramped corridors, framed by doorways, and played out in shadowy back streets amid carefully positioned old automobiles. When they eat Western food at a faux L.A. coffee shop, Mrs. Chan's flowered *qipao* matches the palm trees on the oversized plastic menu. Wong puts the antique bric-a-brac in the foreground but the old music seems overheard at some distance—except for the recurring songs of multiple displacement that Nat King Cole croons in Spanish.

Studied as it is, *In the Mood for Love* might have felt airless or static were it not for the oblique editing. Every artful contrivance is fuel for the fire, ashes of time scattered on the wind. "That era has passed" is the closing sentiment. "Nothing that belongs to it exists any more." Is *In the Mood for Love* Sirkian? Proustian? Can we speak of the Wongian? This 43-year-old writer-director is the most avant-garde of pop filmmakers (or vice versa). Poised between approach and avoidance, presence and absence, *In the Mood for Love* is both giving and withholding. Governed by laws as strict as the old Hollywood production code, it's rhapsodically sublimated and ultimately sublime.

When Mr. Chow finally decides to leave Hong Kong, the camera finds him in his office and the image almost freezes on a gesture. Similarly, the narrative itself disintegrates into a remarkable series of vignettes—a scene predicated on a phone call placed to Singapore, a fleeting glimpse through a Hong Kong tenement door. The coda—set, with wild extravagance, in the jungle city of Angkor—is almost too lovely. The monumental merges with the ephemeral, as the stately camera tracks through the empty ruins of someone else's eternity.

## THE MAN WHO CRIED

Originally published as "Kitsch as Kitsch Can,"
the *Village Voice* (May 29, 2001).

THE GRANDER THE PASSION, THE KITSCHIER; THE CRAZIER THE KITSCH, THE BETTER. Why not cast the whole twentieth century as just another silly love song? Overwrought and underwhelming, Baz Luhrmann's *Moulin Rouge* has been touted as a major-league lunacy, but there's far too much method in the madness; underproduced and overconceptualized, Sally Potter's equally foolish *The Man Who Cried* is truly nuts, in part because it seems oblivious to its own delusions.

Among the more vivid literary recollections of a misspent childhood, I remember a *Mad* magazine parody of horror comics in which a moldering bayou garbage dump came disgustingly to life. Would that Luhrmann's strenuous attempt to revive the movie musical (and *La Bohème* besides) were half so unruly. In a sense, this magpie monument is the opposite of the monster *Mad* called The Heap. Scarcely chaotic, *Moulin Rouge* is a voracious vacuum cleaner of a movie—hoovering up a hundred years' worth of junk with the same monotonously unmodulated hum.

Conventionally worse than *Moulin Rouge* (but far more entertaining), Sally Potter's *The Man Who Cried* is another attempt to reanimate a passé genre: the multistar romantic epic of the 1950s. Part of the charm is predicated on Potter's pragmatic downsizing. Perhaps, as a child, the writer-director dreamt of making a glamorous tale of pogroms and chorus girls, Nazis and gypsies, war and shipwreck, that would span the globe from Russia to Paris to Hollywood, and star Elizabeth Taylor, Marlon Brando, Marilyn Monroe, and, as the fascist baritone, Kirk Douglas. She settles for Christina Ricci, Johnny Depp, Cate Blanchett, and John Turturro.

Rich with arias and inadvertent anachronism, *The Man Who Cried* raises its curtain on a *shtetl* that might once have been home to Fievel the Mouse. A cantor's daughter survives a pogrom in Soviet (!) Russia, then sets off to find her immigrant papa in America. Put ashore in London and renamed Suzie, she grows up in Dickensian foster care and matures into big-eyed Ricci. Naturally, this round and solemn creature goes to France as a chorus girl, sharing her lodging with a rangy Russian named Lola (fabulously histrionic Cate Blanchett). A few quick cuts introduce the Mutt and Jeff team to their respective swains—Johnny Depp's gypsy horse-handler, Cesar (the natives call him El Smolderoso), and John Turturro's Dante, an opera star whose onstage contortions are even more baroque than Blanchett's flouncing pirouettes.

Crazy love and sudden revelation: A Jewish landlady restores Suzie to her roots with the imperative "Eat!" (The chicken soup's ostentatious set of matzo balls reminds me of the old joke in which, brought home for dinner by fiancé Arthur Miller, Marilyn Monroe innocently asks her prospective mother-in-law what she does with "the rest of the matzo.") But the treacherous Dante is busy monitoring Suzie's romance. "Your lee-tul friend has become a jeepsy-lover," he sneeringly informs Lola—and that's before he discovers the secret behind Suzie's sacred photograph of her bearded, *kapote*-clad father.

*The Man Who Cried* heedlessly leaps from one emotional peak to the next. Nothing can top the mad doina of Suzie pedaling her bicycle through nocturnal Paris in mad pursuit of two gypsy horsemen, unless it's the scene of Lola weepily watching the climax of *Footlight Parade* and imagining herself the star. What's truly amazing is that, from a formalist perspective, *The Man Who Cried* is not poorly made. On the contrary, Potter employs a canny minimalism—ingeniously establishing her period mise-en-scène largely through close-ups and interiors—and saves her most elaborate camera angles for the onstage scenes. You know Paris has fallen when Suzie awakes to hear the amplified thunder of Nazi jackboots—thus the thrifty filmmaker economizes in the hiring of costumed extras.

*The Man Who Cried* gives bad movies a good name. Potter's stringent, resourceful filmmaking in handling an extravagantly absurd plot and hopeless acting recalls the genius of the poverty-row maestro Edgar G. Ulmer. Writing on Ulmer's *Daughter of Dr. Jekyll* ("a film with a scenario so atrocious that it takes forty minutes to establish that the daughter of Dr. Jekyll is indeed the daughter of Dr. Jekyll"), Andrew Sarris noted that "Ulmer's camera never falters even when his characters disintegrate." So it is with Sally Potter, except that she is directing her own ludicrous script.

The combination of cool visuals and overheated narrative, as well as the escalating absence of transition shots, renders *The Man Who Cried* increasingly dreamlike. From the moment Suzie and Lola set sail on the World War II equivalent of the *Titanic,* the movie grows simultaneously more austere and delirious. Suzie entertains the passengers with "Gloomy Sunday" (imagined as a *shtetl* melody and dubbed by the Czech art chanteuse Iva Bittova), while Lola does laps in the ship's swimming pool. Immediately upon drifting into New York, Suzie begins searching for Dad on the Lower East Side. No more or less remarkable than the survival of her talismanic photograph is the fact that the Jews know him: Yes, he is The Bitter One who cursed God and went to Hollywood.

Potter seems essentially humorless, but she does not lack for conviction. *The Man Who Cried* is like a Yiddish generational tearjerker told from the perspective of the lost child rather than that of the bereaved parent. Indeed, Potter all but reprises the stunning climax of the Yiddish talkie *Where Is My Child?* wherein the young lawyer turns his back on his fancy-shmancy Park Avenue adopted parents to embrace his long-lost real mother. This indomitable crazed bag lady (Celia Adler no less) stares into the camera for the movie's final shot and triumphantly exclaims, "There is a God!" In *The Man Who Cried*, God is in the details.

## A.I.: THE DREAMLIFE OF ANDROIDS

Originally published in *Sight and Sound* (September 2001).

"**S**TORIES ARE REAL," INSISTS LITTLE DAVID, THE ENCHANTED ROBOT CHILD WHO is the protagonist of Steven Spielberg's *A.I. Artificial Intelligence*. David believes that fairy tales can come true. Do we? Spielberg the humanist historian is in remission; Steven the regressive mystic has returned, with a vengeance.

An occasionally spectacular, fascinatingly schizoid, frequently ridiculous, and never less than heartfelt mishmash of Pinocchio and Oedipus, Stanley Kubrick (who bequeathed Spielberg the project) and *Creation of the Humanoids*, *Frankenstein* and "The Steadfast Tin Soldier," *A.I.* is less a movie than a seething psychological bonanza. None of the year's Hollywood releases have given American critics more to write about—nor is one likely to. Moreover, given the movie's convoluted provenance and charged subject matter, it's not so much the critic as the inner child who has been responding to Spielberg's provocation.

Opening in the United States in late June 2001, *A.I.* reaped a severely mixed crop of reviews—surely the most varied in its maker's career. *New York Times* critic A. O. Scott hailed *A.I.* as Spielberg's "best fairytale," as well as "a more profound inquiry into the moral scandal of dehumanization than either *Schindler's List* or *Amistad*." Writing in the *New Yorker*, David Denby termed *A.I.* as a movie that "weirdly pours treacle over a foundation of despair ... a ponderous, death-of-the-world fantasy." Adding to the mix have been reports in the trade papers and elsewhere recounting the violent antipathy that ordinary audiences have expressed. This disapproval was manifest at the box office; *A.I.*'s grosses dropped 50 percent and 63 percent in its second and third weeks. *A.I.* is not the first Spielberg film to be perceived as a flop; it is, however, the first to be more a critical than a commercial success, which is to say, an art film.

If there is a universal personality in contemporary cinema it is surely Steven Spielberg. As Walt Disney's invented signature used to emblazon the landscape in the comic books and comic strips produced by his enterprise, so Spielberg has managed to affix his name to the Holocaust, slavery, and the European theater of World War II. In that tradition of aesthetic big game hunting, he appropriates Stanley Kubrick.

*A.I.* is adapted from sci-fi writer Brian Aldiss's "Super-Toys Last All Night Long," a story first published 32 years ago in *Harper's Bazaar*. Kubrick, who evidently had a long-standing interest in this tale of an artificial child and his human parents, acquired the rights in 1983. Various accounts suggest that Kubrick was already operating in reaction to Spielberg. Inspired to make

*A.I.* by the success of *E.T.*, Kubrick is said to have abandoned the project after he saw the digital effects of *Jurassic Park*. Afraid that by the time he could finish *A.I.* its special effects would already be obsolete, he proposed to produce the movie for Spielberg to direct. According to Spielberg, he and Kubrick consequently enjoyed a long-term phone relationship complete with a top-secret fax line dedicated to *A.I.* Having inherited the project, Spielberg worked from the 90-page treatment that Ian Watson had prepared for Kubrick, as well as 600 drawings made by comic book illustrator Chris "Fangorn" Baker.

*A.I.* appears then as a curiously hybrid work. One could begin by parsing the title: Does the artifice belong to Spielberg and the intelligence to Kubrick? Or is it vice versa? The unnecessarily complicated premise is brazenly irrational. The script, for which Spielberg has taken sole credit, more than once bogs down in a hilarious morass of Ed Wood gibberish in trying to elucidate the pseudoscientific principles by which robots might be imbued with the capacity to love and to dream—to have an unconscious—or the special circumstance under which human beings can be cloned. Why bother? The movie's appeal is not to reason. Its psychological terrain is far closer to the magical realm of Hans Christian Andersen or E.T.A. Hoffman than to sci-fi as we know it.

Spielberg's first exercise in cine-futurism, *A.I.* is set in a vaguely established, remarkably homogenous, bizarrely suburban, post-greenhouse-effect world of strict family planning and robot sex slaves. These humanoids are known as "mechas," and *A.I.* opens with their benign designer, Dr. Hobby (William Hurt), informing his devoted band of earth-tone imagineers that he has developed something new, "a robot child with a love that will never end." One associate makes an obscure moral objection, but the good doctor silences her with an airy wave of the hand: "Didn't God create Adam to love him?" Yes, of course, and look what happened there.

The proto robo-tot will be given to distraught Monica (Frances O'Connor), whose own terminally ill son Martin has been cryogenically frozen pending discovery of a cure for his disease. The artificial miracle child first appears out of focus, to suggest the elongated embryos who redeemed the world in *Close Encounters of the Third Kind*. Is little David (Haley Joel Osment, scarcely less uncanny here than in *The Sixth Sense*) the baby Spielberg, a holy child with a smooth, open face and limpid blue eyes? Certainly, Spielberg's identification with David will seem absolute. Is he a sort of emotional prosthetic device, the Frankenstein monster of love? Or is this adorable robot child a terrifying metaphor for us all? The acid-ripped runaways and hippies of the Manson Family used to have a mocking chant about the parents they had fled, "I am a mechanical boy. . . . I am my mother's toy."

*A.I.*'s early scenes are exquisitely creepy—perhaps more than intended. Perpetually smiling and always underfoot, David frisks around Monica like an annoyingly needy pet—even bursting in on her as she demurely perches on the toilet. A psychoanalyst might make something of that scene, but it is soon superseded. Once Monica pronounces the magic spell that will eternally bond David to her alone (not, significantly, the husband who eventually becomes David's enemy), the robot boy embarks upon the golden road of unlimited devotion. The movie presents a profoundly bleak view of human nature—a child imprinted by and forever fixated on the parent's need. "Mommy, will you die?" is the newly programmed David's first abstract question, as well as his first use of the maternal noun. Already expressing anxiety, his query does not quite elide the notion that when this slim and pretty woman is a crone of 90, her adoring mecha will still be a child.

David's age is unfixed. He's been described as 11 although he looks to be three years younger and has the emotional development of a preschooler. In any case, his particular instance of arrested development is superseded by the defrosted Martin's return to his now shockingly expanded family. This suspended animation is also part of the fairy tale. Given that Spielberg wanted to use the *Disneyland* theme song for the celestial communication fest that ends *Close Encounters*, it's perfectly appropriate that when Monica visits Martin there would be Disney murals on the walls and Tchaikovsky's *Sleeping Beauty* playing in the background. (Kubrick, for his part, ended *Full Metal Jacket* with a supremely sarcastic use of the *Mickey Mouse Club* marching song.)

Without ever appearing to question the narcissistic assumption that children are put on this earth to love their parents, Spielberg finds his richest material in the family trauma, sibling rivalry, and emotional malfunction induced by Martin's return. One thing this future world clearly lacks is the cyborg shrink in a suitcase extrapolated by novelist Philip K. Dick. There is no one to analyze, let alone treat, the rejected David's desire to reclaim his mommy's love or his magical solution that he might do so by becoming a "real boy." (This idea has been introduced by the malicious Martin, who insists that Monica read her two sons the story of Pinocchio at bedtime). The mecha quest for an impossible authenticity then becomes the movie's driving mechanism.

*A.I.* has been designed to terrorize actual children, even as it cannily harpoons the hearts of empty-nest boomer moms and pushes psychological buttons in kids (of all ages) longing for a return to the mother ship. David is Monica's toy—or rather he was. The scene in which a human mother abandons her crying, clinging, pleading robot child in the woods is as supreme a heart-clutcher as anything in *Bambi*. Although curiously glossed over in most reviews of the movie, this long, painful sequence, which, as Manohla Dargis pointed out in the *L.A. Weekly,* "combines Kubrick's aesthetic of cruelty and Spielberg's aesthetic of bathos into a single devastating encounter," is understandably the film's turning point. The hermetic suburban environment of David's family gives way to the garish dystopia of the outside world.

Spielberg has always been a master of inadvertent disclosure. One of the most powerful images in his entire oeuvre is that of the obsessed Richard Dreyfuss, imprinted by the aliens of *Close Encounters* and constructing a mountain out of his mashed potatoes even as his distressed children look on in terrified amazement at his apparent regression to infancy. What's fascinating is that Spielberg has gone out of his way to characterize *A.I.* as a film made by an indulgent father: "I am particularly, at this point in my life, somewhat interested in going back a little bit to my past, to tell the kinds of stories I'd like my kids to see. You know, between *Schindler* and *Ryan,* I had a lot of complaints from my kids that I'm not making movies for them anymore. . . . I think *A.I.* is a movie for my own kids."

In what sense, one wonders. Does he mean to teach the power of stories? The idea that fantasy is real? Like Spielberg himself in *Close Encounters,* David takes *Pinocchio* as his text, searching the world in the company of Teddy (a sub Jiminy Cricket "supertoy") for the Blue Fairy who can grant his wish to become a real child. Unlike the puppet Pinocchio, however, David has no need to demonstrate emotional growth or, indeed, any sort of negativity. He's been designed as a perfect reproach to humanity, hard-wired for innocence. (Thus, Spielberg circumvents the moral of the Aldiss story—which is also the pathos of *Blade Runner*—namely that the robots are more human than their creators.)

Whereas Pinocchio's greed led to his being trapped in Stromboli's carnival, blameless David is rounded up by the flying storm troopers of the Flesh Fair, a sort of heavy-metal demolition derby cum death camp for discarded mechas. (The sequence seems to have been imported wholesale from *Mad Max Beyond Thunderdome.*) It's been suggested by some that this bloodthirsty mob represents Spielberg's view of his audience—although, no less than these rabid rednecks, the filmmaker evidently loves the effect of the obsolete jerry-built robots running about further decomposing. Actually, in their devotion to so-called reality, the demagogues responsible for the Flesh Fair might equally represent Spielberg's view of his critics. (Rather than the fantasy of *Schindler's List,* these anti-mechas are demanding the documentary *Shoah.*) Devoted to ritual destruction, the Flesh Fair has a religious aspect: "We are only demolishing artificiality," the cult leader explains. Intelligence will come next.

Escaping from the Flesh Fair, David and Teddy team up with (and redeem) a more profane manifestation of cyberlove. Gigolo Joe (Jude Law) is a stiff, absurdly pomaded creature who supplies his own louche sound track—a faraway-sounding thirties version of "I Only Have Eyes for You" (the very thing surely to guarantee that a lonely repressed spinster will lie back, relax, and lose her inhibitions). Joe's line is no less primitive. "Once you've had a robot lover, you'll never want a real man again," he assures a client. Out of concern for his children no doubt, Spielberg resists showing the sex machine in action. (Joe's bionic member is referred to by his timorous partner but, of course, never seen. This does, however, serve to link him to David, who, in an earlier scene, had had the functionality—and existence—of his penis mocked by a human playmate.)

As *A.I.*'s resident embodiment of cynical Kubrick consciousness, Gigolo Joe takes David to Rouge City (an elaborate extrapolation of the milk bar from *A Clockwork Orange*) to there consult the resident oracle, a fragmented holograph who babbles like Robin Williams. David, of course, wants to ascertain the whereabouts of the Blue Fairy. An impossible dream? Sent to the end of the world, a largely submerged New York City, where he is shocked—shocked!—to discover the reification of human relations that mechas represent, little David runs amok. But this single moment of anticapitalist rebellion is brief. David rejects his creator Dr. Hobby to dive from the top of Radio City deep into the maternal vastness of the dream dump.

For an unforgettable moment, I imagined that Spielberg might really leave us with a bizarre, albeit truly despairing image: Pinocchio frozen forever in a world where Jiminy Cricket is mute and Walt Disney dead, praying through all eternity before an inert icon of the irretrievable mother. Not to worry. The shamelessly milked miracle arrives 2000 (and one?) years later, replete with thunderous wonder, appropriate white light, and a mother and child reunion so obliterating in its solipsism that it bids to split your skull. However sentimental its intent, though, this ending may actually be more hopeless than anything in Kubrick.

As in a Kubrick movie, the humans in *A.I.* are universally shown to be vain, treacherous, selfish, jealous and, above all, cruel creatures. But, Spielberg understands that, no less than the robots, we in the audience have feelings too—really big ones. What's more, we can dream. Thus, the spectators are granted a cosmic fantasy of total symbiosis that combines the everyday mysticism of *2001*, the back to the womb climax of *Close Encounters*, and something akin to the last scene of *Tristan und Isolde*. It is a simulation, which is to say, it is a movie. And, although it has been made just for David, there won't be a dry eye in the theater when, having been treated to his first-ever birthday cake, the ageless cyber-child finally goes to "that place where dreams are born." (Some cheeks, however, may be wet with tears of mirth.)

Flattering? The robot extraterrestrials of the future go out of their way to express an insane admiration for the long-gone humanity of which David represents the last "living" artifact. In somewhat the same fashion, Spielberg imagines himself to be keeping the idea of Kubrick alive. *A.I. is* artificial intelligence. "I felt that Stanley hadn't really died, that he was with me when I was writing the screenplay and shooting the movie," the director has said. As *A.I.*'s initial ad campaign put it: "His love is real. But he is not."

*Shadows of Our Forgotten Ancestors* (Sergei Paradjanov, Dovzhenko Studio, 1964).

# III

ONCE AND FUTURE VANGUARDS

## NAKED LUNCH AND TRIBULATION 99

Originally published as "Bugsy," the *Village Voice*
(January 7, 1991).

THE DESIGNATED STRAIGHT MAN IN DAVID CRONENBERG'S COMIC ADAPTATION OF
William Burroughs' *Naked Lunch*, Peter Weller is as unsmiling as an icon
and as unflappable as a forties private eye. The movie opens by casting the shadow
of Weller's fedora on a tenement door; he mumbles his way through every subsequent scene as Burroughs' stand-in, the exterminator in the three-piece suit.

There would scarcely seem to be a movie in Burroughs' hallucinatory, sex-
ually raw, severely nonlinear novel. Still, as early as 1958, Burroughs' pals Allen
Ginsberg and Gregory Corso tried to sell John Huston on the idea. In 1971,
Burroughs himself hoped to see his novel filmed as a musical vehicle for Mick
Jagger; even more bizarrely, Burroughs was brought to Hollywood the follow-
ing year when Terry Southern somehow managed to interest *Gong Show* mogul
Chuck Barris. Discounting such vintage Cronenberg body-horrors as *Rabid* or
*The Brood*, the closest *Naked Lunch* came to the screen was in Howard
Brookner's 1983 documentary *Burroughs*, which included a brief dramatiza-
tion of the book's lavatory operation with Burroughs himself as Doctor
Benway, braying about the time he performed an appendectomy with "a rusty
sardine can" while massaging the patient's heart with a toilet plunger.

Surprisingly, given the material and director's track record, such gross-out
vaudeville is at a minimum. Although Cronenberg's *Naked Lunch* takes as its
motto one of Burroughs' favorite sayings ("Nothing is true—everything is permitted"), the movie is far more absurd than it is disgusting. It's as if
Cronenberg took his cues from the writer's sober demeanor. The movie is a
deadpan riff, deliberate and decorous—shot, with a quiet camera, in brown
tones so drained you wonder why they're not black and white. Ostentatiously
respectful, it's the accumulation of a hundred small, sustained jokes—the audience might well feel as nonplussed as Weller looks. A sitcom without canned
laughter, *Naked Lunch* is something for the malls to ponder.

Although Cronenberg manages to incorporate the *Naked Lunch* routine of the man who taught his asshole to talk, his film is less an adaptation of Burroughs' book than a fantasy on how the book came to exist. Weller is called Bill Lee, the pseudonym Burroughs used to publish his first novel, *Junky*. The movie is unmistakably a period piece. But from the credit sequence evoking *The Man with the Golden Arm*, through the tenement of boho squalor, the Ornette Coleman sax doodling, the sidekicks modeled on Jack Kerouac and Allen Ginsberg and the junkie slapstick (fingers that can't find the cigarette in one's mouth), to the pair of beefy narcs who bring the hero downtown, you have to wonder whose fifties are these? With offhanded sophistication, Cronenberg mixes motifs from Burroughs' writing with allusions to his vita—his job as an exterminator, his accidental killing of his wife, his sojourn in Tangier.

Although most of the movie's visions can be interpreted as drug-induced, the substance to which the characters are addicted is always something else, Mugwump jism or the black meat of the giant aquatic centipede. Joan Lee (the stalwart Judy Davis, one of only two women in the cast) is introduced injecting her chest with bug poison. "It's a very literary high, it's a Kafka high—you feel like a bug," she tells Bill. To watch Davis idly kill roaches simply by breathing on them is to see the real Morticia Addams. Davis and Weller are a pair of hollow-eyed cadavers—all the more so when, like the actual Burroughs, Bill Lee decides that it's "time for our William Tell routine" and, aiming for the glass on Joan's head, undershoots it by several critical inches.

Joan's death propels Lee into the Interzone, Burroughs' name for Tangier and his original title for *Naked Lunch*. As constructed by Cronenberg, this unreal North African city is populated by expatriate writers (including Tom and Joan Frost, stand-ins for Paul and Jane Bowles), Arab boys and, most spectacularly, Mugwumps— envisioned as stooped and stately lizard men. (These outsized, jaundiced ETs almost do justice to Burroughs' own description: in *Naked Lunch*, he writes that their eyes are as "blank as obsidian mirrors" and their lips "thin and purple-blue like the lips of a penis.") Here, the movie *Naked Lunch* becomes an even more elaborate mix of literary and literal Burroughs.

Asked if he's a "faggot," Lee is noncommittal. His typewriter—which, once in Interzone, mutates into a grant waterbug with a ripe New York accent—dictates a line from the novel to the effect that "homosexuality is the best all-round cover story an agent can use." Still, Lee's homosexuality is limited to a bit of affectionate nuzzling with Kiki (Joseph Scorsiani), named for the Spanish boy who was Burroughs' lover in Tangier. Later, Kiki is compelled to have sex with the wealthy Yves Cloquet (Julian Sands) who turns into a centipede and lustfully devours him—the closest any scene comes to the extravagantly nightmarish sex-murders of the novel.

More than anything else, except perhaps Burroughs' insect-fear, Cronenberg's *Naked Lunch* is a movie about writing. The typewriter-bug is his prize invention—a domestic monster that cowers, scuttles, babbles advice. ("Save the psychoanalysis for your grasshopper friends," Lee snarls.) Lee's rivalry with Tom Frost—played by Ian Holm with a tough, prissily jaded edge—is a virtual scene from *The Hellstrom Chronicle*. Tom insists on lending Lee his typewriter, and the two machines transform each other into something resembling congealed tomato paste. Later, Lee turns his attention to Tom's wife Joan (Judy Davis again). In the movie's lone representation of heterosex, Bill seduces Joan into typing erotica on an Arabic typewriter—a giant glistening penis pokes out as they grapple.

Although Jane Bowles did remind some of Joan Burroughs, the notion that Burroughs had an affair with her may be Cronenberg's most outlandish conceit. Ultimately, however, *Naked Lunch* has less in common with such solemnly gaseous cousins as *Henry and June* or *The Sheltering Sky* than with a mythopoeic manifesto like Cocteau's *Orphée*. (Indeed, *Naked Lunch*'s typewriter-bug controller is not unlike the oracular car radio in *Orphée*, and the fatalistic ending suggests *Orphée* as well.) Cronenberg not only assumes a certain audience familiarity with his subject, he uses his movie to theorize on Burroughs. It's clear that, in his view, shooting Joan was what compelled Burroughs to become a writer; it's also what turns the movie into a matter-of-factly delirious noir.

To see *Naked Lunch* is to ponder anew the connection between Burroughs and Poe (or between their interpreters Cronenberg and Roger Corman). Cronenberg has done a remarkable thing. He hasn't just created a mainstream Burroughs on something approximating Burroughs' terms; he's made a portrait of an American writer. There's never been a pithier definition of the artist's relation to art than Bill Lee's remark that he's addicted to something that doesn't exist.

A more hysterical exercise in avant-garde abstract sensationalism, Craig Baldwin's *Tribulation 99: Alien Anomalies Under America* has been described, most aptly, by its maker as "a pseudo pseudo-documentary obsessively organized into 99 paranoid rants." This 50-minute masterpiece is at once a sci-fi cheapster, a skewed history of U.S. intervention in Latin America, a satire of conspiratorial thinking, and an essential piece of current Americana—the missing link between *JFK* and *The Rapture* (and a better movie than either).

"WARNING," the first of many screen-filling titles announces, "THIS FILM IS NOT FICTION—IT IS THE SHOCKING TRUTH!" If this injunction recalls the opening of Edward D. Wood's *Plan 9 from Outer Space*, so do Baldwin's methodology and narrative. *Tribulation 99*'s "revisionist eschatology" begins in 1949 with the explosion of the planet Quetzalcoatl. Fleeing their doomed world, the Quetzals relocate at the hollow center of ours; unfortunately, this sanctuary is agitated by underground atomic tests and the Quetzals vow the destruction of the U.S., using all manner of futuristic weaponry as well as humanoid alien automatons as provocateurs.

The joke, of course, is on the notion of "alien" invaders—particularly as the war with the Quetzals is waged successively in Guatemala, Cuba, Chile, Nicaragua, El Salvador, Grenada, and Panama. The tone Baldwin adopts is one of a cracked right-winger: Quetzal agent Salvador Allende creates a hole in the ozone over the South Pole in a plan to cause cancer in the "planet's most vulnerable inhabitants: white people"; Grenada is taken over by "a rampaging gang of psychic vampires" whose New Jewel Movement is named for "an evil power crystal" and whose leader, an "Atlantean plant," plans to build the largest saucer port in the Caribbean.

Rather than stage this cosmic drama—which ranges from Easter Island to the Bermuda Triangle and involves Howard Hughes, the abominable snowman, Jim Jones, Klaus Barbie and George Bush among many others—Baldwin illustrates it with a heady mix of images culled from a variety of newsreels, travelogues, industrials, commercials, *Godzilla* flicks, Mexican thrillers, and movies shot off the tube. (Barry Goldwater is represented by James Bond, Maurice Bishop by Blacula, Manuel Noriega by the Wolfman, Fidel Castro by a mad, bearded zealot from some fleabitten sword-and-sandal epic.)

Baldwin's unrelenting montage is scored by inexorable monster music, punctuated by psychedelic swirls, organized by supermarket tabloid titles ("Earth in Upheaval," "False Prophets Descend Among the People"), and mediated by his own rapid-fire voice-over: "In red underwear to escape the evil eye, Noriega flees towards the Hollow Earth through a network of interconnecting caves under the canal, leaving behind a ritual bucket of blood, a maggot-infested cow's tongue, and 50 pounds of highly addictive corn flour."

## POISON

Originally published as "Blood, Sweat, and Fears,"
the *Village Voice* (April 9, 1991).

EVERY PROJECT FUNDED BY THE NATIONAL ENDOWMENT FOR THE ARTS, EVERY film targeted by right-wing bigots, should be as intelligent, provocative, and original as Todd Haynes's *Poison*.

"The most sordid signs became for me the signs of grandeur," wrote Jean Genet in *The Thief's Journal*, articulating a credo that could also apply to Kenneth Anger's *Fireworks*, the original Playhouse of the Ridiculous, the

Cockettes, early John Waters, certain R. W. Fassbinder, and numerous manifestations of so-called Queer Theater. *Poison*, which owes as much to Genet as any movie since *Querelle*, accepts this bold inversion with a kind of laid-back, SoCal-bred confidence. The film describes torment without seeming tormented itself. "A man must dream for a long time to act with grandeur" is the Genet quote that serves as Haynes's punch line, "and dreaming is nursed in darkness."

Like Haynes's 1987 *Superstar* (a Toys "R" Us Bunraku that used a cast of Barbie dolls to dramatize the Karen Carpenter story), *Poison* is both stilted and witty. The two qualities may be indistinguishable; for Haynes, awkwardness seems to be a sort of distancing device. But despite his effective deployment of bad acting, tacky special effects, and soap-opera dialogue, *Poison* is neither camp nor satire. An allover, tripart narrative, the film is characterized by an irony beyond irony and, no less than *Superstar* (whose heroine starves herself to death), a mordant appreciation that the body has a mind of its own.

On the surface, *Poison*'s "three tales of transgression and punishment"—distinguished in the end credits as "Hero," "Horror," and "Homo"—are completely unrelated. In the mock-documentary "Hero," a Long Island housewife (Edith Meeks), posed nervously in her kitchen, explains how her seven-year-old son Richie shot his father dead and then ascended to heaven out a second-story window. In the aftermath of this absurd event, which both opens and closes the film, the boy's neighbors, schoolmates, teachers, social workers are interviewed—their clichéd or uncomprehending remarks suggesting that the never-seen Richie had a heroic pathology suburban logic could never explain.

While "Hero" is disconcertingly telenaturalistic, taking the form of a *60 Minutes* segment, "Horror" is shot in black and white with exaggerated, looming noir angles and the exuberantly gross makeup of a fifties monster movie. Young Dr. Graves (Larry Maxwell) isolates the human sexual drive in liquid chemical form; distracted by a female admirer, Dr. Olsen (Susan Norman), he slurps it down instead of his coffee and is gradually transformed into the hideously pustular Leper Sex Killer. Given the strident supernaturalism of "Hero" and "Horror," the most normal (and tender) sequence is naturally "Homo." A lush pastiche of Genet's *Miracle of the Rose*, it details a doomed and brutal prison romance, replete with flashbacks to an incongruously bucolic Borstal, whose rosy light and overgrown foliage suggest a pleasure garden out of Watteau.

Hopscotching narratives like a low-budget *Intolerance*, *Poison* flips from Grade Z horror to open-air lyricism to deadpan interview and back, spiraling ever more emphatically into each tale's abyss. The stories, however, are less rigid than their genre formats—they seep across boundaries, flowing in and out of each other, abetted by James Bennett's ambitious and effective score. "The whole world is dying of panicky fright," Haynes's first title reads, as the police beat down Richie's suburban door, a sequence that segues into one of the adult prisoner Broom (Scott Renderer) being booked. Later, an interview in which one of Richie's schoolmates explains how Richie provoked him into administering a spanking is followed by a romantic scene in which Broom is transfixed by another inmate's scars.

By the time *Poison*'s zap narrative takes hold, the three stories have come to seem like three aspects of a single sexual biography, if not a kind of cosmic condition. The movie is filled with startling displacements. The ambivalence or loathing that accompanies each declaration of love, the (justified) paranoia that each character suffers, the brooding sense that there is no hope of escape are side effects of the same "poison." Haynes is remarkably deft at orchestrating his reversals: The horrified stares that greet Drs. Graves and Olsen, a hetero couple out for an innocent stroll, have implications far beyond Graves's disgusting affliction.

As film, *Poison* is both intensely sensuous and disturbingly visceral. When somebody leaps to their death from the roof, they fall in real time. The bodily fluids (blood, pus, spittle) that leak from the various characters, the relentless equation of love and death, the invisible No Exit signs in each of the narratives, all serve to bind the film in an intricate web of cross-references. Everything amplifies everything else. Dr. Graves's running sores are visually rhymed (and hence "explained") in the film's most appalling sequence. Here, Haynes orchestrates a form of long-distance gang rape, phlegm raining from heaven in a cascade of humiliation.

Despite the uneven quality of its acting and writing. *Poison* has an extraordinary cumulative power—it's even more impressive on a second viewing. Without ever alluding to AIDS by name (except perhaps in the title of his film), Haynes has made what may be the toughest, most troubling, and least compromised movie on the crisis to date. From *Fireworks* on, American avant-garde cinema has been richly informed by homosexual sensibility and subject matter. No film has ever taken this more for granted than *Poison;* its unique combination of bluntness and metaphor suggests it may turn out to be a landmark—regardless of how it affects the NEA.

## AVANT RETRO

Originally published as "Once More With Feeling,"
the *Village Voice* (June 18, 1991).

A S THE MOVIES CLOSE IN ON THEIR CENTENNIAL, A FASCINATION WITH ORIGINS grows increasingly evident. A flurry of ambitious publications has proposed that work on pre-1920 (even pre-Griffith) cinema is the cutting edge of film scholarship, even as the pre–old new world order year of 1939 continues to be sanctified as Hollywood's supposed apogee.

While the industry traffics in nostalgia, a paradox of avant-garde film is that the primitive past has long seemed as seductive as the radiant future. Indeed, one could argue that *le mode retro* affected "advanced" artists first. Since Andy Warhol premiered *Kiss, Eat,* and *Sleep* (if not before), vanguard filmmakers have been preoccupied with returning their medium to its origins and beginning again, unencumbered by history.

In this sense, the so-called structuralists of the late sixties and early seventies were most militant. George Landow blandly presented his *Film in Which There Appear Sprocket Holes, Edge Lettering, Dirt Particles, Etc.,* while, with *Tom, Tom, the Piper's Son,* Ken Jacobs refilmed and renarrativized a 1905 two-reeler, using a welter of close-ups, pans, freeze-frames, and superimpositions, as though to suggest the development of cinema in an alternate universe. Hollis Frampton announced his baldly titled *Information,* a four-minute study of a naked lightbulb, as the "hypothetical 'first film' for a synthetic tradition constructed from scratch on reasonable principles"—but *Information* wasn't Stone Age enough. "At last, the first film!" is how Michael Snow (whose notorious *Wavelength,* a 45-minute zoom across a Chambers Street loft, was hailed by Manny Farber as "*The Birth of a Nation* of the underground") greeted Ernie Gehr's *History,* 40 minutes of seething grain patterns, produced by dispensing with the camera lens and exposing the film through a piece of black cheesecloth.

By those lights, Snow's *To Lavoisier, Who Died in the Reign of Terror,* which has its local premiere this week at Anthology, is maybe the fourth or fifth film. Call it a chemical conflagration. No less than *Backdraft* (itself a throwback to Edison's 1902 blockbuster, *The Life of an American Fireman*), Snow's latest celebrates the original entertainment spectacle. *To Lavoisier* opens, in silence, with a close-up of a wood-burning stove and, then, a hand feeding the flames. After a time, we hear an unmistakable crackle. Sustained more-or-less throughout the film's remaining 40-odd minutes, the sound of the fire comes to seem the song of the medium.

*To Lavoisier* is Snow's longest film in the decade since his 1981 *Presents* and, for the most part, the scenes he chooses to photograph are no less banal— a sleeping couple, a woman soaking in the tub, a bathroom shelf, the filmmaker polishing a glass table, a woman cooking, a man eating, a Ping-Pong match, a game of cards. The camera is typically positioned at some extreme angle, the better to derange gravity and induce a shallow depth of field, and (perhaps in homage to Snow's most famous work), there is often a slow, all but imperceptible, zoom in.

What's extraordinary about *To Lavoisier* is not what the film shows (or how it shows it) but the film stuff itself. Perhaps the woman is the muse of cinema: The footage looks as if it were developed in a bathtub and baked in the oven. The emulsion is scarred, lightstruck, watermarked, solarized, explosively blotched with a deep blue or golden orange overlay. The visual surface "noise" is continually amazing. There's a pattern beneath every pattern and that pattern is as vibrantly random as a toddler's scribble- scrabble.

Structural films such as Snow's encourage the viewer to look for an overall, organizing system. That the card game here involves a chaotic selection of playing cards, as well as the random rolling of dice, suggests that there may be none—the game and the movie are improvised, just as the effect of "home developing" is largely unpredictable. This freeform feeling is reinforced by a coda in which a pink architectural model, suggestive of the Parthenon in its classical order, topples before the advancing camera.

Snow names his film for Antoine Laurent Lavoisier, the founder of modern chemistry, the eighteenth-century scientist who, among other things, explained combustion as oxidation and proved the law of conservation of matter. (The shot of a man "eating" a bowl of water with a knife and fork may refer to Lavoisier's experiments to establish the composition of water.) But even if Snow's reference to Lavoisier's death (as a government tax collector, he was guillotined in 1794) reinforces the sense of aesthetic martyrdom expressed in Snow's last verbal film, *So Is This, To Lavoisier* has no particular agenda other than to make us conscious, again, of what it is to watch a movie.

Concentrated by the lens, light burns traces into sensitive emulsion and these traces, projected, blaze before our eyes. The images here look consumed; there's a visceral sense of scorched silver nitrate. Some shots are superimposed with fire; others give way to the flicker of flames. There's a certain irony that parts of *To Lavoisier* resemble nothing so much as the painstakingly painted films currently produced by Snow's erstwhile (self-identified) rival, Stan Brakhage. But, however much *To Lavoisier* stylizes the photographic image, Snow's is an expressionism that doesn't express anything—unless it's his punning assertion that *To Lavoisier* "makes light of the law of conservation of matter."

▬

The sense of movies as an archaic technology is implicit in labor-intensive, perversely artisanal work as otherwise disparate as *To Lavoisier* and Brakhage's painted films, Lewis Klahr's cut-and-paste animations, and E. Elias Merhige's widely celebrated *Begotten*, currently at Film Forum.

A long-standing rumor on the festival circuit before it had its New York premiere in the fall of 1990 at the Museum of Modern Art, *Begotten* is rightly perceived as something primeval. "It could be taken for a documentary made a few thousand years ago on a previously unknown demented clan, buried beneath the tundra and now miraculously discovered intact," wrote Elliott Stein, while Susan Sontag emphasized the movie as sui generis by terming it "an extraordinarily original first accomplishment." (It's fitting too that film historian Tom Gunning, an authority on early American cinema, is acknowledged as story consultant.)

Personally, I find *Begotten* grotesquely pretentious but no less grotesque, nor technically impressive and abstractly interesting, for that. This metaphysical splatter film is something like *Night of the Living Dead* as it might have been imagined by Georges Rouault. More ritual than narrative, the film opens with a cowled figure—identified in the credits as "God Killing Himself"—rocking spastically back and forth, drooling black pitch and plunging a knife into his gut; the shack where he crouches becomes as blood-spattered as an operating theater.

Coming across God's disemboweled corpse, a masked woman, "Mother Earth," uses his remains to impregnate herself (in tight close-up), then gives birth to something called "Son of Earth-Flesh on Bone," a hideously twitching creature that she trundles through a wasteland suggesting a Sahara of dirty sleet. Eventually, Mother and Son are captured by a tribe of burlap-wrapped nomads who truss Son up, bludgeon him to death, and seem to devour his corpse—not necessarily in that order. (Or, indeed, at all: After the nomads rape Mother with sticks, Son is left disconsolately peering between her legs.) In any case, the sacrifice is not in vain; it triggers the lonely sprouts that push their way up in time-lapse from the barren earth.

Of course, there is more to *Begotten* than plot. The movie seems to exist in an advanced state of decomposition. The brilliantly high-contrast black and white images are continually dissolved in film grain; the exposure flickers wildly within a given shot. Four years in the making, *Begotten* is a mutant descendent of *Tom, Tom, the Piper's Son*—it was rephotographed on a homemade optical bench, one frame at a time, utilizing all manner of filters, at, according to the filmmaker, a ratio of 10 hours' bench time to each minute of screen time.

Although considerably more kozmic than *To Lavoisier*, *Begotten* similarly directs the viewer to its material state—but that which is the subject of Snow's film is more like a gimmick here. The paradox of *Begotten* is that it must have rephotography to work at all. That the film's images are difficult to decipher only encourages one to visualize the worst of them. You need only visualize the actual set (or the action unmediated) to see the film as something merely gross or even comical, instead of disturbing and disturbingly regressive.

## ARCHANGEL

Originally published as "Forgotten," the *Village Voice*
(July 23, 1991).

S TYLIZED, CONVOLUTED, VISIONARY, GUY MADDIN'S *ARCHANGEL* IS A DEADPAN whatzit of the highest order. The movie's stately pace borders on the lugubrious, but its "huh?"-quotient is impressively high. Watching this often impenetrable spectacle, the brain is split between the frustrating task of keeping Maddin's story straight and a gaga admiration for his stylistic conviction.

Although the best known of the Winnipeg Film Group, the 34-year-old Maddin has yet to crack commercial markets. His 1988 *Tales from the Gimli Hospital* was a distinctively musty, mock Nordic gothic that, pitched somewhere between *Eraserhead* and SCTV, was released in New York in 1989 as a midnight film. The more extravagant and less obviously humorous *Archangel* deepens Maddin's enigmatic concerns. As difficult as the film is to characterize, one thing it definitely isn't is a "career move." Indeed, despite a certain amount of hype and considerable expectation at the last Toronto Film Festival, *Archangel* all but emptied the press screening long before the final iris-out.

Taking its suggestive title from the near-Arctic Russian city where it ostensibly transpires, *Archangel* is set during the First World War (when, as part of an international attempt to squelch the Revolution, Archangel was occupied by Allied forces as well as the White Army) and pivots on the romantic delusions of a shell-shocked, one-legged Canadian soldier, Lt. John Boles (named for the WW I espionage agent who went on to become a popular, if bland, Hollywood baritone). As Boles's memory has been further destroyed by mustard gas, he mistakes the beautiful Russian nurse Veronkha for his dead love. That Veronkha is married to a similarly impaired Belgian aviator named Philbin creates a continual erotic confusion, further complicated by the passion Boles inspires in his comely landlady.

Maddin's characters are no less eccentric or obsessive than his film itself. *Archangel* is at once tacky and accomplished, dynamic and fusty, willfully off-putting and bizarrely romantic. The narrative is filled with non sequiturs, dreams, and flashbacks. The most spectacular, induced by hypnosis, has Veronkha remembering her wedding and glamourous, if unconsummated, honeymoon at the "famed" Murmansk hotel ("It was very exciting, a Bolshevik carried our bags"). *Archangel* has the aroma of a Salvation Army thrift store, but it unfolds in a perpetual present. Even combat is a distraction. At one point a motley company of Russian women and international soldiers—the former in medieval wimples, not a few of the latter in elaborate turbans—set off into the mist, picking their way through a tundra of strewn bodies (one of which wakes up and moves on). They arrive at the front, then turn around and march back.

A triumph of shoestring set building, shot in supersaturated black and white, *Archangel* cobbles together an imaginary, expressionistic "Russia" out of all manner of cut-out flats, models, and outsized props—their contours softened by a Vaseline-smeared lens and, a barrage of superimpositions, the perpetually falling fake snow and the chiaroscuro of flickering candles. (Maddin told one interviewer that he "quickly learned that the cheapest prop is a shadow.") Interspersed with titles, *Archangel* sometimes resembles the partial talkies of 1928 and 1929; sometimes the more fluid, as yet uncodified, productions of 1932 and 1933. Most of the movie is overdubbed; dialogue comes and goes, disappearing into the muffled battlefield rumbles Maddin refers to as "audio shadows" or blended into the faint strains of twenties pop. (It's no surprise to learn that the filmmaker collects 78s.)

Maddin further ages his antideluvian mise-en-scène through the illogical use of dissolves and deliberately missing frames; at times *Archangel* suggests *The Scarlet Empress* remade by underground moviemaker George Kuchar. (Like Kuchar, Maddin has a fondness for undergraduate actresses in heavy makeup.) From the archaic studio logo of the credits through the fake newsreel ending, *Archangel* is a pastiche—but of what? Maddin's most distinctive trait is an uncanny ability to exhume and redeploy forgotten cinematic conventions—often to no apparent end. (His next project, made for hand-painted "colorization," he says, is an opera set in an Alpine landscape where the slightest sound can trigger an avalanche.)

Continually absurd if not always laugh-out-loud funny ("Darling there's a dead sparrow on your roof—a good omen for our wedding," is a typical line), *Archangel* is cumulatively and surprisingly poignant. The outlandish couples entwined on a snowy battlefield or the scene in which soldiers asleep in their trenches are beset by a thudding invasion of bunny rabbits are as indicative of the Maddin touch as the lovingly matted sequence in which silhouette "Huns" attack out of an opalescent fog, or the midnight money scene in which a fat peasant is disemboweled, rallying to use the sausages that spill out of his gut to strangle his Bolshevik adversary.

*Archangel* identifies itself as "a reverent dirge," and the film is very delicate in its way—the wilted flowcry dialogue and crazed-soap-operatics waft out like incense. What's haunting about *Archangel* is its dogged quest for an irretrievable, if not unknowable past. As two amnesiacs compete for a woman with two identities, the characters' yearnings merge with the film's link to invented tradition.

*Archangel* is a movie about movies as imaginary memories. Maddin himself claims that by the time he shot it, he'd already forgotten his intentions as a screenwriter: "*Archangel* is a film literally directed by an amnesiac delirious from the strangeness of directing a film."

## SERGEI PARADJANOV

Originally published as "Roots," the *Village Voice*
(May 24, 1994).

THE GENIUS OF CARPATHIAN-ARMENIAN-AZERBAIJANI ETHNO-FUNK, FILMMAKER
Sergei Paradjanov (1924–1990) was best known for a pair of masterpieces,
the delirious *Shadows of Our Forgotten Ancestors* (1964) and the sublime *Sayat
Nova* (1968), as well as for surviving the most arduous martyrdom in the post-
Stalin Soviet cinema.

Cine-Paradjanov is at once avant-garde and kitsch, minimal and lush.
Paradjanov, who has his most complete New York retro this weekend and next at
the American Museum of the Moving Image, was part Robert Flaherty (collector-
explorer of isolated cultures), part Edgar G. Ulmer (impresario of bargain-
basement Yiddish, Ukrainian, all-black talkies), and part Jack Smith (maestro of
underground extravaganzas and admirer of Maria Montez's *Arabian Nights*). His
first feature, *Andriesch* (1954), was drawn from Moldavian folklore; his last, *Ashik
Kerib* (1988), was the tale of a Turkish minstrel, based on a story by a Russian poet,
shot in Azerbaijani and dubbed into Georgian. In the interim, which included 15
years of enforced exile from filmmaking, he invented a unique film idiom.

Paradjanov himself was equally singular: "He's a *creature*," an experienced
publicist said in shell-shocked amazement after the director's brief and only
visit here for the screening of *Ashik Kerib* at the 1988 New York Film Festival.

The most universally ethnic of Soviet filmmakers was born to prosperous
Armenian parents in the Georgian capital Tbilisi. He studied opera during
World War II, attended the State Institute of Cinematography in Moscow after,
then broke into the industry, making Ukrainian-language movies at the
Dovzhenko Studios in Kiev. Shot in the Carpathians and drawing on Gutsul
folk culture, *Shadows of Our Forgotten Ancestors* culminated Paradjanov's first
period with a tale of blood feuds, unhappy love, and village sorcery. The film was
structured like a ballad, scored to near continuous music, filled with traditional
rituals, and (thanks to brilliant cinematographer, later filmmaker, Yuri Ilyenko)
it looked like an acid head's home movie—an explosion of lyrical pantheism
unseen in Soviet cinema since the late silent period.

*Shadows* was also a worldwide hit. The movie won 16 awards abroad but
tarred Paradjanov as a "nationalist" at home—particularly as he resisted dubbing
it into Russian. (Paradjanov's heedless single-mindedness is suggested by
émigré journalist Alexei Korotyukov's recollections of the filmmaker combing
Gutsul villages for heirlooms, costumes, and icons, which he never returned.)
Once his political patron, the first secretary of the Ukrainian Communist
Party, fell from power, Paradjanov had 10 scripts rejected before being permitted

to film *Sayat Nova,* a poetic evocation of the eighteenth-century Georgian-born Armenian poet and troubadour turned archbishop.

Quieter and more studied than *Shadows, Sayat Nova* (also known as *The Color of Pomegranates*) represents the poet's milieu as the backwoods crossroads of Europe and Asia. Paradjanov coaxes a visionary mix of Fra Angelico and barnyard surrealism with the most economical use imaginable of weatherbeaten churches, casually tethered animals, and peasant grandmothers—punctuating his static compositions with jump cuts and Méliès-style movie magic. Any one of the film's linked tableaux is a startling combination of Byzantine flatness, Quattrocento beatifics, and Islamic symmetry.

*Sayat Nova* was shelved until 1973. Later that year, as part of a general crackdown on the Ukrainian film industry, Paradjanov found himself shelved—arrested and charged with crimes ranging from trafficking in art objects and selling currency to spreading venereal disease, engaging in homosexual practices, and "incitement to suicide." Most likely entrapped by KGB provocateurs, Paradjanov was given a closed trial; Tarkovsky, Ilyenko, and veteran writer-theorist Victor Shklovsky were his only prominent defenders.

In 1978, after five years in a maximum security prison and an international campaign on his behalf, Paradjanov was freed. Four years later, he was rearrested. Then came the post–Leonid Brezhnev thaw, and, in 1985, Georgia's studio commissioned him to make the Georgian national epic, *Legend of the Suram Fortress.*

A film whose compositions have the bold patterns of oriental rugs, a series of tableaux in which every third shot seems to be a still life with hookah and peacock, *Suram Fortress* is, in some respects, Paradjanov's most sumptuous production. As the convoluted narrative encompasses visions, daydreams, and digressions (not to mention religious rites and interpolated puppet plays), so the result is at once overplotted and oblique, Christian and pagan, archaic and postmodern.

Begun two years later, *Ashik Kerib* is less stringent and more strident—a payback for the director's years of persecution that, at times, borders on self-parody. It is haunting, nonetheless, that Paradjanov would end by expressing a doomed form of internationalism. Now nowhere at home, *Ashik Kerib* is a film about a Muslim poet and Azerbaijani hero directed in Georgia by an Armenian Christian.

In addition to *Shadows, Sayat Nova,* and the two comeback films, AMMI is screening superb prints of Paradjanov's first four features. Never before shown in New York (indeed, largely disowned by their director), these early works explicate Paradjanov's attempt to "create an expressive structure working directly from folk poetry and mythology."

*Andriesch* is an expansion of Paradjanov's diploma film, *Moldavian Fairy Tale*. An orphaned shepherd boy is helped by various natural spirits to defeat Black Storm, a demon with the power to turn creatures to stone. Clumsily set on a cramped soundstage, this Disney-like conceit is also somewhat petrified, albeit enlivened by a nonstop sound track of juiced-up Romanian folk music and endearingly tacky special effects.

According to Paradjanov, *Andriesch* "vividly expressed an absence of experience, craftsmanship and good taste. And that unfortunately was only the beginning." The "ridiculous" *Ukrainian Rhapsody* (1961) is a far more drastic example of unfunny camp—a lugubrious operetta reveling in nationalist, religious, and aesthetic clichés.

A wholesome village lass returns home having won first prize in an international vocal competition held in an imaginary West European city where, in the first of many surreally stilted phantasmagorias, her aria wafts out of the theater to transfix a street populated by prostitutes and disabled war vets. As the train carries her east, past "Germany in ruins," the singer remembers a jumbled past. Like Paradjanov, she spent the war studying music, hence, perhaps, the bizarre dilettantism. A Russian soldier plays the "Moonlight Sonata" in a ruined theater to a motionless audience of pensive comrades and smashed statuary—the music continuing even after Paradjanov cuts away to attacking tanks and then back to show flames reflected on the piano.

No less strange, if more successful, *The First Lad* (1958) and *Little Flower on a Stone* (1962) exaggerate socialist realist clichés into a kind of Soviet mannerism—artificiality accentuated by references to the sputniks whizzing overhead. The Ukrainian countryside is represented as a perfectly orderly paradise—the fields are lawns, the kolkhoz resembles a park, the "model department store" is a blatant movie set. The harvest celebrations suggest a realm of regulated fertility; a timely radio broadcast inspires the flowers to open and sends a young girl running through the fields at dawn with an apple for her sleeping sweetheart, before triggering an ecstatic montage of birds, crops, and tractors.

Perhaps made to promote the benefits of sports activity, *The First Lad* features a soccer rivalry between two collective farms as well as a romance between a winsome Komsomol secretary and a kolkhoz hooligan. (As she is unmarried, so he has yet to be "led into Communism.") *Little Flower on a Stone* has a related premise—the same actor, here an earthy miner, pursues another proper *komsomolka*. But where *The First Lad* is playful (gags predicated on reverse-action photography, camera mimicking the flight of a soccer ball), *Little Flower* is noirish, melodramatic, and prone to gloomy bursts of Rachmaninoff.

In *Little Flower* a newly dug coal mine has been infiltrated by a morbid religious cult that calls upon believers to demonstrate their faith by sacrificing digits to the "sacred ax." The narrative weirdness is accentuated by Paradjanov's own: He accelerates the action by omitting transitional shots, directs the unctuous cult leaders as though they were acting in a silent movie, provides his hero with prismatic dreams of industrial installations that might have been lifted from Dziga Vertov's *Enthusiasm*. Awkward, experimental, and ethnographic in a way Paradjanov could never have anticipated, *The First Lad* and *Little Flower on a Stone* change the light in which his later films are seen—casting the shadows of his own forgotten ancestors.

## LESSONS OF DARKNESS

Originally published as "The Big Heat," the *Village Voice* (October 31, 1995).

HORRIFIC AND AWE INSPIRING, WERNER HERZOG'S 50-MINUTE DOCUMENTARY *Lessons of Darkness* can most simply be described as a travelogue of hell: white-hot skies, black seas of bubbling pitch, flaming lakes, fiery geysers, billowing toxic fumes, an arid wasteland littered with the dinosaur bones of twisted metal debris.

This powerfully visionary film, which begins with a fabricated quote from Blaise Pascal on the grandeur with which solar systems die and is interspersed with tersely poetic intertitles, could have been made to illustrate the Book of Revelation. Children are reported to weep black tears. Temperatures on the ground are claimed to reach 1000 degrees. A sequence called "Satan's National Park" shows a scorched, gnarled, partially submerged forest. The clouds are reflected on its liquid surface, but "everything that looks like water is, in actuality, oil," remarks Herzog in his measured Vincent Price voice-over.

This catastrophic landscape is the Kuwaiti desert in the aftermath of the Gulf War. "The war lasted only a few hours," Herzog says by way of introducing a few minutes of televised flares and aerial explosions. No further explanation is offered. There's an emphasis throughout on the failure of language. "The first creature we encountered tried to communicate something to us," Herzog explains, adopting the persona of a bemused space traveler. A traumatized woman wants to tell us her tale—two sons tortured to death before her eyes—but finds that she can no longer speak. A young child whose head was trampled by Iraqi soldiers has also lost his power of speech.

Eventually, Herzog and his intrepid director of photography, coproducer Paul Berriff, get down with the firefighters—men wearing Darth Vader helmets and speaking Texan who, spraying oil-rig volcanoes with massive jets of water, precipitate an infernal black rain. Herzog defamiliarizes their attempt to shut off and secure the oil wells through the use of slow motion, so that the sequence titled "The Closing of the Wells" becomes pure science fiction. In the film's final segment, the men torch a gusher and rekindle the blaze. "Others, seized by madness, follow suit," Herzog reports. "Now they are content, now there is something to extinguish again."

One of the most original documentary filmmakers of the past quarter century, Herzog has described himself as a director of landscapes—and not just because of his blatant "creative geography." Here the use of solemn, surging rhapsodies (Grieg's *Peer Gynt*, Mahler's Second Symphony, Wagner's *Parsifal*) to underscore his unprecedented images suggests a desire to conduct cosmic upheaval. Meditating on the perverse grandeur of a man-made apocalypse, flying over a smoldering death star whose sole sign of life is the shadow cast by his helicopter, the filmmaker is totally in his element. *Lessons of Darkness* is a masterpiece—the culmination of Herzog's romantic Doomsday worldview.

The litter of burnt cars and transports, the collapsed radar station, and shattered bunkers are ruins of a vanished city: "All we could find were traces." It is as if Herzog were recreating some primordial memory. If the tortured vistas of *Lessons of Darkness* bring to mind surrealist painter Max Ernst's celebrated canvas *Europe After the Rain*, it may be that those vistas are Herzog's heritage. Born in 1942, he grew up amid the craters and wreckage of defeated Nazi Germany. His earliest recollection, according to the film notes, is "the red sky over the burning town of Rosenheim."

Herzog's passion for destruction has a quasi-religious fervor. Indeed, this "requiem for an uninhabited planet" might have the galvanizing effect on eco-activists that a Gruenwald altarpiece had for believers during the bubonic plague.

## MYSTERY SCIENCE THEATER 3000: THE MOVIE

Originally published as "Lost in Space," the *Village Voice*
(April 21, 1996).

**S**O SELF-CONSCIOUS THAT IT ALL BUT WRITES ITS OWN AMBIVALENT REVIEW, Jim Mallon's movie version of the cable cult show *Mystery Science Theater 3000* presents a unique critical problem. The film invites a dissertation even as it bids to shut down your brain.

*Mystery Science Theater 3000*, which was born in Minneapolis in late 1988 and hailed in 1995 by *Time* critic Richard Corliss as "just about the smartest, funniest show TV has produced," is nothing if not a historical construct. Accompanied as they were by a variety of lecturers, musicians, gramophone recordings, or actors concealed behind the screen, the earliest movies were a form of live performance. *MST3K*, as its fans abbreviate it, automates this practice. For those not wired for Comedy Central, the show's basic premise has the viewer watch a Grade-Z movie from a position behind a trio of wisecracking silhouettes—two of them meant to be robots.

Requiring a double level of attention, *MST3K* is audio graffiti, visual net-chat, a nihilistic version of the information track on a prestige laser disc, a comic variant on the Japanese *benshi* who explicated the action in the silent Japanese cinema, or the Second Avenue actors hired to turn silent Biblical spectacles into low-budget Yiddish-language talkies. None of these forms have quite the *MST3K* attitude. By literally inscribing the audience on the screen, the program manages to flatter, as well as deride, the viewer's intelligence. *MST3K* provided the inspiration, perhaps, for Beavis and Butt-head's music-video critique—if not for Mark Rappaport's more complicated but scarcely less sarcastic exegeses of the Rock Hudson and Jean Seberg texts.

Week after week, *MST3K*'s resident mad scientist (Trace Beaulieu) tortures a hapless janitor-turned-astronaut (Michael J. Nelson) in a dog bone–shaped space station with transmissions of what are said to be the worst movies ever made. Is the audience ever educated? The tiresome elaboration on its cable framing device makes *Mystery Science Theater 3000: The Movie* a candidate for its own treatment. Spanking himself with glee, the crazed doctor cues up another "stinking cinematic suppository" for our delectation. Where the standard *MST3K* fare is a ruthlessly abbreviated piece of fifties drive-in junk, preferably starring Mamie Van Doren, *Mystery Science Theater 3000: The Movie* is inflated with something more spectacular, namely *This Island Earth*.

Universal's first color sci-fi feature, this turgid space-opera was originally released in June 1955 after the success of the studio's far snappier 3-D cheapsters, *It Came from Outer Space* and *The Creature from the Black Lagoon*. Albeit upstaged by *Forbidden Planet* the following year, *This Island Earth* was the first studio movie to attempt to show an alien civilization. (With their deep tans and white pompadours, the denizens of Metaluna became a minor sci-fi trope—as did their triangular two-way color TVs and insect-headed mutant slaves.) *Variety* deemed the effort "Socko . . . one of the best outer-space film entries to date," while the *New York Times* described its special effects as "superlatively bizarre and beautiful."

That was then. Ragging on the opening titles ("Hey, who sneezed on the credits"); flagging lame jokes ("Duh, I made a funny"); offering production advice ("Increase the Flash Gordon noise and put some science around it"); annotating the set and costume design (a lit-up atomic knickknack is a "nice

Hanukkah bush," a mutant suggests "Ted Kennedy in a Barney suit"); making low-level sexual innuendos ("I just know they're going to probe my anus"); and otherwise subjecting the spectacle to a relentless series of random sound effects, Mork imitations, and scurrilous insults, the MST collective succeeds in spinning flax into . . . flax.

Rendering the ridiculous laughable is some sort of accomplishment, although, perverse as it may sound, I prefer to ponder bad movies in silent awe. *MST3K*-ism effectively precludes the use-value of junk as a source of personal fantasy. Years ago, in an essay entitled "The Wedding of Poetry and Pulp," British critic Raymond Durgnat singled out *This Island Earth* as a movie with "everything against it." By ordinary standards, the film was unredeemable: "It's a fantasy, it's science fiction, it's slanted at adolescents, it's a routine product from a studio with no intellectual pretensions, it has no auteurs, its artistic 'texture' is largely mediocre—and for all that, it has a genuine charge of poetry and of significant social feeling. It's not cliché; with its sense of inner tensions, of moral tragedy, it's myth." *MST3K*, by contrast, encrusts the artifact with 40 years of American pop culture.

The urge to desecrate the media environment is hardly exotic. The aggression that *MST3K* directs at those hapless old movies that fall into its deconstruction machine is the inverse of the idiotic positive "reviews" that blurb whores can be relied upon to lavish on the most disposable current release. Those robot silhouettes are our secret sharers: It's a pity we can't turn them loose on *Primal Fear* or *Sgt. Bilko*.

## DEAD MAN

Originally published as "Promised Lands," the *Village Voice*
(May 14, 1996).

JIM JARMUSCH HAS ALWAYS BEEN PROUDLY IDIOSYNCRATIC—A STYLIST AT ONCE stubborn and fey. A dozen years ago, *Stranger Than Paradise* pioneered the neo-beatnik mode of hip Americana—bleak, deadpan, borderline sentimental— that Jarmusch would elaborate in subsequent features with varied success. But the indie landscape has shifted in the nineties, and *Dead Man* marks something of a departure—a fairy-tale western that howls in the moonlight.

Uncompromising from the get-go, Jarmusch's first feature in the four years since his cosmic cab anthology *Night on Earth*, opens on the road with a 10-minute, pure-movie montage of nineteenth-century locomotion. A Cleveland accountant named, like the English poet, William Blake (Johnny Depp) is heading for a job at the Dickinson Metalworks in the frontier town of Machine. In a fragmentary sequence that encapsulates the movie to come, Blake—a dude with lank hair, spectacles, and a vaudevillian's checkerboard suit—rides along with a changing cast of grizzled cowpokes against a wildly shifting terrain. There's no dialogue until the first of the film's several prophets (Crispin Glover) babbles a warning that all Blake will find in Machine is his own grave. To reinforce the notion, the mountain men start shooting at the buffalo grazing alongside the speeding train.

Jarmusch's *Dead Man* picks up where Kafka's *Amerika* leaves off, with the innocent young hero hurtling into the mysterious, limitless West, but it soon returns to Kafkaesque semicivilization by depositing Blake in a realm of sinister absurdity. Machine proves to be a muddy hellhole whose crummy Main Street, the province of rooting pigs and wild-eyed drifters, is marked by mountain goat skulls, dotted with coffin shops, and dominated by the hideous Dickinson Metalworks. To the amusement of the office manager (John Hurt) and his servile clerks, Blake finds another accountant already in his place and only just survives a highly unpleasant run-in with the crazed factory owner (Robert Mitchum, crouching beneath his outsized portrait like a degenerate founding father).

Wandering through the forest of the night, Blake meets the lovely Thell (Mili Avital), named for the unborn heroine of a Blake song, who has been tossed out of the town saloon for peddling paper flowers. Thell brings Blake home, but the loaded gun she keeps beneath her pillow ("'cause this is America") results in an absurd, mid-tryst shoot-out that leaves two people dead and the wounded Blake wanted for murder. Having fled into the wilderness, the hapless accountant is saved by a beefy, solemn Indian (Gary Farmer) who gives his name as "Nobody" and calls his charge "stupid fucking white man" until he discovers that his name is William Blake: "It's so strange that you don't remember anything of your poetry."

Farmer, who steals the movie from the game but necessarily blank Depp, appeared a half-dozen years ago as a similarly massive and placid mystical warrior in the underappreciated *Powwow Highway*—a western road movie that, like Jarmusch's, managed the interpenetration of two historical epochs. For, although set in the 1870s and filled with creepy period details, *Dead Man* equally suggests an imaginary, postapocalyptic 1970s, a wilderness populated by degenerate hippies and acid-ripped loners forever pulling guns on each other or else asking for tobacco. Although beautifully shot in sumptuous black and white by Robby Müller, *Dead Man* resembles the grimmest of Nixon-era antiwesterns—movies like *Bad Company*, *Kid Blue*, and *Dirty Little Billy*—with

Neil Young's discordant electric-guitar vamp providing a further abstraction of their countercultural rock scores.

On the other hand, like *El Topo*, *Greaser's Palace*, and the more Christ-conscious spaghetti westerns, *Dead Man* is a metaphysical journey. Blake is pursued through the forest by three hired killers—the meanest, a cannibal demon, sleeps with a teddy bear. At one point Blake stumbles across a trio of troll-like animal skinners, one (Iggy Pop) in drag, telling the story of Goldilocks. At another, he is surrounded by masked raccoon spirits. There are ample clues to suggest that Blake has died and that Nobody is the spirit who guides his departing soul. Nobody (not to be confused with Blake's more punitive deity, Old Nobodaddy) takes peyote and hallucinates seeing the skull beneath Blake's skin.

Nobody encourages his charge to go even further beyond the law by killing as many whites as he can and thus continue writing his poetry in blood. (Blake's notoriety is clinched when a Christian gun salesman asks for his autograph on a wanted poster.) The landscape grows increasingly uncanny as the pair travels ever deeper into Indian country, eventually paddling by canoe toward the entry to the spirit world: Splayed out along a cold ocean beach, this terminal Indian settlement is as funky and unsettling a frontier necropolis as was Machine.

Trimmed by 14 minutes since its mixed reception at Cannes in 1995, *Dead Man* drifts inexorably at its own pace on the River Lethe into the Twilight Zone. By the time Blake reaches his appointed destination, one's sense of Jarmusch has deepened considerably. (Rather than fey and stubborn, he now seems jive and primeval.) This is the western Andrei Tarkovsky always wanted to make. Even the references to Blake are justified. It's a visionary film.

## FRAGMENTS * JERUSALEM

Originally published in *Film Comment* (January 1998).

**A**T ONCE HOME MOVIE AND CITY SYMPHONY, A FAMILY PHOTO ALBUM AND A national history, Ron Havilio's six-hour *Fragments * Jerusalem* is a monument in time that excavates a space. The streets, ancient or modern, are filled with memories and the memories of memories.

Havilio has taken literally the injunction of the 137th Psalm: "If I forget thee, O Jerusalem, let my right hand forget her cunning." An obsessive 12 years in the making, *Fragments * Jerusalem*—which last fall won the grand prize at the Yamagata International Documentary Film Festival in Japan—is in some ways comparable to the epic, ongoing personal diaries with which Jonas Mekas documented his displacement and exile and, in others, analogous to the form of cine-archival history developed by Ken Burns in his PBS miniseries. Like Mekas, Havilio serves as his own narrator—offering a guided tour through a personally curated museum of photographic artifacts rivaling Burns's for its ingenuity.

Like the city it portrays, Fragments * Jerusalem is a film of unexpected byways. Extending the boundaries of urban flaneurism, Havilio is both a walker in the city and a time-traveler—in Jerusalem, it goes with the territory. The city does not live in the past so much as its history and historical destiny exist in the present. The discontinuous here-and-now of Havilio's "fragments" is infused with intimations of biblical antiquity on the one hand and the realization of a millennial future on the other. Yet, for all the tumult of wars, riots, pogroms, terrorist attacks (Jewish and Arab) which the movie records, Fragments * Jerusalem retains a serene detachment in its chronicle of daily life.

A photographer, an archivist, an urban archeologist, and an instructor at the Jerusalem Film and Television School, Havilio was born in the still-divided Jerusalem of 1950 but spent much of his childhood and adolescence abroad. (His father, an officer in the Israeli foreign service, was variously stationed in Paris, Istanbul, and Cameroon.) In a certain sense, the city is lost to him, even once it has been found. Fragments * Jerusalem opens with an hour-long meditation on the filmmaker's birthplace, the city's no-longer extant Mamila district.

Jerusalem's commercial center during the period of the British mandate, Mamila was divided by a wall after the 1948 war of independence. Once the city was reunited in 1967 under Israeli rule, the shattered neighborhood was evacuated and demolished—albeit remaining a deserted, construction site for the better part of the next two decades. The adult Havilio has returned to Jerusalem but his Jerusalem no longer exists. That he filmed much of the Mamila footage during the intifada emphasizes the no-man's-land feel, even as the images of deserted buildings and urban debris effortlessly evoke the original Jewish disaster—the destruction of the First Temple in 587 B.C.E.

From his own childhood memories, Havilio plunges into the remote past (surfacing frequently for air). Expelled from Spain in 1492, the Havilio family arrived in Jerusalem by way of the Balkans. Some were cabalists, others vendors of sweets. Fired by messianic expectation, his mother's family came to Jerusalem from Vilna (known by Jews as the Jerusalem of Lithuania) some three centuries later. The focus of millennial longing for nearly 2,000 years, Jerusalem was again a majority Jewish city by the mid-1800s. Before the turn of the century, the overcrowded Jewish quarter spilled over into the Arab quarter and precipitated a wave of building outside the city walls—a geography mapped by the peregrinations of the Havilio family within the Old City and finally out to the new center at Mamila and Jaffa Roads. (At the same time, one great-uncle disappears into Paraguay; another part of the family relocates to Sarajevo and perishes during the Holocaust.)

In ways both significant and trivial, Havilio's family history is entwined with that of the city. His mother's grandparents operated the first dairy within the Jerusalem walls—which turns out to be a legendary story in itself. Havilio's father, a youthful hero of the Haganah (underground Labor Zionist defense organization) and hence the family's first modernist, married Havilio's mother (another Haganah fighter) on the same day that the UN voted to partition Palestine into Arab and Jewish states. Havilio himself met his future wife in the aftermath of the Six Day War—both exploring, for the first time, the Old City.

Again and again, *Fragments * Jerusalem* recapitulates that passage through the Jaffa Gate, entering—at various points between 1896 and 1996—the "dark, sloping alleys" of the labyrinth where the layers of historical strata are emphasized by the incredible mix of costumed Bedouins, Hasidim, Ottoman soldiers, European tourists. Time too is a spiral. The film's second cycle begins with the funeral of Havilio's paternal grandmother (who immigrated with her family from the Macedonian capital Skopje on the eve of World War I), then segues into an account of the shift from Ottoman to British rule. The snowfall of January 1992 is used to recall the great snow of 1920 and then, the birth of the filmmaker's father. The intifada harks back to the 1921 pogrom in which, for the first time in centuries, Muslims attacked their Jewish neighbors.

As in the city itself, all periods coexist. Scenes typically combine past and present. *Fragments * Jerusalem* is profoundly anachronistic—among other things, it preserves the sense that motion pictures are a medium of (and not only for) preservation. Film is also a sublimated form of prayer—or study. For the secular Havilio, religious tradition ended with his father's rejection of his father's orthodoxy. In one long section, the filmmaker goes from shul to shul during Days of Awe—visiting congregations of cabalists, Persian Jews, and Kurdish Jews, imagining how it was in the old sephardic synagogues of his father's childhood.

A childhood collector, Havilio mixes tinted postcards with old *actualités* and period lithographs, incorporating both his parents' 8-mm movies as well as archival footage from the period of Zionist idealism, reading from newspapers and period accounts, playing old phonograph records. (The film's score is a mainly Mediterranean mix of Greek laments, Arabic pop, Israeli tangos, Hebrew prayers, and Portuguese *fados*, seasoned with Purcell and punctuated by the click of the slide projector.) The presence of Havilio's three young daughters also serves to mark the passage of the years—as well as introduce another reality principle. "Dad, stop filming," one tells him as he documents their fun at an amusement park outside the Jaffa Gate.

*Fragments * Jerusalem* has a generic resemblance to the family films by other Jewish filmmakers, including Alan Berliner, Ken Jacobs (whose *Urban Peasants* is fashioned entirely from his in-laws' home movies), and Ernie Gehr (whose *Germany on the Air* maps the no-longer extent terrain of his parent's Berlin). In Israel, Havilio's main precursor is David Perlov, local pioneer of the lyrical documentary mode. Intercut throughout with unpretentious domestic scenes, *Fragments * Jerusalem* suggests an enchanted picture book in which time continually folds back on itself. An elderly cousin (identified as a "forgotten author") waves goodbye—forever and not—from his apartment terrace. A sequence on Jerusalem in the 1930s ends a half century in the future as a pet bird flies away. Havilio not only makes use of Lumière *actualités;* he subscribes to the Lumière aesthetic: The rustle of the wind in the leaves, the patterns of light in the family kitchen.

The film's last image is of an illuminated Ferris wheel set up outside the Old City walls in the wasteland of Mamila. The circle is unbroken. Indeed, Havilio is already planning a third cycle—this one to visualize the Israel he missed while living abroad during the 1950s and to bring home Jerusalem's most persistent issue of spatiotemporal authority by focusing on the house in the once-Arab neighborhood of Ein Karem which Havilio renovated and where he has lived with his family for the last quarter-century.

## MOTHER AND SON

Originally published as "Flesh and Blood," the *Village Voice* (February 10, 1998).

**M**OTHER AND SON IS A MOVIE AS ELEMENTAL AS ITS TITLE, AS WELL AS THE MOST rarefied vision its famously uncompromising director, Alexander Sokurov, has yet produced. An artist whose fastidiously crafted movies concentrate on the most elusive, fugitive sensations, Sokurov here outdoes all previous efforts with this astonishing chamber piece—the equivalent of a visual whisper—about the last hours a child spends with his dying parent.

The 47-year-old Russian's trademark twilight zone is here the shadow land between consciousness and oblivion. An enfeebled woman (Gudrun Geyer) is attended by her grown son (Alexei Ananishnov) in an isolated country cabin. Their speech is muffled, even as the noises around them are exaggerated. The light is fading, the perspective seems unfixed, the colors are barely present, and yet these flattened-out, smeared images have a startling precision. How does something so insubstantial project so much authority? The crackle of the logs in the fireplace might be the sound of burning film emulsion, even as the movie appears to float somewhere in space, casting its faint shadow on the screen.

*Mother and Son* (which was screened once at the 1997 New York Film Festival) looks like no other film ever made. Sokurov has fused locations ranging from the Russian woods to the sandy cliffs of Germany's Baltic coast, synthesizing his own version of early-nineteenth-century Romantic landscape canvases. (Caspar David Friedrich is the painter most frequently invoked, although Sokurov's images can also suggest William Turner's quieter compositions in mist and light.) Each shot is an individually worked-out composition. Indeed, *Mother and Son*'s spectacular "creative geography" is doubly invented—the image modified by a system of mirrors and glass filters, some of them hand-painted, positioned both behind and before the lens.

Ethereal as it is, *Mother and Son* makes a stark contrast to Sokurov's most original movie, the 1990 *Second Circle*—a far more materialist view of death, where the protagonist spends most of his time in the miserable Siberian hovel where his father has just died, arranging for his parent's corpse. Shot nearly in real time, this sui generis borderline black comedy had as much to do with dreariness and discomfort as it did with grief. *Mother and Son* is different. "The relationship between a father and a son is more complicated," Sokurov told one interviewer. "Between a mother and son there is virtually only one relationship, that of love, irrespective of how it manifests itself."

Be that as it may, the son here treats his enfeebled mother with a lover's tender solicitude. At times, the son seems the doting parent and his mother the child—refusing to sleep or eat, disdaining her medicine, drinking like a baby from a bottle, fretfully asking to be taken outside for a walk. The movie is triumphantly pre-Freudian, although not in its limning the child's ambivalence, desiring—even as he fears—the release of his mother's death. The dying parent is a literal burden who, for much of the movie, is carried through the world by her son in a sort of reverse pietà.

A movie of incredible stillness, *Mother and Son* evokes overwhelming solitude amid fulsome creation—the filmmaker's not the least. (Sokurov's subtlety and high seriousness were poorly served by the ludicrous trailer that Film Forum had the good sense to cease showing.) Sokurov is driven to strive for the sublime, working without the net of irony that served Lars von Trier in his similarly high-flown *Breaking the Waves*. In the film's most stunning passages, the son leaves his mother alone and returns to the fields, wandering through the deep forest and windswept hills. A storm is gathering; black clouds cover the sky. He turns to watch the gradual progress of a distant railroad train traversing the valley—inexorable time, made tangible to crawl across the screen. (Seeing this, we understand that a life has passed.)

Interviewing Sokurov in a recent issue of *Film Comment*, Paul Schrader linked the director to the austerely spiritual Dreyer-Bresson-Ozu tradition he analyzed a quarter century ago in his book *The Transcendental Style in Film*. Sokurov's, however, is a bleak pantheism. Neither mother nor son makes mention of God. And, although the child speaks to her corpse as a Tibetan Buddhist might, the mother's last words are what hang in the air: "You will still have to go through all I have suffered. It's so unfair."

## PECKER

Originally published as "Watered Down," the *Village Voice*
(September 22, 1998).

**I**F SCANDAL, SLEAZE, AND CELEBRITY WORSHIP ARE OUR NATIONAL RELIGION, THEN John Waters is an American prophet. For the past 30 years, this Baltimore-based sage has been joyfully asserting—in his movies, writings, photographs, and talk-show guest shots—that freedom is just another word for trash cult and tab TV.

Waters was a trial buff whose fascination with criminal justice antedated Court TV, an aficionado of serial killers long before it became fashionable, a gross-out king when the Farrelly brothers were farting around the schoolyard. Waters' self-described "celluloid atrocities," *Multiple Maniacs* (1969), *Pink Flamingos* (1972), and *Female Trouble* (1974)—all underground sensations starring the 300-pound gender-blur Divine—were countercultural manifestos that explored the outer limits of hippie tolerance.

The young Waters thrived on publicity, outrage, and exhibitionism—*Pink Flamingos* concerned nothing less than a contest to determine the "filthiest people alive." But *Pecker* shows the now mellowed provocateur in a self-reflexive mode. A portrait of the artist, it begins with the teenage shutterbug Pecker (Edward Furlong, still button-cute seven years after *T2*) snapping away in downtown Baltimore. His subjects are Waters'—teenage hair-hoppers, roach-infested fast food, copulating rats, the antics of lesbian strippers, and the supposed weirdness of blue-collar Baltimore.

"You're crazy, you see art when there's nothing there," Pecker's shoplifter friend (Brendan Sexton III) tells him—summing up in a sentence the process by which photography, a technology allowing any idiot to produce an image worthy of Da Vinci, drove painters to exhibit their own "found" objects (as when, in a gesture Waters would surely appreciate, Marcel Duchamp exhibited an inverted urinal). "Everything always looks good through here," Pecker explains. Thanks to the camera, as aesthete-of-aesthetes Andy Warhol once put it, "all is pretty."

Pecker is a Warholian joke—a personification of the camera's innocent gaze and capacity to spin gold from dross (or worse). He is able to create art by casting a glance. But no man is an island in Watersworld. As Stefan Brecht was the first to point out, virtually all Waters movies pit one clan (nonjudgmental, unselfconscious, generous) against another (status-seeking, uptight, commercial). Thus, Pecker is surrounded by other primitives. His father is a morose barkeep; his mother is the cheery proprietress of a thrift store stocked with goods rejected by the Salvation Army; his grandmother peddles pit beef and uses a statue of the Virgin Mary as a ventriloquist's dummy; his older sister (Martha Plimpton) is the good-natured MC at a gay male stripper bar; his little sister is a candy-addicted brat who drools white sugar and talks as though she studied elocution with Edie the Egg Lady.

They are all natural performers—an important Waters value. In addition to cultivating his own stock company of Baltimore superstars, Waters contrived to have Tab Hunter romance Divine in *Polyester* and Kathleen Turner hawk a loogie on a crying baby in *Serial Mom*. Johnny Depp first revealed the depths of his ambitions by starring in *Cry Baby* while Sonny Bono donated his last (screen) performance in *Hairspray*. This tradition of courageous self-display predates the current wave of daytime talk shows—indeed, it was Waters' *Hairspray* that gave the teenage Ricki Lake her break.

Not unambitious, Pecker has his first exhibition at the scurvy fast-food place where he works. He's fired (for hanging an artsy close-up of a stripper's pubic bush), but simultaneously discovered by a slumming New York dealer (Lili Taylor) who gives him a show in her Chelsea gallery. The opening, which Pecker photographs, is a great success: The work sells out. Cindy Sherman attends as herself. A rich collector, Waters regular Patty Hearst, goes gaga. Pecker is hailed as a "humane Diane Arbus." An admiring *Village Voice* review dubs his girlfriend and model Shelley (Christina Ricci) a "stain goddess." One of his photographs graces the cover of *Artforum*. The Whitney Museum wants to give him a show.

New York is of course *Pecker*'s vision of the bad scene—mercenary and trendy as opposed to Baltimore's sweet and friendly village. Pecker's innocence is corrupted. After his show even the local Baltimore newspaper cites his "delicious photographs of his culturally challenged family" (whose house is robbed while they are away), although other locals are less impressed. "What they call art up in New York looks just like misery to me." Shelley warns Pecker that he is becoming an asshole, Child Protection Services shows up to monitor his little sister, even Mary stops talking.

Unlike Warhol's, Pecker's creatures (both in Baltimore and New York) are offended by being repackaged as art. But really, what's the problem? What malign magic has transformed Pecker into a paparazzo? And since when has John Waters shied away from the trappings of show business?

To some degree, *Pecker* suggests Waters' own recent reinvention as a gallery artist. His photographic pieces—which he calls "re-directing jobs"—are mainly serial images culled from various movies (his own and others), at once rigorously conceptual and punch-line funny. But there's another cultural re-direction at work. *Pecker* concludes by invoking "the end of irony." Does John Waters feel that things have gone too far?

As recently as April 1997, when *Pink Flamingos* was rereleased in its 25th anniversary edition, it seemed that the cheap and vulgar *Clerks* was the closest contemporary equivalent to *Pink Flamingos*. But that was before *There's Something About Mary* put the gross in grosses. For all its references to dingleberries and teabagging, *Pecker* has nothing that approaches *Mary*'s mock-castration or hairdo money shot. Nor, for that matter, does the perversity of Pecker's family drama remotely approach the agonized ickiness of Todd Solondz's upcoming *Happiness*—a movie that is steeped in a viscerally Watersian sense of Middle American corruption.

The 1980s, when Waters published two books, made two nouveau teen movies (*Cry Baby* and *Hairspray*), and appeared as a guest commentator in *Newsweek*, signaled his arrival in the mainstream. But, although he has managed to release only two features since *Hairspray*, the nineties have been the real Waters decade: the Menendez brothers, Jeffrey Dahmer, Joey Buttafuocco, Tonya Harding, Lorena and John Wayne Bobbitt, Marv Albert, and Dick Morris are all Waters characters—not to mention Jerry Springer and every single one of his guests. And, speaking of the filthiest people alive, what of Lucianne Goldberg, Linda Tripp, Ken Starr, and the stain goddess named Monica?

Filthy? Perhaps we should say *tacky*. Tripp and Starr don't even have the uncouth cool of the evil heteros typically played in Waters' early movies by David Lochery and Mink Stole. Perhaps that Chelsea gallery which transforms the innocent Pecker into a hot commodity is not really the voracious and snobby New York art world but an even more voracious American media culture.

Could it be that Waters is the snob, reacting to the saturation of his own once-rarefied vision?

These days, the President of the United States finds himself playing the Divine role in a real-life remake of *Pink Flamingos*. The spectacle of Bill Clinton eating shit may be enough to make even John Waters gag.

## THE IDIOTS

Originally published as "Arrested Development,"
the *Village Voice* (May 2, 2000).

PUBLICITY, AS ALL GOOD MODERNISTS SHOULD KNOW, IS THE LIFEBLOOD OF ANY successful avant-garde. It may be a bit of a stretch to term the refurbished, mock-militant neorealism of Dogma '95 a vanguard, but the movement's cofounder and best-known exponent, Danish bad boy Lars von Trier, is nothing if not an impressive self-promoter.

Dogma's restrictions—no tripods, no background music, no artificial lighting, no special effects—may be less a serious polemic than a canny branding gimmick. The so-called Dogma Brothers' "Vow of Chastity," allegedly dashed off by a giggling von Trier in half an hour, reinforces its author's position as European cinema's most relentless stunt-meister in the several decades since Werner Herzog was hypnotizing the cast of *Heart of Glass* or schlepping a steamboat through the rainforest for *Fitzcarraldo*.

The main thing that distinguishes Dogma's vaunted realism from that of cinema verité is the presence of actors. Hence von Trier's most notorious provocation to date, finally opening in New York nearly two years after it grossed-out half the 1998 Cannes Film Festival, is a self-reflexive jape. *The Idiots* is a movie about acting . . . out. Operating under some obscure philosophical imperative, the youthful members of a Copenhagen commune confound the local bourgeoisie with a form of dada guerrilla theater, engaging in wildly regressive, sometimes disgusting behavior in public places—what they call "spassing."

Von Trier pushes beyond punk paeans to pinheads and cretins to stage the comic spectacle of adult normals drooling, thrashing, disrobing, and otherwise mimicking the extreme agitation of the mentally disabled. On one hand, this politically incorrect telethon run amok is a further development of the Down's syndrome chorus that von Trier employed in *The Kingdom* or even his heroine's sexually "idiotic" behavior in *Breaking the Waves*. On the other hand, it's the essence of Dogma theatrics. The last two Dogma films to open in New York,

Harmony Korine's *julien donkey-boy*—shot, like *The Idiots*, on video—and Søren Kragh-Jacobsen's *Mifune*, both trade heavily on the entertainment value of having actors play morons.

Designed to provoke laughter at the unlaughable, *The Idiots* opens with a manifestation in which some communards harass the patrons of a genteel restaurant while others pretend to be their embarrassed caretakers. The scene directly addresses the very issue of table manners, which anthropologist Claude Lévi-Strauss famously saw as the bedrock of civilization; it also provides this particular counterculture with an ongoing foil. Thanks to their performance, the idiots pick up a lonely diner named Karin—a strategy that drops this viewer-surrogate in the midst of various infantile antics as they stage a field trip to a factory or invade a public swimming pool.

For the most part, the idiots resemble a gaggle of untalented Harpo Marx imitators. Meanwhile, a dogged wet blanket, Karin keeps trying to understand the meaning of what they are doing. (Their vaguely sixties ideology is never really explained, although as semiserious performance artists, the group holds postmortem discussions complete with psychobabble references to their "inner idiots" and earnest manifestos like "Idiots are the people of the future.") Von Trier, who is credited as director of photography, further ups the ante by shooting the movie in a documentary frenzy of smear-pans and camera-flails.

The filmmaker can occasionally be heard off screen asking questions, and the fictional nature of his film is further complicated by several pranks that seemingly involve innocent bystanders, as when the idiots go door-to-door in a wealthy neighborhood attempting to sell their homemade, hilariously stunted Christmas ornaments. There is also a birthday gangbang, which to judge from *The Idiots'* early reviews, included actual penetration. The U.S. release print obscures this by employing floating black rectangles (often ridiculously outsize) to conceal the actors' genitalia. This outlandish discretion is but one of *The Idiots'* old-fashioned elements. Von Trier uses the orgy as a prelude to a more tender—if scarcely less regressive—one-on-one love scene. (The corniness is further compounded when one participant's father shows up to take her home, explaining that she's a real schizophrenic gone off her medication.)

Von Trier's elaborate metaphor for filmmaking was itself the subject of a feature-length documentary, Jesper Jargil's *The Humiliated*—also a Dogma project, shot like most of *The Idiots* with a digital camcorder—aptly described by its maker as "a day in von Trier's puppet theater." I caught *The Humiliated* before seeing *The Idiots*. Then, it seemed an effective teaser for von Trier's film; now, it appears that, in promoting the documentary, the master may have upstaged himself.

Like *Burden of Dreams*, the Les Blank account of Werner Herzog's travails in the jungle making *Fitzcarraldo*, *The Humiliated* is more powerful than the movie it documents—as well as more successfully Dogmatic. Including most of *The Idiots*' key scenes (without added fig leaves) and more, *The Humiliated* makes clear that von Trier's film was a pretext to make something happen in life as much as on film. Jargil includes not only audiotapes of von Trier's on-set rantings but the spectacle of the artist's idiocy, directing without his trousers and convulsed with laughter at his own mischief.

Ending amid the detritus of the shoot, *The Humiliated* strongly intimates that *The Idiots* was a failed experiment. Of course, von Trier suggests as much with his own ending. Unable to reenter society as idiots, the commune breaks up—only to discover, in a scene of quiet horror, that, liberated by example, their little fellow traveler is the greatest idiot of all. In the fiction of the movie, life trumps art; in the reality of the film, however, it is precisely the reverse.

## THE WIND WILL CARRY US

Originally published as "Wander Land," the *Village Voice*
(August 1, 2000).

"WE'RE HEADING NOWHERE," A DISEMBODIED VOICE COMPLAINS AS A BATTERED jeep crawls up a winding road through harsh, scrubby terrain. So begins *The Wind Will Carry Us*—the latest and, to my mind, the greatest film by Iranian master Abbas Kiarostami. An engineer and his two never-seen assistants are traveling from Tehran to the remote Kurdish village of Siah Dareh. If the directions they attempt to follow are puzzling, so too are their intentions. These outsiders won't say what brings them to Siah Dareh, although they jokingly tell the village boy who has been appointed to guide them into town that they are looking for "treasure." It's soon clear that this treasure has something to do with a sick old woman (also never seen), but it's never directly revealed what that something is.

*The Wind Will Carry Us* is a marvelously assured film—at once straight-forward and tricksy. It's also bracingly modest. For all the self-important claims certain experts have made on Kiarostami's behalf, his films are anything but pompous. Typically understated, *The Wind Will Carry Us* is less amusing than bemusing. Kiarostami's sense of humor feels as dry as the countryside he depicts; the film is in many regards a comedy. The timing is impeccable, the dialogue borderline absurd. The gags, if that's the word, are predicated on formal elements—including the filmmaker's rigorous, somewhat ironic, use of point of view and voice-over. The same routines are repeated throughout, often punctuated by amplified animal sounds, to establish a musical structure. (Shots often end with a herd of goats crossing the screen.) In this sense, *The Wind Will Carry Us* resembles the films of Jacques Tati and, more recently, Takeshi Kitano's *Kikujiro*.

The city folks' obscure mission to Kurdistan is but one of the movie's modernist tropes. The villagers call the protagonist the Engineer in somewhat the same spirit that the outsider antihero of Kafka's *Castle* is known as the Land Surveyor. Indeed, having switched from cosmic long shot to more humanizing medium shot once the Engineer (Behzad Dourani) arrives in Siah Dareh, Kiarostami spends considerable time establishing the village's baffling geography—the steep, whitewashed maze of alleys and courtyards that are terraced into the hillside.

Taken as a documentary, which it is in part, *The Wind Will Carry Us* largely concerns the town's daily life—its laconic customs and puzzling arguments. But Kiarostami's method points toward something more. This is a movie of disembodied voices and offscreen presences, including half the characters and a newborn baby. Like the Engineer's two-man crew, who are always indoors and supposedly eating strawberries, Kiarostami is forever drawing attention to that which cannot be seen—or shown. (This might also include the Kurds, who are an officially "invisible" minority in Iran. The filmmaker has denied that *The Wind Will Carry Us* has any political intent, albeit in suggestively perceptual terms: "If the viewers have the impression of receiving a direct political message, it's up to them.")

In one (literally) running gag, the Engineer is required to scramble to the village's highest point so that his cell phone can receive an incoming signal from Tehran. (When he finally gets the connection, he discovers that he doesn't want the call.) The village graveyard is also located atop the hill—a coincidence that allows for another sort of dematerialized conversation. While catching his breath, the Engineer has a series of conversations with an unseen ditchdigger who is excavating the cemetery to facilitate some mysterious form of "telecommunications." (The Engineer is mildly interested, and in a blithely metaphoric move, the ditchdigger throws him a bone.) In what may be the strangest scene in this extraordinarily subtle and nuanced film, the Engineer uses an excursion to buy fresh milk as a pretext to drop in on the ditchdigger's girlfriend. She too, he discovers, lives in darkness. He finds her in one of the village's subterranean caverns, milking a goat, and is moved to recite the poem about loneliness that provides the movie's title. (The poem is by the late Forough Farrokhzad, a modernist and feminist icon, whose remarkable 1962 documentary on a leper colony was shown at the 1997 New York Film Festival.)

At last, the Engineer has put something in words. Skinny and balding, peering at the village through steel-rimmed glasses, this dungaree-wearing character is an example of what used to be called the intelligentsia. He is also a parody director who makes a few lame attempts to photograph the villagers, while more than once employing the actual camera as a mirror, peering directly into it as he shaves. The Engineer is interested in life. At one point, he idly flips a tortoise on its back—perhaps to see how it will squirm. But at another, more crucial moment, he demonstrates that he cannot take action himself but only direct others to do so. It's part of the movie's formal brilliance that, suddenly, during its final 10 minutes, too much seems to be happening. *The Wind Will Carry Us* is a film about nothing and everything—life, death, the quality of light on dusty hills. (Kiarostami, as made clear by his recent show of photographs in a Chelsea gallery, is a landscape artist.) Confident in its lack of consequence, the film far surpasses the strained allegory that dogged Kiarostami's more stilted and schematic official masterpiece, *Taste of Cherry*. Effortlessly incorporating aspects of documentary and confessional filmmaking into an unforced, open-ended parable, *The Wind Will Carry Us* transforms barely anecdotal material into a mysteriously metaphysical vision.

For all its glorious time-wasting, *The Wind Will Carry Us* is essentially a deathwatch. Late in the movie, it's casually revealed that the Engineer has been hanging out in Siah Dareh for two weeks. When night finally falls, however, it's as though the time he's spent there has been a single golden, purposeless, perpetual afternoon.

## MAKING NEW MEMORIES

Originally published as "Persistence of Memory,"
the *Village Voice* (March 20, 2001).

**M**EMENTO TAKES THE SENSATION OF WAKING UP IN A STRANGE BED BESIDE A complete stranger and totalizes it. The movie is part *Alice in Wonderland* mind trip, part *Point Blank* revenge quest—a tale told in reverse order over a series of overlapping flashbacks. The video stores are filled with examples of retro-noir and neo-noir, but Christopher Nolan's audacious time bender is something else. Perhaps it is a meta-noir.

As in Harold Pinter's *Betrayal* or Martin Amis's *Time's Arrow*, the temporal river flows backward—sequence by sequence, in 10-minute increments. *Memento* opens with a killing, then shows the buildup, then the events that lead up to that. Up until the last scene, it keeps beginning again. Each flashback triggers another. The gimmick serves to keep the viewer hyper-vigilant, but the narrative involves a second complication. Dependent on audience recollection, the movie features a protagonist who, traumatized by the murder of his wife and a blow to the head, has lost his short-term memory. Each scene starts with Leonard (Guy Pearce), blank and "innocent," confronting anew the mystery of how he got there.

Leonard is a former insurance-claims investigator searching, like the protagonist of *The Fugitive*, for his wife's killer—albeit navigating near blind through time and space. He comes to consciousness in the midst of a chase and wonders who is running after (and shooting at) whom. He finds a guy stuffed in the closet and has to figure out if whatever happened took place in his motel room. (And if so, just how many has he rented?) Leonard stares at Natalie (Carrie-Anne Moss), the woman with whom he appears to have arranged a meeting, and puzzles why. Did she set him up to kill the ubiquitous Teddy (Joe Pantoliano)? Or rather, will she?

As befits so meta a movie hero, Leonard is pitifully dependent on camera technology. "Since my injury, I can't make new memories," he explains more than once, sometimes to the same person. Upon meeting anyone for what could be the first time, he has to quickly take a Polaroid and scrawl a caption on the photo. Struggling to find a pen to note down some vital information before it slips away, this wildly unreliable narrator is a walking text. His pockets are full of annotated snapshots and his hands covered with addresses, but the crucial clues are tattooed, in mirror-friendly reversed lettering, across his torso: "John G. raped and murdered your wife."

Watching *Memento* is a unique experience: tense, irritating, and all absorbing. Indeed, there is another chronological strand to consider. Leonard's backward-forward investigation, with each scene supposedly bringing us closer to the meaning of the events we've seen or knowledge of the trauma that inspired them, is intercut with black-and-white footage of Leonard in a motel room on the phone, telling the tale of an insurance claimant who suffered a similar condition. To whom is he talking? And when?

Slight and feral, Guy Pearce seems to tunnel into the movie, hurling himself repeatedly at the all-knowing characters, Natalie and Teddy—who, in perhaps creating Leonard and manipulating him to their own ends, complete the film's bizarre oedipal triangle. (The casting provides another subtext: Two veterans of *The Matrix* confound one of the framed heroes of *L.A. Confidential*.) Teddy, the man Leonard initially—or rather, ultimately—kills, could be his only friend or his cynical controller. In either case, his is the only alternative voice. It's Teddy who asks Leonard how he happens to be driving a Jaguar, or points out that, given Leonard's less than total recall, revenge would be pointless—he'd instantly forget it.

Adding several extra dimensions and considerable confidence to the 29-year-old Nolan's tricksy first feature, *Following* (1999), *Memento* may be a stunt, but it's a remarkably philosophical one. The movie is a tour de force of frustration, a perverse tribute to the tyranny of cinema's inexorable one-way flow, and in effect, an ad for a home DVD player. It's also an epistemological thriller that's almost serious in posing the question: How is it that we know ourselves? Throughout, Leonard insists on the importance of fact over memory and, bravely pragmatic, argues against his own subjectivity: "I have to believe in a world outside my mind. I have to believe that my actions have meaning, even if I don't remember them." The movie's final joke plays on the audience's similar faith. *Memento* may be a Möbius strip, but it snaps like a slingshot in jolting you back to linear time: Now where was I? It's a punch line for all the movies ever made.

Chantal Akerman's *La Captive* is another sort of psycho-epistemological inquiry that asks: How can we know another? An intractable, objectlike movie with many pleasing symmetries, Akerman's gloss on the fifth novel of Proust's *Remembrance of Things Past* begins with a quotidian conquest of time. Wealthy young Simon studies a home movie of his lover, Ariane, as she frolics with several young women on the beach. He repeatedly runs the footage through the projector, staring at the image and painfully enunciating, "I . . . really . . . like . . . you."

As Simon (Stanislas Merhar) casts his shadow on the screen, eclipsing the phantom object of his desire, so Akerman casts him in a version of *Vertigo*. He pursues Ariane's car as it glides through a posh, empty Paris, stalks her in an art gallery, ravishes her in her sleep. Ariane (Sylvie Testud) can be provocatively plain—even homely—but she is fetishized by the unwavering force of Simon's obsession. Like Proust's Marcel and Albertine, the two live together in his family's apartment, but it is what Ariane does when she is apart from him that most fascinates the tormented Simon. (As Proust's narrator explains, "It was in myself that Albertine's possible actions were performed. Of each of the people whom we know we possess a double . . .")

In adapting Proust, Akerman eschews the temporal pyrotechnics of Raul Ruiz's *Time Regained*. Visual as *La Captive* is in its rigorously formal compositions, the filmmaker is straightforwardly concerned with language. She filters her Proust through the old nouveau roman of Duras or Robbe-Grillet to fixate on recurring phrases: "*au contraire*," "if you like," "you think so?" Similarly,

Akerman takes situations from Proust and elaborately defamiliarizes them. The novel's brief description of Marcel and Albertine's adjoining bathrooms occasions a long scene in which the unseen Ariane sings as Simon sits in the tub, instructing her on the precise details of her toilette. (Outrageously, much of the conversation is a deadpan discussion of Ariane's intimate physiognomy, vaginal secretions, and body odor. "If it weren't for my allergy and all the pollen you bring in, I almost wish you would never wash," smitten Simon says wistfully.)

Bedtime is another droll, even more complicated ritual. "Do you want me to come?" Ariane asks, meaning to visit him in his boudoir. "No, not yet," Simon replies so that he can scurry back to his room and then call Ariane on the phone to invite her in. The rules dictate that they play draughts as a prelude to Simon's real desire—absolute knowledge of her past and future whereabouts. Then she sleeps, or pretends to, allowing for the only time—literally as well as figuratively—that Simon can have her, even as she eludes him. (His practice of rubbing himself against her unconscious form until he climaxes is also taken from Proust.)

The seething vacuum known as Simon is animated only by his jealousy. As blank and well turned out as a mannequin, the impassive but twitching Merhar gives an extreme Bressonian performance. He watches, he listens, he checks up on Ariane: following strangers in the street, bursting into some soiree and dragging her out. Whatever he does, Ariane is neither angry nor surprised but rather pliant and unreadable. Always obliging, she suggests a machine on perpetual standby. Refusing to acknowledge Simon's surveillance, she blandly deflects his interrogation. When he demands to know what she's thinking, she replies, "If I had any thoughts, I'd tell you—but I don't."

Like the hero of *Memento*, Simon is a freelance investigator. Suspecting that Ariane is having an affair with an opera diva (if not the woman he has assigned to watch her), Simon interviews a lesbian couple to see if they can offer any insight. "It's different," they tell him. Tormented by Ariane's absence, he picks up a hooker in the Bois de Boulogne. She may resemble Ariane, but she can't play her. Her feigned sleep is too feigned. This material is brilliantly suited to the filmmaker's objective technique. Simon's passion isn't so much mad love as it is impossible love.

Few things are more pathological than Simon badgering Ariane to tell him her lies so that he can rewrite the past in terms of "real memories." The breakup—as dogged and excruciating as everything else—takes its dialogue from Proust but feels like *Vertigo* once more. Akerman has fashioned a great negative love story, a long stare into the abyss of the night.

## MULHOLLAND DRIVE

Originally published as "Points of No Return,"
the *Village Voice* (October 9, 2001).

**M**ULHOLLAND DRIVE **PARTS THE VEIL ON A TOTALLY CRACKED, UTTERLY CONVINCING** world with David Lynch its brooding demiurge. A Denny's-like restaurant on Sunset Boulevard fronts the void: "I had a dream about this place," a smug young creative type explains to someone who might be his agent, even as his nightmare begins to unfold. Crazy!

Fashioned from the ruins of a two-hour TV pilot rejected by ABC in 1999, Lynch's erotic thriller careens from one violent non sequitur to another. The movie boldly teeters on the brink of self-parody, reveling in its own excess and resisting narrative logic. This voluptuous phantasmagoria is certainly Lynch's strongest movie since *Blue Velvet* and maybe *Eraserhead*. The very things that failed him in the bad-boy rockabilly debacle of *Lost Highway*—the atmosphere of free-floating menace, pointless transmigration of souls, provocatively dropped plot stitches, gimcrack alternate universes—are here brilliantly rehabilitated. What was it that Dennis Hopper called Dean Stockwell in *Blue Velvet*—one suave motherfucker? From the absurd midnight automobile accident on the Los Angeles road that opens the movie and gives it its title, *Mulholland Drive* makes perfect (irrational) sense.

Lynch's outlandish noir feels familiar, and yet it's continually surprising, as when a bungled assassination turns into a Rube Goldberg mechanism involving two additional victims, a vacuum cleaner, and a smoke detector, or a scene begins with an abrupt eruption of pink and turquoise and a studio rendition of the Connie Stevens chestnut "Sixteen Reasons (Why I Love You)." The narrative, such as it is, commences when a lush brunette of mystery soon to be known as Rita (Laura Elena Harring) dodges a bullet, staggers out of her crashed car, and descends from the Hollywood Hills into the jewel-like city below to find refuge in an empty apartment. She's suffering from amnesia, which makes her the perfect foil for the flat's caretaker, Betty (Naomi Watts), who arrives the next morning—blond, perky, and inanely optimistic—from the Ontario town of Deep River (named perhaps for the sinister dive where Isabella Rossellini made her home in *Blue Velvet*). Betty is innocently avid to become a star; Rita is forced by circumstance to impersonate one. Their first meeting is a mini Hitchcock film, with the dazed brunette assigning herself a name from a handy *Gilda* poster.

Where did Rita's suitcase full of money come from? What is the significance of the blue key in her pocket? There's a definite Nancy Drew quality as the naively trusting and ever enthusiastic Betty takes it upon herself to solve the enigma of Rita's identity: "It'll be just like in the movies. We'll pretend to be someone else." Although Betty is initially a mass of cornball clichés, possibly modeled on Eva Marie Saint or Lynch himself, it unexpectedly develops that she really can act. (So, too, Naomi Watts.) Betty's audition at Paramount, a sensational performance in a tryout worthy of Ed Wood, presents the possibility that everything she has done and will do is calculated for effect. "You look like someone else," Betty exclaims when Rita gets a makeover to more closely resemble . . . her. Thanks in part to that new blond wig, the women get together in a scene that is not only exceptionally steamy and tender but contains what is surely the greatest amnesiac sex joke ever written.

Whatever *Mulholland Drive* was originally, it has become a poisonous valentine to Hollywood. (This is the most carefully crafted L.A. period film since *Chinatown*—except that the period is ours.) The locations are quietly fabulous; there's a museum quality to the musty deco apartment where Betty and Rita live under the watchful eye of a showbiz landlady (Ann Miller). The cloyingly lit nocturnal landscape and splashy glamour compositions seem pure essence of 1958, as do Betty's ingénue poses. The ominously rumbling city is malign and seductive; the movie industry, or should we say dream factory, is an obscure conspiracy. In a secondary narrative, an inexpressive, self-important young director (Justin Theroux) is compelled to endure a production meeting from hell wherein a shadowy cabal seizes control of his movie—but only so that the presence of a single, unknown actress can be dictated by an irony-resistant bogeyman called the Cowboy (Monty Montgomery, producer of Lynch's *Wild at Heart*, among other credits).

Alarming as the Cowboy is, *Mulholland Drive*'s most frighteningly self-reflexive scene comes when Betty and Rita attend a 2 A.M. performance—part séance, part underground art ritual—in a decrepit, near deserted old movie palace called Club Silencio. The mystery being celebrated is that of the Sync Event, sound-image synchronization, which is to say cinema, and the illusion throws Betty into convulsions. At the show's climax, Rebekah Del Rio sings an a cappella Spanish-language version of "Crying." She collapses onstage, but the song continues—just like the movie. For its remaining three-quarters of an hour, *Mulholland Drive* turns as perverse and withholding in its narrative as anything in Buñuel. Similarly surreal is the gusto with which Lynch orchestrates his particular fetishes. In *Mulholland Drive*, the filmmaker has the conviction to push self-indulgence past the point of no return.

Curiouser and curiouser. From the moment Betty and Rita leave the club, the narrative begins to fissure. *Mulholland Drive* flows from one situation to the next, one scene seeping into another like the decomposing corpse I've neglected to mention that's at the story's center. Characters dissolve. Settings deteriorate. Situations break down and reconstitute themselves, sometimes as fantasy, sometimes as a movie—which is to say, much of what has previously happened, happens again, only differently. Love is now a performance. Rita reverts to femme fatality. The parental demons return. Betty's dream becomes a nightmare—or perhaps the previous story was itself only a dream. Not that it matters. *Mulholland Drive* is thrilling and ludicrous. The movie feels entirely instinctual. The rest is *silencio*.

*Once Upon a Time in the West* (Sergio Leone, Paramount Pictures, 1969).

# IV

THE HISTORY OF FILM,

THE FILM OF HISTORY

## HOW THE WESTERN WAS LOST

Originally published in the *Village Voice* (August 21, 1991).

THE BUFFALO ARE GONE. THE RAILROAD IS FINISHED. THE RED MEN ARE IN DISARRAY. The sun sets on Monument Valley. Once the quintessential Hollywood genre, certainly the mode that dominated Cold War *Kinderkultur*, the western, as we knew it, is virtually extinct. The cowboy movie was typically the way America used to explain itself to itself. Who makes the law? What is the order? Where is the frontier? Which ones are the good guys? Why is it that a man's gotta to do what a man's gotta do—and how does he do it? Each Hollywood western, no matter how trite, was a national ritual, a passion play, a veritable presidential election dramatizing and redramatizing the triumph of civilization, usually personified as the victory of the socially responsible individual over "savage" Indians or outlaws. "They tell me everything isn't black and white," John Wayne growled in 1969. "Well, I say why the hell not?"

Why not indeed? Black and white or Technicolor, it is the western that was our true Fourth of July celebration. For, as historian Richard Slotkin has pointed out, in the national imagination, America's real founding fathers are less those celebrated and enlightened gentlemen who solemnly composed a nation in the genteel city of Philadelphia than "the rogues, adventurers, and land-boomers; the Indian fighters, traders, missionaries, explorers, and hunters who killed and were killed until they had mastered the wilderness."

Add to these the cavalrymen and demobilized soldiers, freed slaves and impoverished homesteaders, picturesque immigrants and miscellaneous riffraff who went west after the Civil War—as well as "the Indians themselves, both as they were and as they appeared to the settlers, for whom they were the special demonic personification of the American wilderness"—and you have the set of characters for what seemed the pageant that could not die.

That the western landscape still holds the promise of liberation and/or redemption, rebirth or reinvention can be seen in such disparate recent hits as *Thelma & Louise* and *City Slickers*, not to mention the phenomenal success of *Dances with Wolves*. The latter's awesome popularity, like the current word-of-mouth resurrection of Forrest Carter's autobiographical novel, *The Education of Little Tree*, demonstrates the enduring fascination of the classic western situation—the confrontation, in the wilderness, between the European and the Native American—even when that situation is presented all but devoid of context.

The continuing significance of the West for American identity is expressed by the panic greeting the possibility that a Japanese company might administer our national parks, no less than in the moral fervor of the Smithsonian's controversial exhibition, "The West as America." If nothing else, the hysterical response to this show—centering, for the most part, on the unremarkable curatorial suggestion that the Western art of the nineteenth and early twentieth centuries may have had its own ideological biases—shows how contested and problematic this territory remains. In that sense, the western is still at the impasse it reached 20 years ago.

Like baseball, the western is a sacred part of America's post–Civil War national mythology—a shared language, a unifying set of symbols and metaphors, and a source of (mainly male) identity. But baseball is all form; the western is heavy, heavy, heavy on content. That the national pastime was successfully integrated after World War II while the demographics of the western remained overwhelmingly white up until the eve of the genre's demise—despite the fact that at least a quarter of the working cowboys in the late nineteenth century were of African descent—should alert us to the possibility that the western was as much concerned with concealing as illuminating historical truth. In his catalog essay for the Smithsonian show, Alex Nemerov makes the point that the cowboy and Indian icons that developed around the closing of the frontier at the turn of the century can best be understood in relation to the urban, industrial culture that produced this iconography.

What is true for Western painting is no less true for the Hollywood oat opera: "Reluctant to give up the spectacular vistas that had already entered the nation's mythology," as Nancy Anderson notes in her contribution to the catalog, "Americans took comfort from the constructed artifice of studio paintings that offered assurance that the West could endure as both iconic symbol and economic resource." Urban cowboy Norman Mailer explicitly linked the development of Hollywood to the closing of the West—"the expansion turned inward, became part of an agitated, overexcited, superheated dream life." We were born to be wild—at least in our hearts.

As a genre, the western was most often but not always confined to a relatively brief era of American history—the 25-year-long mop-up operation between Lee's surrender at Appomattox and the defeat of the Sioux at Wounded Knee. (Fascination with this particular period does not usually extend to the contemporary phenomenon of Reconstruction.)

Similarly, the Hollywood western enjoyed its Golden Age during the quarter-century Pax Americana that followed World War II, a mainstay of early television no less than "grind" movie theaters. In the 1865–1890 period, individuals were armed and the threat of violence was constant; in that of 1948–1973, the nation was mobilized and the fear of war endemic. By focusing on the distinction between legal and illegal killing, the western supported American hypervigilance during an age when, it was feared, widespread affluence might lull the nation into decadent complacence. Not for nothing did John F. Kennedy name his program the New Frontier or Stanley Kubrick choose cowboy icon Slim Pickens to ride a hydrogen bomb bareback to Armageddon.

The celebration of national expansion intrinsic to the western implicitly supported the Cold War ethos of limitless growth and personal freedom. The Cinerama spectacular *How the West Was Won* (1962), which climaxed its epic saga with a vision of freeways, conveniently designates the watermark of this optimistic worldview. Thereafter, confidence in the western began to ebb in response to the struggle for civil rights at home and the question of imperial ambition abroad. If the Eisenhower era represented the western's high noon, an era in which the United States appointed itself global sheriff and the gunslinger supplanted the cowboy as the archetypal western hero, shadows had lengthened by the time Kennedy reached the White House. The old stars and veteran directors were aging. Sam Peckinpah's *Ride the High Country* and John Ford's *The Man Who Shot Liberty Valance* (both 1962) introduced the crepuscular mood that deepened in Ford's *Cheyenne Autumn* (1964) and Howard Hawks' *El Dorado* (1967).

The sixties brought unprecedented domestic and foreign upheaval and, given its privileged place in American popular culture, it was inconceivable that the western would remain immune. In Italy, Sergio Leone made the genre more immediately relevant by raising the body count. At once more abstract and more violently naturalistic than Hollywood westerns, Leone's "Dollars Trilogy" reintroduced TV cowboy Clint Eastwood as the last western hero. First, cynical bounty hunter, then outlaw-lawman, Eastwood was the "dirty" icon who would preside over the end of the western and the birth of the urban anti-Miranda *policier*.

Like the Beatles and the Trinitron, spaghetti westerns (shot in Spain, directed by Italians, starring Americans) marked the internationalization of our popular culture. Leone defamiliarized the genre—his westerns, Vincent Canby observed, were "twice removed from reality, being based on myths that were originally conceived in Hollywood studios in the nineteen-thirties." Perhaps three times removed from reality would be more realistic—the movies were based on myths that were themselves based on myths. Nor was Leone alone. Don Siegel's *Coogan's Bluff*, a vehicle for the new Eastwood, and Andy Warhol's *Lonesome Cowboys* –two self-consciously "modern" examples premiering within a month of each other during the final weeks of the 1968 presidential campaign—each in its way presented the genre itself as a form of Pop Art. By then, however, the western had outgrown the screen.

In the national dream life, Indochina was an extension of the western frontier and Americans were once again settlers, cavalrymen, schoolmarms, gunslingers, and marshals on a mission of protection and progress. The analogy was felt from the very beginning. In 1962, the *Saturday Evening Post* characterized JFK's notion of strategic hamlets as "the old stockade idea our ancestors used against the Indians," while Admiral Harry D. Felt hung a sign in his Honolulu head-quarters that read, "Injun Fightin' 1759. Counterinsurgency 1962." Helicopters were named for Indian tribes and their machine-gunners compared to the men who rode shotgun for the stagecoach; military operations coded "Sam Houston," "Daniel Boone," and "Crazy Horse." This mythology affected our allies as well. The novel *The Green Berets* describes the reaction of a South Vietnamese strike force to the showing of a western against the side of a building. They "loved the action and identified themselves with it. When the Indians appeared the strikers screamed 'VC,' and when the soldiers or cowboys came to the rescue the Nam Luong irregulars vied with each other in shouting out the number of their own strike-force companies."

Nor did America's soldiers, toting guns through hostile territory inhabited by an unseen, uncanny foe of an alien race, fail to grasp the analogy. (A celebrated passage in Michael Herr's *Dispatches* has the combat reporter invited on a search-and-destroy mission: "'Come on,' the captain said, 'we'll take you out to play Cowboys and Indians.'") After all, the men who fought in Vietnam were raised on westerns—presented with cap-firing six-guns and Davy Crockett coonskin caps, deposited in Saturday matinees to watch the adventures of Hopalong Cassidy and Gene Autry. The average recruit was graduating grade school at the 1958 to1960 height of the cathode-ray shoot-'em-up, when eight of the top prime-time TV shows were oat operas. Small wonder then that John Wayne, the greatest of movie cowboys, became a talisman for American soldiers. The unwieldy .45-caliber service pistols were known as "John Wayne rifles," the hard, tasteless biscuits included in boxes of C rations as "John Wayne cookies." Wayne himself made numerous appearances in Vietnam—as well as in Hollywood's only Vietnam movie during the actual conflict. The war was almost his personal crusade.

And why not? With the abdication of that tarnished Texan cowboy LBJ, Wayne was virtually the only establishment authority figure around—his appeal transcended politics. The Duke was asked to run for vice president with George Wallace while, in a cover story that identified Wayne as "the Last Hero," *Time* quoted an SDS organizer's enthusiastic endorsement: "He's tough, down to earth, and he says and acts what he believes. He's completely straight and really groovy. I mean, if they really want to make a movie about Che Guevara, they ought to have Wayne play him."

Wayne's base in *The Green Berets* (1968), described by its producer as "Cowboys and Indians . . . the Americans are the good guys and the Viet Cong are the bad guys," is called Dodge City. Meanwhile, in the real Vietnam, dangerous areas were known as "Indian country," Vietnamese scouts were termed "Kit Carsons," and more than a few grunts echoed the notorious slogan coined by General Phil Sheridan a century before, painting THE ONLY GOOD GOOK IS A DEAD GOOK on their helmets or flak jackets. Lieutenant William Calley complained that the Vietnamese laughingly called him and his men "cowboys." But there's nothing funny about a range hand gone loco. One scene in the documentary *Interviews with My Lai Veterans* has three vets discussing the mutilation and scalping of dead Vietnamese: "Some people were on an Indian trip over there."

In short, the metaphor was irresistible, only this time there was no consensus as to who were the good guys and who were the bad guys. While Lyndon Johnson called upon the nation to "nail the coonskin to the cabin door," the counterculture that opposed his war identified itself with outlaws or worse . . .

---

The western mythology played itself out in Vietnam and, of course, vice versa. No less than the nation's hearts and minds, the western movie was up for grabs. Two of 1969's three key releases, *The Wild Bunch* and *Butch Cassidy and the Sundance Kid* (less dirty perhaps than dirty-blond, albeit the highest-grossing western made before *Blazing Saddles*), embodied a striking inversion of values. At once cynical and romantic, both movies presented the unregenerate criminal as a sympathetic figure, regretful at his elimination by the agents of law and order. In the wake of *The Wild Bunch* and the My Lai massacre, the genre grew increasingly apocalyptic.

After *The Green Berets*, Hollywood produced no movies on the war. Instead, there were such revisionist and counterrevisionist essays as *Little Big*

*Man* (1970), *The Cowboys* (1972), *Bad Company* (1972), *Ulzana's Raid* (1972), and *High Plains Drifter* (1973)—crypto-Vietnam films all. No less than America's increasingly polarized political scene, the western split into radical right- and left-wing camps. Those starring John Wayne and, to a lesser extent, Clint Eastwood took up the cudgels against those directed by Arthur Penn and Robert Altman, while Peckinpah's westerns were divided against themselves. Common to all, however, was a sense of social breakdown, disillusionment, and the distrust of "liberal" mainstream values.

By the late 1960s, parallels between Vietnam and the Indian wars were commonplace (and were to be developed into formidable scholarly treatises by historians Richard Slotkin and Richard Drinnon). Like Boston's Sons of Liberty or the leaders of the Whiskey Rebellion, the hippies of Haight-Ashbury impersonated Native Americans—adopting a wardrobe of long hair, headbands, and love beads. Indians were remythologized as heroic forebears whose traditional way of life was more organic, spiritual, and communal than that of white settler society. Taking up "tribal" lifestyles, rationalizing the use of marijuana, mescaline, and peyote as Indian sacraments, promoting the connection between political and ecological concerns, the hippies more or less suggested that the current and past evils of American history might be redressed by reenacting that history in the guise of Indians rather than cowboys.

Thus, the most overtly ideological of revisionist westerns concerned the Indian wars. The revelation of American atrocities in Vietnam only reinforced their argument that the slaughter of Native Americans was less the distortion than the essence of the white man's wars. *Little Big Man*, *Soldier Blue*, and *A Man Called Horse* identified with the Indians so strongly as to be the equivalent of marching against the war beneath a Viet Cong flag. Released in 1970 and coinciding with the publication of two influential histories, *Custer Died for Your Sins* and *Bury My Heart at Wounded Knee*, these films proposed that any and all Indian barbarities paled before the enormity of white genocide. (Indeed, Sidney Poitier's *Buck and the Preacher* proposed an alliance of red and black men.)

Contempt for soldiering was a given in the dirty western. *The Wild Bunch* and *Little Big Man* make a mockery of the army, while prominent western deserters include Clint Eastwood (*The Good, the Bad, and the Ugly*), Jim Brown (*El Condor*), and Robert Redford (*Jeremiah Johnson*). *Bad Company* portrayed hostility toward the nation's wars as an American tradition—in this case, the refusal to serve in even so "just" a conflict as the Civil War—and linked it to an overall absence of authority. By the middle of Richard Nixon's first term, the quintessential Hollywood genre had clearly come unglued—although, in addition to widespread confusion, the extraordinary succession of revisionist and parody westerns that appeared around the turn of the decade acknowledges a multiplicity of perspectives on the winning (or losing) of the West

The ultimate desecration—*Blazing Saddles* (1974), the highest grossing western before *Dances with Wolves*—capped the assorted anti-, post-, spaghetti, revisionist, psychedelic, black, and burlesque westerns of the early seventies. (It's appropriate that the concept for *Heaven's Gate*, blamed by some for the demise of the genre, also dates from this period.) By that time, *The Godfather* had emerged as a new sort of national epic while, as presaged by *Coogan's Bluff* (1968), *Fort Apache* was relocated to the urban wilderness of the Bronx.

From 1910 through the end of the fifties, a quarter of all Hollywood films had been westerns. As late as 1972, the high point of genre revisionism, the year of *Jeremiah Johnson* and *The Life and Times of Judge Roy Bean*, *The Great Northfield, Minnesota Raid* and *The Culpepper Cattle Company*, *Buck and the Preacher* and *Greaser's Palace*, westerns still represented 12 percent of Hollywood's total output.

But the year that brought Richard Nixon's triumphant reelection was the last in which western releases would reach double figures. The subsequent falloff was dramatic: Four westerns were released in 1973; two in 1974; five in 1975; seven for the Bicentennial; two in 1977; three in 1978; and a total of three between 1979 and 1984, the year of TV western host Ronald Reagan's even more spectacular reelection. As J. Fred MacDonald put it in his history of the television western, "No form of mass entertainment has been so dominant and then so insignificant."

Though the western has bequeathed such enduring American totems as Marlboros and blue jeans, its decline effectively redefined the masculine screen image. After Clint Eastwood, the bounty hunter par excellence, there were no new heroic cowboys. When Dustin Hoffman made a western he impersonated an Indian. Robert Redford played a charming outlaw, Warren Beatty a failed pimp. The seventies saw a whole generation of movie stars who never donned Stetsons or strapped on six-guns (Robert De Niro, Al Pacino, Sylvester Stallone, Richard Dreyfuss). At the same time, the issues that preoccupied the western have either been repressed or else dispersed to other genres—including the Vietnam War film.

That, save for a handful of releases, the western itself has remained defunct since the fall of Saigon suggests that the spectacle by which America came to be America has proved resistant to the re-illusionment of the past dozen years. Although middle-aged generals reflexively referred to Iraqi-occupied Kuwait as

"Indian country," the rhetoric that supported, the commentary that described, and the celebrations that followed Operation Desert Storm were notable for a paucity of western imagery, despite the leadership of our first Texan president since Lyndon Johnson. It's striking that the origin of the yellow ribbon is habitually located in a 1973 Tony Orlando song, rather than a 1949 John Ford Cavalry western.

As the only game in town, and a softer version of the Indian western of the 1970s, *Dances with Wolves* has been attacked from the left, the right, and points unknown. (My favorite critique, from *Spy*, argued that Costner's film is "nothing more than a remake" of the suitably degenerate, mid-sixties cavalry-western sitcom *F Troop*.) Moreover, it is a backhanded tribute to Hollywood's authority in general, and its western franchise in particular, that *Dances with Wolves* has presented the means with which to characterize the revisionism of the Smithsonian exhibition. The Moonie-owned *Washington Times* denounced the show as embodying "the Kevin Costner approach to art history . . . the sort of fantasy approach to an issue one expects from Hollywood movies," and then again as "a crazed, illiterate diatribe against the westward expansion of the United States . . . a product of the Kevin Costner revisionist school of American history." The more sympathetic *City Paper* found the exhibit a less romantic "art-historical counterpart to *Dances with Wolves*," while in *Time*, Robert Hughes dryly observed that "John Wayne would have disapproved."

Response to the show has been no less revealing than the show itself. It's fascinating that while movies are perceived as ideological fantasies, paintings have come to seem neutral representations. Fueled by press reports, political opposition was led by a group of Republican senators from western states—Ted Stevens of Alaska, Slade Gorton of Washington, and Alan Simpson of Wyoming, who maintained that it was "silly" to read "all this religious and symbolic nonsense" into the paintings. At least Simpson saw the show. Stevens, the strong supporter of oil and mineral development who led the charge, told the *Washington Post* that "we from the West live here in the East really under attack all the time. To see that exhibit . . . I'll tell you, that really set me off"—thus imagining himself one of the protagonists of Frederic Remington's extensively interpreted *Fight for the Water Hole*, even though he had yet to actually visit the Smithsonian.

"The West as America" doubled attendance at the Smithsonian, but has since been canceled by museums in Denver and St. Louis. The problem, of course, is not with the reading of individual paintings; the problem is that it is has become impossible to study or think about the West without facing some unpleasant truths. "How can we revel in the glorious self-confidence of the mountain men, the cattle drives, the pioneers, and at the same time know the attendant tragedies that all but destroyed the native cultures? How can we glory in the grandeur of the landscape and still count such burdensome environments as Los Angeles, Phoenix, and Las Vegas as part of the West?" asks Chris Bruce, curator of "Myth of the West," another show of western art that perhaps because it was mounted in Seattle, Washington, rather than Washington, D.C., has avoided the charge of "political correctness."

The man the French called Ronnie Le Cowboy might have brought America back, but restoring the myth of our "innocent" origins defied even his magic. If we date the end of the Cold War to the 1989 Polish election in which Solidarity successfully identified itself with the image of Gary Cooper in *High Noon*, then is history over?

The western as a genre implies a belief in secular progress. Even when the hero kills in revenge he is acting in the name of immanent law and order. (The frontier, by definition, is the sphere where civil rule has yet to be established and thus, from the spectator's point of view, a legitimate arena for the spectacle of violent conflict.) In the workaday world of urban stress, against a civilization complicated by the insights of Marx and Freud, the western argued a form of natural morality; it proposed an instinctive awareness of right and wrong, and granted the freedom to act, often violently, even kill upon that awareness.

For this reason, the western narrative is typically the rationalization of aggression. The climactic murder may redress either a personal wrong or an injustice done to the community, and usually contrives to be both—Manifest Destiny given emotional meaning as a personal vendetta. The western hero is licensed to kill, providing that his adversaries have been characterized as sufficiently atrocious as to warrant extermination. The Indian and the outlaw equally reject and threaten the new order (or rather, the immanent order), which is to say, ours. But who, exactly, are we? And even if "we" are of European origin, does our American History begin at Santa Fe or Plymouth Rock?

It may not be coincidental that the Smithsonian's critics come from northwestern rather than southwestern states—it will be rather more difficult, I suspect, to make so "universal" a movie as *Dances with Wolves* on the subject of the Alamo or the Mexican War. Although acknowledging the presence of blacks and Asians and thus grudgingly "urbanizing" the West, the two most ambitious Reagan-era westerns, Clint Eastwood's *Pale Rider* and Lawrence Kasdan's *Silverado*, were noticeably uncomplicated by the presence of Indians or Hispanics. Indeed, *Dances with Wolves* is itself so antiseptic and well regulated as to reduce our national dark-and-bloody ground to campsite proportions.

My guess is that the born-again western may not be a western at all, but rather, as presaged by *Westworld* (1973) and suggested by the grand climax of *Back to the Future,* a theme park. As *Time*'s recent cover story on the New American Mecca, Orlando, observed, "Disney World is predominantly white and middle class—and so is Orlando. The city, like Disney World, offers relief not just from the pressures of geography (it is flat and still undeveloped) and of history (more than half the area's population arrived during the past 20 years) but, most of all, from contending ethnicity. In that sense, Orlando is a new psychological frontier, a jumping-off place for a society that revels in the surface of things, even if deeper problems remain unaddressed."

Comfortably unicultural, if not implicitly white supremacist, this liberating new psychological frontier is the virtual reality that has supplanted the western as the repository of American order, morals, history, and civilization. Bloody and confused, the iconoclastic last westerns took moviegoers to the end of a long and winding trail—and found less a clearing in the forest than a thicket of ambiguities. It remains to be seen whether the first postwestern generation has any pathfinders with the nerve to push deeper still into that wilderness and reignite a genre that once epitomized America to itself and to the world.

## SCHINDLER'S LIST

Originally published as "Spielberg's Oskar,"
the *Village Voice* (December 21, 1993).

**F**ROM THE DEPTHS OF THE OCEAN TO THE DARK SIDE OF NEVERLAND, FROM RURAL Georgia to occupied Shanghai, Steven Spielberg envelops creation like an infinite expanse of Saran Wrap. His crinkly realm encompasses prehistoric dinosaurs and extraterrestrial aliens; his sacred texts range from the ark of the covenant to *A Guy Named Joe.* The president himself initiated the buzz on *Schindler's List*; New York's David Denby staggered out to proclaim, "It's as if [Spielberg] understood for the first time why God gave him such extraordinary skills."

Is there a higher authority? "Possibly no one ever again will achieve [Spielberg's] clout," wrote the editor of *Variety.* "Nor use it with such magnanimity." Three of Spielberg's movies have in their time reigned as all-time box-office champ— he may be the most universal artist on planet Earth. What challenges remain? The perpetual insider question—will one of his pictures ever win an Academy Award?—is interesting only insofar as it might inspire industry savants to reflect upon another. Can any subject resist recuperation? Could even the Holocaust be Spielbergized? Is it possible to make a feel-good entertainment about the ultimate feel-bad experience of the twentieth century?

*Schindler's List* dramatizes the wartime exploits of Oskar Schindler, a German industrialist and Nazi party member who managed to save over a thousand Polish Jews from extermination by employing them in the enamelware factory that the German occupation had allowed him to confiscate from its prewar Jewish owners. The fullest account of Schindler's life has been provided by Australian novelist Thomas Keneally. Neither a work of fiction nor history, alternately chatty and laconic, padded with imagined dialogue and unnecessary details (as if mere biography would not be compelling enough), Keneally's 1982 book presents Schindler as a given, making little attempt to account for his character.

Extremes of human behavior were the norm in occupied Poland, to help a Jew was to invite death; the 3 percent of Poland's 3.3 million Jews who survived the war in Poland did so through a run of luck so cosmic and inexplicable you'd have a better chance to break the bank at Caesars Palace. That Schindler was such a gambler is part of his mythology. The war transformed him from a charming rogue into something like a saint. (He reverted afterward.) It's an incredible story even by Holocaust standards and, unlike *The Diary of Anne Frank*, for example, races to a happy end—which may be the reason that, with *E.T.* still atop the *Variety* chart, Universal purchased the movie rights for their miracle worker Spielberg.

Played by the sleekly imposing Liam Neeson, introduced making the scene at a smoky Cracow nightclub, Spielberg's Schindler is a bon vivant with an agenda—an opportunist, not an ideologue, who acquires a factory and leases from the SS Jewish slaves, including the former plant manager, to work it. His interest is in making money and living well—he takes over a Jewish apartment even as the former residents are herded into the ghetto—but he has no desire to work his employees to death. This initial enlightened selfishness gives way to a more disinterested heroism with the liquidation of the Cracow ghetto. Out riding with his mistress in the hills above the city, Schindler watches in disbelief as the local Jews are beaten, shot, rounded up, and transported to concentration camps. Thereafter, his factory will become a sanctuary.

Shot on location in luminous black and white, *Schindler's List* has a generic resemblance to Andrzej Wajda's *Korczak*. It's both studied and hectic. Poland is a special effect (this is surely the most expensive movie ever made there), and it gives the movie a distinct chill. Something of the gray, damp countryside has crept into Spielberg's marrow—but even more of sunny Hollywood has remained there. The movie is best when it's a tumble of details. Like more than one artist immersed in this material, Spielberg crams as much in as he can—sometimes sacrificing historical accuracy, but more often lunging for effect.

The terror of Nazi terror was its random, offhanded, unpredictable nature. In the desire to make this comprehensible, Spielberg falls back on what he knows. He tries to be casual when Jews are shot, but he can't resist the punctuating close-up of blood in the snow any more than he can help underscoring the merciful poison administered to Jewish patients as Nazis storm their hospital by framing the beatific looks ghetto doctors exchange, or keep himself from using a cute little kid as a savior, or ending the liquidation sequence by augmenting adventure schlockmeister John Williams' egregiously overwrought score with a saccharine voice-over of children singing the Yiddish nursery song *Ofn Pripitshik.*

Unlike Schindler, Spielberg can't override his instincts. Is there a world beyond Beverly Hills? Spielberg told *Premiere* that if Schindler were alive today he'd be running Time Warner and informed the *New York Times* that a contemporary Schindler would be CAA head Mike Ovitz. *Premiere* entered into the spirit of the discourse by describing the "Darth Vader effect" Spielberg wanted for the termination of the ghetto, while captioning a production still of the Auschwitz scene "temple of doom."

Calling Harrison Ford. With the liquidation of the Cracow ghetto, Schindler's factory is relocated to the Plaszow slave labor camp. This nightmare establishment is run by the hero's evil twin—the sadistic SS commander Amon Goeth (Ralph Fiennes), a dead-eyed, baby-faced Caligula who picks off inmates at random even when he isn't soused. Plaszow affords Spielberg the opportunity to stage an Auschwitz-style selection during which inmates run naked past the Nazi doctors who decide which ones to keep alive. Here again, the horror of the set piece strains the story line, although one might wonder if these narrative breakdowns don't serve to stoke audience longing for the comfort of Schindler's bulky figure.

As early as 1948, the Yiddish feature *Undzere Kinder (Our Children)*, made in Poland with actual survivors, raised the issue of ethical representation by having war orphans criticize as false a sentimental playlet set in the Warsaw Ghetto. Even now, as Auschwitz crumbles (or is transformed into a movie lot), historians and scholars wonder whether it should be preserved and why. How to speak the unspeakable, show the unshowable, how to evoke the reality of systematic mass murder without recourse to horror pornography or sentimental cliché. Masterworks as disparate as Tadeusz Borowski's *This Way for the Gas, Ladies and Gentlemen*, Art Spiegelman's *Maus*, and Claude Lanzmann's *Shoah* all developed strategies to show the Holocaust in its traces and absences—to reflect its horrors in a mirrored shield. Spielberg recognizes this himself, telling

*Premiere* that SS men used to toss babies out of windows and shoot them like skeet: "I wouldn't show that, even with dolls."

Still, the movie achieves its nadir when a group of Schindler Jews, as they are known, find themselves in Auschwitz, heading for the showers. Expanded from a single sentence in Keneally's text, Spielberg unbelievably plays the scene for thriller suspense and last-minute rescue. Will an Allied bomb fall on the gas chamber? Does the Red Army arrive? The U.S. Cavalry? Is there a telegram from Mr. Zanuck? Perhaps you have dreamed yourself into an Auschwitz gas chamber; Steven Spielberg wants to own that nightmare too.

*Schindler's List* is sentimental but it could have been worse. *The Color Purple* was a far shoddier piece of claptrap, and *Sophie's Choice*, in which a Christian Auschwitz survivor is tormented by her Jewish lover, far more contemptible. Perhaps it will even do some good. The abysmal miniseries *Holocaust* served an educational function in Germany, and polls show that nearly 40 percent of the American public is either unaware or dubious that European Jews were systematically murdered during World War II.

For some, the originality of *Schindler's List* may lie precisely in the figure of exceptionalism Schindler provides—as if such exceptionalism were not Hollywood's iron rule. "We have become so conversant with evil in the twentieth century that we are in danger of accepting it as inevitable," writes Denby in *New York*. Yes, *Schindler's List* has the courage of its positive thinking.

In the final hour, Schindler leads his Jews to a new factory in the Sudetenland. There they can keep the Sabbath while suffering neither illness nor starvation. His own transfiguration culminates in a heart-clutching farewell vastly elaborated from Keneally's book. The poster of a father grasping a child's hand is not the only aspect of *Schindler's List* that recalls *E.T.* The pathos of the absent father remains the most deeply felt emotion in the Spielberg universe. Calling himself a "criminal" and protesting that he "didn't do enough," Schindler stands alone on the stage and receives the adoration of the masses. (He asks for three minutes of silence but, because this is a Spielberg movie, there can be no more than three seconds before *Kaddish* rings out.)

And what of the Spielberg Jews? Relegated to supporting parts in their own cataclysm, they hang around the Cracow ghetto . . . making Jewish jokes. There is no debate, no political consciousness, no anguish, no betrayal, no sense of a multitude of classes and castes crammed together because they were Jews. Schindler towers over all. Spielberg's Jews have physical presence only en masse—they're ultimately victims or children. The more individuated assortment of wizened crones and sultry houris, intellectual dreamers and black market schemers, are dignified versions of stereotypes that would hardly have disturbed the Nazi cosmology. The strongest Jewish character (Ben Kingsley) is uptight and prickly, a heroic accountant.

Unafraid to accentuate the positive, *Schindler's List* necessarily focuses on Gentiles. There's a good-looking hero and an easily recognized villain. *Shoah*, for example, is a film about death in which, over and over and over and over, no one ever escapes. Here, most Jews survive and all are properly grateful rather than unpleasantly traumatized. The violin of hope accompanies the presentation of Schindler's list: The pleased nods and satisfied smiles of the designated Jews suggest a transport of underprivileged waifs acting worthy of a special trip to Disneyland. It's total bliss-out, pure enchantment. Evil is not inevitable. "Every time we go to a movie, it's magic," says Spielberg in *Premiere*. "Whether you watch eight hours of *Shoah* or whether it's *Ghostbusters*, when the lights go down in the theater and the movie fades in, it's magic."

One could found a religion on the transformation of Zyklon B into running water. In a single year, Spielberg has reanimated the dinosaurs and brought the Jews of Poland back from extinction. "I was so ashamed of being a Jew," he told *Premiere*, "and now I'm filled with pride." Annihilation *is* disagreeable. You won't have any trouble sitting down to dinner after seeing *Schindler's List*, however. It's a tasteful movie.

## RACE MOVIES

Originally published as "Race to Race," the
*Village Voice* (February 22, 1994).

THE INFLUENCE OF D. W. GRIFFITH ON AMERICAN FILM CULTURE IS ALMOST incalculable. Not only did Griffith develop the language of cinema narrative, he invented the persona of the American film artist: Griffith was the original director as producer, star maker, lonely genius, and national bard.

Ambitious independents King Vidor and Oscar Micheaux began their careers in Griffith's shadow. Micheaux was the anti-Griffith—negating the racist stereotypes of *The Birth of a Nation* and, almost incidentally, undermining the conventions of narrative cinema as well. Vidor, at his best, was a streamlined "modern" Griffith—a muscular antiurban populist working for MGM, the maker of epic pastorals and ham-fisted melodramas that strenuously sung the praises of America singing.

Like his maestro, Vidor was a southerner, and his 1929 *Hallelujah*, the most accomplished talking picture of its day and the centerpiece of the Public Theater's current Vidor retro, supplanted *The Birth of a Nation* as America's fount of racial stereotypes. Whether picking cotton or rolling dice, preaching the gospel or dancing the Swanee Shuffle, the rural African Americans in Vidor's mock ethnographic melodrama—shot in and around Memphis, northern Arkansas, and the MGM lot—were amiable, if passionate, children of nature.

While providing the model for 25 years of Hollywood "race" musicals as well as a precedent for Spencer Williams' more authentic *The Blood of Jesus*, *Hallelujah* was underscored by the same agrarian dream evident in Vidor's subsequent *The Stranger's Return* and *Our Daily Bread*. In the all-black world of *Hallelujah*, sharecroppers are an American peasantry—albeit one with highly developed showbiz proclivities. The sound of wailing spirituals precedes even the appearance of the MGM lion; throughout, the Dixie Jubilee Choir's "traditional" repertoire is augmented with compositions by Stephen Foster and Irving Berlin.

The opening sequence melds cotton field with Cotton Club. As the hero Zeke (Daniel Haynes) and his family return to their cabin, adopted daughter Missy Rose (future blues great Victoria Spivey) breaks into song and the porch becomes a makeshift stage—kids tap-dancing, jug bands wandering out of the wings. Although required to play it wide-eyed and dumb, the principals were mainly experienced troupers and Broadway veterans—the handsome, brawny Haynes understudied Jules Bledsoe in the original *Show Boat*. The baby-faced, endearingly hoarse Nina Mae McKinney—the hip-shaking jazz-baby Chick who leads Zeke astray—was a teenage star of Lew Leslie's *Blackbirds*.

The development of talkies permitted Hollywood to participate in the "Negro vogue" of the late twenties that brought tourists to Harlem and productions like *Shuffle Along, Show Boat, Porgy*, and *The Emperor Jones* to Broadway. MGM perceived *Hallelujah* as a prestige picture (although Vidor was required to invest some of his own money in it), and, for all its pernicious and/or simple-minded distortions, the movie remains a compelling attempt to create an American folk naturalism.

At once starkly documentary in its visual style and utterly dreamlike in its narrative trajectory, *Hallelujah* charts Zeke's circular progress through the fallen world. Set up by Chick to lose his money in a crooked crap game and then causing the death of his brother in the ensuing fracas, Zeke starts spontaneously preaching—traveling by train and mule, addressing tranced-out camp meetings and staging mass baptisms. Chick's reappearance as a potential disciple hopelessly blurs religious and sexual ecstasy, landing Zeke first in a sawmill and then on a chain gang before he's returned to Mammy, Pappy, and Missy Rose.

Universally raved by white critics, *Hallelujah* inspired understandable ambivalence among black writers. W.E.B. Du Bois praised the movie in *Crisis* while noting its inability to represent the white power structure that kept Zeke and his family in their place. This invisible Jim Crow was reproduced by the movie's release. *Hallelujah* had two New York premieres—one on Broadway, the other 85 blocks uptown.

Unlike *Hallelujah,* the films of Oscar Micheaux were made for an African American audience. For years, Micheaux was seen as an abstract symbol, the Father of the Race Movie, rather than a major American filmmaker. Although not infrequently shown, the movies constituting his complex, troubling, out-landish, enjoyable, and unique oeuvre were rarely written about—and then almost always from a historical perspective. Recently, however, Micheaux has become a hot academic property, the subject of essays, conferences, and scholarly newsletters (although appreciations of his films as film remain the exception).

The Micheaux retro currently at the American Museum of the Moving Image is New York's first since the Whitney surveyed his work in 1984, and, in the interim, a number of lost movies turned up—including *Veiled Aristocrats* (1932).

Whereas *Hallelujah* makes a spectacle of African Americana, *Veiled Aristocrats* addresses itself directly to the issue of race. The movie is Micheaux's second adaptation of "talented tenth" writer Charles W. Chesnutt's once cele-brated novel *The House Behind the Cedars*—the story of octoroon siblings, John and Rena Walden. John, who has left their North Carolina town to suc-cessfully pass for white, sends for Rena; she wavers—nearly marrying a white suitor—but ultimately elects to remain in the race. In the novel, Rena dies. Micheaux is more positive, improving upon Chesnutt so that Rena lives to marry the poor but honest black man, Frank.

The movie's opening sequence is classic Micheaux, destabilizing Hollywood conventions of form and content: It's been 20 years since old Mrs. Walden has seen John (Lorenzo Tucker, "The Black Valentino"), yet she knows that he's a "great lawyer." Rena (Laura Bowman), who is 22 and still treated like a child, observes their reunion in a series of cutaways—while mother and son move around the set, she remains fixed at the top of the stairs, listening to John explain why he wants to take her away: "I've heard, right on the street, a coal black Negro declare that he loves her!"

Rena warns Frank what's in store. When she suggests they elope, he demurs: "You are too good and too true to do any but the finest and most noble things." That, of course, is John's plan. In the existing print, found in a

Tennessee garage and restored by George Eastman House, Rena's experience of the white world consists of John's middle-class digs and some ballroom dancing with a young swell who, to her consternation, declares his love. Later, three black servants strain their ears toward the camera to tune in John's reproaches and Rena's declaration that she is "not a white girl but a Negress." Playing to the audience, the eavesdropping trio deduces that her desire is sexual: "Once you've had a black man, you never go back."

Whether or not you take this as Micheaux's comment on the poisonous irrationality of America's racial illness, it's safe to say that, once you've seen a Micheaux movie, Hollywood "perfection" will never seem the same. The word "pragmatic" is insufficient. Micheaux told his stories by whatever means necessary—cobbling together scenes out of imperfect takes and blatant inserts, sound bridges and dubbed dialogue papering over the mismatched shots. Add to this his indifference to continuity and fondness for narrative delirium (the use of titles to superimpose one story upon another), and you have a recipe for avant-garde genius.

Micheaux shot *Veiled Aristocrats* during the summer of 1931 in Montclair, New Jersey, using his mother-in-law's house as the primary set, and like his best films, it has a documentary immediacy. The vaudeville aesthetic is far more radical than Vidor's. The title "A Servant Woman in the Walden Home" announces a rendition of "Many Happy Returns of the Day" accompanied by unseen piano and delivered by the singer as she perfunctorily dusts a table. Micheaux staged his scenes as though recording a screen test or reinventing cinema.

*Veiled Aristocrats* ends with Frank rescuing Rena in a Model T. At once monotonous and hysterical, she describes the ordeal of passing. ("I'm sure it's not as bad as all that," says Frank, still trying to out-John John and do the right thing.) Ignoring the offscreen cry of "Cut, cut!" they kiss and drive off in what seems to be the opposite direction from which Frank arrived. Moments like this make Micheaux's films forever fresh.

## JAWS

INHUMAN, UNSLEEPING, OMNIVOROUS, A MACHINE TRIGGERED BY THE SCENT OF blood. . . . It was with *Jaws* that the culture industry began to contemplate itself.

In April 1974, a week before Steven Spielberg's movie went into production on Martha's Vineyard with three mechanical sharks—collectively nicknamed

"Bruce"—powered with pneumatic engines and launchable by 65-foot catapult, the *New York Times Magazine* ran a detailed analysis on "the making of a best-seller," tracking the novel *Jaws'* development from Peter Benchley's initial one-page description, through the completion of the manuscript, title selection, cover-art development, and sale-pitch creation, to climax with a wild auction for the paperback rights, a full nine months before the hardcover would appear. As the film rights had also been sold before the novel's February 1974 publication, the entire period of *Jaws'* bestsellerdom—much of which coincided with the making of the movie—could be considered a giant publicity trailer for a work-in-progress. Released simultaneously at 460 theaters on an equally unprecedented wave of TV advertising, *Jaws* was everywhere at once—like a television event—needing only 78 days to surpass *The Godfather*'s rentals and become the top-grossing movie of all time (or at least until 1977, and *Star Wars*). By then, Americans had purchased two million Jaws tumblers, half a million t-shirts and tens of thousands of posters, beach towels, shark's tooth pendants, bike bags, blankets, costume jewelry, shark costumes, hosiery, hobby kits, inflatable sharks, iron-on transfers, board games, charms, pajamas, bathing suits, water squirters. Jaws was the greatest marketing bonanza since the 1955 Davy Crockett craze. The beach itself was a virtual-reality billboard (a beneficial side-effect of the movie's extended production schedule—Universal had originally hoped to release it the preceding Christmas): Both *Time* and the *New York Times* ran features reporting that "formerly bold swimmers now huddle in groups a few yards offshore," while "waders are peering timorously into the water's edge."

Could mere advertising explain this orgy of participation? *Newsweek* noted that, "the spell seemed larger than its merchandising hype alone could account for." In a new and particularly self-conscious way, the movie's extraordinary box-office appeal further fed that appeal—transforming a hit movie into something larger, a new form of feedback and a new model for the movies. *Jaws* was the very post-TV multimedia *Gesamtkunstwerk* predicted by Max Horkheimer and Theodor Adorno, in which the total integration of "all the elements of the production, from the novel (shaped with an eye to the film) to the last sound effect," would be totally integrated: "The movie-makers distrust any manuscript which is not reassuringly backed by a bestseller. Yet for this very reason there is never-ending talk of ideas, novelty, and surprise … Nothing remains as of old; everything has to run incessantly, to keep moving." To keep moving—just like the shark which devours whatever comes its way. (Indeed, Carl Gottlieb's paperback quickie *The Jaws Log* opens by comparing producers David Brown and Richard Zanuck to sharks—*nice* sharks, not so much predatory as hyperalert: "Just as the Great White Shark can sense the erratic vibrations of a swimmer in the water, so can Richard and David sense the movement of a literary property in the publishing world.")

The shark is nature's revenge—but revenge for what exactly? Although putatively designed to dispel the idea that the shark is "the cold, mechanical eating-machine of popular myth," the exhibit "Sharks! Fact and Fantasy," currently at the American Museum of Natural History, nevertheless greets visitors (courtesy of Red Lobster) with a facsimile set of jaws, suggesting a creature big as a Greyhound. What is this fish's role in the nation's fantasy life?

Traveling through the United States during the summer of '75, Umberto Eco observed that "the shark in *Jaws* is a hyperrealistic model in plastic, 'real' and controllable like the audioanimatronic robots of Disneyland." Two sequels, several re-releases, innumerable clones later, and 19 years later a *Jaws* ride finally opened at Universal Studios Florida—a six-minute boat trip in which a 32-foot latex and polyurethane shark, moving 20 feet per second with the thrust of a 727 jet engine surfaces approximately once a minute to spook and spray. *Jaws* the film is itself predicated on a ruthless notion of movie as roller coaster. The buildup is certainly as long as the wait for a Disneyland ride—the monster remains invisible until 80 minutes into the movie. Then, with each appearance bigger than the last, it repeatedly violated human space, erupting from below. As visualized on *Jaws*' book jacket and movie poster, the *Jaws* shark is at once monstrous phallus and vagina dentata. Coalescing a whole nexus of submerged feelings and sadistic sexuality, the film opened with one of the most blatantly eroticized murders in the history of cinema—and one which openly encourages the audience to identify with the killer.

In 1975, there were few American fears that were not displaced onto the shark. That summer, the *Jaws* poster was parodied to show the Statue of Liberty menaced by the CIA, Portugal by communism, Uncle Sam by a Soviet submarine buildup, Gloria Steinem by male chauvinism (though here, the swimmer attacked the shark back), American citizens by a tax "bite," American wages menaced by inflation, American drivers by the energy crisis, American workers by unemployment, and Gerald Ford by recession, Ronald Reagan, and a toothless Congress. (Meanwhile, Fidel Castro identified the great white with U.S. imperialism.) Historians of drive-ins noted that the creature's true ancestor was the Japanese monster Godzilla who emerged from Tokyo harbor, disturbed from eternal slumber by the atomic bomb. *Jaws*, too, was haunted by the idea of nuclear holocaust and a fear of retribution: it makes one character retell the story of the USS *Indianapolis*, the heavy cruiser that delivered the atomic bombs meant for Hiroshima and Nagasaki, then suffered a suitably cosmic trial—hit by a torpedo, its crew forced to abandon ship in shark-infested seas with hundreds of seamen dead.

In short, *Jaws* was perceived, correctly, as a political film. Representing a crisis in American leadership, it was in production as the Watergate disaster played its final act and the nation marked the fifth anniversary of Senator

Edward Kennedy's automobile accident on the tiny island of Chappaquiddick, off Martha's Vineyard, with the resultant death of a young campaign worker. Chappaquiddick was consistently in the news during the *Jaws* shoot—in fact, Bruce was filmed gliding through the same channel where Kennedy ditched the car. The *New York Times Magazine* ran a lengthy article on the still-unexplained circumstances of Mary Jo Kopechne's drowning, and the subject was rehashed by *Time*, the *Boston Globe*, and *60 Minutes*.

By the time *Jaws* wrapped, Nixon was gone, and Kennedy had removed himself from the presidential race—both victims of what now, post *Jaws*, would be known as a media "feeding frenzy." (Fittingly, the first recorded usage was by former Nixon press secretary Gerald L. Warren.) Nor were Nixon and Kennedy all that America had tossed into the drink—by the summer of *Jaws* there was no more Vietnam war, no further talk of the space race, no new Miami or Las Vegas to construct. As the summit of American accomplishment there was now only this . . .

"It looked like a Nike missile, but it was one of the [mechanical] sharks," the *Boston Phoenix* had reported from the set, having penetrated Spielberg's security system to note Bruce's "inner workings of pumps, gauges, hoses, and clamps." *Jaws* "should never have been made," Spielberg would maintain and his description of his "impossible effort" was elaborated in *The Jaws Log*: "Launching *Jaws* was a film production problem analogous to NASA trying to land men on the moon and bring them back." Yes, no less remarkable than Universal Studio Florida's $45 million attraction is Landshark—an "incredible state-of-the-art radio broadcast facility on wheels" constructed from the same "space-age polypropylene honeycomb utilized in NASA's space shuttle vehicles" and created to whip the populace into a frenzy of *Jaws* consciousness.

In *The Jaws Log*, Gottlieb recalls a cocktail party at which *New York Times* political columnist and Vineyard regular James Reston buttonholed producer Zanuck and berated him for Hollywood's apparent lack of interest in celebrating the impending Bicentennial. What Reston couldn't know was that in giving America a new source of pride, *Jaws* would be that celebration.

## QUIZ SHOW

Originally published as "Going Down the Tube," the
*Village Voice* (September 13, 1994).

**I**T'S A TRUISM OF LIFE IN THE GLOBAL VILLAGE THAT ANYTHING THAT IS ANYTHING is sure to happen twice—the first time as news, the second time as entertainment (or, increasingly, vice versa). A great media event defines itself by monopolizing our attention and then returns intermittently to reignite the heavens in a comet blaze of publicity: The big-money TV quiz shows that mesmerized America in the mid-1950s reappeared in all the media a few years later to fascinate anew with the revelation that they had been rigged.

For more than 30 years, the story lay dormant. But next week the spectacle's two aspects—crime and punishment—return as one with the release of Robert Redford's *Quiz Show*. Indeed, *Quiz Show* absorbed a rival film treatment of the same material, and it isn't even the only impending replay. Richard Greenberg's ambitious drama *Night and Her Stars*, extensively reviewed when it was staged last spring in Costa Mesa, is scheduled to open at the Manhattan Theater Club in March 1995.

What could the quiz show scandal possibly mean in 1994? Dealing with the mechanics of celebrity and corruption, conspiracy and betrayal, truth and ratings, adulation and shame, the scenario provides a natural history of television—one more opportunity for the media to reflect upon itself and for us to seek our images in the illusory depths of that reflection. *Quiz Show* resonates with such seventies Redford projects as *Downhill Racer* and *The Candidate*. It's *Ordinary People* meets *All the President's Men* (appropriately spiked with strategic references to then vice president and future nation-betrayer Richard Nixon) but without the heavy melodrama—the most polished, least sentimental, and best movie that Redford has ever directed.

Set in a deftly generic mid-fifties, *Quiz Show* never traffics in nostalgia, although as entertainingly jaundiced, literate, dialogue-rich, and performer-juiced as it is, the movie has affinities to certain productions of the period—*All About Eve, Sunset Boulevard, A Face in the Crowd, Sweet Smell of Success*. The mode is glamorously disillusioned. The engagingly primitive backstage manipulation of the TV image, crosscut with the telecast itself, makes it clear from the start that the fix is in. Even so, *Quiz Show* is surprisingly suspenseful.

Redford is not ordinarily the most available of celebrities, but he's eager to talk about *Quiz Show*—as well he might be. Wearing a snug T-shirt and chinos (the previous interviewer was with the *Ladies' Home Journal*), he matches the decor of his relaxed, haute Navajo offices at Radio City, the scandal's former epicenter. "There's a personal view here, I can't deny that," he says of *Quiz Show*. "It has to do with my own experience. My life has spanned this time." Redford associates the quiz shows with his penniless New York period—a struggling actor, he appeared on *Play Your Hunch* in 1959—as well as with his appreciation of showbiz corruption.

A trim and weathered 57, Redford has the laconic cowboy look, but he's more than willing to hold forth on the significance of his subject: "One of the first visibly exposed examples of what really controls our industry—the merchant mentality." For Redford, the televised Army-McCarthy hearings of 1954 were "the first time we experienced the critical mass, gathered over one event, brought together by viewing something at the same time." The deceptive quiz shows that built upon that audience marked "the beginning of the erosion of our public trust," the prelude to "the Kennedy assassinations, Watergate, Iran-Contra, the Savings & Loans debacle, BCCI, the Clarence Thomas hearings." In a word, the whole telehistorical gestalt.

<hr />

*Quiz Show* shoulders a particular historical burden, although, as a movie, it's a canny example of applied Jetsonism. (Michael Ballhaus shot the picture; Jon Hutman's production design is exemplary.) Closer in tone to sociological sci-fi than remembrance of times past, it begins in an automobile showroom—the brand-new deep green Chrysler 300 gleaming, the Soviet sputnik ominously beeping, Bobby Darin belting his Vegas-ized version of the old Brecht-Weill tune, "Mack the Knife."

A few minutes later, a montage suggests everyone in New York tuning their vidscreens to watch Herb Stempel play for $3,000 a point on *Twenty-One*. This is scarcely an exaggeration. Once upon a time, there actually was a moment when America was transfixed by the idea of citizen intellectuals spinning the flax of their arcane knowledge into gold on the air.

By the spring of 1955, nearly a decade into the postwar era, the power of TV was amply apparent. After Disneyland's three-part series on the erstwhile King of the Wild Frontier created a near insatiable demand for Davy Crockett caps, the price of raccoon pelts rose from 25 cents to $6 a pound while other Crockett spin-offs, ranging from toy rifles and lunch boxes to baby shoes and ladies' panties, grossed a quick $300 million.

Looking for an appropriate televehicle with which to wage war on Hazel Bishop lipstick, then sponsor of the popular *This Is Your Life*, Revlon president Charles Revson and his brother Martin were sold on a venerable concept devised and updated by CBS producer Louis G. Cowan. *The $64,000 Question* was based on the old radio quiz shows of the 1940s, but television amplified the jackpot a thousandfold. Contestants would be brought back for several weeks to build up the stakes (which doubled with each correct answer), and even the losers would receive a consolation Cadillac.

On Tuesday night, June 7, 1955, the show "where knowledge is king and the reward is king size" made its debut. Nearly as impressive as the promised largesse was the mise-en-scène. Delivered with theatrical solemnity by a bank representative and two grim security guards, the questions and answers were deposited in an oversize safe that, years later, was revealed to be a cardboard stage prop. Once the quiz reached the $8,000 level, the set was darkened and the contestant placed in a glass "isolation booth." As the tension mounted and the winner agonized over whether to risk all in pursuit of the ultimate $64,000, the camera cut to close-ups of anxious family members sweating it out in the studio audience.

Suitably memorialized in *Back to the Future*, the summer of 1955 was marked by pop culture monuments. No sooner had the Crockett craze peaked than Disneyland itself opened. And as Bill Haley's prescient "Rock Around the Clock" held the Hit Parade's No. 1 spot throughout July and August, so *The $64,000 Question* proved the most dramatic success in the history of American TV. By August, the show had a weekly audience of 47 million—nearly one-third of the total population. CBS was flooded with 20,000 applications per week. Bookmakers quoted odds. Broadway shows were empty on Tuesday nights. Pharmacies had long since run out of Revlon Living Lipstick, and the company was reduced to promoting remaining stocks of its Touch and Glow Liquid Makeup Foundation.

Not since the Depression radio show *Amos 'n' Andy* had a broadcast so mobilized the American people; not until *Roots* would a single TV program command such rapt attention. *The $64,000 Question* was more than a hit, it was a phenomenon—an astounding 97 percent of the television sets in New York City tuned in for one program in October. People were naturally wondering what it meant. *Fortune* was struck by the "awesome" amount of "heavy thinking" that pundits devoted to a mere TV show: "Seemingly every financial writer in the U.S. has taken the program as a case study from which to explore the effect of taxation on higher income groups. In a six-part *New York Post* series on the show, Max Lerner observed portentously that its ability to make ordinary people into national figures overnight 'has far-reaching implications for politics and power.'"

*The $64,000 Question* was television as cornucopia. As the United States scaled the peak of postwar prosperity (there were a record 8 million new cars sold in 1955, as well as an unprecedented million and a half housing starts), the show materialized like a rapturous collective thought balloon to muse upon this astonishing abundance—as well as demonstrate upward mobility, illustrate the dogma of self-improvement, and testify to the hidden potential of the ordinary American.

Like the members of a Hollywood platoon, quiz show contestants represented a cross section of the body politic, albeit typically cast against type. The first stars included the marine with a taste for French cooking, the cop who loved Shakespeare, the Bronx cobbler rewarded with $32,000 for his amazing knowledge of Italian opera. Kids were also good. Baltimore junior high school student Gloria Lockerman not only won $16,000 for correctly spelling "the belligerent astigmatic anthropologist annihilated innumerable chrysanthemums," she was invited to address the 1956 Democratic National Convention. Eleven-year-old Patty Duke amassed $32,000 as an expert on singing groups. Air Force test pilot John Glenn first tasted celebrity teamed as a contestant with Eddie Hodges, child star of *The Music Man*.

*The $64,000 Challenge*, a quickly conceived sibling designed to further exploit the popularity of *The $64,000 Question's* newly minted winners, elevated incongruity to a ruling principle: Turned down as a contestant in her own field of psychology, 28-year-old Dr. Joyce Brothers reinvented herself as a boxing maven and made $132,000. *The $64,000 Challenge* was spangled with celebrities and eccentrics—including Xavier Cugat, Lillian Roth, and Larry Rivers. There were, of course, other winners. Louis Cowan parlayed the success of the *64s* into the network presidency. Revlon's revenues quintupled over two years. (At a January 1956 stockholders meeting, a representative of Hazel Bishop haplessly explained that the year's losses were "due to circumstances beyond our control.")

Cheap to produce and excellent for sponsor identification, the *64s* were cloned by all three networks: *Do You Trust Your Wife?* and *The Big Surprise, Dotto* and *High Low, Name That Tune* and *Nothing but the Truth, Can Do* and *Tic Tac Dough*. And then there was *Twenty-One*, the general-knowledge quiz with an unlimited jackpot. This was the program that, by making contestant Charles Van Doren a national figure and a lifelong recluse—first a supernova and then a black hole in the media universe—provided the subject for Redford's film.

At the height of the quiz craze in 1956, motivational research guru Ernest Dichter praised *The $64,000 Question* for showing that randomly selected Americans were often "remarkable individuals." Unfortunately for Dichter's thesis, the contestants had not only been carefully screened, it would eventually be revealed that—in a kind of Calvinist showbiz theocracy—the winners were preselected as well. The Revsons closely monitored their show's ratings, associating any slump with an unpopular champion; to manage the talent, the *64s* conducted extensive interviews determining the parameters of a contestant's knowledge and devised questions accordingly. This technique was subtle, however, compared to the coaching producer Dan Enright initiated with *Tic Tac Dough* and refined to an art on *Twenty-One*.

Like TV wrestling, *Twenty-One* presented contests between heroes and villains. Martin Revson immediately recognized that to do this, the show had to be rigged; everyone else just signed on. This was, after all, the moment of the revised American pantheon. The Cold War was in remission, the climate sufficiently temperate for new archetypes to sprout. By spring 1956, Elvis Presley was an axiom of TV variety shows. In the midst of "Heartbreak Hotel"'s two-month reign at No. 1, *Time* reported that this worrisome idol was "packing theaters, fighting off shrieking admirers, disturbing parents, puckering the brows of psychologists, and filling letters-to-the-editor columns with cries of alarm." By summer's end, the newsweekly informed its readers of a second "weird new phenomenon loose in the land; a teenage craze for a boyish Hollywood actor named James Dean, who has been dead for 11 months." It was then that *Twenty-One* made its debut, Wednesday, September 12, 1956, at 10:30 P.M. on NBC, sponsored by Geritol, "America's No. 1 tonic."

The basic Enright technique was to rehearse selected contestants with questions that would then be asked again on the air. The first designated winner was so dismayed by the practice that he quit the show. Then Enright, who dominates *Night and Her Stars* as a tele-Mephistopheles, found a more cooperative prospect: Herbert Stempel, a stocky 29-year-old know-it-all from deepest Queens, attending CCNY on the G.I. Bill. (The role was made for John Turturro, who, in *Quiz Show*, gives Stempel an additional manic edge.)

Enright cast Stempel as the working-class geek with total recall—Stempel was compelled to wear threadbare suits, submit to bad haircuts, and address the show's MC as "Mr. Barry." Demolishing all comers, he achieved a brief notoriety as the intellectual equivalent of proletarian sitcom zhlubs like Ralph Kramden or Chester A. Riley. But soon Enright and his associate producer Al Freedman were looking for a more attractive winner and, on December 4, in a show that NBC hyped with regular spot announcements wondering if this would be the night that Stempel broke $100,000, another star was born: Charles Van Doren.

The scion of a distinguished literary family, son and nephew of Pulitzer Prize winners, the 32-year-old Van Doren (played in *Quiz Show* by Ralph Fiennes) was making $4,400 a year as an English instructor at Columbia, the university where his poet father Mark also taught. Stempel versus Van Doren was a match made in heaven: the Troll versus the Golden Boy. It was the crass, working-class Jew against the elegant, patrician WASP, City College schlepper and Ivy League thoroughbred, an instant replay of the 1956 World Series in which the regal New York Yankees reasserted themselves over the upstart Brooklyn Bums.

The previous week, *Twenty-One* producers had arranged several exciting ties. Now, the unbeatable Stempel with his 170 IQ was scheduled to take a dive—instructed by Enright to identify *On the Waterfront*, rather than *Marty* (his favorite picture!), as the Oscar-winning best movie of 1955. As he left the set, cast back into nonentity for blowing a question that everybody knew, the unhappy loser thought he heard someone remark, "Now we have a clean-cut intellectual as champion instead of a freak with a sponge memory." It would not be long before Stempel, after futilely demanding a rematch, came back to blow the whistle—although at first no one cared. To this day, he remains obsessed with Charles Van Doren.

"There's no protagonist, much less a hero," points out scriptwriter Paul Attanasio, born a month after the scandal climaxed in 1959. In fact, *Quiz Show* has two heroes—Van Doren and congressional investigator Richard Goodwin (Rob Morrow), a bright fallen star and a duskier rising one. But Attanasio is correct in considering the project offbeat. "There's no violence, there's no car chase, there's no romance, there's no sex, there's no genre. In a genteel way, this is a very experimental movie." Certainly *Quiz Show* followed a torturous road to completion—in some respects recapitulating the narcissistic personalities, affable opportunism, and corporate cowardice that are the movie's subject.

When he published his memoirs in 1988, former Kennedy aide Goodwin strenuously promoted the chapter about his role as a congressional investigator into the quiz show scandals. (Goodwin, who has never been shy about amplifying his importance in the affair, appears as a minor character in *Night and Her Stars*.) Accruing additional producers at every stage—including Barry Levinson, who commissioned Attanasio's script—the project bounced from studio to studio. Redford got involved when *Quiz Show* was mired at TriStar. Passing through Paramount and Savoy, the project came to rest at Disney, which was developing a similar picture called *One for the Money*. Failing to persuade Redford to direct its script, the studio agreed to produce Attanasio's.

Centered on Stempel, *One for the Money* told the sentimental tale of a little guy who takes on the system. *Quiz Show* casts Stempel as one of three protagonists, along with Goodwin and Van Doren, but rather than dwell on his suffering and vindication (or even Goodwin's role as investigator), Redford's film raises an issue that can scarcely date: the conflict between established, if beleaguered, social values and an ascendent, supremely vulgar, popular culture.

Unafraid to portray class resentment, Redford employs a similarly unflinching ethnic schemata. With the exception of the Van Dorens, the major figures in *Quiz Show* are all Jews, sensitive to anti-Semitism and scrambling after their piece of the American Dream. It is the brilliantly suspicious Stempel who figures out that Enright has fixed it so that whenever a Jew is on *Twenty-One*, he loses to a Gentile who then goes on to win more money. The movie depicts Jewish as well as Gentile anti-Semitism. ("I've observed that condition in my business for a long time," says Redford.) Neither Goodwin nor Enright can bring himself to champion Stempel—as if both men fear that the crass and "pushy" CCNY student will bring further attention to their own ethnicity.

For Stempel and Goodwin, the privileged Van Doren is the epitome of dazzlingly white, Gentile America. If the humiliated Stempel longs to besmirch Van Doren, the upwardly mobile Goodwin yearns just as much to be accepted by him. It is the showbiz savant Enright, adept at meeting the needs of sponsors and the American public, who understands how to give Van Doren what he wants, and is thus able to corrupt him. As the movie (and the facts) suggest, there may have been no one who felt the yoke of WASP tradition embodied by Mark Van Doren more than his son, who at one point had fled to Paris to write a novel about . . . parricide.

During the 14 weeks that boyish, personable Charlie appeared on *Twenty-One*, the show became a smash—moving from Wednesday to Monday nights to challenge CBS's *I Love Lucy*. Geritol sales climbed. Van Doren got 2,000 fan letters a week, a total of 500 marriage proposals, and a promotion at Columbia, where students pasted up signs directing visitors to "the smartest man in the world." Had the professor sold out to TV or merely realized the medium's potential? The *64s* celebrated the average American. In Van Doren—who, by early February made *Time*'s cover as "TV's brightest new face"—*Twenty-One* produced an attractive young scholar to personify television's much-vaunted and equally abused mandate to educate the public.

As recently as 1953, popular historian Leo Gurko had written in *Heroes, Highbrows and the Popular Mind* that "to be suspected of learning or, what is worse, to display it publicly is to invite ridicule." But did the display of erudition invite ridicule or, more to the point, inspire the fear of ridicule? Gurko argued that professors were regarded as "fogies wrapped up in musty and useless books"—a stereotype telegraphed in *Quiz Show* by the polite boredom of the senior Van Doren's students. But in the popular mind, professors were also potentially dangerous, prone to be Jews and commies and queers, an affront to decency and common sense. Democratic candidate Adlai Stevenson's egghead reputation had precluded his being a man of the people, but the quiz shows successfully domesticated braininess—the *64s* locating it in "ordinary people," *Twenty-One* making it the province of an artfully shy, telegenically smiling WASP.

Thanks to television, highbrow trivia was worth Big Bucks, and thanks to Charlie Van Doren, intellectuals could be incorporated into the mass culture they were wont to critique. At the climax of a wittily observed birthday picnic at the Van Doren home in Connecticut, *Quiz Show*'s Charlie presents his father (played in grand fashion by Paul Scofield) with a humongous TV set. They were better and yet . . . they were no better.

For *Time*, Van Doren combined nothing less than "the universal erudition of a Renaissance man with the nerve and cunning of a riverboat gambler and the showmanship of the born actor. . . . Just by being himself, he has enabled a giveaway show, the crassest of lowbrow entertainments, to whip up a doting mass audience for a new type of TV idol—of all things, an egghead." *Time* noted that when Van Doren appeared as a guest on *The Steve Allen Show*, its rating topped that of the rival *Ed Sullivan Show*. "Oddly enough, Allen had beaten Sullivan only once before—when one of his guests was Elvis Presley." The analogy was out: "Many a grateful parent regards [Van Doren] as TV's own health-restoring antidote to Presley."

As a sneering Elvis enacted copulation, so Van Doren's "weekly torment of concentration" pantomimed cogitation. Coached by Al Freedman, Van Doren performed answers to the questions he had already received. Earphones clamped to head, he sweated and stuttered, rolled his eyes, knit his brow, bit his lip in an agony of concentration. *Time* was enchanted: "Breathing heavily, Charlie coaxes elusive answers out of odd corners of his brains by talking to himself, muttering little associated fragments of knowledge." And yet, even then, there was the suspicion that Van Doren's agony was an act, that he was playing with the audience. "Some viewers get the feeling that he knows most of the answers immediately and simply makes the audience squirm for the money he gets. But Charlie and those who know him best insist that it is actually his technique of ferreting out the answers."

"I remember watching Van Doren and, as a young actor, thinking, 'That's not a really great performance,'" says Redford. "But why didn't I doubt the show?"

---

Redford's notion of a great actor was no doubt closer to James Dean than Charles Van Doren (who was, it should be noted, a talented amateur thespian), but Van Doren was playing an equally existential drama. Increasingly uncomfortable as his fame spread and winnings mounted, he pleaded for release.

Finally, on March 12, 1957, with more than half the viewing public tuned in to watch their protracted battle, lawyer Vivienne Nearing beat the Smartest Man in the World, who left the show with the record sum of $129,000. (The next morning, *The $64,000 Question* announced that it was raising its jackpot to $256,000.) Stempel, who was smart enough to figure out that this was the show where Van Doren would take a dive, lightened his bookie by $10,000. But he was outraged to discover that while he would live out his life as a hapless loser, Van Doren remained a TV superstar—hired by NBC at an enormous $50,000 a year to bring a soupçon of high culture to the viewers of *Today*.

In a general sense, the quiz show story follows the trajectory of the fifties. The shows' heyday marks the 1955–57 period of abundance; their decline and eventual disgrace underscored the traumas that closed out the decade. (In *Quiz Show*, the chronology and thus the good times are necessarily compressed in such a way as to offer a suitably revisionist look at our official *Happy Days*.) A psychohistorian might date the recession of 1957–58 to September 4, 1957. The very same day that a jeering mob prevented nine black students from integrating Central High School in Little Rock, Arkansas, the Ford Motor Company unveiled its 1958 Edsel. Lured by months of publicity, 3 million potential customers mobbed Ford showrooms, but by the time events compelled an unwilling Eisenhower to send paratroopers into Little Rock, the Edsel had flopped—at a cost of $350 million.

As unemployment climbed to a postwar high, automobile sales fell to a decade low. Then, on October 4, with the spectacle of American soldiers occupying an American city still before the eyes of the world, the Soviets launched humankind's first artificial satellite—Sputnik! Within hours, politically ambitious Democratic senators were invoking Pearl Harbor, pointing at the sky and howling that the Free World faced extinction. To add to the national humiliation, the Russians orbited another sputnik a month later, this time with a canine passenger.

Rampant Edselitis! January 1958 polls showed that 82 percent of the electorate thought the country "behind" the Soviet Union and 61 percent were willing to "sacrifice" for stronger defense. (Elvis had just received his induction notice.) Worse, European public opinion revealed a weakened confidence in American know-how and the NATO alliance. Meanwhile, former quiz show contestant Reverend Charles Jackson—a Tennessee minister whose category had been "Great Love Stories"—was telling *Time*, the *New York Times*, and the *Nashville Tennessean* that *The $64,000 Challenge* was fixed.

In March, another contestant on *The $64,000 Challenge* discovered that his opponent was given "warm-up questions" that were somehow re-asked on the show. The program's representatives assured him that it was inexplicable coincidence. That spring, amid the negative publicity surrounding Vice President Nixon's nightmare tour of Latin America (he was spat upon and his car was stoned in Caracas), a standby contestant on *Dotto*—the highest-rated daytime show, soon to go prime time—came across a notebook wherein the current champion, Marie Winn, had jotted down answers to the very questions she was even then being posed on the air. Winn disappeared from the show (having subsequently seen the light, she reappeared in 1985 as an expert on the baleful influence of TV with her bestseller, *The Plug-In Drug*). Her standby was given a $2,666 payoff in an inept cover-up that led sponsor and network to hastily cancel the program.

▬▬▬▬

The *Dotto* debacle lit the fuse. In August, New York D.A. Frank Hogan began investigating, and Herb Stempel reappeared to repudiate his earlier repudiation of his original charges that *Twenty-One* was fixed—an allegation denied, on the air, by Van Doren, then summer host of *Today*. That fall, as the novel *The Ugly American* climbed the bestseller lists, NBC dropped *Twenty-One* and CBS canceled the *64s*. Throughout the first half of 1959, Van Doren and other former contestants, as well as their handlers, perjured themselves before a New York grand jury.

Perjury was the crime—not participating in the fix. Most contestants chose to break the law rather than admit that they were less than they seemed. But because, in a virtually unprecedented decision that has never been adequately explained, Judge Mitchell D. Schweitzer sealed the findings, the scandal would not climax until the following autumn.

It was at this point that Goodwin, then an ambitious young lawyer attached to the House Special Subcommittee on Legislative Oversight, entered the picture. In his memoirs, he describes how, amazed by Schweitzer's actions, he persuaded the subcommittee to continue the probe and was sent to New York to interview the protagonists.

Asked why he thought Schweitzer had sealed the presentment, Redford flashes the sly grin of a man whose investigative reporting had brought down a president . . . at least in our celluloid dream life: "The real question is whether the network was implicated. NBC managed to engineer things in such a way that it was never culpable." (Schweitzer resigned from the bench in 1972— charged with judicial misconduct and conspiracy to obstruct justice in his apparent leniency with known mob figures.)

When the House hearings commenced on October 6, 1959, star witness Stempel was anxious to see his nemesis testify. But Goodwin, who admired Van Doren, persuaded the subcommittee to omit Van Doren's name from the list of witnesses—until the professor sealed his fate by sending a telegram to the subcommittee that insisted on his innocence. Once subpoenaed, Van Doren admitted what was, at last, obvious: he had been given questions and otherwise coached by the producers of *Twenty-One*.

Treated with extraordinary sympathy by the subcommittee (a scene Redford stages with hyperrealist clarity), Van Doren was fired first from Columbia and then from the *Today* show. (Along with 17 other contestants, he would eventually receive a suspended sentence for second-degree perjury.) Networks blamed producers, producers blamed sponsors. Louis Cowan was forced to resign as CBS president, and the network even briefly banned the deceptive practice of canned laughter. Barry and Enright were banished from TV for more than a decade.

Not all quiz shows were fixed and, even on those that were, not all participants were coached. The process even produced some lasting winners. Revlon decisively beat Hazel Bishop. Mike Wallace survived his stint cohosting *The Big Surprise* with a chimp named Zippy. Dr. Joyce Brothers not only won $132,000 but went on to become a regular on Johnny Carson's *Tonight Show* (and Johnny himself got his break as the host of *Whom Do You Trust?*). In the movie, it's the Geritol mogul played by Martin Scorsese who has the last word. The shows will be back, he assures Goodwin, with "easier questions."

Like TV itself, the quiz show scandal was cataclysmic and trivial: In 1987, when Ronald Reagan still hosted the national media spectacle, cover stories in *Time* and *Newsweek* made light of the public dismay that greeted the exposure of the fraud. Reporting on "America's Newest Obsession," the success of *Wheel of Fortune, Jeopardy, The $100,000 Pyramid*, and 30 other game shows, *Newsweek* noted that "from the perspective of a more cynical, or at least less gullible age, the reaction to the quiz shenanigans seems almost quaintly overwrought."

Vanna White, the star of our own mid-eighties quiz show revival, was distinguished from Charles Van Doren for not only being safely supply-side but also publicly mute. Still, in reacting some months later to the crisis in ethics precipitated by the near simultaneous falls of Ivan Boesky, Jim Bakker, and Gary Hart, *Time* echoed the era's sleaziness. Forgetting the consternation of the American people, the newsweekly suavely blamed the victim in rewriting the past to recall that "intellectuals reacted to the TV-show scandals with an outrage that now seems comically disproportionate to the offense."

───────

Whether public response now seems ridiculous or prescient, the quiz shows involved a national suspension of disbelief—and hardly for the last time. Not the least remarkable aspect of the affair is the amount of time the pretense that the shows were honest was maintained, particularly in view of the numerous citizens involved in the charade. As early as April 1957, around the time Stempel made and recanted charges of fraud, *Time* began a story on the shows by asking if they were "rigged," going on to report that "even the chitchat between contestant and quizmaster on *Twenty-One* and *The $64,000 Question* is composed and drilled in advance," and further remarking on the coincidence that "most big winners have been blessed by crucial questions right up their alleys." But then *Time* backed off, concluding that something like Van Doren's defeat could scarcely have been desired.

Even more explicitly, a *New York Times Magazine* piece appearing in the midst of the 1957–58 season observed that if TV dramas always end the way they should, why not quiz shows? "How long would wrestling have lasted on television without scripts? By the time a man [*sic*] works his way up to the $64,000 question, the viewer wants him to answer it as surely as he wants the Sheriff to outdraw the heavy. The fact is, of fourteen contestants who have gone for the $64,000 question, only two have missed."

Allowing both *64* producer Steve Carlin and *Twenty-One*'s Dan Enright to "wearily deny" that they ever know enough about the shape of a contestant's mind to tailor the questions, the *Times* concluded that "despite diligent research, nobody has yet turned up evidence that the fix is in on any of the big money quizzes." But then, nobody wanted to. The movie and broadcast industries had only recently undergone a massive purge of com-symp subversives and un-American intellectuals. Wasn't the public now getting what it had wished?

With "some heat," Carlin told the *Times*, "Some people have said our contestants are too good to be true. Well, the typical American has many facets, and those who doubt it show little faith in the American way." Carlin was stating the truth. The business of America is show business and rigging the shows was business as usual. Particularly on TV, where commercial imperatives are indistinguishable from the principles of dramaturgy, the plot had to be regulated through strategic pauses and interest built up with exciting ties. Some saw the fix as a betrayal of television's vaunted spontaneity or an exploitation of the medium's spurious sense of intimacy. But more than dramatizing TV's potential for deception, the scandal exposed the nature of televisual rhetoric: Was TV primarily a source of information or entertainment? Could the two even be distinguished?

From then on, the United States would be ruled by central casting. Emerging in the aftermath of Adlai Stevenson's crushing defeat, Van Doren was the egghead as Elvis. In his history of the fifties, David Halberstam logically suggests that Van Doren's replacement as a TV star was the similarly "young, attractive, upper-class, and diffident" Senator John F. Kennedy. Even then, however, observers recognized that the quiz show premise lived on. Daniel Boorstin's *The Image*, published a year into the Kennedy administration, remarked upon "the application of the quiz show format to the so-called 'Great

Debates'" between candidates Kennedy and Nixon. (Of course, if Boorstin had been up on his quiz show trivia, he would have recognized that Nixon had cast himself as the hapless Stempel to Kennedy's coolly poised Van Doren.)

Like all great media spectacles, the quiz show scandal is a text. A clever novelist might have humiliated Herb Stempel by contriving to have him deliberately miss the question on *Marty*—particularly as it would be clear to every TV viewer in America that Stempel himself was alter ego to the homely Bronx butcher. But only a genius would have instructed Stempel to give as his wrong answer *On the Waterfront*—a movie whose most famous scene is an account of an ex-boxer's lament for taking a "one-way ticket to Palookaville" by throwing a fight. No one knew better than Herbert Stempel, who went on to spend years teaching social studies in the New York City public schools, that he coulda been a contender.

Like most of us, Redford filters history through himself. For him, the quiz show scandal represented "the earliest sign of what has been an ongoing struggle between capitalism and ethics." Typically, he traces his awareness of class distinction and anti-Semitism to his experiences as a second-grader in a Santa Monica school populated by the children of the rich and their servants. He segues from that to a mention of his father, a CPA who moonlighted as a milkman during the Depression but achieved a measure of prosperity working for Esso during the war.

Redford's worldview is tinged with alienation—the sense that he could (and *should*) pass for normal. "I grew up in that kind of privileged place although I wasn't of that privileged set. I grew up looking like one of those people, but not really being one. I saw how they were perceived . . . and I found it offensive." As refined over his career, the Redford persona is that of the cynical idealist whose sense of mischief belies a sober social conscience. A professional Man of the West who has spent much of his life living, with remarkable invisibility, in New York, he's a prim hipster, intellectual jock, a serious joker, the star who directs ordinary people but understands the appeal of the rancid golden boy. He refers to *Quiz Show* as "the fall from grace." (In *Night and Her Stars*, the "defeated" Van Doren asks Enright if "we only recognize grace once we've fallen from it.")

Redford has enacted versions of both Van Doren and Goodwin. With which man does he identify? Is it even a question? Taking Goodwin's attraction as a given, Redford says he's fascinated by Van Doren's perversity—the "dance" between beautiful culprit and ardent investigator, the degree to which Van Doren plays Raskolnikov to Goodwin's Petrovich: "Van Doren brings Goodwin in and then he deflects him. He never answers Goodwin's question. He never says, 'I did it,' or, 'I didn't get the answers.' He only asks, 'Do you really think I'd do something like that?'"

Ralph Fiennes reconnoitered Van Doren's Connecticut home, but Redford made no attempt to contact the now 71-year-old recluse. Having retreated out of camera range to work for *The Encyclopedia Britannica* and edit worthy literary anthologies, Van Doren has done penance through a kind of middlebrow intellectual public service, yet is still so traumatized that he cannot tour to promote his own books. In any case, Redford says tartly, "the other two"—Goodwin and Stempel, still wanting in!—"were so busy climbing all over you they left teeth marks." The lust for fame is something that Redford experiences only from the other side.

Attanasio suggests that the reason it took Redford so long to cast Van Doren was because he himself "could do every line of it." Van Doren's anguished confession speech actually uses the same phrase with which Redford's character, the 24 karat Hubbell Gardener, begins his short story in *The Way We Were*: "Everything came too easily." As did Bill McCoy in *The Candidate* and Robert Redford in real life, Van Doren experienced the horror of celebrity—his privacy invaded by the little people. The sense of America as an audience is made grotesquely explicit in the final shot of the chortling quiz show audience, which effectively turns the screen into a mirror.

No less than Van Doren, Redford has had to wonder if he was a fraud. Asked if he has imagined Charles Van Doren's emotions at having to relive his youthful crime, Redford concedes that Van Doren "may have mixed feelings about being exposed again, but I like to think that he gets more than fair treatment." Attanasio agrees, pointing out that the movie suggests Van Doren falling into corruption more reluctantly than he may actually have done.

■■■■■■■■■■■■■■■■■■

Van Doren is the least-developed major character in *Night and Her Stars*, but he is a veritable psychic battlefield in *Quiz Show*. Redford reworked Attanasio's script to put the relationship between the Van Dorens, father and son, at his movie's center. Charlie's inability to live up to his father's expectations is matched by Mark's failure to grasp what exactly is happening to his son. The burden of being a Van Doren is equaled by the shame that Charlie brings upon his family. The casual infantilization of the son, sneaking a nocturnal wedge of chocolate cake and washing it down with milk slugged from the bottle, sets the table for the ultimate expression of patriarchal anguish. "Your name is mine," the elder Van Doren thunders when he is at long last compelled to see the nature of Charlie's deception.

The Van Dorens resemble the tragic WASP families of *Ordinary People* and *A River Runs Through It*, not in the depth of their catastrophe (no one dies, although Redford maintains that "there is incredible violence in this picture—there is murder of the soul"), but for their world historic role. Some ideal of intellect and knowledge is consumed before our eyes. An infinite capacity for co-option shimmers in the haze. What's more, everyone—with the exception of Herb Stempel (who, in the eclipse of *One for the Money* by *Quiz Show*, has lost to Van Doren yet again)—has a stake in Van Doren being what he appeared to be.

Why should Redford care? "We really didn't want him to be guilty," says the sometime movie star. "We really do have a need for heroes at almost any cost."

## NIXON

Originally published as "Bugging Out," the *Village Voice* (December 26, 1995).

H E MAY BE JUST A HOMELY LITTLE FACE ON A POSTAGE STAMP, BUT AS CANDIDATE Bob Dole last year eulogized our 37th president: "The second half of the twentieth century will be known as the Age of Nixon." Now, thanks to Oliver Stone's *Nixon*, we may climax that epoch in the second half of December 1995.

Attempting to make sense of Nixon's rise and fall and rise and fall and current rise, the long and winding road from Whittier to Watergate to Eternity, Stone has clearly bitten off more than he can swallow. And yet, however the director may quote the New Testament, cite Shakespeare, and genuflect toward *Citizen Kane*, his cautiously self-described "dramatic interpretation," with Sir Anthony Hopkins miscast in the title role, arrives so thoroughly chewed over in the media, it already seems regurgitated.

Something less than a total rehab job, *Nixon* finds Stone chastened but still in *JFK* mode. The movie is markedly more "responsible" than his last presidential election year extravaganza, albeit a kindred chronology-jumbled, all-format mix and match. Hopkins is repeatedly gumped into historical events—facing off against the actual Kennedy in the 1960 TV debate, for instance—but the nudging visual interpolations are here more restrained. There will never be a *Nation* symposium on this three-hour morass. Unlike *JFK*, *Nixon* is more often turgid than flashy, explicitly devoted to the reality principle. "When they look at you, they see what they want to be," Stone's Nixon tells a JFK portrait late in the movie. "When they look at me, they see what they are."

Satisfying as it is to at last have Nixon as a Disney character, Hopkins' overheated, self-consciously self-conscious performance doesn't get the overall nuttiness of Nixon's unctuous rage, his failed regular guy–ness, his sonorous gloom, his vicious opportunism, his iron-butt single-mindedness. Nixon's blatant, cheesy neuroses have provided juicy fodder for a variety of actors—Jason Robards, Jr., in the 1977 miniseries *Washington: Behind Closed Doors*, Rip Torn in the 1979 miniseries *Blind Ambition*, Philip Baker Hall in Robert Altman's 1984 *Secret Honor*, Lane Smith in the 1989 *The Final Days*. Not here. Hopkins swills Scotch and curses, maladroitly pulls the doorknob off a door and repeatedly twitches into a mirthless public smile—his performance is an inorganic checklist of "Nixonian" traits. Hopkins is having less fun than even the real Nixon. When he perfectly reproduces the demented free association of Nixon's farewell address, he's upstaged by Stone's decision to show a bit of the actual thing on tape.

Given his penchant for inadvertent exposure, Nixon was made for psychohistory. It's a pity that Warren Beatty turned down the role, particularly since Stone pegs Nixon as terminally unloved. The movie's most painful sequences are the black-and-white flashbacks to the grim Nixon childhood—working with his brothers in the family gas-pump grocery, in thrall to his severely "saintly" Quaker mother (Mary Steenburgen). She's reincarnated in the movie in the person of Nixon's wife Pat (Joan Allen), a near perfect simulacrum who shows up every once in a while to reintroduce the notion of the psychosexual and provoke her husband's displeasure: "Brezhnev is coming in three days—I don't want to deal with him and them and you!"

Oliver Stone, it's well known, can't make a movie without finding himself in it. No less than Nixon, the filmmaker must feel himself underappreciated, if not persecuted. Stone is no stranger to truculent self-pity; Nixon, moreover, may be the only American politician whose paranoia matches his own. In the Stone schemata, E. Howard Hunt, the former CIA op turned spy novelist and Watergate burglar, signifies conspiracy. "I know what he is and what he tracks back to," Nixon mumbles in the course of the famous missing 18 minutes on the June 20, 1972, White House tape.

The erased conversation is, as Stone suggested in *Newsweek*'s cover story, Nixon's "rosebud"—Nixon's fear that the murder of JFK was blowback from the CIA-Mafia plot to kill Castro that, according to Stone, Nixon helped organize. This of course somewhat contradicts the premise of *JFK* but, seizing upon the coincidence (coincidence?) that brought Nixon to Dallas on the eve of the Kennedy assassination, Stone introduces Larry Hagman as a kind of politically minded J. R. Ewing and takes the opportunity to reprise Dealy Plaza—this time superimposing some sort of God brooding over the sky.

*Nixon* is basically conceived as its subject's slow-motion assassination. Thus, Nixon's legendary post–Kent State, 4 A.M. visit to the young protestors camped out at the Lincoln Memorial is less an instance of stunted, perhaps alcohol-sodden sentimentality (surrounded by bewildered students, the president droned on about football and Neville Chamberlain, unable to make eye contact with anyone) than the mystical moment when he receives the revelation of what Stone calls "the Beast." One coed realizes that, much as Nixon may want peace, the System won't let him stop the Vietnam War.

Nixon, per Stone, regards his greatest triumph as having extricated the United States from Vietnam without precipitating a right-wing revolt. What the movie more usefully hints is that Nixon's opening to China, his Soviet détente, and "peace with honor" Vietnam settlement, were all founded on a demonstrable capacity for mass murder. Stone makes much of the *Macbeth* or *Richard III* notion of Nixon advancing to power "over the bodies" of the fallen Kennedys but rather less of Nixon's role in the slaughter of hundreds of thousands of Vietnamese and Cambodians. While the movie's most effective bit of business has Nixon talking mad bomber as his too-rare steak starts bleeding all over his plate, Stone is hardly immune to the realpolitik scenarios invariably used to justify Nixon's foreign policy.

Sub-Carlyle hero-worshiping romantic that he is, Stone ultimately buys Nixon's Great Man self-explanation, although, of course, in that he's not alone. Played for maximum, sepulchrally croaking buffoonery by Paul Sorvino, Henry Kissinger is the movie's biggest kiss-ass until the real Bill Clinton enlivens the interminable final credits to deliver a mealymouthed eulogy at the real Nixon's funeral.

This may be Stone's final trip to the sixties, and he can scarcely bear to let the movie end. In a final *Citizen Kane* flourish, Stone reintroduces his cast. The pomposity factor is raised by his choice of the Mormon Tabernacle Choir's "Shenandoah" for the walkout music. If *JFK* was scurrilous hero worship, *Nixon* is uplifting whitewash. To achieve the full Shakespearean grandeur, Stone really should be showing a pile of corpses.

## GET ON THE BUS

Originally published as "Journeying Men," the *Village Voice*
(October 22, 1996).

**W**AS THE MILLION MAN MARCH OF OCTOBER 1995 A HISTORICAL TURNING POINT— a genuinely populist, constructively positive expression of racial identity? Or was it a brilliantly promoted hustle—a belated 1980s feel-good pseudo-event like Hands Across America or the Conquest of Grenada—at which, as Adolph Reed put it in the *Village Voice*, for the first time in history, "people gathered to protest themselves"?

Opening to coincide with the happening's first anniversary, Spike Lee's *Get on the Bus* burnishes the director's status as topical showman and political mythmaker. As *Malcolm X* helped compensate for the eclipse of Jesse Jackson in 1992, so, in this presidential election year, *Get on the Bus* resurrects the chimera of collective action or, at least, guerrilla filmmaking, in part by offering itself (independently financed by 15 African American men) as proof that the march was not in vain.

Lee, who has rarely shot a boring scene, has his usual head full of ideas and knack for juggling contradictory images as, directing from Reggie Rock Bythewood's script, he tracks the cross-country odyssey of a charter busload of black men from South Central L.A. to Washington, D.C. No less than last spring's wacky *Girl 6, Get on the Bus* is a roots trip. Shot (often handheld) on Super-16 in three weeks for only $2.4 million, the movie is loose, light, and jaunty—a prolonged rap session punctuated by Terence Blanchard's trademark doodling. On the one hand, Lee frequently recaptures the edgy agitprop of *Jungle Fever* and *Do the Right Thing*. On the other, this is a movie in which everything gets aired but not much sticks.

A programatically diverse group in terms of religious affiliation, class origin, and sexual orientation, the bus mates include the biracial cop Gary (Roger Guenveur Smith), the beatific reformed gangbanger Jamal (Gabriel Casseus, who smiled his way through *New Jersey Drive*), the self-important actor Flip (André Braugher), a gung-ho student filmmaker immediately dubbed "Spike Lee Junior" (Hill Harper), and the salt-of-the-earth driver George (Charles Dutton). At core a melancholy meditation on fatherhood, the movie gives greatest weight to two failures looking for redemption—dour and pitted Evan (Thomas Jefferson Byrd), who comes aboard with his long-abandoned teenage son chained to his waist, and old and grizzled Jeremiah (Ossie Davis), who rips off his hospital bracelet as he climbs on to lead the guys in an inspirational prayer.

The ensemble premise creates numerous opportunities—not the least for a spontaneous roll call–and–response demonstrating Lee's fondness for interpolated musical numbers. Still, the performances are often more credible than the characters: Isaiah Washington, for example, triumphing over the theoretical notion of an ex-marine Log Cabin Republican with beard, single earring, and dreadlocks. As Jamal compares his first gang killing to a bar mitzvah, so Lee and Bythewood use the movie didactically to define and explore different notions of black manhood.

Although the bus offers a number of binary pairings, black maleness is also defined against various straw persons, beginning with the irate objections of Gary's inordinately petulant buppy girlfriend. As in the march itself, the gender dialectic is a bit underdeveloped: would that the bus had stopped off at a mall to critique *Girl 6*. In the most startling example of gender ambivalence (as well as racial essentialism), the guys wax nostalgic for the mother-administered childhood whippings that one character, having been born of a white woman, never received.

Conspiracy crackpot Lyndon LaRouche may have put in an appearance at Farrakhan's last conclave, but white characters are here kept to a minimum. Randy Quaid cameos as a jovially malevolent Tennessee state trooper, while Richard Belzer has a more substantial role as a relief driver named Rick. We know Rick's riding for a fall when he announces that he is "color blind." Seconds later, he's citing his parents' civil rights credentials and, having identified himself as a Jew, invoking the Holocaust.

According to the movie's press kit, Belzer first learned of his role when the director phoned him at home: "Spike started reading my lines to me and laughing." Funny is as funny does. By the time the bus reaches Memphis, Rick has revealed himself to be a closet racist and, ranting about O. J. and Farrakhan, bails out, leaving the disgusted Charles to cover for him. (Given the aggrieved anti-Jewish jibes that find their way into Lee's films, I wish he'd adapt *The Merchant of Venice* as a musical and get it out of his system.)

Rick's fears notwithstanding, when the movie arrives in D.C., Farrakhan—unlike, say, Maya Angelou—is nowhere to be seen. The minister's absence is all the more intriguing in view of the ensemble's refusal to interact with their most enigmatic co-passenger. Throughout the movie, a bow-tied Nation of Islam member can be seen sitting impassively with them on the bus. Adding to the mystery, the actor has neither lines nor a credit—was he dispatched to the set as an NOI observer or included as a form of semiotic tokenism?

If you know your *Midnight Cowboy*, *On the Bus*'s mournful ending won't be much of a surprise. Less expected is the nod to *Network* added to the movie's nonconclusion: "We're tired of this shit and we ain't gonna take it!" Was that what the march was about? By the time the men bow their heads in the Lincoln Memorial (!), asking not for a handout (!!) but a job and a second chance (!!!), you realize that, no less than Belzer's perfidious Hollywood Jew, Lee has jumped off the bus as well.

## UNDERGROUND

Originally published as "Lost Worlds," the
*Village Voice* (June 24, 1997).

THE DRINKING, DANCING, SCHEMING ANTIHEROES OF EMIR KUSTURICA'S *Underground* are the ultimate wild and crazy Balkan party animals—they're jerked through History's convulsions as if by some hyperactive cosmic puppeteer. This extravagant, controversial movie—sniffed at and passed on by several American distributors—is a bravura succession of bitter japes, not least the use of two heedless, indestructible blockheads to lament the dissolution of a nation.

*Underground* won the Palme d'Or at the 1995 Cannes Film Festival and (as chronicled in the *New Yorker*, the *Voice*, and elsewhere) was immediately thereafter subject to a full-scale Parisian contretemps as, per philosopher Alain Finkielkraut, "a rock, postmodern, over-the-top, hip, Americanized version of the most drivelling and lying Serbian propaganda." Now, thanks to Anthology Film Archives and New Yorker Films, local intellectuals can have their opportunity to denounce Kusturica—or not. Is it cinephilia or political sin? The passions of the early nineties already may be more passé than Yugoslavia itself.

*Underground*'s Serbian title could be translated as *Once upon a Time There Was a Country;* "catastrophe!" is the recurring exclamation. Kusturica, a nominally Muslim native of Sarajevo and hence the newly established Bosnia's best-known artist, was effectively stateless when he made *Underground*—as well as without effective political cover, being a public supporter of the no-longer-viable Yugoslav federation. Reviled as a traitor in his hometown, the filmmaker invoked the first several years after Josip Broz Tito's death, corresponding to the early phase of his career, as a golden era. "Great movies. Beautiful novels. Great rock-and-roll. We became a superpower in basketball."

This may be the closest Kusturica will come to greatness. Outraged and outrageous, fueled by a host of comic performances and the mournful frenzy of Goran Bregovic's infectious brass score, *Underground* opens with a band charging through the outskirts of Belgrade—the fantastic succession of falling-down drunken antics celebrating the induction of two petty black marketeers into the Communist Party and previewing the grotesque spectacle to come. Part gypsy saber dance, part sped-up Fellini film, *Underground* is a would-be national allegory, aspiring to the class of magic realist novels like *The Tin Drum* and *Midnight's Children*.

World War II is staged as a series of bloody pratfalls. Set free by a German bombing raid, Belgrade's zoo animals wander off through the rubble of collapsed buildings. Throughout the Nazi occupation, the bluff and hearty Blacky (Lazar Ristovski), his hawk-nosed, sad-eyed, duplicitous blood brother Marko (Miki Manojlovic, eponymous star of Kusturica's other Cannes laureate, *When Father Was Away on Business*), and a clueless German officer all vie for the affections of the actress Natalija (Mirjana Jokovic, as supple and rubber-faced as her character is opportunistic). The rondo of romantic betrayals climaxes with Blacky's onstage abduction of the actress and is supplemented by his and Marko's no less madcap commando raids.

Jumping ahead to the early sixties, *Underground*'s middle section is a convoluted allegory suggesting that Tito's Yugoslavia was dependent on preserving the memory of World War II while keeping the population in a condition of mobilized ignorance. The authorities unveil a statue of the partisan martyr Blacky even while he remains alive in the basement (giving the movie its English title), persuaded by Marko that the war wages on, still producing arms to defeat the Germans. In the midst of this, Kusturica stages a subterranean wedding party—the longest, funniest, most apocalyptic thing of its kind since the Russian Orthodox nuptials that kicked off Michael Cimino's similarly reviled (but far less accomplished) *Deer Hunter*.

To further complicate an already exhausting narrative—and, in a way, parallel Kusturica's gumping his characters into wartime newsreels of Tito's victory parade—*Underground*'s first third is reprised, after a fashion, by the ridiculously heroic film that is being shot about Marko and Blacky's wartime exploits. (When Blacky finally leaves his shelter, he inevitably emerges onto the movie set to mistake it for the climactic battle against the fascists.) A final section has the ageless characters enthusiastically playing their gangster roles on opposing sides of the post-Yugoslavia civil wars. The St. Vitus dance continues. To complete the bloody farce, the galvanized corpses have one last celebration even as their little piece of heaven splits off and floats into oblivion.

A nearly sustained marvel of convoluted takes and choreographed energy that never once loses its sardonic brio, *Underground* is truly maniacal. This is the sort of movie in which characters break bottles of slivovitz over their heads. The oompah rhythms could drive even the members of the New York Institute for the Humanities to do the Zorba, critiquing Kusturica while pounding on the closest seat. Perhaps it's this tone that put off the French. Finkielkraut, who launched his first attack on the movie without even having seen it, would complain to the *New Yorker* of "all that terrible Slav sentimentality that I hate—all these weddings and drunken embraces, spilling over into the love of violence." The movie may look like a wedding, but it's more like a wake. Indeed, *Underground*'s vision of Slavs at their most Yugo is a merciless satire of volkish bombast, about as sentimental as a Roadrunner cartoon.

Kusturica responded to the debate over *Underground* by publicly renouncing filmmaking. At last report, however, he is said to be at work on a new movie. Good news to be sure, although I daresay he would have to lose a second homeland to have the rage to ever again let loose so ferocious a howl.

## POINT OF ORDER

H EGEL SAW THE RITUAL READING OF THE DAILY NEWSPAPER AS THE SECULAR
equivalent of morning prayer. If so, the great televised Media Events that
periodically transfix the nation must be something akin to religious festivals.

Less exalted than the new form of collective expression developed in ancient
Athens, Media Events—watched and parsed by millions simultaneously—are
equally dramatic. Whether the subject is a presidential cover-up or a trial for
double murder, these spectacular narratives are alike in certain key elements:
Powerful stars crash and burn while supporting players (even members of the
chorus) become new-minted celebrities; phrases are turned and buzz words
introduced. Afterwards, the images will be recycled and refracted through
ancillary deals until the debris-littered national landscape suggests a New
Orleans street on the day after Mardi Gras.

Such ghosts of Media Events past haunt *Point of Order*—the 1964 documentary assembled by Daniel Talbot and the late Emile De Antonio from TV
footage of the 1954 Army-McCarthy Hearings. Opening Friday for a two-week
revival at Film Forum, *Point of Order* is a portrait of the first American politician
to achieve full media symbiosis. Senator Joseph R. McCarthy of Wisconsin, the
flamboyant hunter of Communists, real and imaginary, built a career on events
created to be reported. McCarthy's means were less photo ops and sound-bites
than tabloid headlines and wire-service bulletins, but long before the term
"news cycle" existed, he knew how to manage it: As Richard Rovere wrote in his
book, *Senator Joe McCarthy*, McCarthy "invented the morning press conference
called for the purpose of announcing an afternoon press conference."

While televised hearings had made a national figure of Senator Estes
Kefauver in 1951, the same format would destroy McCarthy. His problems
began with the 1953 inauguration of Dwight D. Eisenhower and the installation
of the Republican administration the Wisconsin senator had helped elect.
Having rocketed to fame by denouncing Democratic "treason," McCarthy was
disinclined to abandon the issue. He used his chairmanship of the new
Permanent Subcommittee on Investigations to probe Communist infiltration of
the Voice of America, the International Information Administration, and finally,
in a direct challenge to the former general now President, the army itself.

But the military was not without its own resources. March 11, 1954 (two
days after CBS fired a shot across the Senator's bow with Edward R. Murrow's
critical report on *See It Now*), the Department of the Army released documents
chronicling the attempts made by McCarthy's aide Roy Cohn to obtain special

treatment for the newly-drafted Private G. David Schine, the Subcommittee's erstwhile "chief consultant." McCarthy responded with charges that the army had attempted to forestall further investigation, by taking Schine hostage. The Senate authorized televised hearings to begin on April 22.

Media interest was not a given. CBS passed on the telecast; NBC dropped out after two days. The full hearings were carried by ABC, a network then so weak it had no daytime schedule to preempt. This gamble proved to be a brilliant coup. Public response was enormous. As the hearings built to a climax in June, CBS and NBC affiliates dumped their afternoon soaps to pick up the ABC feed while the Gallup Poll reported that an astounding 89% of adult Americans were following the show. On some afternoons, the audience was estimated at 20 million. Among them was Talbot, then an unemployed writer living in Queens. "I was hooked," he recalls. "I watched every second. I was totally apolitical but this was a fascinating piece of Americana. I read McCarthy as a kind of W.C. Fields character selling snake oil."

Six years later, when he had become the owner of the New Yorker theater, Talbot wondered whether it would be possible to present excerpts from the Army-McCarthy kinescopes at his West Side revival house, perhaps charging viewers a dollar an hour. He joined forces with De Antonio, then an artists' agent, raising $100,000 to secure the rights to all 188 hours of televised footage. Although, according to Talbot, "neither of us had ever seen a movieola before," the partners spent three years distilling the material to 97 strictly chronological minutes.

*Point of Order*, named for McCarthy's frequently employed interjection, remains a remarkable chamber drama. As in *A Midsummer Night's Dream*, the narrative motor is the abduction of a princeling; Schine was the scion of a wealthy hotel family. Here too, confusion is rife. As *The New Republic*'s Michael Straight wrote in his 1954 account of the hearings, *Trial by Television*, McCarthy "understood that the investigation was not a court proceeding, where order would reign and rules of evidence would prevail, but a vast, disorderly drama whose plot would be shaped and whose end would be written by the actors possessing enough power to take command of the stage."

Who is investigating whom? Generals, cabinet officers, senators, even lawyers are placed under oath. Senator Karl Mundt becomes the Subcommittee's temporary chairman. The chaos produces a series of one-on-one confrontations, predicated less on rational discourse than on volume, quips, and personality. The inquiry meanders from Schine to alleged Communist (and homosexual) infiltration of the armed forces, the question of McCarthy's sources, and finally, in a stunning non sequitur, the political associations of a young lawyer who is not part of the hearings but a junior partner in the firm of the army counsel Joseph N. Welch.

McCarthy is playing to something larger than the Committee or even the Senate. The television audience, he says more than once, is "the jury in this case." That the spectacle is being produced for the camera is underscored by the various debates on the quality of color-coded charts and photographic evidence. The crudeness of the TV image only serves to render the antagonists more iconic. But, although appreciated by his fans as a sort of roughneck Mr. Smith gone to Washington to purge the Communists, McCarthy's sepulchral urgency and mirthless laugh proved perversely untelegenic. (So too his five o'clock shadow, despite the "cream-colored make-up" noted by Straight.)

It was the prim and puckish Joseph Welch, a skilled trial lawyer (as well as a lifelong Republican), who blossomed under the lights. The army counsel also badgered witnesses—alluding even to Cohn's rumored homosexuality—but where McCarthy specialized in menace, Welch proved a master of deflationary humor. Although the frustrated Senator attacked his nemesis as "an actor" who "plays for laughs," the Army counsel could also take the high moral ground.

The hearings and *Point of Order* climax when, exasperated by Welch's cross-examination of Cohn (and over Cohn's silently-mouthed objections), McCarthy exposes Welch's partner Fred Fisher as a former member of the leftwing Lawyer's Guild. This gratuitous guilt by association exposed McCarthy himself to Welch's withering scorn: "Have you no sense of decency, Sir? At long last, have you left no sense of decency?" Welch exclaims to a round of spontaneous applause. *Variety* subsequently hailed him as "one of the great performers ever to appear on the small screen" and Otto Preminger cast him as the presiding judge in his 1959 movie *Anatomy of a Murder*.

After seeing *Point of Order* in the sixties, critic Dwight Macdonald suggested a revisionist view of Welch's *cri de coeur*. "It seemed to be a spontaneous cry of moral indignation—'seemed' because on this viewing, at least, I thought I detected a calculated artistry in [Welch's] performance." In fact, according to Nicholas von Hoffman's *Citizen Cohn*, McCarthy had recklessly violated a "back door"—or should we say "backstage"—agreement not to mention Fisher if Welch avoided bringing up the subject of Cohn's draft record. Performance defeats character: McCarthy's psychology dictated his divergence from the script. He could not help himself. Nor, perhaps, could Cohn whose irrational devotion to Schine had dragged the McCarthy juggernaut onto the rocks.

Even before the hearings ended, a week after Welch's outburst, McCarthy was the butt of TV comedians like Steve Allen and Milton Berle who mimicked his constant interruptions and shouted points of order. Although the subsequent Subcommittee report was ambiguous, the Wisconsin senator's hold was broken. On December 2, the Senate voted 67–22 to censure him. Still, perhaps because McCarthy was America's preeminent media politician before John F. Kennedy, his fictional doppelgangers populate the Washington thrillers that characterized the Kennedy era.

McCarthy is reconfigured as a liberal appeaser in *Advise and Consent* and, even more outrageously, as a Communist invention in *The Manchurian Candidate*. *Point of Order* is the documentary correlative. The movie premiered two weeks into 1964, still the disorienting aftermath of the Kennedy assassination, at the posh Beekman theater. There it played through the end of February—a run overlapping the Beatles on Ed Sullivan's show, the opening of Barry Goldwater's presidential campaign, and the release of two more political fantasies predicated on the sedition of rightwing generals, *Seven Days in May* and *Dr. Strangelove*.

Reviewing the latter for *Partisan Review*, Susan Sontag called *Point of Order* "the real comédie noire of the season." Indeed, in successfully repackaging "live" political theater as a sort of filmed political cabaret, the movie began new careers for its creators. Talbot branched out into distribution the following year while De Antonio would establish himself as a leading political documentary filmmaker. (*Milhouse: A White Comedy*, which De Antonio directed and Talbot released in 1970, landed both men on the Nixon enemy list.)

Senator McCarthy is as far from us today as the red-hunting Attorney General A. Mitchell Palmer was from *Point of Order*'s original audience. What remains startlingly immediate is the televisual. Treating the Army-McCarthy hearings as a form of found Pop Art, *Point of Order* is a movie about TV—literally. The kinescopes from which it was fashioned were filmed off the TV screen. The public drama was already mediated for maximum human interest; its spectacle anticipates C-Span and Court TV as well as Watergate and Iran-Contra.

The most powerful demagogue is not McCarthy at all. Nor is Welch the real hero. An electronic cave-painting from the dawn of the media-saturated age, *Point of Order* demonstrates the way that television inevitably recasts news as entertainment, subsumes politics in personality, elevates anecdote to history, and in the final analysis, substitutes its own flickering image for collective memory.

**APOCALYPSE NOW AND THEN**

Originally published in the *Village Voice* (May 19, 1998).

THE TIME OF TRIBULATIONS APPROACHES, BUT THUS FAR THE RUN-UP TO THE millennium has been characterized by cataclysms averted—stock markets rebounding, wars sidestepped, sexual harassment cases thrown out of court. Nevertheless, ever since the earthshaking of *Jurassic Park* revived the disaster cycle in 1993 and the powerfully monopolizing *Independence Day* served to unite the world behind one movie in 1996, the special effects houses have worked overtime to bring home the apocalypse.

*Titanic*, of course, is the greatest catastrophe of all—and, since it's the most expensive and the highest-grossing movie in Hollywood history, this is true in more ways than one. But even many of the past year's art films—*Crash, The Sweet Hereafter, The Ice Storm*—have doomsday subtexts. True believers know the Rapture is imminent; they may be raised to Heaven at any moment. For the rest of us, however, the latter days are canned—this will be the summer during which the Earth is attacked by all manner of rogue asteroids, comets, and meteors; suffers deadly viruses and big weather; and even endures Godzilla's return.

Bill Clinton was barely out of law school when the last disaster cycle played itself out in the mid-1970s, but even then cine-catastrophe was scarcely a novel concept. As early as 1902, Georges Méliès was producing fake newsreels of volcanic eruptions; the Italian cinema emerged as an international force with feature-length spectaculars like the 1913 *Last Days of Pompeii*; and the animated cartoon asserted itself as a source of choreographed mayhem with Winsor McCay's graphic 1918 rendition of the Lusitania sinking. You might even say the mode is intrinsic. It was only the movies, Susan Sontag observed in her 1965 essay "The Imagination of Disaster," that allowed one to "participate in the fantasy of living through one's own death and more, the death of cities, the destruction of humanity itself." No wonder Hitler, Stalin, and Nixon were all movie fans; cinema elevated schadenfreude to the heights of megalomania.

Writing during the year that American involvement in Indochina passed the point of no return, Sontag argued that the Armageddon-minded science-fiction films that enlivened drive-in screens in the period between the Korean and Vietnam wars were not really about science at all. Their subject was rather the aesthetics of destruction—the beauty of wreaking havoc, the pleasure of making a mess, the pure spectacle of "melting tanks, flying bodies, crashing walls, awesome craters, and fissures in the earth."

In the 1960s, the aesthetic of destruction was globalized: After the prodigal *Cleopatra* (1964) nearly capsized an entire studio, Arthur Penn created the doomsday gangster film (*Bonnie and Clyde*, 1967) and Sam Peckinpah the disaster western (*The Wild Bunch*, 1969). *Night of the Living Dead* (1969), still the greatest and most apocalyptic horror movie ever made in America, circulated for several years to achieve full cult status in 1971 with a late-night run in Washington, D.C., that, over the remaining years of the Nixon presidency, would inexorably spread to other cities and college towns.

Nor was *Night of the Living Dead*, in which fresh corpses rise from the grave to feast upon the living, the only vivid representation of Judgment Day. Hal Lindsey's *The Late Great Planet Earth* (1970), an interpretation of biblical prophecy that extrapolated current geopolitical events to predict an impending worldwide catastrophe followed by the return of Jesus Christ, appeared as a mass-market paperback in February 1973. (This after running through 26 printings in its original edition.) Lindsey's tome was the best-selling American nonfiction book of the seventies—a decade for which its predictions included an increase in crime, civil unrest, unemployment, poverty, illiteracy, mental illness, illegitimate births, and increasing dominance of astrology, Oriental religions, and Satanic cults, as well as the greatest famines in world history and the election of open drug addicts to public office.

Years before it was filmed, *The Late Great Planet Earth* inspired a host of underground, homemade premillennialist disaster films with names like *The Final Hour* and *The Road to Armageddon*, which circulated among the faithful first on 16-mm and then on video. (It has been estimated that the most famous, *A Thief in the Night*, has been seen by some 100 million Americans since 1973.) Still, the direct stimulus for the 1970s disaster cycle was neither the Book of Daniel nor the collapse of the counterculture, but rather the surprising success of two movies: *Airport* (1970) and *The Poseidon Adventure* (1972), which, released shortly after Nixon's reelection, proved the number one box office attraction of 1973.

The disaster cycle gathered momentum along with the Watergate scandal, approaching its climax as the president resigned in August 1974. By then, *Time* had offered its readers "A Preview of Coming Afflictions," reporting that Hollywood's "lemming-like race for the quintessential cataclysm" had spawned some 13 disasters at various stages of production. *Earthquake*, cowritten by Mario Puzo, *The Towering Inferno*, Irwin Allen's spectacular follow-up to *The Poseidon Adventure*, and an *Airport* sequel were scheduled to open by Christmas— to be followed by moves whose major attractions were an avalanche, a tidal wave, a volcanic eruption, the explosion of the dirigible Hindenburg, a plague of killer bees, and an earthquake permitting a horde of giant, incendiary cockroaches to exit the center of the earth and overrun Los Angeles.

"There is absolutely no social criticism, of even the most implicit kind," Sontag had noted of her science-fiction films. But movies like *Earthquake* and *The Towering Inferno* were scarcely perceived as anything else. Indeed, the explanation of the trend arrived even before the trend itself. "Every couple of years, the American movie public is said to crave something. Now it's calamity, and already the wave of apocalyptic movies—which aren't even here yet—is being analyzed in terms of our necrophilia," wrote Pauline Kael shortly after *Time*'s piece, thus staking out the counter-pundit position that disaster films were nothing more than meaningless pseudoevents.

Necrophilia, however, was not the explanation offered by most commentators. Disaster films were more often discussed as reflections of the economic crisis (perceived as "natural" in capitalist society) precipitated by the OPEC oil embargo in late 1973 or else as manifestations of Watergate—as if Watergate were not the most enthralling disaster film of all. (Vietnam may have been too painfully obvious to mention, although Kael evoked it in spite of herself when she characterized the directors of disaster movies as "commanders-in-chief in an idiot war.")

In his influential essay "The Me Decade and the Third Great Awakening," published in *New York* magazine during the summer of 1976, Tom Wolfe mocked "the current fashion of interpreting all new political phenomena in terms of recent disasters, frustration, protest, the decline of civilization . . . the Grim Slide." Nevertheless, the Disaster Film cycle roughly coincides with the collapse of the Bretton Woods international financial system in 1971, the 1973 OPEC oil crisis, the 1973–75 recession, the 1975 collapse of South Vietnam—the very period which, according to historian Eric Hobsbawm, marked the end of the twentieth century's post–World War II "golden age" and the reemergence of those social problems which, largely dormant for a generation, had previously characterized the critique of capitalism: "poverty, mass unemployment, squalor, instability."

It was also the period that would incubate Hollywood's rebirth as the world's preeminent packager of presold, pre- (or post-) literate properties, well stocked with stars and spiffy special effects.

Typically, in the disaster cycle of the 1970s, calamity arrives as a punishment for some manifestation of the boom-boom sixties. Crypto Titanic stories both, *The Poseidon Adventure* and *The Towering Inferno* heighten the moralizing thrill by arranging for disaster to strike in the midst of gala parties; in the 1975 *Tidal Wave*, the volcanic eruption that triggers the eponymous cataclysm is synchronized to the lovemaking of an unmarried couple on a targeted beach.

Some disaster movies offered a populist critique by blaming the catastrophe on rapacious corporations and, in most cases, the disaster was worsened by greedy, corrupt, and inadequate leaders. Thus, along with the TV cop shows and vigilante films of Nixon II, disaster movies questioned the competence of America's managerial elite. Kael extended that elite to include the captains of America's film industry: "The people who reduced Los Angeles to rubble in *Earthquake* must have worked off a lot of self-hatred: you can practically feel their pleasure as the freeways shake, the skyscrapers crumble, and the Hollywood dam cracks." Worked off a lot of self-hatred but made a lot of money.

It was the iron rule of disaster films that individuals were at fault, never the system itself, while the natural leader who emerged from the chaos was almost always a white male, usually in uniform (pilot, naval officer, policeman, fire chief, priest). Heroism under stress was practiced by nearly everyone except the top public officials, who were typically upper class and devious.

Like the Senate's televised Watergate hearings, disaster films offered the spectacle of all-star casts impersonating ordinary, middle-class people coping, as a group, with a limited Armageddon—the breakdown of an institution hubristically imagined to be safe; and the ocean liners, airplanes, skyscrapers, theme parks, and cities were, of course, microcosms of America. And yet, despite their overt fatalism, the disaster films were fundamentally reassuring. The cycle celebrated the inherent virtue of decent, everyday Middle Americans, linking their survival skills to traditional gender roles and conventional moral values—a particularly Darwinian form of sociological propaganda.

Disaster films updated the Ancient World epics that had in the 1950s and early 1960s been Hollywood's favorite demonstration of cinematic might. Not only were disaster films more economically produced and rationally conceived (everything centered upon a single gigantic special effect); they were also set in the present. Even if the notion of God's will was only implicit, the cataclysm effectively disciplined an overly permissive social order. On an interpersonal level, the reversals wrought by the disaster were often positive. (Reviewing *Earthquake* in the *New York Times*, Nora Sayre experienced a "sense of ritual cleansing.") As previously atomized individuals formed a community, class distinctions disappeared. Marriages were reinforced. Middle-class virtue prevailed.

In a sense, the disaster cycle denied that Americans had truly become jaded or that traditional values had broken down. They insisted rather, that, when tested by catastrophe, these values proved to be intact and, contrary to the scenario illustrated by *Night of the Living Dead*, enabled people to help one another through the crisis to guarantee society's survival. Disaster films were additionally comforting in that they revived the old-time entertainment religion. (In this sense, *Airport*—like the same year's *Love Story*—can be seen as the trial balloon for a return to proven, pumped-up Hollywood formulae.) Disaster films were populated largely by Nixon supporters and Reagan peers: Charlton Heston, William Holden, Dean Martin, Shelley Winters, Ava Gardner, Jennifer Jones, Myrna Loy, Dana Andrews, Gloria Swanson, Helen Hayes, Fred Astaire, James Stewart; hardy show biz survivors all.

In short, movies returned to their fairground origins by offering the treat of spectacular cataclysms. It was the return of the potlatch, tempting Hollywood's alienated audience with the promise of conspicuous consumption and spectacular effects. The *New York Times* unsarcastically called *The Towering Inferno* "old-fashioned Hollywood make-believe at its painstaking best" while whimsically hailing *Earthquake*'s "awesome" advance toward the total cinema of *Brave New World*'s feelies (in which an on-screen kiss made the "facial erogenous zones" of 6,000 spectators tingle with "an almost intolerable galvanic pleasure.")

But there was something else as well. "Use value in the reception of cultural commodities is replaced by exchange value," Adorno and Horkheimer had observed in *The Dialectic of the Enlightenment*. "The consumer becomes the ideology of the pleasure industry." Or, put another way, the Hollywood modus operandi is less producing movies than mass-producing the desire to see movies. In the years following *Bonnie and Clyde*, this desire had gotten out of control—the audience was actually elevating sleepers to blockbuster status. After the disaster films (and particularly the summer-of-'75 sensation *Jaws*), there would be regular Events that everyone felt compelled to see in order to fully participate in American life.

By recuperating the apocalyptic visions of the previous decade, disaster films suggested, as Herbert J. Gans noted in the journal *Social Policy* in 1975, "that the 1960s never happened." *Titanic* extends the principle.

Not the least of *Titanic*'s cataclysms is its reorientation of film history. It's as if the movie effected the time-travel fantasy articulated by James Cameron in *The Terminator*—the present enables the future to rewrite the past. The critics who compare King Cameron to founding father D. W. Griffith have essentially bookended the birth and death of the medium.

"When a film achieves a certain success, it becomes a sociological event and the question of its quality becomes secondary," François Truffaut once observed. Clearly *Titanic* is that sort of event—and more. The most profligate movie ever made sneers at the rich and puts a "progressive" feminist spin on a disaster that 94 percent of the boat's first-class women survived (as opposed to 47 percent of the women and 14 percent of the men in steerage). A director proudly desecrates the mystery of their watery tomb, then demands a moment of silence for those—represented mainly by digitalized "extras"—interred within.

Thanks in part to *Titanic*, the notion that film might have a documentary, indexical relationship to reality is nearly as quaint as the idea of silent movies. Mass memory meanwhile is identical with the mass media. The actual *Titanic* disaster offered an uncanny prophecy of the nineteenth-century European order wrecked two years later in World War I. Cameron's Ship of Dreams carries the cultural baggage of the twentieth century—advanced Freudian ideas, incomprehensible modern art, Marxist class awareness, technological grandeur, and even the movies (from which the Leonardo DiCaprio character learned his society manners).

"And now, the end is near . . ." we'll soon enough be hearing vanished Frank Sinatra sing. It must be. The response that audiences have for *Titanic*'s awe-inspiring spectacle of modernity sinking below the computer-generated waves can only be called enraptured.

## BACK TO IRAQ

Originally published as "Burn, Blast, Bomb, Cut,"
*Sight and Sound* (February 2000).

ONE OF THE MOST ECCENTRIC HOLLYWOOD RELEASES OF THE PAST FEW YEARS, David O. Russell's *Three Kings* would be novel for its subject matter alone. In his first megabuck production after the indie hits *Spanking the Monkey* (1994) and *Flirting with Disaster* (1996), writer-director Russell attempts to represent the hitherto all but unrepresentable 1991 Persian Gulf War, otherwise known as Operation Desert Storm.

"Will the Gulf War Produce Enduring Art?" the *New York Times* worried back in June 1991, a month after Jean Baudrillard published his science-fiction novella *The Gulf War Did Not Take Place*. There was, of course, the instantly forgotten docudrama *Heroes of Desert Storm* telecast by ABC that October (complete with introduction by then President George Bush) while, on a somewhat higher level of achievement, Werner Herzog's horrific and awe-inspiring documentary *Lessons of Darkness* (1992) used the blasted Kuwaiti desert as the catastrophic projection of his own romantic Doomsday worldview. Edward Zwick's 1996 *Courage Under Fire* was actually the first Hollywood movie to treat the war against Iraq and, Paul Verhoeven's underappreciated sci-fi satire *Starship Troopers* notwithstanding, it was also the last—until Russell's rambunctious *Three Kings*.

Saddam Hussein remains a bit player in American culture, intermittently invoked by defense hawks (and appearing last summer as Satan's abusive boyfriend in the scurrilous animated feature, *South Park*). But, although Operation Desert Storm could be considered the founding moment of the so-called New World Order, its scant cinematic representation is, according to conventional wisdom, a factor of its initial oversaturation. As broadcast live and round-the-clock by CNN, the Gulf War was a highly successful made-for-TV movie even while it was happening. Never before in the annals of instant history had an international combat situation so merged with its own representation. The journalistic first draft turned out to be the final draft as well.

Call Vietnam a living-room war? January 16, 1991, the evening Operation Storm opened with a dazzling *son et lumière* display of bombs falling on

Baghdad, was America's second-most-watched telecast ever (exceeded in percentage only by the number of TVs tuned to the JFK funeral). Not a single serious crime was reported that night in Washington, D.C. Where the Vietnam War produced a frenzy of alienation, Desert Storm inspired fascinated disassociation. The viewing experience was routinely compared to Nintendo and *Top Gun* or, as the event was almost immediately theorized by postmodern academics, the aesthetic pronouncements on the beauty of war made by the Italian futurists.

New military oxymorons—"surgical strikes," "collateral damage," "smart bombs"—palcd before the Pentagon's mise-en-scène. TV watchers were routinely placed inside a missile sensor-system even while military officers acted as assigning editors in determining where to dispatch the reporter-pool. Show business or simulation? Historian Elaine Scarry would compare Desert Storm to Jean Genet's *The Balcony*: "All possible political positions began to orient themselves in relation to the theatrical spectacle rather than to the reality of the events themselves." Although the Gulf War followed by two years Ronald Reagan's departure from the scene it was the perfect postscript to his presidency (as well as Baudrillard's reign as *philosophe du jour*).

Was the Gulf War a police action in the Global Village or a hyperreal exercise in national narcissism? For the first time in a generation, Americans were one nation under the Yellow Ribbon which, throughout Desert Storm (and even after), was emblem of participation, worn by superpatriots, moderate supporters, and antiwar demonstrators alike—the latter using it to signify their opposition to American policy but support for American troops. (This negation of the Vietnam syndrome was a bit of a paradox, given that the earlier war had been fought by conscripts whereas, in another American first, Desert Storm was the province of volunteers—if not mercenaries.)

Used to advertise everything from motorboats to condoms, the Victory over Saddam Hussein not only occasioned all manner of commemorative collectibles (T-shirts, engraved guns and knives, model Patriot missiles) but, beginning with General Norman Schwartzkopf's February 27 Riyadh news conference, was commodified in a succession of videos produced for the home market. These included CNN's *Desert Storm: The War Begins* and *Desert Storm: The Victory*, a confidently jazzed-up alternative to the more sober CBS boxed set *Desert Triumph*. The British perspective was provided by the Independent Television News's *Gulf War: The Complete Story* while the National Football League put out *Victory in the Desert*, complete with Whitney Houston's melodramatic Super Bowl XXV (Desert Storm Day XI) rendition of the "The Star-Spangled Banner."

The O. J. Simpson trial and Monica Lewinsky revelations notwithstanding, Desert Storm was the last great American festival of the twentieth century.

Enemy casualties outnumbered those of the anti-Iraq coalition by a ratio of 500 to one; the U.S. victory celebration lasted far longer than the actual hostilities. In the first flush of triumph, once-wimpish George Bush was imagined to be U.S. President for Life. But the Gulf War turned out to have a Warholian 15-minute half-life as the giddy triumphalism of the New World Order gave way to a sense of gloomy recession.

Desert Storm has been largely forgotten—although it will surely be resurrected in some form during the 2000 presidential campaign as Bush's eldest son, Texas governor George W. Bush proceeds (against an authentic war hero, Arizona senator John McCain) in his seemingly unstoppable quest for the Republican nomination. So where does this partial amnesia leave *Three Kings*?

Russell's bold and messy feature is not a movie about the nature of war, like Terrence Malick's *Thin Red Line*, so much as it is an attempt to fathom war's purpose—as seen in retrospect. The action begins in March 3, 1991, just as the cease-fire takes effect and the operation is declared successful. ("We have finally kicked the Vietnam syndrome," President Bush asserted in his remarks.) "Are we shooting?" one private (Mark Wahlberg) wonders upon spotting a perhaps-surrendering Iraqi. Not waiting for an answer, he nervously splatters the desert with befuddled "rag head" brains—much to his comrades' delight. The war happened after all: They finally got to see someone shot.

The morning after an American party-on bacchanal, staged as a "we're number one" sports-team locker-room celebration, Russell's noncommissioned "kings"—inexpressive Wahlberg, scowling Ice Cube, and, as a goofy redneck, *Being John Malkovich* director Spike Jonze—find a treasure map stuffed up a captured Iraqi ass. (The psychosexual implications are evident and comic, given the American wartime rhetoric, which focused on Saddam's own person.) Led by an opportunistic, dissolute career soldier—George Clooney, another one-note performer—who somehow recognizes the map as a guide to captured Kuwaiti gold, the would-be freebooters hatch a quick plan to commandeer a Humvee, zip behind Iraqi lines and make themselves rich. The war had a use-value after all. If the premise suggests a vintage Uncle Scrooge comic book—with Clooney playing a tough-guy Donald Duck to the kings' Huey, Dewey, and Louie—the movie's relentlessly contemporary, which is to say flippant, attitude is rendered iconic in the Beach Boys–scored close-up juxtaposing an American flag with a Bart Simpson doll.

As though to dispel Desert Storm's magical aura, *Three Kings* is a movie of gross textures: blood flows, milk spills, oil pours. The ragged-jagged look suggests third-generation color Xerox. At once high-contrast and bleached-out, it's purposefully cruddy. As intimated by his nouveau screwball *Flirting with Disaster*, Russell has a knack for choreographing mad confusion. Here, the exciting adventures are set amid sickening violence, the chaos heightened by the use of swish pans, slow motion, and eccentric camera placement. *Three Kings* is not only given to new wave tonal shifts but is shot as wildly spontaneous combat-*verité*.

The spectacle of things flung through the air is a recurring one. There are almost no establishing shots, although when a cow gets blown up, you can bet its head will bang down on the Humvee hood. In his most celebrated stunt, however, Russell claims to have filmed a real bullet going through an actual cadaver—a cross-section of punctured internal organs. Although abstracted from the film's narrative, the shot is as visceral as anything in *Saving Private Ryan*'s D-Day, reminding the viewer that the actual purpose of war is, as Scarry has pointed out, to injure—"to burn, to blast, to shell, to cut"—human tissue.

Embraced with greater enthusiasm by critics than audiences (despite its demographically designed cast), *Three Kings* is—from an entertainment point of view—something of Desert Storm's opposite. The movie has been described as everything from an MTV-inflected *Treasure of Sierra Madre* to the most visionary Vietnam movie [*sic*] since *Apocalypse Now*. Be that as it may, there certainly hasn't been so bloodthirsty a Hollywood service comedy since the Vietnam era. Robert Aldrich's *The Dirty Dozen* (1967) and Robert Altman's *M*A*S*H* (1970) come to mind. But, unlike these, *Three Kings* isn't exactly antipatriotic.

Born at the end of the Baby Boom, Russell was a teenager when the last American troops returned from Vietnam and he has a post-*M*A*S*H* sensibility. *Spanking the Monkey* and *Flirting with Disaster* were both extremely dark sex comedies predicated on convoluted genealogical issues. Here, the inquiry into origins is made collective. Russell says that he spent months researching Desert Storm, which may be why his characters regale each other with the war's conventional wisdom: "They say you exorcized the ghost of Vietnam," a TV correspondent begins one interview. "This is a media war," a commanding officer later insists. "I don't even know what we did here," the hero admits, later adding that "the war is over and I don't know what the fuck it was about."

Once more the search for identity: Was any foreign war was ever so intimately involved with its home front? The Yellow Journalism practiced by William Randolph Hearst during the Spanish-American War had mutated into the Yellow-Ribbon Tele-Journalism of the war against Iraq. American TV regularly covered the families of those soldiers stationed in Saudi Arabia. In one of Russell's best bits of business, the Wahlberg character is able to reach his wife in

Detroit using one of the pile of confiscated Kuwaiti cell phones filling an Iraqi bunker ("Gotta go, goony bird," he signs off as Saddam's soldiers burst in).

Desert Storm also complicated traditional macho as America's first coeducational war. Indeed, back then, the home front gave evidence of a powerful yen to watch movies about women with guns. Opening a month into the bombing of Baghdad, *The Silence of the Lambs* thrived well beyond critical and box-office expectations on the image of ascetic female heroism—as well as a not unrelated fascination with bad and good-bad serial killers. Some months later, as the *New York Times* posed its question on the war's cultural production (and the House Armed Services Subcommittee on Military Personnel announced hearings to investigate the new role of woman in active service), the smiling faces of the scandalous Thelma and Louise shared newsstand space with the pixie redhead in desert fatigues featured on the cover of the fashion magazine *Mirabella*: "Hail the Conquering Heroines: Our Women in the Gulf."

Appropriately, *Courage Under Fire* (an extremely traditional combat movie, albeit made without the Pentagon imprimatur) was a fastidious *Rashomon* story in which America's sweetheart Meg Ryan played Capt. Karen Walden, a chopper pilot (and mother) killed in the action and up for posthumous Congressional Medal of Honor. *Three Kings* recaptures the war for the guys. Don't ask, don't tell. The film's only American women are two TV correspondents. The first is introduced *in flagrante* with Clooney (and thus may be considered a bimbo of no consequence); the other, her older rival, is a misfired parody of CNN reporter Christine Amanpour played by former *Saturday Night Live* regular Nora Dunn.

Hardboiled yet overemotional, the Dunn character swears like a drill sergeant, but can be reduced to tears by the sight of oil-soaked birds. She is regularly confounded by Clooney yet, as immediately recognized by both Iraqis and American brass, several times saves the day. Her compassion is crucial. For where *Starship Troopers* gave the Desert Storm mindset a pronounced fascist inflection, *Three Kings'* more swinging cynicism mixes absurd slapstick with intermittent nods to those helpless huddled Third World masses yearning to breath free.

*There is one further problem for those who believe that this war took place: how is it that a real war did not generate real images? Same problem for those who believe in the Americans' "victory": how is it that Saddam is still there as though nothing had happened?*

—JEAN BAUDRILLARD, *The Gulf War Did Not Take Place*

If the Gulf War did not in fact take place—a notion dramatized by *Wag the Dog* and, even more, the novel on which it was based—Russell at least deserves credit for rethinking the combat movie genre in the weird we-are-the-world terms that Desert Storm established.

Operating at the far frontier of TV space, his heroes cannot help but find America. Along with concealed landmines and subterranean torture chambers, the desert sands cover a veritable Neiman Marcus of war booty. The kings need no open sesame to find this Ali Baba horde of captured computers, Cuisinarts, Rolexes, Louis Vuitton luggage sets, Rolexes, Nordic Tracks, Infiniti's, Walkmans, TVs and VCRs. One of these even transmits the world-historical home video of motorist Rodney King being beaten by the L.A. police. (Although the King video would not go into heavy rotation until the following year, when it helped precipitate the April 1992 L.A. riots, there is the mystical coincidence—presumably noted by Russell—that King was stopped for speeding on the very day the Gulf War ended.)

Unlike most Hollywood movies, *Three Kings* does not consign the Arab foe to absolute cultural Otherness. Russell not only visualizes bombed Iraqi children but even has the guts to point out that, having tilted toward Iraq during its war with Iran, the United States helped to train Saddam's killers—even if he does put the thesis that Desert Storm was fought for Kuwaiti oil in the mouth of the scariest of the movie's "wog" villains (Said Taghmaoui), who makes his point by forcing some handy petrol down captured Wahlberg's throat. It's a scene in which George Bush and Saddam Hussein would each find something to appreciate.

The Iraqis are familiar insofar as the American spectacle fascinates them as well. Specialist Melissa Rathbun-Nealy, the first American servicewoman taken prisoner since World War II, reported that the Iraqis who held her captive were "beautiful people" who "took excellent care of her" and innocently asked whether she knew Brooke Shields and Sylvester Stallone. So it is, after a fashion here. "What is the problem with Michael Jackson?" Wahlberg's captor demands in accented but highly vernacular English, before answering his own question. "Michael Jackson is pop king of a sick fucking country."

As Desert Storm consecrated America's sole superpower status, it also illustrated the limits of U.S. power (or interest), as in the decision to remain aloof from the anti-Saddam rebellions precipitated by the war. It is here that *Three Kings* starts searching for its own heart of gold. His mind blown by the sight of Saddam's soldiers shooting down an unarmed civilian before her small daughter's horrified eyes, Clooney takes his place in the Humphrey Bogart tradition of seemingly mercenary, secretly idealistic Hollywood heroes. The action actually grinds to a halt so he can explain to the audience what's happening, even though (again like Bogart in *Casablanca*) he seems slightly ahead of actual developments on the ground: "Bush told the people to rise up against Saddam. They thought they'd have our support. They don't. Now they're getting slaughtered."

Each generation gets the *Casablanca* it deserves. Increasingly muddled, cumulatively monotonous, and would-be heartwarming, *Three King* ultimately becomes its own entertainment allegory—fighting, Hollywood style, to occupy the position at which blatant self-interest can turn humanitarian, while still remaining profitable. In a pragmatic bit of turn-around, the kings even draft the pidgin English rhetoric needed to recruit the suspicious Iraqi rebels, never identified as Shiites, to help their American quasi-liberators get back to base. ("We will rise up together, many races, many nations. . . . We're united. George Bush wants you!")

Opening with the war's end, *Three Kings* winds up perhaps two days later— just around the time that Iraq expelled all remaining Western journalists, as Saddam's Republican Guard battled Shiite rebels and the Iraqi army prepared for redeployment against the Kurds. The kings have received their baptism under fire, sustained wounds and even losses, to become the real heroes of a nonexistent war of liberation. In a final burst of wish fulfillment, television is thanked for preserving this tacked-on happy ending.

Given the degree to which the American media fulfilled its officially mandated function during the Gulf War and after, this tribute to an independent press is something of a puzzler. But then, in trying to integrate Desert Storm into the American national narrative, *Three Kings* has a unique trajectory. The movie keeps trying to go conventional and ultimately it does.

"President of the U.S.A., saxophonist Bill Clinton,"
by Bill Potts c. 1993 (gift to Clinton from Potts).
From *www.nara.gov/exhall/treasures/clinton.html*.

# V

## OUR ROCK 'N' ROLL PRESIDENT

### CLINTON VS. BUSH: A LOVER OR A FIGHTER?

Originally published as "Living Room Warriors," the
*Village Voice* (September 22, 1992).

*Pat Buchanan is* Cape Fear *and Ronald Reagan is* The Way We Were.

—GEORGE STEPHANOPOULOS, Clinton campaign communications
director, critiquing the opening night of the 1992 Republican Convention

PRESIDENTIAL ELECTIONS TURN POLS INTO ARTISTS—AND NOT JUST POLS. YOU CAN hear America singing. Focus groups free-associate scenarios for 60-second extravaganzas, pundits wrestle with metaphors, campaign managers choreograph happenings for spin doctors to spin, newspapers sculpt public opinion.

A wonderful exhibit could be made from the 30 or 40, increasingly grotesque, portraits that the *New York Times* ran of George Bush this August; there's a potential op-ed thumb sucker in Bushman Kevin Costner's decision not to make a commercial praising the president's environmental record. *Feed*, Jim Ridgeway and Kevin Rafferty's new documentary on the New Hampshire primary, zeroes in on "off camera" candidates constructing their images: Jerry Brown fussing over his tie, Bob Kerrey working on his smile, and Bill Clinton fine-tuning his twinkle.

*Feed* shows the pols so tangled up in feedback, they imitate their *Saturday Night Live* simulacra: "This is the real thing, this isn't Dana Carvey," George Bush mumbles in one air check, while Arnold Schwarzenegger teases the Democrats as "a bunch of girlie-men." There's no escape from the echo chamber. The pols monitor TV to find out what we think they think about us thinking about them. At the very least, *Saturday Night Live* is a useful barometer of public taste. (Bush & Co. were ecstatic in February '91 when the show made fun of reporters, rather than the Pentagon, during Desert Storm.)

*Bob Roberts*, the eponymous hero of Tim Robbins' mock documentary and the most recent of the season's political apparitions, following Murphy Brown and the ghost of Harry Truman onto the media stage, is another *SNL* spin-off—he first appeared several years ago as yuppie Bob Dylan whining about the secondary smoke in a MacDougal Street cafe and singing about capital gains. The new Bob Roberts is a thirty-something multimillionaire "folk singer" with a David Byrne wardrobe and a *sieg heil* wave who successfully runs for United States senator.

A self-proclaimed "rebel conservative" who fronts for a cabal of multinational pirates, Roberts smears his old-fashioned opponent (Gore Vidal, who in real life twice ran for the House of Representatives) and baits media liberals while wrapping himself in the American flag. (The movie is set against the pre–Desert Storm, yellow ribbon delirium of late 1990.) Roberts' rallies are concerts in which he sings songs that preach self-interest and rail against drugs, trash "bleeding hearts," and, in the grand finale, promote a jihad against "Godless Men"—this last delivered as he's seated in a wheelchair, like George Wallace (or Franklin Roosevelt).

*Bob Roberts* anticipates Ross Perot's request to use the Woody Guthrie anthem, "This Land Is Your Land," as a campaign song. (The movie changes it to "This Land Is *My* Land.") But if Bob's speeches are songs, so are they all. Hell, I'll be the only one in America to admit that it was precisely the juxtaposition of Perot on *Larry King Live* and Bill Clinton on *Arsenio* that made me think that I really had to vote for the latter. At least he was openly tooting his horn.

———

*As he sleeps, we live his nightmare.*

—Negative campaign ad, *Bob Roberts*

Granted, just when you think you've seen the worst our system has to offer, you haven't. Richard Nixon is succeeded by Ronald Reagan is succeeded by Pat Robertson is succeeded by Pat Buchanan is succeeded by a slick, corn-fed yuppie with a great big smile, rearing up on stage to yodel an updated version of the old Wallace anthem "Welfare Cadillac": *Some people will work, some people will not—but they'll complain and complain and complain . . .*

*Bob Roberts* demonstrates that—if nothing else—there's a sizable chunk of the left, as well as the right, that sees something dangerously unwholesome in American pop culture. No less than the citizens of Roberts' Pennsylvania, the local media has embraced Bob—their enthusiasm understandably stoked by the spectacle of the Republican Convention. *Bob Roberts* pushes its concept farther than "even the most hopeful liberal could have anticipated," writes Terence Rafferty in the *New Yorker*. "The movie sustains its energy and holds our interest right to the end. . . . [It] keeps inventing new ways for its protagonist to horrify us."

But who is this "us"—the society of hopeful liberals, the Queen of England, the cultural elite—and what exactly is that horror? Surely not the "Elvis economics" George Bush accused Bill Clinton of espousing? Would the movie have been so rapturously received had it opened on the heels of the Democratic Convention? With a pair of "glib," blow-dry boomers heading the ticket?

Few reviews have mentioned *Bob Roberts'* obvious precursor—even though Robbins himself is quite witty in his allusions. In essence, *Bob Roberts* replays that despairing liberal chestnut *A Face in the Crowd*, released in 1957 (the year before Robbins was born). Directed by Elia Kazan from Budd Schulberg's script, the movie is even less subtle and more hysterical than *Bob*. Lonesome Rhodes (Andy Griffith), a hillbilly guitar-picker discovered in an Arkansas jail, becomes, almost overnight, a major-league demagogue. A raucous hayseed combination of Will Rogers and Huey Long, he graduates from radio to TV, from making fun of his sponsor's commercials to refurbishing the images of political candidates just as Hollywood actor-director Robert Montgomery coached Ike. Lonesome seems on the verge of running for office himself when his jilted mistress (Patricia Neal), the Ivy League radio reporter who first found him, destroys his career by opening a mike so that the American people can see the true nature of the monster they've embraced.

In production from the summer of 1955 through the 1956 campaign, *A Face in the Crowd* synthesized all manner of current enthusiasms—Uncle Miltie and Tricky Dick, Billy Graham and Davy Crockett, the Actors Studio and *The Hidden Persuaders*. Although Schulberg told a *New Yorker* reporter, "Don't, for God's sake, identify [Lonesome Rhodes] with Elvis Presley," that's exactly what *Life* did, calling Rhodes a "guitar-thumping demagogue" who inspired "scenes of frenzied bobby-soxers behaving like Presley fans." How could they not? Who else could he be? This guy is truly something else—particularly as played by Griffith with a slaveringly avid ferocity that would never break the practiced affability of his corn pone persona again. Lonesome Rhodes is a force of nature—a nightmare vision of pop culture run amok.

*A Face in the Crowd* is not particularly good (the alleged popularity of Lonesome's bleatings are a mortal insult to the American people), but, as American political rhetoric, it has never ceased to be relevant. The movie was darkly alluded to in 1960 and quasi-remade as *Wild in the Streets*, American-International's contribution to the madness of 1968 in which a sleazy liberal running for senator creates a Frankenstein monster in the person of the 22-year-old rock star he's recruited to help.

Re-released (with a nod to George Wallace) in 1972, *A Face in the Crowd* was invoked to explain Watergate in 1974 and reconfigured as *Nashville* in 1975. Although *A Face in the Crowd* might be considered to have discharged its prophetic duty after the election of Ronald Reagan (1980), the idea of a bona fide remake was floated throughout the Reagan era, with figures as disparate as Barry Gibb, Burt Reynolds, and Don Johnson in the Griffith role. Currently, it's being reworked by Eric Bogosian. The only difference, as *Bob Roberts* knows, is that it's too late to pull the plug. (Credit *Feed* for trying.) Anyway, it takes no stretch of the imagination to see Lonesome Rhodes as Ross Perot and only a mild sense of tabloid melodrama to appreciate Hillary playing Patricia Neal to Bill's Andy Griffith.

*A Face in the Crowd*'s real kick, as Leonard Quart noted in *Cineaste* after the last presidential election, is the sequence where Lonesome shows a prissy eastern candidate how to smile and comb his hair, instructing him on the need for a nickname and a hound dog—the sequence only came into its own in 1988, when Roger Ailes and Lee Atwater made over George Bush by teaching him to talk tough, eat pork rinds, swear by *Hee-Haw*, and make ads claiming "it's the president who defines the character of America . . . the heart, the soul, the conscience of the nation."

---

*How many people do you think have a picture of George Bush in their college dorms?*

—PAUL TSONGAS, *Feed*

*We are not going to lose to some man who wears a pocket protector.*

—CLINTON CAMPAIGN WORKER ON PAUL TSONGAS, *Feed*

*I just wanted them to look at me and think I could be president.*

—BILL CLINTON, *Feed*

You can ponder all this at "The Living Room Candidate," a terrific show at the American Museum of the Moving Image. The exhibit is a succession of 11 sofa-and-television clusters, one for each presidential election since 1952. Bounce along and study the progression from crude slide shows to deluxe studio production. Or stand in the middle of the gallery room, bombarded by images of crowds and missiles in the unending dharma of the economic cycle, watching the candidates' lapels expand and contract and their sideburns roll down and up like window shades.

The main image is always the house we live in (shown as newly built by incumbents, as mortgaged—or trashed—by insurgents) or else the big White one. In a 1956 minidrama, a D.C. cabbie walks his dog down Pennsylvania Avenue and wonders what his "neighbor" is thinking about. (Turns out that, although Ike is unseen, his eye is on the sparrow.) The Democrats' clumsy rejoinders show Adlai Stevenson in what purports to be his living room talking into an oversized microphone on a cluttered desk or posed on the front porch, absurdly holding a grocery bag and complaining about the high cost of living.

In general, though, the Democrats seem to have pioneered a number of modes used to far better advantage by the Republicans—the apocalyptic scare film, the conjugal endorsement, the celebrity endorsement, the imperial president at work. In 1976, Jerry Ford introduces the feel-good ad and Jimmy Carter, posing in a Western shirt before a log cabin to symbolize a "new beginning led by a man whose roots are founded in the American tradition," trumps it. Carter not only produces his wife but, in a campaign first, his mother, Miss Lillian. The '76 campaign creates a fascinating confusion: Ford in the Oval Office wears a leisure suit without a tie and refers to his "nonimperial presidency," while Carter employs a dissolve from Mount Rushmore to his own smiling face. Only four years later, Carter all but self-destructed showing himself alone in his cardigan, burning the midnight oil and realistically kvetching about the "endless pressure of the presidency."

While the 1984 Republican commercials are state-of-the-art evocations of some American virtual reality—idyllic neighborhoods filled with friendly folks, slow-motion weddings, factory theme parks, flags raised over Main Street, the Reagan express going through a Disney town, the Democratic spots are supremely incoherent. Small wonder that the party that attempted to cast Walter Mondale as JFK to Ronald Reagan's Goldwater—while using the insipid hippie injunction "Teach Your Children Well" to criticize the sublimely irrational Star Wars scheme—got its brains beat out four years later with a series of tacky horror films and slapstick comedies. (The latter are really cheap: Dukakis in a tank with a laugh track.)

"The Living Room Candidate" also offers coming attractions for the fall: the use of defeated rivals to bash the candidate (Democrats, 1964); the pre-emptory ridiculing of the presumptive vice president (Democrats, 1968); the deployment of toy soldiers to illustrate candidate's defense policy (Republicans, 1972); home-state voters recruited to "expose" the candidate

(Republicans, 1976); the angry wife answering personal attacks against her husband (Republicans, 1980).

First out of the gate is another spot (this one by Democrats) from 1980. Harry Truman prophetically paraphrasing Ross Perot (and everybody else) in suggesting you "vote for yourself. You don't have to vote for me." I am your mirror.

<hr />

*In a small Southern town that looked like a set for Andy Griffith's Mayberry, President Bush raised doubts today about the Democrats' vision of family, and his surrogate [Representative Newt Gingrich] cited Woody Allen as symbolizing the party's values.*

—*NEW YORK TIMES*, August 23, 1992

Hard not to enjoy the hyperreality of the scene: In a town that resembles a TV facade, politicians bad-mouth each other's families, and employ actors to symbolize the values of millions of individuals. Finally, they're speaking our language.

All happy families are alike, we might paraphrase Tolstoy, but each American family is dysfunctional in its own way. Born on a rural commune, Bob Roberts denounced his parents as potheads and ran away to military school, studied business at Yale, and orchestrated a "phenomenal rise on Wall Street," singing folk songs all the while—a résumé that suggests a militant version of Ronald Reagan's favorite sitcom, *Family Ties*.

Like *Bob Roberts*, the current election is one more referendum on the sixties, that fantastic generational quarrel Bob calls a "dark stain" on American history. So is it Bob or Bill who has his kisser on the cover of the *Rolling Stone*? Bob may talk the talk but, lifestyle-wise, he's at best a Madonna Republican. Tim Robbins' slick smile can't cover for the candidate's unrealistic shortage of Christian piety and demonstrable family values. (Conspiracy buffs have to wonder if the wraithlike wife figure who barely flits through the film was, in an earlier cut, meant to be a parody of Tipper Gore.) Robbins has described Roberts as a "young George Bush," but the movie Bob Roberts is at least as much a satire of folkie self-righteousness as of right-wing rhetoric, and thus a belated critique of the left. For my money, Bruce Springsteen—the Democratic-Republican white hope of 1984, the man whose tragic ballad of post-Viet angst was widely heard as a rousing patriot anthem—would have been a more provocative model.

After all, nothing is beyond co-option when you're born in the U.S.A. *The Candidate*, another *Bob Roberts* precursor, written by a former aide to Eugene

McCarthy and directed by a onetime media adviser to Senator John Tunney, featured the Sundance Kid as a left-wing lawyer who, although he thinks "politics is bullshit," is tempted by a bearded Mephistopheles to run against the current senator. The elderly incumbent talks like Ronald Reagan; the challenger is a probusing, prowelfare, proabortion eco-freak. No problem, his media handlers script the election as a referendum on youth versus age—it's campaign by photo op and victory by tele-debate and it ends with Sundance hypnotized and bummed out, asking his guru, "What do we do now?" *The Candidate* appeared the year of the McGovern debacle. Popular legend has it that a good-looking, if dim-witted, law student named Dan Quayle mistook the movie for a burning bush and realized his mission was to enter politics.

Some metaphors never die. The day I saw *Bob Roberts*, Quayle was also out searching for Andy Griffith's retreat. The *Times* reported that the vice president's acceptance speech "made his life as the grandson of an Indiana newspaper publisher who left a trust fund now valued at a billion dollars sound like the biography of Mayberry's Opie." But Bob Roberts isn't the only "rebel conservative" and the Republicans aren't the only people born in Mayberry.

*The Man from Hope*, the Clinton biopic produced by the makers of *Designing Women,* opens in a black-and-white small town with a young widow going to see the 1946 weepie *Tomorrow Is Forever* (a movie about a young war widow) and, the next day, giving birth to a future president. You could design a postmodern altarpiece around this particular silver-screen annunciation.

It's as if Quayle's attack on single-mother Murphy Brown was designed as a preemptive strike on Clinton's myth. Indeed, the entire Republican Convention can be seen as a reaction to the family values expressed in this brief allegory in which fatherless Bill grows up in poverty, defends his mother, and, according to the now recovered stepbrother he once put in jail, learns to identify his family with the nation. As the film's emphasis on martyred mentors John F. Kennedy and Martin Luther King suggests, Hope is a town that's lost its father. (The candidate for the job is the first to be endorsed as "a great parent" by his actual child.)

Bush, by contrast, is the Man from Nowhere. *Feed* is framed by a sequence of the president waiting for his cue to speak, utterly vacant, features frozen in a goofy grin before he becomes the tough guy who "led America to victory in Desert Storm and the Cold War." As his convention film makes clear, Bush will campaign as Sky God, self-proclaimed "Keeper of the Flame." The movie has him presaged by the Founding Fathers, emerging out of the strobe blitz of American history—a thousand points of light, 200 frenzied years scored to an angst-producing disco drone, Elvis flickering briefly as the bridge from Jackie Robinson to Fidel Castro. It's come to this, George Bush, sum of the zeitgeist: He is the Man. Those are the real family values.

"The battle is joined," the president promised at the end of one of his early commercials. The gloves are off, the masks are on, the channel zappers in hand. Will America choose a lover or a fighter, Top Cat or *Top Gun*, a young Bob Roberts or an old Bob Roberts, a Harry Truman of the left or a Harry Truman of the right, JFK or John Wayne, the King or the Man?

## THE CLINTON SHOW

Originally published as "It's the Mr. Bill Show," the
*Village Voice* (January 25, 1994).

OUR PRESIDENT IS NOT ONLY THE DEACON OF THE AMERICAN CHURCH, WIELDER of the Nuclear Thunderbolt, and Captain of the Starship Enterprise; he's at once the subject and object of the nation's popular culture. Producers seek us through his validation, while he himself is driven by overnight ratings and election-time sweeps.

Does the tree that falls in the wilderness make a sound? Or, put another way, do American presidential polities have a life apart from television? Thanks to our president, America can be envisioned in the nonexistent eye of a statistically conceived beholder. Indeed, the president is only truly manifest as seen by this imaginary focus group. For it, Bill Clinton's first year in office was a sitcom with variety interludes, not to mention a melancholy festival of image warts, live makeovers, and perceived misperceptions.

Initially conceptualized by Arkansas-based sitcom moguls Harry Thomason and Linda Bloodworth-Thomason as "The Man from Hope," Clinton has provided a roller-coaster ride through a new and diminished American history. For, as the media spectacle organized around him is the virtual definition of our united state, the president is also master of the mix—the videodrome Happy Hunting Ground where the living mingle with the dead, fictional characters consort with celebrities, and no one truly knows a simulacrum from a droid.

Seeking to represent that dream life, last spring's political comedy *Dave* vouchsafed its realism, secured a place in the national docudrama, and sent the White House press corps into a tizzy by incorporating cameos of pols and media figures ranging from Tip O'Neill and Jay Leno to Nina Totenberg and Oliver Stone. (The latter is significant in that *Dave* was also a comic *JFK*—a conspiracy in reverse, a coup against the Washington insiders who foist off a mediagenic presidential dummy.)

In *Dave*'s genial world—Washington as well as Hollywood—one's performance under the lights and before the camera in the constructed scenarios of the ongoing news cycle is at least as important as one's performance in waking reality—although that, too, is continually modified by the ceaseless process of feedback, pundit hermeneutics, and image recirculation we call spin.

Just as *The Player* "exposed" movie producers to the spotlight of public attention, *The War Room* focuses on their political equivalents. D. A. Pennebaker and Chris Hegedus's cinema verité account of the Clinton campaign was embraced by Washington insiders as definitive precisely because it has nothing to do with Clinton (or his ideas) and everything to do with the professionals who sculpted his image—and, in a sense, the movie itself.

For those who see *The War Room*, the sense that image rules will hardly be dispelled—despite the best efforts of the spin doctors depicted. The more contradictions, the brighter the star. As Bush handler Mary Matalin puts it after the first Bush-Clinton- Perot debate: "This is not a sports event— people don't get out their peanuts and hot dogs and rate these things. . . . We're not trying to create drama—we're not a made- for-TV candidate." Of course—not.

What she means is had George Bush been able to freeze-frame his image at the moment of his most frenzied triumph, Operation Desert Storm, thus appearing to be the uncontested winner at the center of his own improvised miniseries, he might have been reelected. Instead, he puked into the lap of the Japanese prime minister and was defeated by a hustling glad-hander who most successfully defined himself as an anti-Democrat Democrat.

Unlike any previous president, Clinton enjoyed his honeymoon in the few months before he was inaugurated—when he was the blankest of slates, just The Man from Hope. Back then, *TV Guide* hallucinated that even Ronald Reagan had voted for the lad he would reward with a big jar of red, white, and blue jelly beans. The morning after Clinton's inauguration, he was already in decline, his skull split in a migraine hangover as the talk radio drumbeat a tattoo: Gays in the military . . . Zoë Baird . . .

## LOOKING FOR MR. TRUEMAN

*This is a real John Doe goes to Washington. It's Rocky! A classic movie motif. An underdog. Some guy in his mid-40s who went to Oxford and Yale. Wanted to be president. Wanted to be champion. You would have said, "No way, that wouldn't play in Peoria." He kept getting knocked down like Rocky. He had an Achilles' heel. People counted him out. But he came back. He became champion. It touched a chord in some primal way. This is like the Academy Awards. This is when the guy stands up and wins best picture. You want to show up!*

—PETER GUBER, chairman of Sony Pictures, explaining why Hollywood sees the Clinton inauguration as a "seminal event."

When the last Democrat to be elected president first blipped across the national radar screen, he seemed to confound traditional political categories. Jimmy Carter lacked a coherent public philosophy but had an uncanny ability to please both liberals and conservatives. Carter made his peculiar persona a central issue, yet he was not a particularly charismatic personality. What *was* charismatic was his rocketlike political trajectory.

Instant feedback creates a moving consensus—the so-called Big Mo. Just as the commentators on *Monday Night Football* root for whoever appears to be winning, so David Gergen morphs from Republican to Democrat; Tina Brown abandons the Reaganite *Vanity Fair* to reinvent a Clintonian *New Yorker*, the Steven Spielberg theme park mutates from Neverland to Auschwitz, positing a bon vivant savior readymade for presidential identification. We're all vulgar Hegelians on this bus.

There is nothing more inevitable than an election after the fact; witness Clinton's coronation by a fawning Ted Koppel who flew to Little Rock to be with the governor on November 4, 1992, the night after his triumph. To Koppel, Clinton already *looked* different; it was as if the telejournalist suddenly saw the president-elect for the first time—on his own show. Clinton had instantly acquired presidential aura that *Nightline* itself was bestowing.

To become president, one must first appear Presidential. To appear Presidential one must first seem Electable. To seem Electable, one must appear destined to win—at least in retrospect. Thus, as openly schlepped by operatives of both parties during the Bush-Clinton campaign. David McCullough's bestselling *Truman* became the spin doctor's *I Ching*. The candidates were competing for "the mantle of Harry S. Truman" the *New York Times* reported as the campaign officially got underway.

The Mantle of Truman (like the Robe of Rocky) is the sacred cloak that permitted a feisty underdog to bamboozle an arrogant media establishment with his glorious upset victory of 1948. But the real question in any presidential election is far simpler: Who is fit to be the Father of Our Land?

Bill Clinton may have been the first presidential candidate to have been endorsed as "a great parent" by a filmed image of his actual child (one of the many deft touches in Linda Bloodworth-Thomason's 14-minute biopic *The Man from Hope*). But, during the 1992 campaign, it was Bush who appeared trapped in the role of a shrill and ineffectual dad, haunted by his empty threat: *Read my lips*. Like the American Revolution itself, this election would perpetuate patriarchy through patricide. Pat Buchanan had already tagged Bush "King George," and Clinton defined his own defining moment as the night in 1960 when he stood up to an alcoholic stepfather and warned him never to hit his mother again.

Powerful stuff. Yet, in the Bush cosmology, Clinton was a parvenu punk who deserved to be grounded—a draft-dodging hippie, an Oxford-educated comsymp, a low-rent gyrating Hillbilly Cat. Ignoring the message of the May 1992 postal service plebiscite in which a hot young Elvis resoundingly trounced the fat, aging, Nixon-affiliated Elvis, "ol' Bush" (as Young Bill slyly took to calling him) accused his opponent of making Elvisoid visitations on both sides of various issues. In the struggle, between "touchy-feely" Democrats and "blood and guts" Republicans (to use Maureen Dowd's characterization), this rhetorical strategy backfired—just as Paul Tsongas's labeling Clinton the Pander Bear only reinforced the cuddly side of Bill's image.

You could choose a lover or a fighter— and as Election Day grew near, ol' Bush reinforced the point by repeatedly using the word *lust* to characterize his opponent's desire for power. This rearguard struggle is not yet over. Even now, in a would-be Rabelaisian account of the president's prepresidential sex life, flagged in *The American Spectator* as "His Cheatin' Heart," David Brock calls Clinton "a man of gargantuan appetites and enormous drive." Eyewitnesses describe the Arkansas governor grabbing a baked potato and gobbling it down in two bites or, in a feat of razorback bravado, devouring entire apples, including the stem and core. By contrast, Bush's appetites were negative (his distaste for broccoli) or invented (his yen for pork rinds).

Clinton may be as manic as Bush, but he also looks to be built for comfort rather than speed. Caricatured in the press as a big-bellied, bulb-nosed bozo, mocked on *Saturday Night Live* as an American Sisyphus—the man who jogs to McDonald's for breakfast—Clinton embodies the frailties and comforts of the flesh. It is precisely because Clinton has accepted the mandate to restitch our social safety net that we regard him as a well-upholstered human Barcalounger. On the second day of the New Year, after hilariously documenting the president's recent, most excellent orgy of jalapeño pizza, seconds on cannoli, and frozen yogurt for everyone, the *New York Times* predicted that "'EAT, DRINK AND BE MERRY' MAY BE THE NEXT TREND"; the same week, *New York* magazine was heralding the return of red meat.

Bush's defeat was echoed by the well-publicized death of the last World War II hero. "IT'S TIME FOR HIM TO GO," the *Times* headlined Superman's demise, appropriating the anti-Bush chant led by Al Gore at the Democratic Convention. But, unlike George Bush, Superman is far too usefully familiar a trademark to ever really die and so, eight months into the Clinton era, the Man of Steel was reborn—or rather reconfigured—on television, as a supporting player on *Lois and Clark*.

Like the Clinton administration itself, the new, improved Superman is the joint fantasy of a male-female working team. As the key sitcom mutation of the eighties may have been the two-career household (*The Cosby Show, Family Ties, Growing Pains*), so the great subject for future Clinton biographers will surely be the nature of the Clinton marriage—and how it relates to the notion of *Addams Family Values*, not to mention the tradition of TrueManhood.

The subject is even addressed by Harry and Linda in their still-running *Evening Shade*, in which a high school football coach (played by Burt Reynolds) and a district attorney reign as the "first couple" of a rural Arkansas town. (Hillary herself suggested the poetic title.) Unfortunately, following candidate Bill's co-presidential sales offer, "Buy one, get one free," irate public opinion demanded that Hillary be muzzled and mummified, stripped of her headband, forced to bake cookies, and banished to a supporting role. Throughout the campaign, she was relegated to cheerleader, her place as running mate filled by Al Gore. But if the campaign was Bill and Al—Bill and Ted, Wayne and Garth, Beavis and Butthead, Pander Bear and the Ozone Man— the reign would be Bill and Hill, or, as Rush Limbaugh had it, the gene-spliced freak called Billary.

Throughout the spring of '93, the uncanny Hillary would be persecuted in the form of legal eagle Zoë Baird, crypto-commie Lani Guinier, dizzy diva Barbra Streisand—until finally deemed acceptable as the hulking, neuter Janet Reno. Reno was an invaluable addition to the Clinton sitcom—joining the supporting cast of daughter Chelsea, nutty Uncle Rog', rich neighbors Al and Tipper, droll Mr. Gergen, new character Bobby Ray Inman, the ripe-for- spinoff workplace team of Carville and Stephanopoulos, town eccentric Ross Perot, and mortgage-holding meanie Bob Dole. In the show's *Munsters*-like opening credits, America gets a government that looks like itself; Reno is flanked by colorful ethnic extras Joycelyn Elders and Robert Reich.

Confusingly, though, costar Hillary reconfigured her name and, spinning the wheel like a self-actualizing Vanna, in the heat of the ratings war, undertook her own succession of makeovers. Was she First Lady Macbeth or a dishrag of a wife? Why did this putative man hater pose for *Vogue* as Catherine Deneuve? Had she been hypnotized by Michael Lerner? Was she a failed Tammy Wynette? A legal genius? The sex slave of Vincent Foster? Evita of the Ozarks? A feminazi from Hell? The Florence Nightingale of Socialized Medicine? Donna Reed or Designing Woman? Was she the new Eleanor Roosevelt or (as one editorial cartoon suggested) an admirer of Lorena Bobbitt? And just what did that make Bill? Dagwood to her Blondie? John Goodman to her Roseanne? And, the ultimate sitcomic question: *Who's the Boss?*

*Demolition Man*, the first eighties-nostalgia film, is a nightmare version of Hillary's World. Supercop Sylvester Stallone and archcriminal Wesley Snipes, mortal enemies in fin de siècle L.A., are sentenced to cryostasis and defrosted 40 years later to continue their epic battle in a postearthquake, p.c. environment where nonviolent cops spout New Age jargon and electronic thought police issue tickets for violations of the "verbal morality standard." Consenting adults engage in secretion-free, telepathic sex; the ruler is an effete mad scientist with a fat sissy sidekick. Reality, as Snipes puts it, has become "a pussy-whipped *Brady Bunch* version of itself." It only remains for Sly to restore a healthy measure of masculine aggro and destructive energy.

*The American Spectator*'s white-lightning exposé of Clinton's piney woods peccadillos is actually a far more savage attack on his wife. At one point, the narrative becomes a full-fledged Southern gothic, redolent of overripe magnolias and sweaty satin slips. The "innocent" state trooper finds himself in the governor's mansion, overhearing scarlet Hillary hurling the vilest curses at her tomcat husband: "I went into the kitchen." the stolid trooper recounts. "The cook, Miss Emma, turned to me and said. 'The devil's in that woman.'"

### BILL CLINTON: BUBBA OR BOOMER?

*It's awesome to see somebody who looks like me, and who has been given this tremendous burden. I feel it all the more, because I could be in those shoes.*

—Rolling Stone founder and publisher JANN WENNER
to the *New York Times* on the occasion of *Rolling Stone's*
25th-anniversary party, held two weeks after the
Clinton victory

*Awesome* is the word. As amplified in the media, the president's foibles are at once grandiose and quotidian, a combination of *Star Wars* and the Weather Channel, scripted by James Joyce and directed by the wise guy who hosts *Talk Soup*. Defined anew with each unconscious gaffe or calculated appointment, our president inspires a cult of personality so rich it makes Mao Zedong's seem like a Warhol exercise in serial monotony—and more shoddily effervescent than the Nehru suit.

How to construct that cult? As Jann Wenner told Clinton during the course of a mid-campaign *Rolling Stone* interview, he had been particularly impressed with the spectacle of Bill and Hill and Al and Tipper singing and swaying along to "Don't Stop (Thinking About Tomorrow)" at the climax of the Democratic Convention: "It warmed my heart, and I thought, 'This is a generational ticket.'"

Dr. Hunter Thompson, also seated at the *Rolling Stone* table, would be mesmerized by the enthusiasm with which the garrulous frontier candidate scarfed down a plate of french fries. The good doctor reminded his editor that

Jimmy Carter had memorized Bob Dylan lyrics, but for Wenner, the times were definitely a-changin'. Gone were the anti-hippie, pro-yuppie ads with which *Rolling Stone* had promoted itself at the height of the Reagan Revolution. Here were Bill and Hill and Al and Tipper, who had grown up watching *Howdy Doody* and *Leave It to Beaver*, wearing coonskin caps and playing with Ginny dolls.

Weren't we all, in various degrees, products of that very youth culture that, in the West at least, was a surrogate proletarian internationalism? Before candidate Clinton graced the cover of *Rolling Stone*, he'd already been seen on the campaign trail parked on a Harley in a black leather jacket. He'd sung "Shout" with Whoopi Goldberg, gone on MTV and said that he should have inhaled, and, most crucially, played the sax line in "Heartbreak Hotel" for *Arsenio*. Aides opened his rallies with white classic rock like "Here Comes the Sun" and the evergreen "Good Vibrations."

The key sixties artifact for the Ozark-to-Oxford Clinton might well have been *The Beverly Hillbillies*, identified by vid historian David Marc as "probably the most popular sitcom—if not the most popular show—in television history." No matter. Candidate Clinton had successfully fabricated a new American Heritage—the Boomerography. Never mind that his musical taste ran more to Kenny G than Sonny Rollins: that when he was at Oxford the bellow of Tom Jones's "Green, Green Grass of Home" reduced him to soggy Kleenex; that his daughter was named for a song that, by her birth, made even the elevators weary. He was Sixties Man.

*Rolling Stone* was not alone in this effusion of generational solidarity. As Phil Hartman succeeded Dana Carvey in the *Saturday Night Live* oval office, the show which did so much to define and, ultimately, to defeat George Bush rolled over for Clinton—affectionately mocking the president's fondness for Big Macs or his hounddog lust. The most savage satire was Wayne and Garth's ridicule of the musical fare at the Inaugural Balls: "Hey, it's the nineties." It took a literary assassin like Fran Lebowitz to locate Clinton's totalitarian, yet promiscuous, deployment of Adult Contemporary Lite: "He has the soul and mind of Andrew Lloyd Webber and he's one Häagen-Dazs bar away from having the body."

Talking 'bout my generation. The New Democratic quartet that one *New York Times* headline characterized as "MIDDLE-OF-THE-ROAD FASHION PLATES" signify middle age. If he does nothing else, Clinton has drawn the line between the Boomers and Generation X by exploiting a gross and self-important sentimentality. Just as the election of JFK (who dug Sinatra and not Sam Cooke) precipitated a vault from World War I veterans to those who fought in World War II, Clinton's election has effectively canceled two generations—

Bush's and the Silent Generation of Korean War vets, Brando worshipers, Kerouac followers, and actual Elvis contemporaries.

What sort of hoodoo exactly did Clinton learn in the Arkansas outback? As a master of oxymorons, he had already established himself as an Oxford-educated Bubba and a hippie square. As president, he would appropriate Ronald Reagan's image maker (and then attack the media as "cynical" when they squawked). He would learn to blame the "knee-jerk liberal press" for withholding credit from the liberal programs they should reflexively support, and establish his credibility as a military leader by appointing a secretary of defense who established *his* credibility by announcing that he hadn't trusted the new president enough to vote for him.

In the dream life, however, Bill Clinton's greatest feat was conjuring up the spirits of the dead—namely two American deities, both of whom died in their mid-forties—at approximately the age when Bill prepared to install himself in the national unconscious. For it is written in Boomerography: Washington and Lincoln will be replaced by Elvis and JFK.

## I THINK ICON

*Clinton learned his politics the same way most baby boomers did: By watching television. At 10, he was captivated by the 1956 party conventions, reporting the plot lines to his family as if he was watching a Western.*

—HOWARD FINEMAN, "Sixties Coming of Age," *Newsweek*, July 20, 1992

Were it not for the precedent set by Ronald Reagan, the idea of a President Elvis might be terrifying rather than amusing. Al Gore telling DemCon delegates he'd always dreamed of being Elvis's "warm-up act" could've been a hideous example of redneck demagoguery; the *New York Times* report on the president's "LONG DAYS, LATE NIGHTS" and Elvis tie collection would've reported a clinical degree of necrophiliac fetishism; the president's trademark Elvis lip-bite and slack-jawed country boy grin should be the sinister ultimate in media dissembling.

Never mind that Clinton's analogue is less Elvis than the onetime advertising major Garth Brooks—another touchy-feely Southern showman who, like Clinton, set his demographic sights on suburban Boomers. (The nostalgic sixties imagery in Brooks's video "The Dance" anticipates *The Man from Hope*.) Clinton's identification with Elvis may be less calculated than sincerely sentimental—as Arkansas attorney general, he phoned his mother himself to break the news of the King's death—but it would have been impossible for so astute a politician to ignore that ceaseless yammering clamor for a resurrected King so vividly documented in Greil Marcus's *Dead Elvis*.

By 1990, the Disciples of Elvis communed across a cacophonous nationwide network of tabs and zines, pop and avant-pop music, conceptual art works and postage stamps, TV shows and movies. (The '92 campaign brought an apotheosis of sorts with *Honeymoon in Vegas*, a comedy set in two mythical Elvislands, Las Vegas and Hawaii, wherein a squadron of El impersonators effectively save the character played by Nicholas Cage—who'd already done his Elvis in *Wild at Heart*.) On the one hand, give them a reborn King: on the other . . . a reconstitution of the atomized JFK.

Clinton is certainly the culmination— perhaps the termination—of the Dead Elvis cult, though he was only 10 when its subject exploded on the scene. His adolescent role model was the first political "Elvis," whose own cult received a massive booster shot from Oliver Stone during the 1991–92 political season, and whose image resaturated the media this past November.

John Kennedy was not only the last non-Southern Democrat to be elected president, but the party's last viable icon. No American politician, least of all Ted Kennedy, had so assiduously linked himself to JFK as has the Man from Hope. The sacred heart of Clinton's campaign bio was the priceless newsreel footage of Teen Bill shaking hands with President Kennedy. *Newsweek*'s post-election special upgraded this anointment from "mere advertising to the realm of prophetic history"—but why not call it the anti-Zapruder film?

Like Kennedy I, Kennedy II has been dissed by the military and criticized for nepotism, assailed by right-wingers for destroying the nation's moral fabric, and admonished by liberals for pandering to public opinion. Like Kennedy II in his first year in office, Kennedy I presided over a number of conspicuous PR failures (the Bay of Pigs fiasco, the sudden appearance of the Berlin Wall, the humiliating multiorbit flights of Soviet cosmonauts Gagarin and Titov). Moreover, Kennedy I vacillated on civil rights and proved incapable of moving many of his programs—including federal aid to schools and federal health insurance for the elderly—through a Democratic Congress irritated by the pushy attitude of his aggressive young aides.

But despite the lack of any conspicuous domestic triumph or international success, America loved him. Kennedy I began his second year in office with a 75 percent approval rating. He had shaken off the character questions that had dogged his long campaign (youth, religion, lineage). America was amazed by his displays of wit, televised press conferences, personal communiqués to movie stars and athletes. It was under Kennedy that the president became a TV personality and the White House a perpetual human-interest site.

Kennedy was only *like* a movie star; Ronald Reagan really was one. As the first Republican to appropriate Kennedy (as well as FDR and Truman), Reagan was the JFK who survived his assassination attempt, appealed to youth, and "won" the Cold War. As Rush Limbaugh loves to demonstrate, Reagan cashed the check that Kennedy wrote. Kennedy's irony was trumped by Reagan's self-deprecating "irony." After his first year in office, even *The Nation* allowed that he seemed "stable, decisive, charming, and damn nice," that he was "doing as well as his devotees had hoped and better than his critics had expected."

Reagan's foreign policy may have been largely reactive, yet even in his first year in office, he projected resolve. As an unnamed White House adviser pointed out to *Newsweek* at the one-year mark, Reagan made the American people "feel good," and as *Newsweek* pointed out to the American people, Reagan knew "that an important part of being a president is looking and acting like one." Reagan, the weekly concluded, seems to be "an activist President [yet] he is not an active President." Clinton, on the other hand, appears to be precisely the opposite: "LIGHTS! CAMERA! CLINTON AT WORK: IS MOTION THE SAME THING AS ACTION?" the *Times* asked last October, days before he prepared to re-relaunch his administration by sending Gore to joust Perot on *Larry King Live*.

As with Jimmy Carter, the media theme of Clinton's first year has been precisely his failure to project a positive image. The nadir of this perceived ineptitude came last May with two remarkably self-reflexive stories. First, the president was caught with his pants down and acting like a performer, treating himself to the sort of $200 haircut Ted Koppel's stand-ins get as a matter of course. (The incident is credited with triggering a boom in anti-Clinton collectibles which persists to this day.) Next, Clinton drew attention to the media's symbiotic relationship with the presidency by purging the White House Travel Office that booked their tickets. Finally, when these stories refused to disappear, he got on *CBS This Morning* to denounce the press.

Who added the laugh track? Within a week, Clinton was "THE INCREDIBLE SHRINKING PRESIDENT" per *Time*—so deliriously sycophantic six months earlier when it declared him Man of the Year. ("Clinton's campaign, conducted with dignity, with earnest attention to issues and with an impressive display of self-possession under fire, served to rehabilitate and restore the legitimacy of American politics and thus, prospectively, of government itself.")

The presidency was now in "free fall." *Time* pointed out that Clinton's 36 percent approval rating was worse than any recent president's after four months in office. Meanwhile, with unexpected pathos, *Dave* reigned as the nation's number one box-office attraction. Simultaneously cynical and uplifting, as well as viewer flattering, *Dave* had its vapidly self-important president (Kevin Kline mimicking George Bush) replaced by an unpretentious, idealistic everyman (Kevin Kline acting "natural"), a premise that could have served to allegorize either a Clinton victory or the comeback for a newly humanized incumbent. Was the movie the Capraesque fantasy of an ordinary citizen taking charge? Was it a plea for a president to slay his Goliath handlers? Or was it merely a spin on business as usual?

When that old-time Reagan handler was appointed Clinton adviser in early June, his former colleagues at *U.S. News & World Report* celebrated the event by presenting him with a doctored *Dave* poster, substituting Gergen's puss for the star's. The show had found its producer. Everything could now be bracketed in quotation marks. At last, the president had a "human" face.

## THE PRESIDENT'S FAVORITE MOVIE

*If one knew what one expected of one's president, one wouldn't need a president would one?*

—JACK SMITH, 1968

Given the historical inevitability of President Bill, it's hard to remember the squalid conditions under which Campaign '92 began. In late 1991, when it was reported that two-thirds of eligible voters were dissatisfied with the contenders, candidate None of the Above began to evolve from neo-Nazi David Duke to paleoconservative Pat Buchanan to crypto-Republican Paul Tsongas to insider-outsider Jerry Brown to supersalesman Ross Perot.

The sour mood of the electorate was reified in *Falling Down,* Hollywood's nightmare reflection of the Way We Live Now—images of breakdown and need, urban decay and foreign invasion, inciting vigilante fantasies of omnipotence and revenge. Conceived when Bush appeared invincible, shot during the Los Angeles riot, and released like a seedy acid flashback several weeks into Clinton's reign, it portrayed a wimpy cold warrior in the form of a laid-off defense worker driven mad by the New World Order. Populist hero or potential wife killer? Audiences reportedly applauded as license plate D-FENS (Michael Douglas) trashed a Korean grocery, shot a Latino gang-banger, and even terrorized a fast-food joint.

*Falling Down* was a psychotic version of *High Noon*—the president's official favorite movie, which he claims to have seen 19 times. *High Noon* is the story of the one TrueMan in a town (political party? nation? NATO alliance?) of cowards. The clock is running down and only he recognizes the threat and is brave enough to stand against it—in the process converting his wife from mealymouthed pacifist to cold-blooded killer. Thanks to the maudlin quality of its Cold War tough realism, *High Noon* has been the official favorite movie for all American presidents from Eisenhower up until now. (There will never be a president hip enough to cite *Johnny Guitar*.)

Nobody's asking for *High Noon* back . . . yet. Still, with obsolete NATO replaced by bankrupt Euro Disney, the formerly all-defining Cold War evaporates into a trickle of declassified revelations: Uncle Walt was an FBI informer, J. Edgar dressed in drag, American bombers and Soviet MIGs played a 15-year-long game of tag over Kamchatka, the U.S. government built a gigantic bomb shelter to preserve itself in the Virginia hills, hundreds of American civilians were used as radioactive guinea pigs. D-FENS has to be wondering what makes a man now?

Clinton's domestic agenda led him to a sitcom universe, and the end of the Cold War marooned him there. How else to account for his regaling a Belgian audience with inexplicable saxophone references, or the bizarre bonhomie with which he compared Chancellor Kohl to a sumo wrestler, or his totally calculated, hilarously sodden tour of Prague after dark with Václav Havel? As the first president without the benefit of the apocalyptic Soviet threat, Clinton is automatically diminished—compelled to live out the cruel Boomer nightmare of downward mobility. Don't stop thinking about tomorrow, to be sure.

The parade is over. Clinton's election coincided with the deflation of the Age of Reagan's most pumped up helium balloons—Bruce is over, Madonna shaky, Arnold domesticated, Stallone in suspended animation, the Gloved One teetering on the brink of a colossal fall. It's a poignant footnote to the Clinton inauguration, and a mad flashback to 1984, that Michael's handlers reportedly proposed to combine all 10 balls into one gigantic Jacksonalia.

In the midst of the gaudy debris, Bill stands alone. His rise came during the futile search for a new Johnny Carson, that is, for a detached jester to frame the spectacle and put the president in his place. (Given the end of network hegemony, there can never be another Carson. Nevertheless, not only Jay Leno and David Letterman but Howard Stern, Rush Limbaugh, and Ross Perot all pretend to the Carson throne.) Numerous commentators have pointed out that President Reagan was something like a national TV host. A quick study who tries to please, can operate on five hours' sleep, and likes to talk, Bill would seem even better suited for the job. "He puts Geraldo to shame!" *The War Room* records Mary Matalin's furious wail after Clinton bested Bush in the second, explicitly *Donahue*-like debate.

Throughout the campaign, the candidate handled himself like a veteran channel surfer, hopping from the Evening News to *Donahue* to MTV to *Arsenio* and back. Having lost his postinaugural momentum to talk radio, the president opened the 1993–94 television season by commandeering *Nightline*, then dispatched Gore to smash ashtrays with Letterman leering on. Clinton equaled Nixon's Checkers speech when he confessed his marital difficulties on *60 Minutes*—and that was just the beginning. With every appearance, another comeback. There's got to be a morning NAFTA; it's just Whitewater under the bridge.

The fact is that Clinton is at once talk-show supremo and stellar guest. He's not just the telepastor who feels your pain; he's also a champion telepenitent. His résumé offers one potential *Oprah* after another: sons who survived the prenatal deaths of their fathers, children of single-parent families, Yanks at Oxford, husbands whose wives bring home the bacon, siblings of recovered substance abusers, spouses who are compulsive philanderers, joggers who can't lose weight, cat owners with multiple allergies. No wonder the president is supposedly addicted to watching the Menendez trial on Court TV. Where Reagan chose to deny the dysfunctional family, Clinton rushes to embrace it.

As Gergen mused to the *New York Times Magazine,* "To think that you can turn off the Government's information machine and still run the Government is—why, it's hard to imagine it. It requires an enormous leap into a wholly different approach, and one that would probably bring about some unforeseen consequences to the whole system. You know, the Presidency probably would just become dysfunctional." Self-serving but self-evident: The information machine to which Gergen owes his ultimate allegiance is, after all, addicted to itself. It may be the president's life-support, yet sooner or later, that same fabulous apparatus has plunged every president from LBJ through George Bush into perceived dysfunctionality.

In the Bill Clinton Show, the presidential ego appears stripped of its D-FENS to disarmingly comic and deceptively personal effect. Appearing so, Clinton may hope to escape the fate of his predecessors, who never thought to prep the audience for the flaming despotism that proved their undoing. But at the same time that this obsessively placating, seemingly hapless figure moves us, he moves us ever further from direct contact with political power. Knowledge of Bill Clinton replaces knowledge of how things actually stand. It scarcely matters why the president is in trouble. We just want to know he's on the road to recovery.

The media need the president. We and he both know that, just as he and we know that the media need us to need him too. The Laws of Gergenomics maintain that the president appears dysfunctional in order to save the relationship—or rather, in order to preserve the presidency. The virus of empathy is loose in the system. Bill Clinton isn't just our commander in chief, he's our first media codependent.

## BORN AGAIN AGAIN

THE DELIGHTFUL TRUISM THAT SIGN SUPERSEDES THAT WHICH IS SIGNIFIED AND, consequentially, image rules in America received additional support during an unusually self-conscious midterm election where the most popular political special effect was the morph that transformed Democratic congressional candidates (despite their best efforts) into a sinister image of President Bill Clinton. Late '94 was a political season when the likelihood of the comprehensive national medical plan that was to be the chef d'oeuvre of the Clinton administration vanished even as NBC's high-powered hospital series *ER* proved itself to be the most successful new television drama in 18 years—"A Health-Care Program That Really Works" per *Newsweek*'s enthusiastic cover story. (Note: While the conventional tele-wisdom has it that medical shows usually appeal to women, network savants determined that *ER*'s numbers were swelled by the male viewers who believed it to be an action show.)

When not avidly immersed in *ER*'s benign cathode rays, one half of the national brain agonized over the distopian vision put forth by Professor Charles Murray in his best-seller *The Bell Curve*: America was becoming a society hopelessly polarized between a "cognitive elite" and a growing, unredeemable underclass of criminal types with submoronic 75 IQ's. Meanwhile, the brain's other hemisphere continued to dote upon the mentally retarded hero of *Forrest Gump*— a movie repeatedly cited for its positive, counter-countercultural values at the "conservative summit" on Hollywood sponsored by *The National Review* and the Center for the Study of Popular Culture. (Note: Murray's antisocial underclass is overwhelmingly black while the virtuous Forrest Gump, of course, is white.)

No sooner had the election results arrived than the allegedly liberal mass media joined its triumphant opponent, Rush Limbaugh, in characterizing the hapless Clinton as the first half-term president in American history. Then they punished themselves further by transferring its attention and hence the trappings of power to another glad-handing silver-haired scamp, a fellow bubba-boomer—our new Speaker of the House, Newt Gingrich. Never mind that this improved Clinton had himself, once upon a time, been a deferment-seeking draft dodger—he was an authentic tough guy, not to mention a divorced and remarried deadbeat dad. (Note: Republican support was overwhelmingly white male.)

Like his demographic cohorts Clinton and Gump, Gingrich had been raised, at least initially, by a single mother. And, no less than they, he had been a countercultural fellow traveler: his youthful indiscretions include opposing the Vietnam War, leading a student protest against the Tulane administration's attempt to censor nude photos in the student newspaper, co-coordinating the Louisiana effort in support of Nelson Rockefeller's foredoomed campaign for the 1968 Republican presidential nomination, starting a program in environmental studies at West Georgia College, and maintaining his sideburns into the mid-seventies. But Gingrich, who had no interest in feeling anybody's pain, was far more successful in the presidential role of designating enemies than was affable empathetic Bill.

In a reference to another current Hollywood movie, released under the rubric "The children of America need heroes" and concerning the abrasive rascality of an unpleasant, win-at-all-costs Georgia baseball player, former Clinton aide turned telephone industry lobbyist Roy Neel warned that our "national politics [was] now a sport played by the Ty Cobbs, not the Forrest Gumps." At the same time, Gingrich taunted Clinton as a Gump wannabe, warning the President that it would be "very, very dumb" to attempt to obstruct the Republicans' vaunted Contract with America. (Clinton's reflexive response was to sign onto the contract's most magical clause—the return of school prayer as cure for the epidemic of teenage violence, sexuality, and anomie.)

Unlike the Democrats, the Republicans had grasped the electorate's desire to inflict punishment. They also understood the irrational power of denial. Defending Gingrich's belief in so-called family values, his openly lesbian half-sister remarked that she was "surprised" to see the press demanding of the new Speaker "that he *be* his vision. I don't think anyone is. I think it's to his credit that he aspires to be better than he is." Something old was being reborn, as Republican icon Arnold Schwarzenegger demonstrated to millions of his fellow Americans over the long Thanksgiving Weekend in *Junior*, his latest monster hit.

Was the fantasy of a self-impregnating white macho man merely one more symptom of mass regression? Was it a corrective celebration of idealized single motherhood? Or was it the poster image for the Contract with America, a tantalizing promise of a Reaganism without Reagan? Indeed, in the midst of the campaign, the old Charmer briefly surfaced with his own recovered memory that he, too, was having difficulty remembering.

### THE REMAKING OF THE PRESIDENT

**T**HE POLITICAL QUESTION, AS 1996 GREW NIGH, WAS THIS: WOULD THE AMERICAN electorate remember Bill Clinton as the last liberal—a funny fat boy cum dysfunctional ditherer? Scarcely a month before the primary season began, the *Louisville Courier* had caricatured our president as *Saturday Night Live*'s Stuart Smalley reassuring his mirrored reflection: "I'm good enough. I'm smart enough, and darn it, people like me."

Step one in the Clinton recovery had been *The American President*—a *muy simpático* portrait of an affable, narrowly elected, pragmatically waffling baby-boom Democrat characterized by a lack of military service, a teenage daughter, and a vague sense of some personal compromise. (Thanks to the subtext Michael Douglas brought to the role, that weakness was sexualized.) Critics had no trouble identifying President Andrew Shepherd. "Bill Clinton on his best day" per *Time*. The verisimilitude was duly certified by former White House press secretary Dee Dee Myers who told *Premiere* that "everything down to the cover of the daily-news summary is exactly as it was during my tenure there."

Not everything, perhaps. As the makers of *The American President* hadn't factored the Brave Newt World of Republican Nation into their entertainment equation, the suspense of politicking the president's program through Congress proved quaintly obsolete. On the other hand, the filmmakers had intuited the Clinton reelection strategy. *The American President*'s sanctimonious opening credits evoked the very 1984 Ronald Reagan TV spots the Clinton team was reportedly studying: stately music, Old Glory, the Constitution, portraits of George Washington and JFK. When *The American President* was still in previews, Clinton svengali Dick Morris imported neofeminist Naomi Wolf (married to White House speechwriter David Shipley) to brainstorm strategy. Wolf warned that, as the Republicans would attempt to cast Clinton as a child, the President needed to establish his image as the "Good Father." *The American President*, even more utopian, dumped the problematic notion of the First Lady to render the president as that nurturing single father romance writers call the "Fab Dad."

*The American President* was, as film critic Andrew Sarris noted, "the first salvo of the Clinton reelection campaign." The second was the State of Union address dubbed "East Coast Oscar Night" by the *Washington Post*'s editorialists. As *The American President* airbrushed Clinton's imperfections (the old ball and chain among them), the State of the Union—culmination of the president's year-long attempt to crash the Republican party—gumped him into Reagan's "Morning in America." Draped in the ceremonial trappings of office, Fab Dad appropriated a host of conservative social issues while reiterating the death of the New Deal—his genial reasonableness was only reinforced on TV by a glowering Newt Gingrich and repeated cutaways to the glaring Republican majority.

Burnishing the president's triumph, Senator Dole's rejoinder was taken as the campaign's first debate. Not only was Dole's speech panned in the media, the Senator himself was perceived as a geriatric automaton. Dole's advisers had dissuaded him from attacking Clinton as *The American President*—the line "no President has been closer to Hollywood" was dropped—still, the Republican frontrunner was characterized on *NewsHour with Jim Lehrer* as "a grumpy old man." (Soon, Hollywood wags would be calling him "Dead Man Walking.") Clinton's notices, by contrast, were sensational. Reviewing his performance on *Good Morning America*, Cokie Roberts declared the address—which invoked the word "children" some 37 times—as "the most presidential speech that I have seen him give."

Clinton's third step came with the anonymously published, best-selling roman à clef *Primary Colors*. Mythologizing the 1992 Clinton campaign already "documented" by the spin-doctor cinema verité *The War Room*, the novel was sensationally vivid—at least in its representation of candidate Governor Jack Stanton and his wife Susan as they vie for the Democratic nomination. Here at last was a plausible portrait of political animal *Homo Clintonus*—his all-encompassing handshakes and "aerobic listening," the way he "snagged a cold, congealed slice of pepperoni, peppers and onions on his way to the bedroom—where Susan was working the phone with a finger stuck in her ear."

What Anonymous made clear was that Clinton/Stanton had the conviction of his appetites. As a college girlfriend tells the novel's narrator: "He loved me. He loved every stray cat in the quad. That boy is not deficient in the love zone—he's got more than enough to go around, and it's all legit. He's never fakin' it." Nor was the love-machine prepared to stop. "It had reached the point of disgust," the narrator observes of the temporarily faltering Stanton campaign, and the press "didn't understand why he wouldn't just quit. Didn't he know he was history? Everyone had written it."

History for sure. Inside the Beltway, speculation as to which Clinton campaign insider or Washington journalist wrote *Primary Colors*—interest promoted by the book's hefty movie sale and the president himself, who taunted the press corps by calling the author's identity "the only secret I've seen kept in Washington in three years"—all but upstaged the Republican candidates preparing for '96's first caucuses and primaries.

The key moment in *Primary Colors* comes when Governor Stanton agrees to deal with yet another burgeoning scandal by talking to Geraldo. "Jack, don't," his wife pleads, "A president doesn't do that sort of thing. We've got to think about keeping whatever dignity we have left." To which the campaign's hardnosed media adviser replies, "Excuse me, ma'am. But who knows what the fuck a president does these days?" Who indeed? Anonymous has packaged Clinton as destiny's darling—or at least, as the best we can expect. Only nine steps to go.

## BOB DOLE, AMERICAN HERO

**H**ADN'T WE SAID GOODBYE TO THE WORLD WAR II GENERATION WITH GEORGE BUSH? Hadn't D-Day turned 50? It's been years since *Time* ran a commemorative cover: "So long soldier". . . and thanks for the memories. But suddenly, like the thing that will not die, it's 72-year-old vet Bob Dole seeking one last mission as your president.

As sumo wrestlers attempt to shove each other out of the ring, so Washington insiders Bill Clinton and Bob Dole will bump and jostle for the presumed electoral center. Less a matter of party affiliation or ideology, their contest for possession of the national phallus can only be appreciated as generational. As Russell Baker articulated the two sides in the *New York Times*: "We are now being governed by the people we used to spank. We are now being threatened by the people who wouldn't let us have the car on Saturday night."

Human nature being what it is, one can well imagine the taxpaying spankees voting for the social-security-collecting car owners and vice versa. (In fact, the *Washington Post* has noted that Dole's contemporaries support Clinton by the greatest margin of any age group.) Nevertheless, the issue comes down to who's Dad. Or as a little girl says in the opening minute of the $167,000 campaign film *Bob Dole: An American Hero*: "The President is the most important person in the whole country." Trying to outflank Clinton's paternal strategy, Dole presents himself as Babysitter Bob. "If something happened along the route and you had to leave your children with Bob Dole or Bill Clinton," he told a Pennsylvania rally, "I think you'd probably leave your children with Bob Dole." Is that because we know that Bob can't spank?

Back in January, *Time* noted that, while Dole only exploited his war wounds after he began losing his quest for the Republican nomination in 1988, "now he's practically flaunting them." Indeed, once Dole clinched the nomination, the *New York Times* ran a detailed story to mark the 51st anniversary of Dole's battlefield injury, headlined "War Wounds Still Mold Life, And Some Politics, for Dole." Bob Dole brings back the World War II narrative, but with a difference. He would be the first physically disabled president since wartime leader FDR. Dole's right arm and hand remain useless: "I still use a buttonhook every day."

No longer the saga of European appeasement and American freedom, Japanese sneak attack and Nazi evil, Dole's war story is a talk show spectacular of triumph over agony and mutilation. ("President Clinton says, I share your pain. I can say, I feel your pain, or whatever.") A 22-year-old college athlete,

Lieutenant Bob Dole was hit by German mortar fire on April 14, 1945, near Bologna, Italy. The shrapnel crushed his spine and broke his collarbone, his right shoulder and his right arm. Unable to move, he nearly bled to death on the battlefield and was shipped back to Kansas in a body cast on which, his mother would discover, other GIs used to stub out their cigarettes.

A human ashtray, paralyzed in both arms and legs, Dole spent 39 months in recovery. "I couldn't feed myself, I couldn't dress myself. I couldn't walk." Dole's right arm was fused to his body at a 45-degree angle until an adventurous orthopedic surgeon carved a new ball and socket for his shoulder and, using transplanted thigh muscle, rehung the arm at Dole's side. This prolonged hospitalization, involving years of therapy and nine operations, seems more than likely the source of Dole's sardonic humor, his dark moods, his mirthless grin, his explosive bitterness, and who knows what bodily secrets. It is suggestive that his first wife and longtime executive aide were both former nurses; his high-powered second spouse is, of course, the head of the American Red Cross. (In *Bob Dole: An American Hero*, the second Mrs. Dole suggests that the Senator signaled a proposal of marriage in part by unveiling his wound for the benefit of his prospective mother-in-law.)

Just as *Bob Dole: American Hero* presents the candidate's recovery as a miracle, so the Dole candidacy bids to arrest the flow of time and reconfigure the logic of our history, reinstall the Vets and send the Boomers back to school. The venerable *High Noon* (1952), Bill Clinton's professed favorite movie (as it has been for most American presidents since Dwight D. Eisenhower) would be replaced as a Rorschach Test with an earlier Stanley Kramer/Carl Foreman/Fred Zinneman opus on the nature of the masculine imperative, namely *The Men* (1950).

Marlon Brando's first movie, *The Men* tells the story of a midwestern college sports hero (Brando) turned infantry lieutenant who, wounded and paralyzed from the waist down, must endure the nightmare of rehabilitation. Brando's epochal performance aside, the movie is distinguished mainly by its unusual recognition of the ephemeral nature of life, irrationality of existence, situational nature of manhood, and existence of suffering, as well as the absence of an unambiguously happy ending. Shot in late 1949, *The Men* opened the following July—two weeks into the Korean War and a few months before the rebuilt Bob Dole successfully ran for Kansas legislature.

A paraplegic Brando for president—or a galvanized cadaver? Despite his miraculous resilience, Dole embodies mortality. On the eve of the New Hampshire primary, *Time* called him "the National Mortician." Even once his opposition collapsed, the best the *Washington Post* could say was that Dole had "risen, if not from the grave, at least from his political sickbed to reclaim the mantle of front runner." The corpselike picture of the young Dole on a hospital bed (prominently displayed in his campaign film) was rhymed this spring by the much-remarked-upon candid snap of Babysitter Bob splayed out in T-shirt and swimming trunks, phone glued to his ear as he "relaxed" by the pool at the Sea View hotel in Miami Beach. (Running this photo next to the headline "Dole's Ideal Vacation: Doing Nothing, or Close to It," the *New York Times* portrayed the Sea View as a sort of nursing home with palm trees: "On any given day [there are] more people with canes or in wheelchairs than children.")

Dole's age and injury will only heighten public fascination with the presidential body. *Times* columnist Maureen Dowd, who has missed little opportunity to draw attention to the state of Dole's torso ("Seeing a politician's thighs is always alarming") noted that his vacation reading was Richard Brookheiser's George Washington biography *Founding Father,* which "breathlessly celebrates Washington's physique." In 1932, Franklin Roosevelt was photographed swimming, as was the cancer-surviving candidate Paul Tsongas 60 years later. Reagan, who went topless and invited the media to document his capacity for yard work in 1980, went on to merge with Rambo as the national symbol of a restored national Hard Body. Still, the trauma of presidential mortality haunts the movies *JFK, In the Line of Fire, Dave,* and even *The American President.*

Bill Clinton may represent appetite, but Bob Dole signifies the void. If the president is as comfy as a Barcalounger, the senate majority leader is as chilly as the grave. As much as we the people tried to resist it, there was an inevitability to this contest—a race which, in addition to World War II vet against Vietnam peacenik, would seem to pit Death against Taxes.

## INDEPENDENCE DAY 1996

Copyright © *Artforum*, January 1997, "Poll Stars," by J. Hoberman.

A STIRRING VISION OF INTERPLANETARY DANGER IN WHICH AMERICA'S YOUTHFUL President, a slick neolib waffler married to an intimidating warrior-woman, reversed his fallen approval ratings by taking a firm stand against the aliens: "Let's nuke the bastards!"

Can it only be six months ago that this cold *latka*—in which a bunch of hopped-up flyboys of varied ethnic persuasions made believe to join forces and decimate a horde of computer-and-latex extraterrestrial locusts—had all Terra in its thrall? The overlong, vaguely camp appreciation of blood and guts, God and country, ultimate sacrifice and cheap thrills copyright throughout all universes known and unknown as *Independence Day* seemed to evaporate from the mind faster than the memory of the Steve Forbes juggernaut. Did the premise of last year's top-grossing movie leave room for a sequel? (And having pretended to join the Republican Revolution to hold the line on Medicare, in the parallel universe production, *Dependence Day*, what can our reelected Bill Clinton possibly do by way of an encore?)

A celebration of American military and cultural hegemony, *Independence Day* was the pure cultural expression of that which *The Nation* had dubbed the National Entertainment State—the spectacle for which the Republican attack on the Clinton White House and the revelation that life had once upon a time existed on Mars were but part of a three-month publicity buildup. Yet another spin on the War of the Worlds scenario, *Independence Day* looked tacky enough to suggest a mega-million-dollar remake of Ray Harryhausen's 1956 *Earth vs. Flying Saucers*—but without the Cold War subtext. This was a feel-good Armegeddon that knowingly quoted R.E.M. ("It's the end of the world as we know it, and I feel fine") and cleverly rewrote *Dr. Strangelove* (Slim Pickens drafted to replay his rip-roaring nuclear suicide).

For Americans, it's a patriotic duty to be entertained. Among other things, *Independence Day* afforded the key negative moment in the year's other Show Biz extravaganza—namely the interminable presidential campaign (which, given its estimated $800 million budget, cost out at roughly $8.50 per vote, or the price of a first-run movie ticket in New York). Mired in the polls, Bob Dole had created a midsummer media event out of his wife's 60th birthday by treating her to a box of Goobers, a basket of popcorn, and a matinee showing of *Independence Day* in a nearly empty Century City cinema. What did the candidate see? Accurate as far as it went, Dole's thumbs-up review ("Leadership—America—Good over Evil") only underscored his cultural cluelessness. By failing to comment on the movie's "money shot" of the White House blown to smithereens, Dole served notice that he had missed the most successful trailer in recent memory.

Dole's hapless attempt to appropriate *Independence Day* underscored a campaign predicated largely on successful Show Biz mergers. With voters indistinguishable from consumers, publishers subsidized potential presidential candidates (and vice versa). Colin Powell's and Newt Gingrich's lucrative book tours amounted to privatized, profit-making test-pilots underwritten, respectively, by S. I. Newhouse's Random House and Rupert Murdoch's HarperCollins.

Even as Hillary Clinton's *It Takes a Village* supplied a readymade campaign issue, Bob Woodward's campaign book (*The Choice*) appeared mid-campaign, and the hooplah surrounding the initially anonymous *Primary Colors* (Random

House) provided a substitute for the actual primary season, the campaign itself was now understood to be a representation (a "campaign opportunity" in the words of Murdoch employee *Weekly Standard* editor William Kristol). Bill Clinton posing as the President while Bob Dole invented a fictional "Bob Dole" as his real self explained to reporters that "We're trying to get good pictures. Don't worry very much about what I say."

Historical depth was provided by the "Richard Nixon" thoughtfully resurrected by Oliver Stone (for the Walt Disney Company) just as the campaign (for which Disney contributed $532,000 to the Democratic Party) got under way. As former Nixon henchmen, from William Safire to candidate Dole himself, cast the President and First Lady as Nixon redux, predicting a Clinton II as scandal-ridden as Nixon II, so the loser would be lambasted by conservative cheerleader Peggy Noonan as the last Nixonian. The crafty Clinton, she bemoaned, won only because he had contrived to run as her former boss Ronald Reagan.

True enough. As predicted by *The American President*, Clinton had simply merged with Hollywood. "The biggest contributing zip to Bill Clinton is 90210," *Variety* bragged (not referring solely to the Murdoch-produced television show). "Politicians and movie stars spring from the same DNA," Jack Valenti crowed. Never mind the polls showing that the professions American parents wished least for their children were president and movie star, by the time the conventions rolled around, even the erstwhile Bushman Kevin Costner switched his allegiance to Clinton. And as the President was reelected First Celebrity, so the *National Enquirer* opened a bureau in the nation's capital: "We refer to Washington as Hollywood East."

The two parties were now in effect, rival studios—the respective producers of Clinton's *Twister* and Dole's *Mission: Impossible*. To the dismay of *Nightline*, which found its convention reportage reduced to the level of E! network publicity, Democrats and Republicans had joined forces to merge the aesthetic of daytime TV with the hooplah of the prime-time conventions. Where else could it end, if not with stars staging public squabbles with their screenwriters and directors? Dole's speechwriter, novelist Mark Helprin, stalked off the Republican set after the candidate rewrote his dialogue; Clinton was upstaged by his philandering chief image-maker Dick Morris—first on the cover of *Time* and then, thanks to the *Star*, during the convention itself.

Pundits complained but, in fact, these spectacles (complete with scandalous interruptions) were as redolent of American might as any blockbuster. Indeed, in the midst of the U.S. election, *Time* was pleased to report how a cadre of American advisers used polls, focus groups, and negative ads to help the living corpse of Boris Yeltsin win reelection to the Russian presidency. In the most spectacular coup, a one-time Dick Morris associate (with White House connections) stage-managed the April summit meeting as a Yeltsin photo op: The American president was directed to just grin and bear it while the Russian leader lectured him about great-power prerogatives . . . for tele-consumption by the folks back in the former USSR. Bringing Independence Day to Moscow: in the New World order, That's Entertainment II.

## BOOM'S END

**N**OW THAT AMERICAN SOLDIERS HAVE LEARNED TO MAKE LOVE AND NOT WAR, THAT the FBI has been humanized as its own public enemy, and a draft-dodging, pot-smoking, free-loving, TV-weaned ex-longhair approaches the second half of his second term, we understand that the personal truly is the political.

Jim Bakker's Christian theme park and Pat Robertson's TV network notwithstanding, family values are a relative nonstarter in the supermarketplace of multiple lifestyles and consumption identities at least in comparison to those of the old counterculture. You can find "free love" pornotopia at just about any video store. Marijuana is the major cash crop of Northern California. Robert Johnson and Bugs Bunny are honored as U.S. postage stamps. Nathan Glazer publishes a book called *We Are All Multiculturalists Now*, and Gay Day has taken its place among the pagan rites of Disney World.

Che Guevara—martyred and resurrected 30 years ago next month—may have been conspicuous by his absence in the series of ads that drafted rebel males like Chet Baker and James Dean to promote Gap khakis, but the revolution's Great Trademark is active in Europe selling shoes and neckties, gracing a top-selling Swatch watch, and giving his name to a brand of British beer. (And that's just the start—forget the disastrous Che biopic of 1969; two new movies are in the works.) The use of Jimi Hendrix to flack Internet access may not be what candidate Bob Dole had in mind when he attacked "the mainstreaming of deviancy" in the last election but—as foretold by Herbert Marcuse back in the day—Repressive Tolerance rules.

The Dodge Rebellion that the advertising agency BBD&O declared on behalf of Chrysler Motors in 1965 (same year that Marcuse published his notorious formulation) was the original Baby Boom–directed instance of what is now called Liberation Marketing: Consumers unite, you have nothing to lose but the inability to change . . . your image. Dodge had formerly been a car for middle-aged squares—its spokesman was TV bandleader Lawrence Welk. Suddenly gramps was gone and, instead, the car was being promoted by Pam Austin, a 24-year-old California blonde whose résumé included two movies with Elvis. "There's a revolutionary leader whose face is getting to be better known than Fidel Castro's, and is certainly less bearded. And she's a she," the *New York Times* noted of Pam with giddy approval.

Did the counterculture take capitalism at its emancipatory word, demanding only the freedom, plenty, and democracy that the program promised—or was it vice versa? Because supermarket democracy is largely a matter of demographics, Time Warner and Walt Disney can comfortably place their bets on red, black, and double zero—encompassing their own critiques, negations, and alternatives even within the same product. (How can parents explain to kids that Disney's *Hercules* is a marketing event when the movie itself satirically pre-empts this criticism?) In *Conglomerates and the Media,* Thomas Frank argues that the market works to "occupy the niche that dissident voices used to occupy in the American cultural spectrum." Moreover, "the most effective identities are found when a brand takes on the trappings of a movement for social justice." With shopping the most universal form of unalienated labor, advertising shoulders the utopian dreams of the left. Jeep Cherokee's off-the-road gas guzzlers equal freedom; Benetton celebrates a politically correct diversity; Nike promotes spiritual self-improvement; the Body Shop protects the rain forest; Ben and Jerry's ice cream makes gluttony taste like communal spirit.

Resistance anyone? How about the already passé resurrection of late fifties lounge culture—Vegas nostalgia, cocktail chic, the canonization of Tony Bennett and Burt Bacharach, a decadent taste for the swinging bachelor pad music of Esquival and Les Baxter. To appreciate the Rat Pack Revival one need look no further than the 40-minute infomercial telecast late last spring over Time Warner's VH-1: *Bill Clinton: Rock & Roll President.* Coproduced by Sarah Staley, the daughter of Clinton's high school friend Caroline Staley, replete with Carly Simon's smugly unctuous commentary and a bunch of vintage prop albums, *Rock & Roll President* is a sub–*Forrest Gump* distillation of the Boomerography, replete with weighty pronouncements: "Eleanor Rigby" is "one of the most powerful songs I ever heard." (Feel the pain?) *Rock & Roll President* intercuts candidate Clinton's epochal *Arsenio* appearance with early Elvis on TV—although the Prez is seen to best advantage in an ancient 8-mm home movie with his hair slicked back and the short sleeves of his dress Madras shirt fashionably double rolled, already biting his lip as he essays the cha-cha-cha.

Will rock 'n' roll never, ever die? Let's take the Bridge to the Twenty-first Century. The very same week that VH-1 chose to showcase the President's faux record collection, the official organ of the Time Warner empire raised the generational stakes: "You called us slackers," *Time*'s cover warned, pretending to speak on behalf of those Americans born after the 1965 Dodge Rebellion. "You dismissed us as Generation X. Well, move over. We're not what you thought." (And what was that again, sonny?)

Hello Geezerdom. Like Ronald Reagan before him and TV itself, the Rock 'n' Roll President is a conservative hedonist. By comparison, the mainly dead Rat Pack appears to those who missed it the first time to be a bunch of heedless reactionaries. These drinking, smoking, cursing grown-ups embody the last moment before Liberation Marketing and the Baby Boom conquered the world.

## ENTERTAINER-IN-CHIEF

Originally published as "The Show Biz President," the
*Village Voice* (February 10, 1998).

A VAST RIGHT-WING CONSPIRACY? ONLY TO AMUSE, FELLOW VIEWERS.
The Zippergate miniseries is under way. But what we are really watching is the next stage in the marriage of politics and popular culture.

What began with our first radio president, Calvin Coolidge, and accelerated to warp speed with JFK (if only Lee Harvey Oswald had the foresight to sign with William Morris) is now a wrap. The distinctions between show biz and hard news have completely collapsed. Under TV-bred Bill Clinton, fan magazines drive journalism, tabloids drive TV, cyberchats drive talk radio, reporting drives the movies.

As for the current scandal, let no one say the protocols of entertainment were ignored. In the beginning was the book deal. Well before the story broke last month, the literary rights were secured. *All the President's Women; Sex, Lies, and Audiotape; Zippergate; Bill and Monica's Excellent Adventure*, or whatever we finally decide to call the scenario, it was first packaged by agent-ghostwriter Lucianne Goldberg and then offered to Kenneth Starr, desperate director of the $30 million nonstarter *Whitewaterworld*.

In Hollywood East as in Washington West, everyone's got a script to peddle. Disgruntled bureaucrat Linda Tripp had been pitching her White House treatments for years, most recently working uncredited on rogue FBI agent Gary Aldrich's Clinton exposé *Unlimited Access*. "She's like Forrest Gump," a former Bush aide told *Newsweek*. "Time and again, she keeps showing up in the middle of these things." Finally, the would-be screenwriter lucked into a starstruck ingenue from the Land of 90210.

Life is like a box of chocolates. Just as Tripp was looking for the right high concept, Beverly Hills brat Monica Lewinsky had been searching for a vehicle throughout her entire adult life. Lewinsky's high school yearbook listed her as "MOST LIKELY TO HAVE HER NAME IN LIGHTS," no small achievement in itself; her college classmates recall her fanciful accounts of chilling with Tori Spelling and Lyle Menendez.

Exiled from the White House mailroom, this daughter of destiny would inform Tripp that she'd been intimate with the costar she code-named Schmucko, and insist she had the cum-stained dress to prove it. Will even Sotheby's be able to put a price on that trophy? Or will it end up in the Smithsonian, alongside George Washington's wooden teeth?

---

Politics and popular culture are what bring us together. We are defined as a people by our participation in Hollywood blockbusters and media spectacles. To be ignorant of Anita Hill and Rodney King, Murphy Brown and O. J., Desert Storm and *Independence Day*, Dick Morris and *Seinfeld*, Princess Di and *Titanic*, Oscar night and the Super Bowl is to be actively un-American. In the National Entertainment State, the president rules as First Entertainer, and the whole whatevergate he happens to be mixed up in is just too gosh darn much fun for us to let it go.

Sooner stifle your startle reflex than ask Ted and Cokie and Dan (and Dave and Jay) not to react to the sexual scent of political scandal. The media seizes the narrative, preempts regular programming, and expands its round-the-clock team coverage to report on—not to mention protest—its own fascination, soliciting public opinion all the while. None of us think it matters, but no one can get enough.

Who can forget the near hysteria of Monica's opening weekend, with her ID photo on every newsstand, the presidential rope-line video slo-mo'd, in heavy rotation, and—as the scandal's rival release, *Havana Honeymoon,* played to empty houses—the national nervous system focused on a single subject. Mike McCurry merged with *Melrose Place, Nightline* with Dr. Ruth ("We are going to talk about oral sex," Ted warned), and the on-line gutter-rag *Drudge Report* was invited to *Meet the Press.*

"I did it because it's fucking fascinating! I love dish! I live for dish!" Lucianne Goldberg cackled when the *New Yorker* asked her if she had a political agenda. The fact is, dish is political. The tapes that Goldberg conjured into existence, slipped to director Starr, and then leaked to the press, are just one more part of the process by which, to quote historian Benedict Anderson, "fiction seeps quietly and continuously into reality, creating that remarkable confidence of community in anonymity which is the hallmark of modern nations."

As an episode in American show business, the Clinton presidency has oscillated between wacky sitcom and confessional talk show—*The Beverly Hillbillies* meets *Oprah*—with long intervals programmed by VH-1, particularly around election time. Now, with no presidential campaign to distract us, the presidency might become Fox's newest prime-time soap.

William Safire was only the most persistent of those who predicted that *Clinton II* would be as scandal ridden as *Nixon II*. (He has even written the president a Buddy broadcast to complement Nixon's career-saving Checkers speech.) Our desire for that scenario may be gleaned, not only by the Vincent Foster conspiracy cult—the political equivalent of a midnight movie—but from the eager flurry of salacious thrillers released to set the mood of Clinton II. With uncanny prescience, *Shadow Conspiracy, Murder at 1600*, and *Absolute Power* all feature the White House as crime scene.

In his 1993 *In the Line of Fire*, Clint Eastwood played a heroic Secret Service agent protecting an empty suit; but by 1997, in *Absolute Power*, Eastwood put the suit on display, watching himself as presidential sex escalated from merely adulterous to kinda rough to ultra violent. It's President O. J.!

Bill Clinton has twice offered America the choice between a lover and a fighter—and we bought it, twice. As a would-be Elvis defeated first a John Wayne wannabe and then a Humphrey Bogart retread, Woodstock eclipsed D-Day as the ruling generational metaphor. Having beaten the last hero from Big Two, Clinton has remained a lover. Lawyers may dispute whether being serviced by a big-haired groupie may constitute dictionary-definition love—but whatever it is, it sure ain't war.

In the absence of military or economic crisis, Hollywood is free to set the agenda. And increasingly, it prefigures politics. As the president geared up to run for reelection, we chuckled at the spectacle of sleazebag Michael Douglas as his surrogate trying to date lobbyist Annette Bening in the Oval Office. Now we must face the possibility that *The American President* fed Monica Lewinsky's Aaron Spelling fantasy by presenting the president as that eligible and nurturing figure romance writers call the Fab Dad.

It's only a matter of time before Jay Leno features the Dancing Clintons while, in the tape loop that serves as national sound track. "Hail to the Chief" is replaced by the catchy Hot Chocolate pick-up anthem revived by *The Full Monty*: "I believe in miracles. . . . You came along, you sexy thing."

The suits at Universal are wondering about possible negative fallout for their $65 million adaptation of *Primary Colors*—starring a tubbed-out John Travolta gone salt-and-pepper as the Clinton clone who may have knocked up a 17-year-old girl. Will audiences pay to see a fantasy that, for all intents and purposes, has already happened?

Because box-office results can't be legislated, Hollywood serves as a source of electoral feedback. No wonder Clinton dreams of running a movie studio, according to Cindy Adams. (Where else can you get regular under-the-desk head?) No wonder the Clintons spent Meltdown Weekend at the White House, hunkered down in the same Family Theater where, it would soon be reported and denied, an unidentified Secret Service man spied Monica being "intimate" with Bill.

The Clintons were immersing themselves in movies, communing with the masses by catching up on *Titanic* and *The Apostle*. The former could only have enhanced the president's self-pity. (Even worse would have been *The Gingerbread Man*, in which a transparently Clintonian lawyer is led by his dick to the brink of catastrophe.) But *The Apostle* features Robert Duvall as an adulterous, murderous, yet triumphantly righteous Baptist evangelical preacher. Just as the oft-screened *Patton* reinforced Nixon's decision to invade Cambodia, *The Apostle's* libidinal preacherman could only strengthen President Hound Dog's will to deny.

Bill's been here before. His ratings-enriched State of the Union speech was dedicated to the memory of Sonny Bono, even as Hillary took to performing the equivalent of "I Got You Babe" on *Good Morning America*. Unfortunately for the president, however, Judge Starr would only have to let La Lewinsky twist two or three days in the wind to recapture the headlines. The world may laugh at us, but as citizens of the Entertainment State, we do understand these things—witness the ease with which the "*Wag the Dog* syndrome" (as the Pentagon has named the fear of mimicking the movie by starting a war) instantly insinuated itself into the highest reaches of op-ed punditry and— such is the nature of the Global Village—the calculations of Saddam Hussein.

The embarrassingly prescient *Wag the Dog*, like many things Boomer, is really a nostalgia for the Cold War, the Great Days when permanent crisis—the threat of nuclear armageddon and the international communist conspiracy— insured that sexual peccadilloes would not dominate the news cycle. This suggests that only bombing Baghdad could blast little Monica from her page one niche. Even the hyper-jingo *Post* would have to drop her. A nation is defined not just by what it remembers but by what it forgets.

If Monica has legs, the show must go off. But who will tell the president it's time to leave the screen? Last time, it was senior Republicans who made that call. But this time, the new Democratic wise men—Michael Eisner, Steven Spielberg and Barbra Streisand—will visit the White House. The helicopter can wisk Bill and Hill (and Buddy and Socks) over the rainbow, but the klieg lights will remain. Ready for your close-up Mr. Gore?

## *PLEASANTVILLE:* SOMEWHERE UNDER THE RAINBOW

Originally published as "Under the Rainbow,"
*Sight and Sound* (January 1999).

**A**T ONCE GENEROUS AND TOTALIZING, PATHETICALLY EAGER TO PLEASE AND RUTHLESSLY inclusive, outgoing and self-absorbed, American entertainment has a natural desire to be everything to everyone—its human embodiment would be Bill Clinton on the campaign trail. But can such an other-directed force ever truly reflect upon itself? With *Pleasantville*, Hollywood strains to ponder just this epistemological question.

The latest example of that American strain of magical realist fantasy rooted in Frank Capra's *It's a Wonderful Life* and Rod Serling's TV series *The Twilight Zone*, *Pleasantville* is Gary Ross's first directorial outing, after writing speeches for Democratic candidate Michael Dukakis and crafting sound bites for President Bill Clinton—not to mention the scripts for the hit comedies *Big* (1988) and *Dave* (1993). It is also the most fanciful political allegory produced in Hollywood since *Forrest Gump.*

If *Dave* was the first consciously Clintonian movie, the 42-year-old Ross (son of screenwriter Arthur *Creature from the Black Lagoon* Ross, a liberal described by Gary as "dark gray–listed" during the 1950s) is himself a living embodiment of the Washington-Hollywood connection that has made Bill Clinton the most popular movieland president since John F. Kennedy—and perhaps ever, supported and defended as he is by Barbra Streisand, Madonna, and the moguls of Dreamworks.

*Dave* was a canny pop culture synthesis with a premise recalling, among other things, *The Phantom President*, a 1932 comedy in which a good-natured snake-oil salesman (all-round entertainer George M. Cohan) secretly doubled for, and ultimately supplanted, a corrupt and stuffy presidential candidate (also George M. Cohan). More flattering to the viewer, *Dave* had its vapidly self-important, philandering president (Kevin Kline mimicking George Bush) replaced—after he suffers a stroke in a staff assistant's bed—by his lookalike, an unpretentiously idealistic everyman (Kline acting "natural").

Thus, a regular guy came to power—although in *Dave*'s genial world (Washington no less than Hollywood) one's performance under the lights and before the camera in the constructed scenarios of the ongoing news cycle was at least as important as one's performance in waking reality. *Dave* defined the president in terms of his image. The real President was introduced posing for a phony photo opportunity; Dave, by contrast, first appeared atop a pig, impersonating the President as a shill for a used-car dealer. Dave's is honest hokum—a postmodern oxymoron that suggests candidate Bill Clinton's playing his saxophone on a TV talk show. Was Gary Ross then the new Capra? "A political film works if it's also an idealistic film," he explained. "People want to feel renewed about their politics. . . . Those films in the 1930s succeeded because they understood what the right hero was; they weren't afraid of populism."

Simultaneously cynical and uplifting, moderate-liberal in tone, *Dave* maintained a consensus by sticking to safe issues. Like his Biblical namesake, the hero tackled a huge adversary—during his brief term in office, he brought in his accountant pal to balance the national books, cut a bit of wasteful spending, and restored funding to a single homeless shelter. Small wonder that Clinton asked for a special White House screening and consequently drafted Ross as a presidential joke writer—the movie proved to be an uncanny prophesy of his agenda.

Like *Big* (in which Tom Hanks played a 12-year-old boy in the body of a man) and *Dave*, *Pleasantville* is a fish-out-of-water movie with a didactic spin. And even more than in *Dave*, the setting is a media hall of mirrors. A pair of contemporary teenage twins David (Tobey Maguire) and Jennifer (Reese Witherspoon) are transported from their troubled suburban home, not into the 1950s (per *Back to the Future*), but into a representation of the period—the *echt*, ersatz fifties TV situation comedy, *Pleasantville*, shown (as the fifties have been lo these 25 years) in perpetual rerun on American cable TV.

The trip from the crass, oversexed, broken-family present day to a homey black-and-white fantasy world is something like *The Wizard of Oz* in reverse. Set in a sort of small town populated by polite adolescents, affable white-collar dads, and housewife moms who bake pies in pearls and vacuum in heels, the *Pleasantville* program evokes family sitcoms like *The Donna Reed Show*, *Ozzie and Harriet*, and *Father Knows Best*. The movie *Pleasantville* is just clever enough to recognize its imaginary namesake as a form of sociological camp, attractive for its corny negation of the modern world. Ross takes care to set the table by juxtaposing the TV show's simpleminded cheerfulness with 1998 kids absorbing all manner of depressing statistics on jobs, AIDS, and ecology.

The *Pleasantville* sitcom is essentially the same artificial world as the made-for-TV location of *The Truman Show*. But Ross gives his theme park a less paranoid, more obviously political, inflection by having it promoted on the film's equivalent of Nick at Nite (a cable network specializing in just such canned nostalgia) with such post-fifties Republican party buzz terms as "family values" and "kinder, gentler." It is also blatantly a fiction. Because this is TV, in its initial triumphantly innocent incarnation, the rain never falls and the temperature is always 72 degrees. Toilets and double beds do not exist. Firemen are only around to rescue kitty cats from trees, and the high school basketball team never loses a game.

Albeit exaggerated, the *Pleasantville* show is nevertheless a pleasingly skillful simulation, not least in the hyperreal casting of William H. Macy and Joan Allen (who, having played Pat Nixon, is the icon of fifties womanhood) as the ideal parents whom Jennifer and David have suddenly inherited. But the place Pleasantville is also the fantasy of a perfect, conflict-free social order available to anyone with a television set—even if its dated qualities make it seem less paradisal than, for example, more recent let-us-entertain-U-topias as *Bay Watch* or *Beverly Hills 90210*. "We're like stuck in nerdville," Jennifer moans as, correctly re-outfitted in a cardigan and poodle skirt, she joins her new peer group filing into school under the American flag.

In an era when old television shows are regularly recycled as overblown movies, it seems absurd for Hollywood to critique TV for its lack of verisimilitude. (Ross himself worked on the script of *The Flintstones*.) Perhaps, with the new power of the Internet, it has become easier for the movies to imagine their old enemy as America's sole cultural referent. What constructs Pleasantville? Jesus Christ may be conspicuous by his absence from this moral regime, but Ross has no difficulty imagining God's representative as a cosmic television repairman (veteran sitcom star Don Knotts).

The twins themselves, as noted by Andrew Sarris, are "secular missionaries from the advanced '90s." Schooled in pop trivia, David is familiar with every *Pleasantville* episode and can hence alter the show's "reality," while the less cerebral Jennifer employs another strategy to broaden Pleasantville's horizons. Having already nibbled the apple back in the world, she introduces sex into this sterile Eden—and by thus raising the excitement quotient, makes it more entertaining (for the audience not the least). This transformation is signified in showbiz terms by the gradual introduction of color.

Funny for about half an hour, *Pleasantville* thereafter becomes an increasingly lugubrious, ultimately exasperating mix of technological wonder and ideological idiocy. The sexual metaphor is wildly inconsistent. Having seduced the gee-whiz captain of the basketball team and precipitated the first flush of color into Pleasantville's video gray world, Jennifer is free to sublimate—putting on a pair of glasses to hit the books and, in general, leave the orchestration of the Pleasantville cultural revolution to her brother. *Pleasantville* has no laugh track, but given the simplicity of its moral universe it scarcely needs one.

Soon all the cool kids are out on Lover's Lane participating in a Technicolor orgy of secular humanism as they devour *Huckleberry Finn* and *Catcher in the Rye*, two books which have been often targeted for censorship in the ongoing war for the soul of America's school children. The goofy malt-shoppe proprietor (Jeff Daniels) has taken up fauvist painting and, before too long, mom has left dad to take up with him (as a nude model no less). Eventually, these proponents of nonmarital sex, fifties rock 'n' roll, and western culture become Pleasantville's persecuted "colored" people; with the black-and-white "no-changists" of the all-male Chamber of Commerce conducting themselves, in menacing low angle, like book-burning Nazi brownshirts.

*Father Knows Best* as *Triumph of the Will*? Exactly where is Ross going? As a political statement, *Pleasantville* is seemingly haunted by the specter of the Reverend Pat Robertson's cable network (a mix of Christian fundamentalism and family-oriented TV shows from the black-and-white fifties) and responding to the early stages of the 1996 presidential campaign wherein the Republican candidate Bob Dole focused his geriatric fire on the "mindless violence and loveless sex" being foisted on the unwilling American people by liberal Hollywood: "There are few national priorities more urgent." Dole's public attacks on Antonia Bird's *Priest* as hostile to "family values" and Oliver Stone's *Natural Born Killers* as a "nightmare of depravity" were among the most publicized episodes in the ongoing culture war that had been declared at the 1992 Republican convention. The Evil Empire was dead, but nature abhors a vacuum. "There is no 'after the Cold War,'" neoconservative godfather Irving Kristol proclaimed in *The Public Interest*. "So far from having ended, my cold war has increased in intensity, as sector after sector of American life has been ruthlessly corrupted by the liberal ethos. . . . Now that the other 'Cold War' is over, the real cold war has begun."

The battle against the Soviets was only a rehearsal. The true jihad was the post–Cold War cleanup that demonized liberals, rappers, femi-nazis, illegal aliens, counterculture McGoverniks, welfare mothers, and homosexuals—a virtual who's who of Unpleasantville. Indeed, such types would soon receive their just desserts at the movies. Released during America's last midterm election season, *Forrest Gump* was another ambitious special effects–driven comedy that addressed the recent past. "I imagined Norman Rockwell painting the baby boomers," was how director Robert Zemeckis put it. Here, history was dissolved in a bleak yet saccharine tale of simpleminded goodness triumphing over the social ills associated with the Vietnam era.

Amazingly popular and absolutely prescient in anticipating the outcome of the 1994 election, *Forrest Gump* literalized the notion of American popular culture as a spectacular form of political theater in which actual leaders assumed the same symbolic weight as star performers and headline personalities. *Pleasantville* was similarly well timed to underscore the lessons of recent American politics. The movie opened, at number one, in the midst of an off-year election that had been framed by right-wing Republicans and the powerful Christian Coalition as a referendum on Bill Clinton's morality. Just as in the movie, the 1998 congressional races pitted black-and-white Pleasantville against the Clinton palette of rainbow relativism. And despite widespread predictions that the President would drag his party down in flames, voters proved surprisingly tolerant of their leader's peccadilloes.

It was quite a difference from the *Forrest Gump* election which had been universally explained as the white man's revenge. Back then, the *Wall Street Journal*'s postmortem interview with a 33-year-old unemployed male Memphisite, mesmerized by the spectacle of women driving to work each morning, put it on the line: "You just know that has got to emasculate a die-hard, big-ego, male chauvinist. Men have got to have a scapegoat . . . and Clinton is just perfect for everybody's ailment." In 1994, right-wing talk radio hosts taunted Clinton as the first half-term president in American history, as the allegedly liberal media punished itself by transferring attention and hence the trappings of power to the new Speaker of the House, Newt Gingrich. But that was only a strategic retreat to Pleasantville. And in 1998, it would be Gingrich's turn to go.

One more episode in the ongoing debate over the 1960s that continues to characterize American politics, *Pleasantville* is scarcely the sort of frontal attack on suburban complacency and family values found in independent films like Todd Solondz's *Welcome to the Doll House* and *Happiness*. For a Hollywood insider like Ross, show business is the only frame of reference that exists. From that perspective, it is nothing less than a patriotic chore to correct the out-moded entertainment of the 1950s that has somehow lodged itself in the mind of the fundamentalist right as the simulation of the American past. Thus does Hollywood defend itself against itself. The clichés are summoned to the rescue. Ross may believe that he is liberating the uptight Eisenhower era with a zipless sixties sexual and cultural revolution, but, if anything, *Pleasantville* is a colorized imitation of New Dealish Capracorn.

While it's unlikely that anyone ever mistook *Ozzie and Harriet* for reality, *Pleasantville* is no less predicated on denial than the TV shows it purports to critique and even more smug in its attitudes. Is it churlishly politically correct to note that, all diversity-babble and color metaphors to the contrary, the new and improved Pleasantville is no less comfortably white and heterosexual (or middle-class and suburban) than the old place? That the official anthem of liberation is a four-decade-old Buddy Holly song rather than gangsta rap? That the we-are-the-world epiphany that ends the movie is completely mediated by the (newly color) TV? Or that the coda is a nauseating replica of a 1984 Ronald Reagan "Morning in America" TV ad (even if it is set to Fiona Apple's cover of a sentimental John Lennon song)?

It's wild to see a big-budget Hollywood movie lifting the cudgels for "modern art" (or at least the modern art of 75 years ago). But in proposing that entertainment will solve the "problems" that entertainment has itself created, this hilariously self-absorbed, hermetically sealed package gives a whole new meaning to the term *bubble brain*.

## CINE CLINTON: *THE CONTENDER* ET AL.

Originally published as "Creatures of Appetite,"
*Sight and Sound* (February 2001).

T'S A SAD FACT OF SHOW BUSINESS THAT THE GLAMOUR OF THE AMERICAN PRESIDENCY has been unavoidably diminished by the fall of the Evil Empire and end of the Cold War. It was precisely this state of affairs that entertainment journalist turned filmmaker and self-described political junkie Ron Lurie addressed in his first, low-budget feature, *Deterrence* (1999). The pre-credit sequence of Lurie's tepidly received thriller, written over a long weekend and filmed in 18 days, presents a newsreel montage of presidents from Dwight Eisenhower through the original George Bush all talking nuclear war; the movie itself is a single-set chamber drama in which, trapped in the Rocky Mountains by an unexpected blizzard even as Saddam Hussein's son overruns Kuwait and pushes on to Saudi Arabia, America's first unelected Jewish president (acting not unlike a movie mogul) converts a Colorado greasy-spoon diner into an ad hoc war room from which he argues about and orchestrates the nuking of Baghdad.

Brinkmanship redux: In the *Deterrence* fantasy, the Cuban Missile Crisis fused with Operation Desert Storm. *The Contender*, Lurie's considerably more lavish follow-up, is a scenario that takes the New World Order as a given. There's a sense in which post–Cold War Washington, D.C., resembles post–World War I Hollywood as a celebrity-stocked City of the Plain. Foreign policy pales before domestic affairs. In *The Contender*, the Washington shenanigans begin with a reporter somewhat ironically asking an ambitious politician if he would be willing to "take a bullet for abortion rights or the flat tax" or any of the other issues of the day. That the pol is even then preparing a daring media stunt to advance his career retrospectively puts the joke on the journalist. That the stunt echoes the infamous incident whereby Senator Edward Kennedy effectively terminated his presidential viability by driving his car off the bridge at Chappaquiddick and drowning a young woman in the process, gives *The Contender* all the historical contexts it needs.

American presidential politics has, for some time now, been an entertainment pageant that the electorate stages for itself. And, given the nonstarter, preelection weekend revelation of George W. Bush's long ago drunk driving arrest and the failure of the media to pay any attention to *Hustler* publisher (and Hollywood movie hero) Larry Flynt's allegations of the Republican candidate's even more ancient sexual improprieties, *The Contender* proved to be just about as enjoyably lurid as the 2000 campaign got. Of course, the film, no less than the actual race, was eclipsed by the election results—a statistical tie essentially decided by the vote of a single Supreme Court justice.

The Democratic and Republican conventions had received only minimal TV coverage; the three presidential debates were watched by a bored and steadily shrinking audience. Media pundits compared the race unfavorably to the reality TV smash *Survivor* until the election blossomed into a monthlong 24–7 telefestival, replete with sideshows in which the current president's wife, the vice presidential candidate, and the dead governor of Missouri were all elected to a Senate now split 50–50 between the two parties, prelude to years of conspiratorial revelations concerning the irregular voting practices in the very state governed by the new president's brother. Fond as he is of outrageous coincidence, Lurie could have scarcely anticipated *that*. But then filmmakers, like generals, are always fighting the last war.

Eight years of Bill Clinton took the politics of entertainment to a new stage. Hollywood got the message early, responding not only with unprecedented financial support but with a cycle of presidential movies—although not the infamous Joe Eszterhas screenplay about a president caught *in flagrante* with a cow. Far more extensive than the apocalyptic thrillers of the Camelot era, although only *Air Force One* was a blockbuster and *The American President* but a minor hit, the cycle was complemented by a number of specifically Clintonian novels, among them Joe Klein's *Primary Colors*, Eszterhas's *American Rhapsody*, Erik Tarloff's *Face Time* (about a President's adulterous affair with his chief aide's girlfriend), and Charles McCarrey's *Lucky Bastard* (in which a love child fathered by JFK grows up to be a draft-dodging, woman-izing, KGB-controlled U.S. president). The one indisputable piece of literature, *The Starr Report: The Independent Counsel's Complete Report to Congress on the*

*Investigation of President Clinton*, will doubtless find its place alongside such other epics of puritanical obsession as Cotton Mather's *Magnali Christi Americana* or Benjamin Church's *Entertaining Passages Relating to Philip's War*.

Clinton nostalgia began to surface during the late-1999 run-up to the campaign in the form of the NBC-TV dramatic series *The West Wing*, starring Martin Sheen as President Josiah "Jed" Bartlet, a liberal Democrat from New Hampshire. Never mind that a New England Democrat had not served as president in nearly 40 years, nor that it seemed most unlikely that one would soon again; Jed Bartlet was in show business. Implicit in the success of Ronald Reagan, the notion of President as Entertainer in Chief received further validation in June 1992 when candidate Clinton, then trailing in the polls behind President George Bush and third party gadfly Ross Perot, managed to reverse his fortunes with a late night TV appearance, wearing his shades and playing his saxophone like a third Blues Brother on *The Arsenio Hall Show*. Indeed, the notion had since been enshrined by *Saturday Night Live* and its animated feature "X Presidents," a cartoon in which Reagan—along with Gerald Ford, Jimmy Carter, and the first George Bush—plays a simpleminded action hero.

By the start of its second season in September 2000, *The West Wing* had zoomed from a viewership of 14 million to 25 million, rising from 30th place among American TV shows to the very stratosphere, alongside the sitcom *Friends* and hospital drama *ER*. The latter became America's number one show in the aftermath of the Clinton administration's failed attempt to legislate a total health care package; similarly, *The West Wing* presented a remarkably blatant compensatory fantasy.

Throughout the campaign, Bartlet—who shared Clinton's Hollywood constituency and demographics, complete with college-age daughter, but not his hound-dog tendencies—consistently outpolled the actual candidates. After all, polls suggested that nearly half of Americans between the ages of 18 and 29 (and a quarter of all adults) derived most of their information about the campaign from the late-night comedy shows that had rigorously conceptualized the race as a struggle between the Stiff Guy (or Gore the Robot) and the Dumb Guy (or Bush the Moron). Sheen, meanwhile, had ample preparation for his current role. He played Robert F. Kennedy in 1974 telefilm *The Missiles of October* and graduated to big brother JFK in the 1983 miniseries *Kennedy*—as well as serving as Michael Douglas's chief of staff in *The American President*, the movie which, written by *West Wing* creator Aaron Sorkin, was that show's big screen prototype.

Television mediated the campaign's key events. (Well before the election was decided, the makers of *South Park* announced that they would be producing a scurrilous situation comedy on whoever occupied the White House come

2001.) The kiss which George Bush planted on the cheek of afternoon talk queen Oprah Winfrey allowed the Republican to regain the lead in the polls, apparently taken by Al Gore after his televised smooch with wife Tipper at the Democratic Convention (an event which featured an MTV-style, rough-and-ready biographical portrait of Gore and family that the candidate had specially commissioned from *Being John Malkovich* director Spike Jonze). The first presidential debate may have been an overhyped flop, but Gore's loss was ratified by the front page news that he had studied tapes of the parody on *Saturday Night Live* which presented him as a shameless know-it-all who capped his overbearing performance by attempting to deliver two closing statements. No less an authority than *West Wing* executive producer Lawrence O'Donnell appeared on NBC's cable affiliate to declare this sketch "the most important political writing of this election year." So integral had *The West Wing* become to the political process that it seemed only natural when the series' big Christmas show would be preempted by what NBC called *Decision 2000: The Final Chapter* in which Al Gore conceded defeat and George W. Bush announced his victory. That movie has yet to be remade.

Taking off from America's last great political festival, the 1998–99 impeachment of Bill Clinton, *The Contender* may be considered the culminating example of cine Clinton—not because it's any better than its precursors or because it managed to cram together a host of Billious, Hillarian, and even Gorey themes just in time for the election, but because—in its emphasis on sexual misconduct and public confession—it's the closest the political film has come to merging with daytime TV. Graceless writing and mechanical plotting are part of the fun. Lurie has designated *All the President's Men* as his favorite film. But while *The Contender* takes as a given the post-Watergate notion of Washington as a sewer of slimy ambition, the movie more closely resembles the Senatorial drama of *Advise and Consent* and backstage skullduggery of *The Best Man*—both movies about ambitious politicians with guilty secrets. Adding to the film's magpie construction are bits of business swiped from *Blow Out*, *The Candidate*, and *Air Force One*, not to mention the hearings with which accused sexual harasser Clarence Thomas was confirmed as a justice of the U.S. Supreme Court.

For all the hot air expended on prescription drug benefits and mandatory school testing, the theatrics of the Bush-Gore TV debates were all about projecting alpha maleness and strategic empathy. Lurie similarly understands American politics as a matter of image and targeted demographics. Much is made in *Deterrence* that the president, played by short, charmless, and feisty Kevin Pollack, is distinctly unpresidential. *The Contender* revolves around a second-term president's look to look presidential in attempting to replace his deceased running mate with America's first unelected female vice president. (This announced look to his "legacy" presumably means a decision that is not motivated by public opinion.) This historic feat is rendered all the more problematic by the public's— or is it the media's—insatiable thirst for tabloid trash. As in some nightmare episode of *The Jerry Springer Show*, the vice president designate, Senator Laine Hanson of Ohio (Joan Allen) is confronted with the revelation of a frat-house gangbang in her teenaged past. And, as with the identity of Monica Lewinsky back in early 1997, this information is first leaked on a Matt Drudge–like Internet website.

Although the vice president designate is introduced to us having sex atop her office desk—albeit with her husband—her reserved demeanor is more suggestive of a Supreme Court justice than a party girl or even politician. By comparison, "Hillary Rodham Clinton begins to seem almost down-home." Stephen Holden observed in the *New York Times*. (Not for nothing did Allen play the bride of Nixon.) Because she had changed her party affiliation from Republican to Democrat her nemesis is the Republican chairman of the House Judiciary Committee, Ohio representative Shelly Runyon (a nearly unrecognizable Gary Oldman, hilariously tricked out in fake hair-plugs and masking his twitchy surplus of nervous energy with a flat Midwestern accent).

The nominee's indiscretion is scarcely a crime, but to the relief of audiences everywhere, it insures that her confirmation hearings can be all about sex—or rather about sexual propriety, the defining issue of the Clinton administration. As a resident media-savvy wise man puts it, "the one thing that the American people will not stomach is a vice president with a mouth full of cock." *The Contender* is a movie where you are what you eat—the damning evidence against Senator Hanson is passed from one Congressional aide to another over a table full of junk food. Politicians are shown as creatures of appetite. President Jackson Evans (Jeff Bridges) is a cigarette-smoking, glad-handing blowhard whose main psychological quirk seems to be that he's always hungry. Bridges moves through *The Contender* like a champ, brandishing a shark steak sandwich at the young representative (Christian Slater) who seems inclined to defy him. Despite the West Point sweatshirt he affects (Lurie, too, attended the U.S. military academy), this president is a figure of sly, affable menace—less a statesman than a pure political animal, Clinton reinvented one more time, unencumbered by family or personal relations.

Evidently the man whom Evans beat in the last election, Runyon reveals his unhealthy if not murderous instincts in the grotesque gusto with which he's twice shown tucking into a big slab of bloody steak. (Hanson, of course, is some sort of vegan.) Runyon is intended to evoke Representative Henry Hyde and the other smugly moralizing Republican congressmen who attempted to bring down Bill Clinton. The actual Hyde's impossible dream of Clintonicide was reportedly reinforced by repeated listening to the score from the old Don Quixote musical *Man of La Mancha*. Runyon stands up to the president's men and rallies his troops by telling them that Hanson embodies the "cancer of liberalism [and] virtuous decay." In a bizarre disconnect, this speech is underscored with vaguely inspirational patriotic music.

Just before its U.S. release, *The Contender* was denounced by Oldman as an example of a left-wing Hollywood conspiracy. Douglas Urbanski, Oldman's manager and one of the film's four producers, was quoted in *Premiere* as calling *The Contender* "a Goebbels-like piece of propaganda." Urbanski accused the DreamWorks honchos, Steven Spielberg, Jeffrey Katzenbach, and David Geffen (who double as Hollywood's chief Democratic fundraisers, having raised some $15 million for the party during Clinton's administration) of recutting the movie. "If your names are Spielberg, Katzenbach, and Geffen, you can't have a film with a Republican character—who is at all sympathetic—being released on October 13 [three weeks before the election]." The studio denied in any way changing the movie although, back in August, Lurie had told the *Los Angeles Times* that *The Contender* was tracking equally well with Democrats and Republicans, while Urbanski was quoted as saying, "The liberals in the film definitely say things that make you feel warm and fuzzy. But the one true patriot in the film is the rascally Republican. He's the only character who doesn't say anything insane, who puts his career on the line for what he believes in."

As *The Contender* stands, however, Hanson becomes the object of Runyon's jihad. Largely because she is identified with liberalism, affirmative action, and a woman's right to chose, she must be hillary'd. "We have to gut the bitch in the belly," a member of the Republican cabal smirks moments before the story of her long ago frat-house indiscretion breaks. Reading the script—if not the situation—clearly, President Evans warns his candidate that "the whole world [is] thinking you're something out of a crazed soap opera." He advises her to take a leaf from the Bill Clinton playbook and make a public confession. Hanson, however, refuses to answer any questions about her sexual history, let alone confess to any indiscretion despite the brutal pressure applied to her by the president's advisers. The close-up in which she drops a single silent tear provides an unmistakable, if insane, reference to *The Passion of Joan of Arc*. (Endearingly, Lurie pushes the movie further into science fiction by making his heroine an open atheist.)

As the president tells his nominee to go beyond embarrassment, so Lurie himself ventures beyond cynicism. (Astonishingly, Evans has no truck with the focus groups that his precursor Bill Clinton made integral to American politics.) As an evocation of scandalous politics, *The Contender* is then an attack on itself—

or maybe a defense. The president's big speech is the riposte Clinton never made, even quoting the rhetorical question attorney Joseph Welch famously asked Senator Joseph McCarthy during the televised Army-McCarthy Hearings, "Have you no decency, sir?"

*The Contender* creates a situation in which his heroine can self-righteously invoke the House Committee on Un-American Activities, sexual McCarthyism, and the "ideological rape of all women." Essentially feminist, the movie—which is dedicated to "our daughters"—appears to demonstrate the threat that unbridled female sexuality poses in the ultra patriarchal order. The candidate suffers through hearings in which she is grilled as to her fertility, forced to discuss her birth control, held responsible for the "holocaust of the unborn," and interrogated about her affair with her husband when he was her campaign manager and married to someone else.

Less uncompromising than Senator Hanson, *The Contender* decries the existence of a double standard—the better to demonstrate its dramaturgical necessity. In other words, the movie allows Joan Allen to play Bill to her own Monica and emerge from the Washington cesspool satisfyingly unbesmirched. Far more than Al Gore, new Senator Hillary Rodham Clinton was Hollywood's 2000 candidate. In this sense, the movie may well be ahead of its time—a prophesy of 2004.

*The Long Day Closes* (Terence Davies, Sony Pictures Classics, 1992).
Courtesy of Channel Four Television Corporation (U.K.).

# THE FILM CRITIC OF
# TOMORROW, TODAY

Originally published in *The Crisis of Criticism* (1998).

**W**E'VE BEEN HERE BEFORE. AS THE AESTHETICIAN (AND ERSTWHILE MOVIE reviewer) Rudolf Arnheim predicted in 1935:

> One of the tasks of the film critic of tomorrow—perhaps he will even be called a "'television critic"—will be to rid the world of the comic figure the average film critic and film theorist of today represents: he lives from the glory of his memories like the seventy-year-old ex-court actresses, rummages about as they do in yellowing photographs, speaks of names that are long gone. He discusses films no one has been able to see for ten years or more (and about which they can therefore say everything and nothing) with people of his own ilk; he argues about montage like medieval scholars discussed the existence of God, believing all these things could still exist today. In the evening, he sits with rapt attention in the cinema, a critical art lover, as though we still lived in the days of Griffith, Stroheim, Murnau, and Eisenstein. *He thinks he is seeing bad films instead of understanding that what he sees is no longer film at all.* [The italics are mine.]

The crisis in film criticism has been variously linked to the consolidation of entertainment conglomerates, the proliferation of home video, the dumbing down of the movie audience, the toxic fumes of film theory, the death of cinephilia, the retirement of Pauline Kael. True enough, but is the crisis not even more fundamentally related to the disappearance of movies?

Not literally, of course. Indeed, the Movies occupy more cultural space than ever before. *Entertainment Tonight* commands as much broadcast time as the Evening News. Entire cable stations are devoted to the promotion of new movies and stars—who exert more power and make more money than at any time in human history. Grosses too are generally up, and Oscar night, the annual festival of self-congratulation, has become a "feminine" counterweight to the "masculine" Super Bowl in the celebration of national identity. For busy people, there is Time Warner's *Entertainment Weekly* to provide a convenient substitute for actual consumption. Freed from the obligation to see-hear-read all this stuff, you can flip through the magazine, glom the letter grades, and be knowledgeable. You can have opinions.

(And just what is it that you, reader, want to know about a movie that you have never seen—and may never see? Is it an account of the narrative action—stopping short to protect of the various twists and surprises? Is it an amusing description of the physical appearance of the—hot? cold?—stars? A sober evaluation of the competence of the cinematic technique? An assessment of the manifest directorial personality? Is it speculation on the movie's place in—movie?—history, the degree to which it embodies the way we live now? Did you really care if I liked it—and why? Is the question whether to buy a ticket to see the movie now—or wait for video?)

What else is there to say? Familiarity may breed contempt but commercial cinema trades on prior acquaintance. (In no medium is the stigma of the "difficult"—which range from the absence of stars to the presence of subtitles—more damning.) Stars are a form of living trademark, scripts a kind of organized cliché. Genres rule. Movies are made in cycles and recycled as remakes. Anything sold once can be sold again . . . and again. Moreover, the movies are the nexus for an endless series of cross-references and synergistic couplings. Just as movies are now routinely based on old TV series, so plays are adapted from old movies. So-called novelizations used to be written after a movie was released; now they are published before the film is made.

The more old Hollywood movies are sentimentalized as art, the more crass our appreciation of the current crop. A flop is, by definition, an aesthetic failure; quality is synonymous with economic success (or at least notoriety). Although critics continue to grouse over the decline in narrative values, the story line that everyone in America has learned to follow is the fever chart of box-office grosses. Every major production brings its own ephemeral *Entertainment Tonight* metadrama. Each summer, audiences are invited to be a part of History by queuing up to see *Independence Day* or *The Lost World*—the resonance of these titles!—on their first mega-million-dollar weekends.

A movie is almost by definition a record of that which once was—and how we long for that which no longer exists! Fifty-eight years after *Mr. Smith Goes to Washington*, *Variety* reported that the most trusted man in America was still Jimmy Stewart.

The moment of national self-analysis that followed Stewart's death marveled over his old-fashioned virtues, his lack of pretension, the miracle of his actorly "ordinariness," the positive values of his persona. The fact is, however, that stars are our supreme public servants. The mild gossip their doings and vehicles inspire promotes the socially cohesive illusion of an intimate America where everyone knows (and even cares) about each other. The stars—and the entertainment media that showcase them—create what the theorist of nationalism Benedict Anderson has called an imagined community. And not just ours—by 1995, as American movies filled the vacuum left by the declining indigenous film industries of Europe, Latin America, and Asia, foreign rentals had surpassed those of the domestic box office.

In the totalitarian Soviet Union, entertainment was an obvious aspect of the state ideological apparatus—merging politics with show business. Of course, we can't say that of America (at least not on television). Nevertheless, this Imagined Community—predicated on the existence of shared tastes, feelings, desires—is an economic necessity. For if the prerequisite of mass production is mass consumption, that mass consumption is itself predicated on the production of mass desire—for movies, among other things. And, because virtually all reviewers are compelled (as journalists) to write about films before most people have a chance to see them, they are only one more part of a vast machine devoted to inculcating the mass urge-to-see.

Although movie reviews are historically the favor with which newspapers acknowledge the placement of movie advertisements, the ads now in effect commission their own six-word reviews (while serving the secondary function of providing free publicity for the reviewers and, of course, the periodicals or broadcast outlets that employ them). To be a movie reviewer is to strike a Faustian bargain with the industry. You can have your name (and your words) emblazoned on a newspaper ad or poster as large as that of Tom Cruise. Does anyone doubt that many reviewers write to be quoted or paraphrased? Some phantom reviewers exist only as pull quotes. (The industry term for them is "blurb whores.") In 1989, Rex Reed complained to *Variety* that studio publicists had asked him if he would polish a quote; eight years later, *Variety* was reporting that at least one studio had taken to faxing readymade quotes to freelancers, inviting them to attach their name to the one found most agreeable.

United in their need to promote the latest blockbuster, studio press agents and movie journalists enjoy a symbiotic relationship. (*Premiere*, a periodical at which I worked for a half dozen years, transformed on-set reportage into a—marginally—more literary form of the studio press book.) Studios typically mark the opening of a major investment by organizing an industry junket, flying reviewers from all over the country to Los Angeles or New York to preview the movie, enjoy a hotel banquet, and then attend a succession of five-minute group interviews with the stars. Categorizing journalists in terms of their use-value, publicists trade early screenings, film clips, and access to the talent for sound bites and advance superlatives.

The magazine journalist is thus a part of the movie's anticipatory build up as well as the magazine's own competitive struggle to secure the star-image for its covers. Celebrity is the coin of the realm—the ultimate in surplus value, which, through the magic of endorsement, transforms, as Marx wrote in *Capital*, "every product of labor into a social hieroglyph." Publicists routinely vet writers, stipulate format and ground rules, and barter for cover placement (and, when they can, other aspects of editorial content). While publicists understand the press as a potential rival in the creation of a star's persona, the underlying assumption is that journalists, like reviewers, are too stupid or star struck to realize how much more money they could make writing screenplays or even press releases.

Once upon a time, media commentator James Wolcott wrote in the April 1997 *Vanity Fair*, film critics "had the oral swagger of gunslingers. Quick on the draw and easy to rile, they had the power to kill individual films and kneecap entire careers." Then the frontier closed. Faced with the silence of his idol Pauline Kael, Wolcott laments that, "movie criticism has become a cultural malady, a group case of chronic depression and low self-esteem." Reinforcing his point is the fact that the vehicle for his screed is a journal devoting an extraordinary amount of space to movies and movie stars without apparently feeling the need for regular film criticism.

▪▪▪▪▪▪▪▪▪▪▪▪▪

In addition to bankrolling remakes, Hollywood studios are primarily interest-ed in recycling movies as theme-park rides, interactive video games, CD-ROMs, and computer screen-savers. This is one meaning of André Bazin's "Myth of Total Cinema." Anticipating by some decades his compatriots Guy Debord and Jean Baudrillard, Bazin forsaw the historical logic by which the movies and their more perfect successors would inexorably seek to supplant the world: Virtual Reality.

The key development, but only thus far, in the Myth of Total Cinema was development of "talking" pictures in late 1927—the magical simultaneity of sound and image is what the Austrian avant-garde filmmaker Peter Kubelka called the Sync Event. It was, in fact, this particular technological advance that prompted Rudolf Arnheim to declare of the film critic that "he thinks he is seeing bad films instead of understanding that what he sees is no longer film at all."

Time Warner and Walt Disney, the world's two largest media conglomerates, were both founded upon the miracle of synchronous sound. Talking pictures brought forth first *The Jazz Singer* and then, the far more durable blackface entertainer, Mickey Mouse. The Mouse is prophetic of Total Cinema's next stage, namely the overthrow of camera authority by computer digitalized imagery: More and more, the future begins to look like Paula Abdul's four-minute "remake" of *Rebel Without a Cause* or the computer-animated Diet Coke ad where her fellow flack Elton John jams with Louis Armstrong for the amusement of Humphrey Bogart. The living party with the dead under the sign of the trademark, the gods dwell among us from here to eternity.

The very name Time Warner suggests the fusion of news and entertainment—indeed Warner's summer 1996 blockbuster *Twister* was featured on *Time*'s cover as the hook for a news report on tornados. Rival retail outlet Walt Disney is named after the corporate artist supreme—the single most important figure in mass culture, the first to saturate America with cultural trademarks, to use television to create a system of self-perpetuating hype, a creator so universal his quirks must be stamped on our DNA and his Magic Kingdom now incorporates a substantial chunk of midtown Manhattan. (Might we not balance the budget simply by establishing the American flag as a registered trademark, licensed exclusively to Walt Disney?)

Following Disney, the successful Hollywood movie is an increasingly uninteresting bridge between the multimedia barrage of prerelease promotion and a potential package of spinoffs, career moves, and tie-ins. (Such ancillary income exceeded even the box-office grosses for such megablockbusters as *Batman* and *Jurassic Park*.) As reported in *Time*, Time Warner chairman Gerald Levin heralded the media conglomerate's Christmas 1996 release—an epic synthesis of an animated Looney Tune and a Michael Jordan sneaker commercial—with unusual candor: "*Space Jam* isn't a movie. It's a marketing event." Disney's summer 1997 animated feature, *Hercules*, went even further (while preempting any criticism) by satirizing itself as a marketing event.

Awaiting the fulfillment of Total Cinema, Americans already live in the world of Total Docu-Drama. (Think of it as the live-action and cartoon mix of *Who Framed Roger Rabbit?* or for that matter *Titanic*.) The television-induced symbiosis of entertainment, history and politics is so complete that no one complains when *Star Trek* memorabilia are enshrined, alongside actual moon rocks and Lindbergh's authentic *Spirit of St. Louis,* in America's equivalent of the Sistine Chapel—the National Air and Space Museum in Washington, D.C. This technology for manufacturing evidence is what we have to remember us by—shared projections of an imaginary past.

As predicted by George Lucas's *American Graffiti* and demonstrated by his *Star Wars*, as illuminated by the careers of Steven Spielberg and Ronald Reagan, Hollywood is the main repository of cultural memory—and authority. In her introduction to a recent collection of scholarly essays on *Schindler's List*, Israeli professor Yosefa Loshitzky notes that making the film had effectively made Spielberg more than an artist: His "testimony in the summer of 1994 before a congressional committee examining the issue of 'hate crimes' itself testifies to the fact that the most successful commercial filmmaker in Hollywood's history has suddenly achieved 'expert' status on a controversial and complex social phenomenon—purely by virtue of having directed a film whose subject is the rescue of a handful of Jews from the Nazis."

Any news story in the cinema-saturated world can burgeon into a media spectacle, played like an old-fashioned pinball machine to ricochet from one mirrored surface to another. Within weeks of the now barely remembered tale of Tonya Harding's alleged assault on her Olympic skating rival Nancy Kerrigan, the *New York Times* reported that no less than ten film production companies "as well as networks and studios" were seeking the rights to the story. Since then magazines have begun aggressively shopping the movie rights to material they publish, while the Disney studio has taken the lead in directly commissioning journalists to investigate stories—eliminating the magazine middleman. Similarly, the Heaven's Gate cult (named for a film) is but the bridge from *Star Wars* and *Close Encounters of the Third Kind*, from which it drew its theology, to a made-for-TV movie.

"Fiction seeps quietly and continuously into reality," writes Benedict Anderson, "creating that remarkable confidence of community in anonymity which is the hallmark of modern nations." In the context of a world inexorably transformed into a representation of itself, the big-budget biopic or historical reenactment—once the ultimate middlebrow made-for-TV mode—had come to seem the quintessential Hollywood genre. Self-proclaimed countermyths like *Patty Hearst*, *Born on the Fourth of July*, *The Doors*, *JFK*, *Ruby*, *Malcolm X*, *Quiz Show*, *Hoffa*, *Schindler's List*, *Panther*, *Apollo 13*, *Nixon*, *The People vs. Larry Flynt*, and *Evita*—as well as their fictional, satirical, or avant-garde counterparts (*Forrest Gump*, *Ed Wood*, *I Shot Andy Warhol*)—are to the post–Cold War Bush-Clinton transition what the Spielberg-Lucas megafantasy had been to the Age of Reagan or the epic of antiquity to the early 1950s—spectacular displays of pure movie might, would-be interventions, contributions to (or, perhaps, substitutions for) a national discourse.

In the absence of what had been considered film, Arnheim reminded the critic of 1935 to recall that "second great task"—often neglected by virtue of the demands required by "aesthetic criticism"—namely, "the consideration of

film as an economic product, and as an expression of political and moral view-
points." How can we do anything else? As Arnheim's colleague and contemporary Siegfried Kracauer put it, "the good film critic is only conceivable as a critic of society." (Now, of course, the reverse is also true.)

▪▪▪▪▪▪▪▪▪

As explicated by Terence Davies' 1992 masterpiece, *The Long Day Closes*,
movies are both the most subjective of individual experiences and the most
public of public arts. Davies' ten-year-old alter ego is charged by a love for the
ineffable—a fascination with that world on the screen we never see.

Is that love gone? It was just past the hundredth anniversary of the
Lumière brothers' first public exhibition of their cinematograph that Susan
Sontag lamented the death of cinephilia, with an article published in the *New
York Times Magazine:* "Cinema's 100 years seem to have the shape of a life cycle:
an inevitable birth, the steady accumulation of glories and the onset in the last
decade of an ignominious, irreversible decline."

Readers of the *Times* were quick to point out that Sontag's view of cinema was
a highly selective one. She maintained, for example, that only France produced
"a large number of superb films" for the first 25 years of the sound era (and presumably thereafter). She made no mention of current Chinese movies or even
American independents (or Chantal Akerman or Atom Egoyan or Raul Ruiz or
Lars von Trier or Stan Brakhage or Beat Takeshi or Abbas Kiarostami . . . ). She
capped her career-long disinterest in American movies by mourning the
blighted careers of Francis Coppola and Paul Schrader.

As ahistorical as it was, Sontag's piece nevertheless partook of a now-familiar
melancholy. The approaching millennium, the AIDS plague, the collapse of
"existing socialism," and the end of the Cold War have inspired many such
obituaries to mark the real or perceived disappearance of many wondrous
things—modernism, historical consciousness, oppositional culture, the literary
canon, American industry, the Democratic Party, New York City, baseball, the
Broadway theater, downtown nightlife, labor unions, print journalism—all to be
replaced by the bogus virtual reality of an impoverished cybertopia. In truth,
the movies have merged with the spectacle of daily life.

The cinephilia of the 1960s is over—it required not only the films of the
sixties but also the social moment of the sixties. If the 1960s and 1970s brought
a film culture of unprecedented plurality, the last 20 years have been characterized by increasing self-absorption, a profound ignorance of world cinema and
a corresponding disinterest—among American critics, as much as American
audiences—in other people's movies. More disturbing, perhaps, than dimin-

ished film enthusiasm is the failure of the sixties film culture, which Sontag herself helped create, to establish itself as a lasting intellectual presence. (After Reagan, one might expect that moveiology would be the central pursuit of the age. But, there is still something suspect in taking the movies too seriously—except, of course, as a business.)

Sontag's two-page spread included a cover image of *Cahiers du cinéma* but failed to note the French journal's ongoing debate on the nature of movie-love. "Is it necessary to cure cinephilia?" was the question posed by *Cahiers*'s January 1997 issue, which in sampling the writings of Ricciotto Canudo (1879–1923) resurrected a cinephilia no less intense than that of the sixties. "What is striking, characteristic, and significant, even more than the [cinematic] spectacle itself," Canudo wrote in 1911, "is the uniform will of the spectators, who belong to all social classes, from the lowest and least educated to the most intellectual." Canudo saw, in movies, a "desire for a new Festival, for a new joyous unanimity, realized at a show, in a place where together, all men can forget, in greater or lesser measure, their isolated individuality."

That festival is "Hollywood"—the quaint name for an international mass culture, based in the United States but drawing capital, talent, and audiences from all over the world. A celebration of American military and cultural hegemony, *Independence Day* was the pure cultural expression of the formula PR + F/X = USA #1. As *Independence Day* united America before one movie, so the movie showed America organizing the world to establish July 4th as a global celebration of independence—from what? Surely not Rupert Murdoch, the immigrant lad who bankrolled the flick.

Is movie criticism then inevitably a form of publicity? Or, put another way, is it even possible to position oneself outside the media system? (For most of the 1990s, the national film industries that have inspired the greatest degree of cinephilic enthusiasm have been those of the designated outsiders China and Iran.) Who wants to be the festival's spoilsport?

There is a sense in which print criticism is obsolete anyway. After all, that which television ignores can barely be said to exist. While making his bitterly confessional *Ginger and Fred* (1985), Federico Fellini—for decades the popular notion of the individual film artiste—spoke about "the enchanted palace of TV." Taking its title from a pair of star-imitators, *Ginger and Fred* is set in a hermetic, controlled environment—the Cinecittà studio transformed into something like a mall—where entertainment feeds on entertainment. This is Fellini's complaint: In an image-glutted world aspiring to the complete commercial saturation of cable stations like MTV or the E! Channel, the movies have disappeared. Even the great Fellini has been out-Fellini'd by TV.

Sneering at the ersatz, *Ginger and Fred* is filled with celebrity imitators—but, as Andy Warhol understood, celebrity is infinitely recuperable. Tim Burton's 1994 *Ed Wood* results from one of the most bankable filmmakers who ever lived expending the credit of his success in sincere, black-and-white tribute to the obscure, tawdry vision of the alcoholic, heterosexual transvestite and sometime pornographer known affectionately as "the world's worst director." There is no such thing as negative publicity, and to be the World's Worst Filmmaker is to personify a particular high concept.

Celebrity is absolute, and *Ed Wood*, of course, is absolutely flawless—as fastidiously crafted as any previous Burton production. Burton's painstaking replication of Wood's haphazard compositions suggests a vanished Hollywood landmark, the Buena Park Palace of Living Art where the Mona Lisa or Whistler's Mother are reproduced as garish wax dioramas and the Venus De Milo is improved upon, not only for being colorized, but through the restoration of her lost limbs. *Ed Wood* is the Palace of Living Art in reverse. Art is not reproduced as kitsch; living kitsch is embalmed as art. Deliberately or not, Ed Wood served to deconstruct all manner of Hollywood pretense. *Ed Wood* builds it all back up, better than new—the movie's greatest irony is the liquidation of irony itself.

▪▪▪▪▪▪▪▪▪▪

*We know very well that occasionally—and this will also be true in the future—in the hand of an avant-gardist, a narrow-gauge film amateur, or a documentary hunter, a true film is still made, but the work of a critic cannot be concerned with such exceptional cases. It must instead deal with everyday production, which can only be subjected to aesthetic criticism when a production falls into the realm of aesthetics in principle; that is, when it has the possibility of creating works of art. Formerly, good films differed from mediocre ones only insofar as their quality was concerned; today they are the outsiders, remnants, things of a basically different nature from that which normally passes through the cinemas.*

—RUDOLF ARNHEIM, "The Film Critic of Tomorrow"

Yes but . . . how does one resist? Is it by defending underground movies on the Internet? Extolling entertainment that refuses to entertain? "*Mars Attacks!* is meant to be a kind of anti-entertainment," the critic for the celebrity-driven *New Yorker* wrote increduously of Burton's mega-million-dollar dada jape.

Similarly, the 1996 Jim Carrey vehicle, *The Cable Guy*—a jarringly violent, slapstick meditation on role-playing, performance, and the E! Channel totality—was attacked precisely for its own, unexpected attack on the system that produced it. "The shocking sight of a volatile comic talent in free fall," per the *New York Times* review. Explicitly playing a stellar public servant (and architect of the E!-magined Community), Carrey's $20 million "cable guy" was mass culture, precipitating the latent hostility felt even by the festival's most dogged celebrants.

*Mystery Science Theater 3000*, for several seasons a regular feature on cable's Comedy Channel, inscribed an animated pair of wise-cracking humanoid spectators over their presentation of the worst, most inept drive-in features of the 1950s—including, of course, those by Ed Wood. The aggression that *MST3K* (as its fans abbreviate it) directed at those hapless old movies that fell into its deconstruction machine is the inverse of the idiotic positive "reviews" which blurb whores can be relied upon to lavish on the most disposable current release. *MST3K* is a rearguard action to be sure, but we might learn from it.

Why settle for a mere laudatory blurb when the entire enterprise is available? Total cinema is our second nature and, as D. W. Griffith, Sergei Mikhailovich Eisenstein, and the Surrealists long ago demonstrated, cinematic meaning is a factor of context and juxtaposition—not to mention purposeful derangement. (In a social sense, we might call this reeducation.) Sooner or later—or rather, sooner and sooner—the most elaborate $100 million block-buster will fall into your hands as a $19.95 videocassette.

Just as the most radical recent examples of film criticism have, by and large, been "found footage" compilations like Craig Baldwin's *Tribulation 99*, Mark Rappaport's *Rock Hudson's Home Movies*, Oleg Kovalov's *Garden of Scorpions*, and Chantal Akerman's *Chantal Akerman by Chantal Akerman*, so the most important film critic of the past 35 years has, of course, been a filmmaker. "The greatest history is the history of the cinema," Jean-Luc Godard told Serge Daney.

That history will force those critics refusing the role of underpaid cheerleaders to themselves become historians—not to mention archivists, bricoleurs, spoilsports, pundits, entrepreneurs, anticonglomerate guerrilla fighters, and, in general, masters of what is known in the Enchanted Palace as "counter-programming."

*Sátántangó* (Béla Tarr, Hungarofilm, 1995). Courtesy of Béla Tarr.

# Appendix

## TEN "10 BEST" LISTS (1991-2000)

A movie reviewer's annual service to his or her readers, the traditional 10 best list is also a side bet with history, made with one eye on the past 12 months and the other on eternity. Thus, I have resisted the temptation to tamper with these lists, all of which appeared in the *Village Voice*, even though Jean-Luc Godard's *Germany Year 90 Nine Zero* was somehow cited twice. In some cases, a few sentences have been added to the capsule descriptions; movies treated elsewhere in the book are generally listed without comment.

## 1991

1. **WHITE DOG** (Sam Fuller, U.S.)
2. **DROWNING BY NUMBERS** (Peter Greenaway, U.K.). Will future generations regard this as the movie Greenaway made before he lost it? Unlike the mind-bludgeoning studio extravaganza *Prospero's Books*, *Drowning by Numbers* is a light and airy landscape film. Greenaway not only treats serial killing as a form of serial music, he proposes another way to watch a movie— *Drowning* is a countdown in reverse with a plot based on repetition and inevitability.
3. **TRIBULATION 99** (Craig Baldwin, U.S.).
4. **EUROPA, EUROPA** (Agnieszka Holland, France-Germany). Radically non-judgmental, Holland's account of a Holocaust survivor suggests that "passing" is a universal fate. As the uprooted hero casts about for a home, taking refuge in alternate ideologies and national identities, the film comes to seem an allegory for the Jewish experience of modern Europe.
5. **THE ARCHITECTURE OF DOOM** (Peter Cohen, Sweden). Cohen uses all manner of archival material to evoke the totality of Nazi notions of artistic, medical, and racial "deformity." As an argument, the movie is lucid and shocking—explaining the gas chambers of Auschwitz as the culmination of a campaign to "beautify" the world.
6. **NAKED LUNCH** (David Cronenberg, Canada)
7. **MY OWN PRIVATE IDAHO** (Gus Van Sant, U.S.). At once a story cycle and a collage, Van Sant's third feature draws on Shakespeare, Welles, Dostoyevsky, and Warhol; the director's self-conscious erudition is balanced by the reckless innocence with which River Phoenix throws himself into his role.

8. **THELMA & LOUISE** (Ridley Scott, U.S.). It doesn't get any more American than this—the freedom to reinvent yourself, take pleasure in the road, drive your eight-cylinder Alamo off the edge of a cliff.

9. **THE SILENCE OF THE LAMBS** (Jonathan Demme, U.S.). This is as vivid an immersion in the American landscape as *Thelma & Louise*, except that here the environment is somber, impoverished, musty: the flight to freedom a chthonic quest through back wards and backwoods, rural funeral parlors and makeshift morgues, abandoned rooms in decrepit Rust Belt towns, and storage facilities so moldy the cobwebs look like jungle creepers.

10. **PARIS IS BURNING** (Jennie Livingston, U.S.). An invaluable text, as well as a superb showcase for underdog fantasy, *Paris Is Burning* needs neither narrative nor narration to make absolutely explicit the relationship between vernacular and dominant culture. Is it a coincidence that the two movies to most boldly attack the notion of "natural" identity, this and *Europa, Europa*, were both directed by women?

# 1992

1. **UNFORGIVEN** (Clint Eastwood, U.S.). The miraculous resurrection of a genre that expired some 15 years ago, *Unforgiven* is a great western that harks back to 1776 to define the American character and illuminates the territory for miles around.

2. **SIDE/WALK/SHUTTLE** (Ernie Gehr, U.S.). Cinema's virtuoso minimalist uses a glass-enclosed outdoor elevator as a readymade crane for a series of serial views of San Francisco. The movie is pure sensation: *Side/Walk/Shuttle* has the effect of a slow-motion roller coaster. The camera's stately swoops and stomach-dropping descents obliterate all sense of gravity. San Francisco is so viscerally and obsessively transformed that Gehr might honorably have titled his film *Vertigo*.

3. **GERMANY YEAR 90 NINE ZERO** (Jean-Luc Godard, France-Switzerland). As critics once cited *Alphaville's* "East Berlin" ambience, so Godard tracks *Alphaville's* anachronistic hero (tough guy Eddie Constantine) through the decomposing DDR of December 1990. A wealth of twentieth-century history is compressed in a single reference to the famous "surreal" intertitle from Murnau's *Nosferatu*: "Once I crossed the frontier, the phantoms came out to meet me," Constantine murmurs at the site of the no-longer-extant Wall.

4. **THE MATCH FACTORY GIRL** (Aki Kaurismäki, Finland-Sweden). Humming with relentless comic logic, the most pared-down and presenta-

tional of Kaurismäki's film is a marvel of narrative Taylorism. The precision camera placement and carefully measured durations suggest a shaggy-dog story told by a robot. Meals complement assembly lines; the movie's first spoken words issue from a television set; each surge of feeling the narrative-machine produces is as neatly packaged as the matchboxes its heroine helps manufacture.

5. **NIGHT AND DAY** (Chantal Akerman, France-Belgium-Switzerland). More deadpan comedy, this tale of all-consuming love amid spectacular dailiness satirizes, even as it celebrates, romantic youth, urban anonymity, minimalism, the nouvelle vague, and its own gorgeously diagrammatic structure.

6. **BAD LIEUTENANT** (Abel Ferrara, U.S.). A hardcore scuzzmeister elevates himself to a new place with this startling, powerfully restrained portrayal of sin and salvation in godless New York. Harvey Keitel's inarticulate *maudit philosophe* is the most uninhibited performance in this disco inferno that also offers religious hallucinations, sports-ranter "Mad Dog" Russo, and the most distanced representation of fellatio since Andy Warhol's *Blow Job*. As sordid as the material is, the movie isn't oppressive.

7. **RAISING CAIN** (Brian De Palma, U.S.). Even more than *Bad Lieutenant*, *Raising Cain* resembles a pageant staged by De Sade and performed in a mental institution. This lurid, comic, relentlessly experimental exercise in psychosexual delirium is De Palma's strongest movie in a dozen years. Although the treatment of narrative causality can be as baroque as anything in Raul Ruiz, *Raising Cain* is also a mediation on childhood and a critique of *Psycho*—the movie which moved the locus of horror from the old world of Transylvania to the heart of the American family.

8. **WINDOW SHOPPING** (Chantal Akerman, France-Belgium-Switzerland). Like *Night and Day*, this 1986 feature maps a romantic triangle in an artificial world. But the Barbara Kruger koan "I shop, therefore I am" underscores the musical mall-o-drama, set in a glamour factory devoted to the social construction of women and populated by shop girls, the very people for whom it used to be said that movies were made.

9. **ZENTROPA** (Lars von Trier, Denmark). Another sort of pomo movie-movie, this action-romance, set on the eve of the Cold War in the murky depths of Germany Year Zero and slyly evocative of the present moment, satirizes America's European entanglements. Von Trier brazenly attempts to recapture the primitive magic of popular cinema. "No trick is too crass, no method too cheap, no effect too vulgar for this film," he told one interviewer. As Kaurismäki has inherited Fassbinder's poker-faced humor, von Trier aspires toward his flashy hubris.

10. **TETSUO: THE IRON MAN** (Shinya Tsukamoto, Japan). A virtual one-man production, this impeccably gruesome cult film not only features special effects worthy of David Cronenberg but takes the desire to be a machine to the limit. It seems to dredge up the unconscious fantasies latent in "normal" robo-pop—like viewing *Total Recall* through the prism of Arnold's *Terminator* brain.

# 1993

1. **THE PUPPETMASTER** (Hou Hsiao-hsien, Taiwan). Hou is one of the few working narrative filmmakers who, in his fusion of a strong personal style, cultural specificity, and humanist scope, can be compared to the generation of directors who defined international cinema during the fifties and sixties. Indeed, he might be their belated sibling. Neither documentary nor fiction, the story of Taiwan's most famous puppeteer is a structuralist's treasure trove—an unpredictable anthology of narrative ploys in which stage performances alternate with scenes from an ongoing family melodrama. To a typically economical use of detail and synecdoche, Hou adds a startling advanced use of editing. A single cut can span a dozen years even as the voice-over loops over and around the scene, knotting a story line so unobtrusively complicated it makes a time traveler like Alain Resnais seem all thumbs. How tiresome it is to reiterate that not one of Hou's movies has ever had an American theaterical release.

2. **THE LONG DAY CLOSES** (Terence Davies, U.K.)

3. **A CHILD'S GARDEN AND THE SERIOUS SEA** (Stan Brakhage, U.S.). A tour de force of formal elegance and sensuous surfaces, Brakhage's first feature-length film in nearly a decade is biography once removed—an evocation of his wife's childhood. The indefatigable filmmaker, who recently turned 60, employs a lifetime of techniques—prisms, diffusion lenses, sudden camera moves, percussive shifts in exposure, oversaturated colors, tricks of scale—to suggest an enchanted island in the midst of some pellucid sea. Nearly as miraculous, Brakhage had his existence recognized by the *New York Times*: "Mr. Brakhage (pronounced BRACK-idge) floats placidly in a brightly colored, very strange cinematic universe of his own devising." Don't we all.

4. **ROCK HUDSON'S HOME MOVIES** (Mark Rappaport, U.S.). It scarcely matters if Rappaport is rereading or rescripting the Hudson text (taking moments from various Hudson vehicles that, in one way or another, confirm or deny—and thus reconfirm—the actor's concealed homosexuality). Addressing the medium no less than the actor, *Rock Hudson's Home Movies*

is an act of criticism . . . and love. Rappaport has reinvented the image called "Rock Hudson" with a passion and pathos only barely evident in Hudson's original imitation of life.

5. **THE OAK** (Lucian Pintilie, France-Romania). A railroad bridge floods, a mob of besotted miners shove onto the rescue train, punching the passengers out of their way; the heroine disembarks at a grim factory nexus and is first gang-raped, then subjected to pointless police interrogation, and finally denied service at a fairground hot dog stand. Hospitals double as charnal houses; the world runs on booze and resentment. Long-exiled Pintilie, a wild man who routinely placed the camera inside a crematorium or rubs the viewers's nose in a spinning propeller, is reexperiencing Romania.

6. **NAKED** (Mike Leigh, U.K.). The angriest in a long tradition of British angry young men rants and fucks his way to the end of the night, encountering a succession of brain-dead night workers, demonic yuppies, and sundry candidates for the dog collar. Paired with Pintilie's, Mike Leigh's grim-as-a-gulag apocalyptic farce would afford the King Kong double bill of the year—indeed, under any circumstances, the respective stars, Maia Morgenstern and David Thewlis, would be a monumental matchup.

7. **A BRIGHTER SUMMER DAY** (Edward Yang, Taiwan). At once coolly distanced and desperately romantic, this four-hour teenage epic is like an Antonioni version of *West Side Story* or a Wenders remake of *Rebel Without a Cause* transposed to 1960 Tapei and set to the music of the Fleetwoods.

8. **GARDEN OF SCORPIONS** (Oleg Kovalov, Russia). Sifting through the rubble of official truth, a former Leningrad film critic mixes and matches all manner of archival footage to frame a didactic spy movie from the mid-fifties that, given the montage and sense of grandiose delirium, might be a flashback in the mind of a mental patient.

9. **GROUNDHOG DAY** (Harold Ramis, U.S.). The funniest comedy I saw all year manages to conflate a Hindu sense of eternity with the endless repetition involved in any studio production, satirizing (even as it embraces) the vacuity of everyday American mass-mediated life while actually contributing a concept to that culture.

10. **JACQUOT** (Agnès Varda, France). Like *The Long Day Closes*, the biography of Jacques Demy dramatizes a future director's precocious obsession with cinema. As made by his wife, however, it's also an act of explication, predicated on continual cross-referencing Demy's movies and life. Switching between her footage and his, *Jacquot* is a complex work of reconstruction as well as Varda's means for keeping Demy alive. The narrative ends with the young hero going to Paris to become a filmmaker; the last indelible image is of the dying Demy, weathered and resigned, on an autumnal Brittany beach, the sands of time running through his hands.

## 1994 (alphabetical)

**THE BLUE KITE** (Tian Zhuangzhuang, China). Rigorous, tough-minded, metaphor-charged antipropaganda, *The Blue Kite* is remarkable for its unsentimental view of childhood, for the tact with which it handles historical sweep, for its honest evocation of the Cultural Revolution's heady thrills. Banned at home, the movie has effectively terminated the career of the most gifted, least compromising member of China's Fifth Generation. Despite favorable reviews ("the most amazing act of political courage and defiance I have ever seen in the cinema," for example), this fiercely restrained, cumulatively moving family melodrama was overshadowed here first by Chen Kaige's glitzier *Farewell My Concubine*, then by Zhang Yimou's coarser *To Live*.

**CHUNGKING EXPRESS** and **ASHES OF TIME** (Wong Kar-Wai, Hong Kong). That other Chinese cinema brought the year's most insouciant avant-pop. Wong used an enforced hiatus in the production of his lavish new wave sword film, *Ashes of Time*, to knock off a kinetic, chronology-pulverizing exercise in manic noir and absurdist comedy. Incidentally, *Ashes of Time*, which ran briefly in Chinatown, proved no less stylized.

**FAUST** (Jan Svankmajer, Czech Republic). Did the Velvet Revolution permit the brilliant Czech animator to renegotiate his deal with the devil? Underscored by Prague's transformation from depressed, moldy ruin into booming, sanitized tourist mecca, Svankmajer's "civil version" of the Faust myth perversely posits its antihero as a passive opportunist. *Faust* is less flashy but more coherent than Svankmajer's 1991 adaptation of *Alice in Wonderland*, with a typically surrealist emphasis on slapstick dismemberment and duplicitous geography as well as the filmmaker's characteristic fondness for disconcerting textural juxtapositions.

**HEAVENLY CREATURES** (Peter Jackson, New Zealand). Like *Faust*, this seriously sensational account of a tabloid murder mixes puppet animation with live-action drama in the service of a cerebral gross-out. Where Svankmajer tends toward the depressed and ironic, however, Jackson is overwrought and romantic. His teenaged heroines laugh to keep from screaming—or is it vice versa? The film's madcap brio belies its bleak finality and unexpected pathos.

**HÉLAS POUR MOI** (Jean-Luc Godard, Switzerland). The title, which can be roughly translated as *oy vey iz mir*, suggests the problem Godard sets his exegetes. This updated version of the Greek myth in which Zeus impregnates Alcmene by taking the form of her husband, Amphitryon, is hilariously fragmented, elegantly layered, rhythmically complex and willfully impenetrable. With the possible exception of Stan Brakhage, no other living film artist is so utterly in command of his particular, private vocabulary.

**HOOP DREAMS** (Steve James, Frederick Marx, and Peter Gilbert, U.S.). An old-fashioned social documentary of highly charged fantasy material, *Hoop Dreams* puts athletic ability in the context of race and class, rendering the sports inspirational problematic by showing it to be an all-or-nothing proposition.

**PULP FICTION** (Quentin Tarantino, U.S.).

**QUIZ SHOW** (Robert Redford, U.S.).

**THREE COLORS** (Krzysztof Kieślowski, France-Poland-Switzerland). Greater than the sum of the parts, the trilogy is best seen as one movie that is fully revealed only when time throws itself into reverse in the final movement. Indistinguishable from a bemused cynicism in the face of an unknowable universe, Kieślowski's mysticism suggests no underlying belief system—his fascination with coincidence seems telling in a film artist who leaves so little to chance.

**AN UNFORGETTABLE SUMMER** (Lucian Pintilie, France-Romania). A sort of sardonic East European *Fort Apache*, with the "civilized" military family exiled down on hostile terrain populated by primitive natives and policed by a battalion of brutal operetta soldiers. All nostalgia for the Good Old Days must been seen in the context of the newly rebalkanized Balkans. Bland title notwithstanding, it's a work of savage disillusionment.

# 1995

1. **LESSONS OF DARKNESS** (Werner Herzog, Germany).
2. **EXOTICA** (Atom Egoyan, Canada).
3. **A SHORT FILM ABOUT KILLING** (Krzysztof Kieślowski, Poland). Kieślowski's Polish films have been overshadowed by his more recent French coproductions, but this 1987 feature shows him in top form. Not for the squeamish, it's a harrowing, expressionist account of two murders—one committed by a Warsaw punk, the other by the Polish state—both dramatized in excrutiating real time.
4. **GERMANY YEAR 90 NINE ZERO** (Jean-Luc Godard, France-Switzerland).
5. **BOILING POINT** (Takeshi Kitano, Japan).
6. **THE CONVENT** (Manoel de Oliveira, Portugal). The last working director to have begun his career in silent movies got his first US commercial release thanks to the uncanny presence of Catherine Deneuve. Like many of de

Oliveira's autumnal works, *The Convent* is at once a distillation and a parody of European high culture—elegant, enigmatic, and serenely characterized by the director's acerbic sense of humor.

7. **CRUMB** (Terry Zwigoff, U.S.). As the critics' awards this year lavished on performers playing dipsos, hookers, and sociopaths suggest, American movies have caught up to American TV in celebrating our national dysfunction. Thus, this portrait of the artist-as-survivor has to be the American movie of the year. Indeed, its strengths are codependent with its flaws. The kind of movie only an insider could make, it's a myopic revelation.

8. **THE KINGDOM** (Lars von Trier, Denmark). This is my guilty pleasure. For one thing, it's really TV—a four-episode miniseries, perhaps inspired by *Twin Peaks*, that brews hospital soap opera, Saturday-morning supernaturalism, and genteel detective story, spiking the punch with cheap gross-out effects and an abundance of sneering attitude. Totally addictive, *The Kingdom* establishes an absorbing atmosphere of smoldering idiocy—trashing New Age spiritualism as well as medical science, not to mention the Scandinavian sense of a rational, orderly society.

9 & 10. **THE ADDICTION** (Abel Ferrara, U.S.) and **NADJA** (Michael Almereyda, U.S.). The year's best double bill would be these two gloriously black-and-white, Lower Manhattan–set, wildly revisionist vampire sagas, each centered on a bravura female performance. Where *Nadja* is an ethereal, drolly postmodern textual mélange, *The Addiction* is ferociously premodern. Ferrara actually believes in mortal sin. This is one vampire flick that insists on blaming the victim.

# 1996

1. **SÁTÁNTANGÓ** (Béla Tarr, Hungary). I've been talking for several years now about Tarr's astonishingly staged seven-and-a-half-hour bleakly comic allegory of social disintegration on the muddy vacuum of the central plain Hungarians call the puszta. This summer, thanks to Anthology Film Archives, the movie had something like a theatrical release.

Recognized as a landmark from its first screenings at the 1994 Berlin Film Festival, *Sátántangó* is a characteristically East European tale of charismatic swindlers casting their spell on hapless peasants. Indeed, Tarr's hypnotic film constructs somewhat the same relationship with its viewers. A movie in which emptiness becomes amazingly rich, textured, and visceral, *Sátántangó* is a multiple tour de force—for the actors, as the camera circles them in the lengthy continuous takes that Tarr adapts from Miklós Jancsó, and for Tarr, who constructs his narrative out of these morose blocks of real time. The final shot, in which one character boards up his window, provides a superbly materialist fade-out. More experiential than narrative, *Sátántangó* has fewer shots than the average 90-minute feature, and two hour-long chunks of it would be remarkable movies in their own right. In one, a fat, drunken doctor spies on his neighbors, runs out of booze, and is forced to make an epic trek through torrential rain to get another bottle; in another, a 10-year-old girl poisons a cat and then herself.

The titular performance is a remarkable composition in repetitive ranting, drunken strutting, and befuddled dancing to the same mind-breaking musical loop. After everyone collapses, the accordionist finishes all their drinks and pukes (offscreen). Not until halfway through the movie is it apparent that much of the action is unfolding simultaneously.

2. **THE GEORGETOWN LOOP** (Ken Jacobs, U.S.). Here, on the other hand, is a masterpiece that's 11 minutes long. Elegantly reworking some 1905 footage of a train trip through the Colorado Rockies, the dean of radical filmmaking printed the original image and its mirror side by side to produce a stunning wide-screen kaleidoscope effect. Did it really take 100 years of cinema for someone to execute this almost ridiculously simple idea?

3. **DEAD MAN** (Jim Jarmusch, U.S.). What does it take to get the media's attention? Miramax released *Dead Man* as if with tongs; the *New Yorker* couldn't even be bothered to give it a capsule review.

4. **BREAKING THE WAVES** (Lars von Trier, Denmark). The year's second-most-visionary commercial release—also shot by Robby Müller—at least managed to garner a few critics' awards. This saga of spiritual anguish is alternately excrutiating and exalted, a true test of faith, as raw as the Scottish weather.

5. **AVENTURERA** (Alberto Gout, Mexico). Forty-seven years ahead of its time.

6. **PORTRAIT OF A LADY** (Jane Campion, U.S.). Genuinely weird, Campion's gloss on Henry James stands virtually alone as a time-machine return to the nineteenth century.

7. **LA CÉRÉMONIE** (Claude Chabrol, France). This supremely intelligent and discomfiting domestic thriller is a bourgeois nightmare—precise, expert, cynical, and rich with female characterizations.

8. **A SINGLE GIRL** (Benoît Jacquot, France). If the ambition to transfigure daily life into spectacle is the oldest impulse in motion pictures, the desire to place human beauty at the center of the cinematic flux is surely the most persistent. Both urges underlie the premise of this minimalist tour de force—a movie that, despite its modest means, manages to wax as philo-sophical as it is physical, in elevating an hour in the life of a new hotel employee into a cosmic adventure.

9. **MOTHER** (Albert Brooks, U.S.). Having dealt with one life-crisis after another in his oeuvre, Brooks casts himself as a rejected child. Costar Debbie Reynolds has referred to *Mother* as "a wonderful warm movie," but the cuddliness is continually subverted by an underlying hostility.

10. **THE CABLE GUY** (Ben Stiller, U.S.). Ranging from the painfully creepy to the terrifyingly obnoxious, Jim Carrey's $20 million "cable guy" *is* mass culture—especially since the movie surrounds him with such a crew of blandly malleable idiots. Don't even dream of taking the children, Janet Maslin advised *New York Times* readers, "They'd be better off reading supermarket tabloids and watching the evening news."

# 1997

1. **CONSPIRATORS OF PLEASURE** (Jan Svankmajer, Czech Republic). The last Surrealist presents his obscure object of desire—a radical mix of de Sade, Freud, and Rube Goldberg, in which a sextet of Prague kinkmeisters play out their elaborate, ultimately interlocking, autoerotic fantasies. There's no dialogue (albeit plenty of sound), and the homemade special effects (machines, animated mannequins) are wondrous. Tactile, funny, disturbing, it's a great film.

2. **CRASH** (David Cronenberg, Canada). Brilliant science fiction—witty, poetic, uncompromising in its melancholia.

3. **IRMA VEP** (Olivier Assayas, France). A mock-verité movie about a new wave burnout's failed attempt to remake a 1916 serial with HK star Maggie Cheung, *Irma Vep* is enjoyably steeped in six sorts of cinephilia.

4. **LE SAMOURAI** (Jean-Pierre Melville, France). The achieved distillation of the nouvelle vague godfather's B-movie worldview, as austerely abstract as anything by Bresson, this gleaming nocturne is the most Cartesian of hit-man flicks—not to mention the essence of macho camp.

5. **NENETTE ET BONI** (Claire Denis, France). The everyday gets a patina of eroticized tropical splendor in this coming-of-age film. Claire Denis may be the most talented Euro cineaste to never have a movie in the New York Film Festival. Her lyrical impressionism has affinities to avant-gardists Warren Sonbert and Bruce Baillie, but what sets her apart from the current generation of Americans, industrial and independent, is an interest in getting the texture of life on film.

6. **THE SWEET HEREAFTER** (Atom Egoyan, Canada). As brilliantly edited as *Nenette et Boni*, Egoyan's most conventional movie is not on the level of *Exotica* (although the *New Yorker* praised him for finally learning how to tell a story). What the director has done in this restrained, devastating

account of the ways in which disaster resonates through the communal psyche is find his own themes in someone else's material.

7. **HAPPY TOGETHER** (Wong Kar-Wai, Hong Kong). Even more romantic in its neo-new-wavism than *Irma Vep*, Wong's long jagged still life looks away from the Crown Colony to map a love affair between two of its major male stars. The narrative fragmentation recalls—without imitating—Godard.

8. **BOOGIE NIGHTS** (Paul Thomas Anderson, U.S.). Why did I get as much hostile mail for praising this as for panning *Titanic*? Even so, my designated pull-quote, "the American movie of the year on what is surely the subject of the age" [that is, cock size], was insufficiently enthusiastic to be cited in the ads. Should I have called this wildly ambitious meditation on the Dream Factory "the kickiest family romance since *Oedipus Rex*"?

9. **CHANTAL AKERMAN BY CHANTAL AKERMAN** (Chantal Akerman, France). Neither avant-garde nor mainstream, the most formally innovative European filmmaker of her generation has always worked in the gap between fiction and documentary. In this hour-long self-portrait made for French TV, she treats her previous films as rushes for a new, obliquely autobiographical work.

10. **UNDERGROUND** (Emir Kusturica, Yugoslavia).


# 1998


1. **MOTHER AND SON** (Alexander Sokurov, Russia).

2. **FALLEN ANGELS** (Wong Kar-Wai, Hong Kong). The last installment of Wong's long goodbye to the now lost paradise of colonial Hong Kong is the acme of neo-new-wavism, the ultimate in MTV alienation, and the most visually voluptuous flick of fin de siècle. Hou Hsiao-hsien's only rival as director of the decade, Wong is a rootless cosmopolitan whose movies have less to do with the weight of the past than a nostalgia for the ever vanishing present. Like the Iranian directors whose relative lack of historical perspective gives their cinema, at once neorealist and self-reflexive, its unique postmodern flavor, he is a harbinger of twenty-first-century cinema.

3. **OUTER AND INNER SPACE** (Andy Warhol, U.S.). Doomed superstar Edie Sedgwick copes with her video image. Unseen in any form for over 30 years, this double-screen film installation, premiered at the Whitney Museum, proved to be a masterpiece of video art made before video art was invented.

4. **SONATINE** (Takeshi Kitano, Japan). Kitano's 1993 masterpiece opened on the strength of his more recent *Fireworks* but, for me, this remains the actor-director's most fully achieved film—abstract and implacable, it ranks with Sam Fuller's *Underworld USA*, Jean-Pierre Melville's *Le Samourai*, John Boorman's *Point Blank*, and John Woo's *The Killer*.

5. **THE THIN RED LINE** (Terrence Malick, U.S.). Melding combat confusion with a meditation on the nature of nature, Malick's austerely hallucinated battlefield vision is an exercise in nineteenth-century transcendentalism. Although this hugely ambitious adaptation of James Jones's 500-page novel gives evidence of having been hacked into its final shape, the violence only adds to the movie's serene, despairing nobility.

6. **AFFLICTION** (Paul Schrader, US.). Low-key and downbeat, character-driven, and well-written, the sort of American movie nostalgically associated with the first half of the 1970s, Paul Schrader's orchestration of a male self-destruct act could be a belated follow-up to *Five Easy Pieces*. It's as chilly a spectacle as you're likely to see—like watching a comeback in an empty stadium.

7. **THERE'S SOMETHING ABOUT MARY** (Peter and Bobby Farrelly, U.S.).

8. **THE DISENCHANTED** (Benoît Jacquot, France). As fetishistic in its way as the Farrelly film in "stalking" a nubile young woman, this admirably brief feature is terse and fragmentary, set in a psychologically charged realm of fairy-tale archetypes and childlike games.

9. **BUFFALO 66** (Vincent Gallo, U.S.). Actor-director Gallo regards himself with something like the awestruck wonder Jacquot lavishes on his enigmatic gamine. Would that every vanity production were this funny, soulful, and genuinely experimental.

10. **BULWORTH** (Warren Beatty, U.S.). Another mock-grandiose actor-directed psychodrama—less generous than Gallo's in its narcissism but more provocative in its self-revelation—this grab-bag synthesis of Michael Moore, *The Magic Christian*, the RFK campaign, and Beatty's own *Shampoo* made for the most overtly political and even inflammatory studio movie since *Malcolm X*.

# 1999

1. **FLOWERS OF SHANGHAI** (Hou Hsiao-hsien, Taiwan). Hou's third master-piece of the decade—following *The Puppetmaster* and *Goodbye South, Goodbye*—is a story about storytelling that takes a highly material view of prostitution in the course of a near mystical reverie on the nature of film. The movie was shown eight times during the Walter Reade's Hou retrospective and every screening was sold out. Not since the Museum of Modern Art's 1985 Tarkovsky retro had an "unreleased" filmmaker drawn such crowds—evidence that a sizable chunk of the local film culture is far ahead of the local film media.

2. **KHRUSTALIOV, MY CAR!** (Alexei German, Russia). Each 10-best list has its rules. Mine is that if a movie has three public screenings, it's eligible.

German's phantasmagoric account of Stalin's passing may never get a commercial release but it was shown twice at two Russian series.

3. **TOPSY-TURVY** (Mike Leigh, U.K.). This is the last twentieth-century movie; Leigh already got the millennium out of his system with *Naked*.

4. **ROSETTA** (Luc and Jean-Pierre Dardenne, Belgium). The best Marxist remake of a Bresson movie ever.

5. **EXISTENZ** (David Cronenberg, Canada). Cronenberg's comic cyberthriller finds body horror's acknowledged high muckety-muck in a relatively benign mind frame, riffing on virual reality games—or rather, their primitive precursor, the motion picture. Great props, great gags (that can make you gag), *eXistenZ* is a parody of *The Matrix*, avant la lettre—being as it's an art film, Miramax released under its genre label.

6. **MAGNOLIA** (Paul Thomas Anderson, U.S.). This manic meditation on karmic craziness, a mosaic of dark cross-purposes in which just about each scene plays like the big one, is not a perfect film. For one thing, the performers are a lot more believable than their characters. It isn't perfect, but as Anderson is not yet 30, I'd read this show biz apocalypse as a sign of hope.

7. **HOLY SMOKE!** (Jane Campion, Australia). Mischievously deconstructing the May-September sexual relationship between an old Method actor and a brazen ingénue, *Holy Smoke!* justifies its exclamatory title as a sort of emotional slapstick in which characters react to stimulation as directly as they would to a kick in the pants.

8. **DIVINE** (Arturo Ripstein, Mexico). Perhaps Ripstein's most personal film is a comedy about the end of cinema as collective fantasy. This fable of a doomsday cult that takes its cue from the biblical epics of the 1950s and is led by two venerable icons of Mexican cinema, Francisco Rabal and Katy Jurado, is ultimately less a matter of narrative than mise-en-scène, more a ritual than a melodrama. There is a monotonous quality to most end-of-cinema dirges, but *Divine* is a movie on the subject that is also a triumph of celluloid. Incredibly frustrating that this hilarious and soulful movie could only be seen as part of the Walter Reade's late-summer "Latin Beat!" series.

9. **THE HOLE** (Tsai Ming-liang, Taiwan). Tsai's most distilled, droll, deftly realized allegory is an apocalyptic comedy with numbers by Grace Chang and intimations of Jacques Tati.

10. **BEING JOHN MALKOVICH** (Spike Jonze, U.S.). The most offbeat studio comedy since *Rushmore* drafts the brain-twisting conundrums of Jorge Luis Borges, the grotesque humor of Jan Svankmajer, and the narrative extravagance of *Celine and Julie Go Boating* in the service of a pop, Warholian riff on celebrity—which is to say, this droll, uncanny, live-action puppet show is actually something new.

# 2000

The melancholy that's supposed to shroud the end of the century—romantic myth or self-fulfilling prophecy? These unending literary adaptations—are they a way for films to convince themselves of their lasting importance? Half the movies on my list use the medium to reflect either on *temps perdu* or on the decade when the motion picture age began or, in some cases, both.

1. **FRAGMENTS * JERUSALEM** (Ron Havilio, Israel).

2. **TIME REGAINED** (Raul Ruiz, France). *Fragments * Jerusalem* is profoundly anachronistic—among other things, it preserves the sense that motion pictures are a medium of (and not only for) preservation. Raul Ruiz ponders the same paradox of memories fixed in emulsion in his eccentric and triumphant meditation on the labyrinthian volume that brings Marcel Proust's *In Search of Lost Time* to its magnificent conclusion. It's posh stuff to be sure, although Ruiz still manages to project a certain cultural disrepute— the flavor of a third-world *Last Year at Marienbad*.

3. **THE HOUSE OF MIRTH** (Terence Davies, U.K.). Another unlikely literary adaptation, this customer treats Edith Wharton's bleak society satire as material for Mizoguchi geisha drama—the tragic heroine is tricked, abused, or betrayed by almost every character she meets. Davies resists the idealizing soft-focus glamour or nostalgic, ostentatious opulence of similar period pieces. This is no fetishized lost world but one that is fiercely, uncomfortably present.

4. **THE WIND WILL CARRY US** (Abbas Kiarostami, Iran). Kiarostami may be the last international filmmaker to grow up under the influence of Italian neorealism—its tendencies may be seen in his use of nonactors and "ordinary" situations, his uninflected camera style and eschewal of mood music, his interest in children and taste for open endings. But as the last neorealist, Kiarostami is a necessarily self-reflexive one.

5. **BEAU TRAVAIL** (Claire Denis, France). "I've found an idea for a novel," a Godard character once announced. "Not to write the life of a man, but only life, life itself. What there is between people . . . space, sound, and colors." His words could describe Claire Denis's sensational transposition of *Billy Budd* to a French Foreign Legion post on the Horn of Africa. This movie could be projected upside down and backwards, it would still look great.

6. **TABOO** (Nagisa Oshima, Japan). *Beau Travail*'s perfect double-feature complement is similarly set in an all-male military universe, but rather than a rapt meditation on the erotic obsession that one officer develops for an

individual soldier, *Taboo* is more detached and analytical in its concern with love's flowering within a repressive system. Japan's greatest living filmmaker had not made a theatrical feature in 14 years—who could have predicted this action film, at once baroque and austere, hypnotic and opaque?

7. **SHADOW OF THE VAMPIRE** (E. Elias Merhige, U.S.). Premised on the notion that F. W. Murnau's *Nosferatu* was actually a documentary, *Shadow of the Vampire* manages to turn a highly dubious premise into a subtle and delicately mordant comedy. More than a footnote scrawled in the margins of film history, it has a philosophical weight that allows it to make light of that history.

8. **SUZHOU RIVER** (Lou Ye, China). On paper, transplanting *Vertigo* to Shanghai sounds scarcely more promising than *Shadow of the Vampire's* recycled *Nosferatu*; on the screen *Suzhou River* (named for what amounts to an urban stream of consciousness) looks fabulous. Indeed, this adroit, concise, poetic city symphony is almost too stylish for its own good.

9. **KIKUJIRO** (Takeshi Kitano, Japan). Japan's king of all media is a man with more than one face; there's the tough guy, the funnyman, and the rank sentimentalist. The overpraised *Fireworks* attempted a synthesis; the unfairly dismissed *Kikujiro* does the same thing to funnier, more complex effect. A true *film maudit*, this superficially mawkish fairy tale is subverted by a remarkable combination of comic brutality, acute formalism, and inconsolable sorrow.

10. **THE LITTLE GIRL WHO SOLD THE SUN** (Djibril Diop Mambéty, Senegal). Mambéty's last film is a wondrously affirmative marketplace-legend-cum-political-allegory about an indomitable crippled girl, granddaughter of a blind street singer, who reinvents herself as a newspaper vendor. The score is infectious, and the metaphor overwhelming.

# Index

Note: *Page numbers in italics indicate illustrations.*